Jacobinism and the Revolt of Lyon
1789–1793

JACOBINISM AND THE REVOLT OF LYON 1789–1793

W.D. EDMONDS

CLARENDON PRESS · OXFORD
1990

Oxford University Press, Walton Street, Oxford OX2 6DP
Oxford New York Toronto
Delhi Bombay Calcutta Madras Karachi
Petaling Jaya Singapore HongKong Tokyo
Nairobi Dar es Salaam Cape Town
Melbourne Auckland
and associated companies in
Berlin Ibadan

Oxford is a trade mark of Oxford University Press

Published in the United States
by Oxford University Press, New York

British Library Cataloguing in Publication Data

Edmonds, W. D.
Jacobinism and the revolt of Lyon 1789–1793.
1. France. Lyons. Revolutions, 1789–1799
I. Title
944'.582304'1
ISBN 0–19–822749–3

Library of Congress Cataloging in Publication Data

Edmonds, W. D. (William D.)
Jacobinism and the revolt of Lyon, 1789/1793 / W. D. Edmonds,
p.   cm.
Includes bibliographical references.
1. Lyon (France)—History. 2. France—History—Revolution,
1789–1793. 3. Jacobins—France—Lyon—History—18th century.
I. Title.
DC195.L9E36   1989
944.04—dc20
ISBN 0–19–822749–3

Typeset by Butler & Tanner Ltd,
Frome and London
Printed and bound in
Great Britain by Bookcraft Ltd,
Midsomer Norton, Bath

**To
Lindsey**

Acknowledgements

Barrie Rose, who introduced me to the challenges of French revolutionary history, has provided indispensable support, advice, and encouragement during the long process of researching and writing this book. Richard Cobb has always been generous with his time and his knowledge of Lyon, the Revolution, and the people who experienced it. I am also grateful for help from Colin Lucas, Antonino De Francesco, and Paul Mansfield. In Lyon, I have had invaluable assistance and advice from people of all kinds during several most enjoyable visits.

I could not list, much less adequately thank, the archivists and librarians in three countries who have gone out of their way to assist me in my research. But I must mention René Lacour, formerly *archiviste en chef du Rhône*, who took great pains to familiarize me with the rich collections under his care, and with sources for Lyonnais history generally.

The University of Sydney provided the Hannah Fullerton Scholarship which enabled me to study in France in the first place. Macquarie University granted leave and financial assistance for later research in England and France. An Honorary Visiting Fellowship at the University of Tasmania provided a valuable opportunity to rethink my approach to this study. Thanks are also due for permission to reproduce sections of some of my previously published work: 'The Rise and Fall of Popular Democracy in Lyon', *Bulletin of the John Rylands University Library of Manchester*, 67 (1984); 'A Study in Popular Anti-Jacobinism: The Career of Denis Monnet', *French Historical Studies*, 13 (1983); 'Successes and Excesses of Revisionist Writing about the French Revolution', *European History Quarterly*, 17 (1987).

At Macquarie University I have had the benefit of countless discussions with students and colleagues, particularly George Parsons, Michael Roberts, John Ryan, and Duncan Waterson, whose historical interests overlap with my own in various ways. Jean Scott's typing triumphed over a much-revised manuscript, and she has been most generous with her time, skill, and patience. I would also like to thank the editorial staff at Oxford University Press, and particularly Robert Faber and Nicola Pike.

My parents, my sister, and my son have helped me in more ways than they could have known. My greatest debt is to my wife, without whom this book would not have been written.

Sydney   W. D. E.
January 1989

Contents

List of Maps

ERRATUM

KEY TO MAPS

A. Pont Saint-Vincent
B. Place des Terreaux
C. Hôtel de Ville
D. Comédie
E. Saint-Clair
F. Pont Morand
G. Pont de Pierre
H. Prison de Roanne

I. Pont Volant
J. Cathedral of Saint Jean
K. Hôtel-Dieu
L. Pont de l'Archevêché
M. Place Bellecour
    (Louis le Grand)
N. Arsenal
O. La Charité
P. Prison de Saint-Joseph

Sections:
1. Le Gourguillon
2. Saint-Georges
3. Porte-Froc
4. Place Neuve
5. La Juiverie
6. Le Change
7. Port Saint-Paul
8. Pierre-Scize
9. Bellecour I
10. Bellecour II

11. Port du Temple
12. Place Confort
13. Rue Belle-Cordière
14. L'Hôtel-Dieu
15. Rue Thomassin
16. Plat-d'Argent
17. Bon-Rencontre
18. Rue Tupin
19. La Croisette
20. Rue Buisson
21. Saint-Nizier

22. Rue Neuve
23. La Pêcherie
24. Place Saint-Pierre
25. Le Plâtre
26. Les Terreaux
27. Le Griffon I
28. Le Griffon II
29. Saint-Vincent I
30. Saint-Vincent II
31. La Grande-Côte I
32. La Grande-Côte II

Source to Map 1: based on C. Riffaterre, *Le Mouvement anti-jacobin et anti-parisien à Lyon et dans le Rhône-et-Loire en 1793* (Lyon, 1912–28), i. 106; and E. Herriot, *Lyon n'est plus* (Paris, 1938–40), i. 406.

Abbreviations

The archives most commonly referred to are given thus:

AN   Archives Nationales
AD   Archives Départementales du Rhône
AC   Archives Communales de Lyon
AG   Archives de la guerre

The Coste collection in the Bibliothèque Municipale de la Ville de Lyon is referred to as Fonds Coste (for printed material) and Coste MSS (for manuscripts).

Other abbreviations:

CSG   Committee of General Security
CPS   Committee of Public Safety
CM   *Procès-verbaux des séances des corps municipaux de la ville de Lyon 1787– an VIII*, 4 vols. (Lyon, 1900–4).
CP   *Procès-verbaux des séances de la Commission populaire, républicaine et de salut public de Rhône-et-Loire*, ed. G. Guigue (Lyon, 1899).

Note on French quotations:

These follow the sources cited, even though many of the contemporary documents are full of solecisms. The use of *sic* has been limited as much as possible, but in some instances the quotations are unavoidably peppered with it.

Introduction

That the Revolution of Fraternity culminated in civil wars was a cause of disillusionment to its sympathizers at the time and has been a source of contention amongst historians since. Conservatives have blamed Jacobin fanaticism, and neo-Jacobins have blamed counter-revolutionary conspiracy for the fratricidal conflicts of 1793 in rural and urban France. More recent academic studies have attempted to locate their causes in processes of political change and social conflicts.[1]

Clearly, the study of these episodes requires a good deal of work in the field of *histoire événementielle* from which the French *annalistes* and some of their British and American admirers have recently withdrawn their attention in favour of analysing longer-term structural developments or cultural and linguistic aspects of the revolutionary phenomenon. But as long as there is interest in the disappointment of so many of the aspirations of 1789—amongst them the rule of law, the realization of a true national community, civil peace, and unanimity in virtuous citizenship— there will be a need to assess and reassess the disasters of 1793.

In the case of Lyon there is a particular need. The savage repression which followed the defeat of its rebellion is perhaps the most notorious episode of the Great Terror, one of the Revolution's worst blood-lettings, in which nearly two thousand people were shot, guillotined, or blown apart by cannon-fire. It left a stain on the history of the Republic, and its legacy of political conflict helped bring the Republic down. Yet the explanations we have are contradictory and incomplete. The only detailed scholarly study, written by Riffaterre more than half a century ago,[2] stressed the local causes of the insurrection of 29 May 1793 which began the rebellion of Lyon. But neo-Jacobin historians have persisted in seeing it as part of a nation-wide campaign linked more or less directly with the

---

[1] e.g. A. Forrest, *Society and Politics in Revolutionary Bordeaux* (Oxford, 1975); W. Scott, *Terror and Repression in Revolutionary Marseilles* (London, 1973); G. Lewis, *The Second Vendée: The Continuity of Counter-revolution in the Department of the Gard, 1789–1815* (Oxford, 1978); C. Tilly, *The Vendée* (Cambridge, Mass., 1964).

[2] C. Riffaterre, *Le Mouvement anti-jacobin et anti-parisien à Lyon et dans le Rhône-et-Loire en 1793*, 2 vols, (Lyon, 1912–28).

Girondins' parliamentary campaign against the Montagne.[3] This has led
to confusion about matters as fundamental as the order of events: Soboul,
for example, wrote that 'news of the insurrection [of 31 May–2 June] in
Paris and the elimination of the Girondin deputies ... precipitated the
revolt in Lyons ...',[4] yet the revolt in Lyon had begun two days before
the insurrection in Paris. Of the few extended accounts of the rebellion
available in general works, one is marred by serious mistakes of fact.[5]
Two others make good use of Riffaterre and other local studies, but tend
to follow the former in what I will argue is excessive concentration on
local causes of the rebellion.[6] And, like Riffaterre, they leave unresolved
the intriguing question of why, in Lyon, did so many artisans and
labouring men join the wealthy and the formerly privileged in their war
against the Jacobin Republic?

Much of this can be cleared up by looking at the extensive, though
still fragmentary, documentary remains of political activity in Lyon and
responses to it in Paris from the crisis of September 1792, which ended
a cautious experiment in populist municipal government, to the end of
the siege. But one crucial question can be resolved only by investigating
the earlier history of the Revolution, and it was that investigation which
turned a thesis on the rebellion into this book. Estimates of popular
participation in the Lyonnais rebellion, which was strongly anti-Jacobin,
vary wildly from minimal to massive. If it turns out to have been massive,
characterizations of the rebellion as bourgeois are obviously misleading,
and questions would have to be asked too about Professor Soboul's social
interpretation of the Parisian Jacobin-*sans-culotte* alliance—why, for
example, were the *menu peuple* anti-Jacobin in Lyon when they were pro-
Jacobin in Paris? In fact, their political behaviour was not radically
different to their Parisian counterparts', and where it differed was in the

---

[3] See e.g. J. M. Thompson, *The French Revolution* (Oxford, 1943), 365–6; M. Bouloiseau,
La République jacobine (Paris, 1972), ch. 2; A. Soboul, *The French Revolution 1787–1799*,
trans. A. Forrest and C. Jones, 2 vols. (London, 1974), ii. 317–18.

[4] Soboul, *French Revolution*, ii. 317.

[5] J. Godechot, *The Counter-Revolution* (London, 1972), 236–41. The more serious errors
include the claims that the revolt was precipitated by the need to prevent Jacobin victory
in elections to form *Comités de surveillance* on 29 May (the elections had in fact been won
by the anti-Jacobins ten days before), and that the Montagnard *député* Dubois-Crancé was
sent as a conciliator to Lyon after the revolt (he had been in the region for over a fortnight
before 29 May, and his extremely unconciliatory behaviour was an important factor in the
revolt).

[6] N. Hampson, *A Social History of the French Revolution* (London, 1963), 171–5;
D. M. G. Sutherland, *France 1789–1815: Revolution and Counterrevolution* (London, 1985),
176–82, 187–91.

timing of their interventions and of their disillusionment with the Jacobins who sought their support. In the 1970s work by several historians helped considerably to clarify these issues.[7]

The timing of popular political mobilization came to seem more and more important. It threw light not only on the causes of the rebellion, but on other aspects of Lyon's revolutionary history: on its extreme turbulence in 1789 and 1790 and its relative quiet during 1791 and early 1792; on the failure of its élites to achieve dominance during the constitutional monarchy; and on the apparent inconsistency between its role as the cradle of the popular societies and its reputation as a haven of counter-revolution.

It soon became apparent that putting the rebellion into an adequate context meant writing not just an introductory chapter, but an extended essay on Lyon's history from 1789 to its capture by government troops in October 1793. The latter event opened the way for Lyon's revolutionary colonization by Paris, beginning a new pattern of local politics and, for the historian, a new set of problems which could only be fully explored in a separate work. This book, then, has two primary aims: to explain why Lyon suffered the disaster of civil war; and to make available in English a history of the first five years of revolutionary politics in the second city of France. It also aims to meet the need stressed by Georges Lefebvre fifty years ago for a social reinterpretation of Lyonnais politics developed from 'un tableau de la vie économique et de la structure sociale à Lyon en 1789 et durant les premières années de la Révolution'.[8]

Recent work on Lyon[9] and broader developments in the historiography of the French revolution have made a re-examination of these questions seem all the more necessary. Revisionist historians, following the example of Alfred Cobban and François Furet, have made damaging attacks on the neo-Marxist interpretation, which, they argue, became an orthodoxy during the period when Lefebvre and Albert Soboul held successively

---

[7] R. Cobb, *The Police and the People* (Oxford, 1970); T. Koi, 'Les "Chaliers" et les sans-culottes lyonnais', Thèse de doctorat, IIIᵉ cycle, Université de Lyon II (1974); and A. De Francesco, 'Montagnardi e sanculotti in provincia: Il caso lionese (agosto 1792–maggio 1793)', *Studi storici*, 19 (1978), 589–626.

[8] *Compte rendu* of E. Herriot, *Lyon n'est plus*, Annales historiques de la Révolution française (hereafter *AHRF*), 15 (1938), 123.

[9] See above, n. 7, and A. De Francesco, *Il sogno della repubblica: Il mondo dell lavoro dall'Ancien Regime al 1848* (Milan, 1983); id., 'Conflittualità sul lavoro in epoca pre-industriale: Le agitazioni degli operai cappellai lionesi (1770–1824)', *Annali della Fondazione Luigi Einaudi*, 13 (1979), 151–213; D. L. Longfellow, 'The Silk-Weavers of Lyon during the French Revolution, 1786–1796', Ph.D. thesis (Johns Hopkins University, 1979).

the chair in the history of the French Revolution at the Sorbonne. One result has been to turn this field into something of an ideological battleground where on occasion more heat has been generated than light.[10] As I have argued elsewhere, some revisionists have been premature in declaring extinct what they variously call the 'social', 'neo-Marxist', or 'neo-Jacobin' interpretation and proclaiming the primacy of purely political and ideological factors over social ones in revolutionary history.[11] For one thing, the empirical evidence on which Cobban rightly insisted is still too incomplete even to proclaim the demise of the old orthodoxy, much less to establish a new one, though sufficient is becoming available to permit well-founded generalizations at least on a regional basis.[12] For another, the evidence we have suggests that although the outbreak of the revolution can no longer be seen as the inevitable culmination of a long-developing conflict between two distinct classes, nobility and bourgeoisie, a social interpretation of it is still possible, one, moreover, with wealthy commoners playing the dominant role in revolutionary politics and emerging with the victory they had sought in 1789, permanent integration with the political élite.[13] This, of course, is a long way from the teleological schema of some Marxists, in which the overthrow of feudalism by the capitalist bourgeoisie created a new social order bearing the seeds of socialist revolution. But it is also a long way from viewing the 'Lefebvre school' as having tied revolutionary studies into an ideological strait-jacket by focusing on social conflict and on the role of the bourgeoisie.

In the case of Lyon, the importance of these factors is evident from the beginning of the revolutionary crisis. The collapse of the absolute monarchy came at a time when the city's main industry, silk, was in deep economic difficulties, and when discontent amongst its working population, particularly weavers and hatters, was particularly intense. Only in this context is it possible to understand the response of bourgeois Lyon to the political crisis. With the exception of an isolated *patriote* minority, the propertied classes united in defence of order and kept revolutionary initiatives to a minimum, setting Lyonnais politics on the

[10] A convenient summary of the controversy, with extracts, is in R. W. Greenlaw (ed.), *The Social Origins of the French Revolution* (New York, 1975).

[11] 'Successes and Excesses of Revisionist Writing about the French Revolution', *European History Quarterly*, 17 (1987), 195–217.

[12] A good recent example is H. C. Johnson, *The Midi in Revolution: A Study of Regional Political Diversity* (Princeton, 1986).

[13] See ibid., ch. 8; W. Doyle, *Origins of the French Revolution* (Oxford, 1980), 203–4, 208; L. Hunt, *Politics, Culture and Class in the French Revolution* (London, 1984), ch. 5.

course which was to bring the city into conflict with the Montagnards in 1793.

It is not intended, however, to present a reductionist interpretation in terms of 'ultimate' socio-economic forces. One of the most valuable outcomes of the revisionist controversy has been a clearer definition of the role of revolutionary ideology, a role particularly evident in Lyonnais politics. François Furet has sought to replace the neo-Jacobin 'catechism' with a version of the revolution as ideologically driven, according to which 'a *mental representation of the social sphere* ... permeated and dominated the realm of politics'.[14] As a reinterpretation of the Revolution this remains an elegant speculation, and although Hunt has since fleshed out some aspects of it, it is probably still true, as Hugh Gough wrote in 1980, that many historians will prefer 'to argue that ideological factors need to be balanced against social conflict and economic circumstances in order to explain the rapid radicalization of revolutionary politics'.[15]

But Furet's work contains brilliant insights, most notably (as Hunt neatly summarizes it) into 'the obsession with conspiracy [which] became the central organizing principle in French revolutionary rhetoric'.[16] 'The "aristocratic plot" thus became the lever of an egalitarian ideology that was both exclusionary and highly integrative ... the nation was constituted by the patriots only in reaction to its adversaries, who were secretly manipulated by the aristocrats.'[17] This goes a long way towards understanding the world-view of the Jacobins considered not just as members of Jacobin clubs, but more broadly as the 'specialists and experts' of 'the language of revolutionary consensus'.[18] While it would be absurd to maintain that Jacobins everywhere accepted this orthodoxy, or took the histrionics of the orators literally, this was a period when rhetoric was of paramount importance.[19] Not only perceptions but policies could be affected by it, above all when what looked like opposition to the Revolution was encountered. The obsession with conspiracy patterned the thinking of both Jacobins in Lyon and Jacobins outside Lyon, and it will be argued here that their tendency to identify the second city with the

[14] *Penser la Révolution française* (Paris, 1978). This quotation is from the English translation, *Interpreting the French Revolution*, by E. Forster (Cambridge, 1981), 63.

[15] *Historical Journal*, 33 (1980), 978.

[16] Hunt, *Politics, Culture and Class*, p. 39.

[17] Furet, *Interpreting the French Revolution*, p. 55.

[18] Ibid. 50.

[19] See Hunt, *Politics, Culture and Class*, ch. 1.

counter-revolution, apparent from 1790 but continually strengthening, contributed indirectly to its revolt and directly to the severity of the Convention's policies against it in the second half of 1793.

In this limited sense, my study supports Furet's criticism of the neo-Jacobin claim that the Terror was the product of circumstances, an explanation involving 'the overriding consideration of national survival' and repeating 'yet again the type of interpretation current at the time of the events themselves . . . a free-floating version of the plot theory'.[20] Marc Bouloiseau's verdict on 'federalism' exemplifies this way of thinking: 'Le Fédéralisme se distinguait des rébellions fomentées et encadrées par la contre-révolution, mais tous deux attaquaient dans le dos une France débordée sur ses frontières. Ils trahissaient la nation et la République.'[21] For a patriot this might justify a Terror at Lyon, in Jacobin eyes the centre of the most virulent outbreak of 'federalism'. But considerations of national survival can only partly explain why the repression of Lyon was so severe. For that, we must look again at revolutionary ideology and Jacobin perceptions of Lyon.

As Barrie Rose has suggested,[22] a synthesis between some of the conclusions of the Lefebvre school and the revisionists seems not impossible, despite all the verbal barrages they have exchanged. This book attempts to move in that direction, which unfortunately involves sacrificing the neatness and symmetry achieved by exponents of both the rival schools. But seekers of neatness and symmetry would perhaps be wise to avoid the French Revolution and the Jacobins. The former can no longer be seen either as a class struggle which created a new social order or as a political collapse with little social significance. The truth lies in between. The latter cannot be seen simply as semi-religious fanatics or as the vanguard of the revolutionary bourgeoisie, the historically necessary hammer of feudalism. Bourgeois though they were, the Jacobins were 'deeply troubled by the corruption associated with commerce'[23] (one reason for their hostility to Lyon). Men of egalitarian principle, they were inspired by 'a mixed vision of a society that did respect private property but which would also be virtuous and communitarian'[24] once the last

[20] Furet, *Interpreting the French Revolution*, p. 62.

[21] Bouloiseau, *La République jacobine*, p. 80.

[22] R. B. Rose, 'Reinterpreting the French Revolution: Cobban's "Myth" Revisited Thirty Years On', *Australian Journal of Politics and History*, 32 (1986), 238–44.

[23] Hunt, *Politics, Culture and Class*, p. 50.

[24] P. Higonnet, *Class, Ideology, and the Rights of Nobles during the French Revolution* (Oxford, 1981).

debris of aristocracy had been cleared away. The history of Lyon from 1789 to 1793 reveals—perhaps more clearly than any other episode of the Revolution—how tragically inappropriate this was in a deeply divided society.

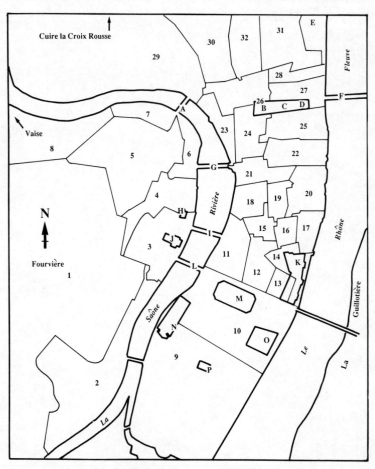

1.   Lyon and its *sections* 1789–1793

1

Lyon in the 1780s

THE URBAN ENVIRONMENT

Taking into account its *faubourgs* and a floating population of something like 20,000, Lyon's population in 1780 was about 150,000, which made it less than a quarter the size of Paris but still the second largest French city.[1] There were about 50,000 more Lyonnais than in 1700, but the increase was not from natural population growth. Large excesses of live births over deaths were frequently recorded, only to be wiped out by high rates of mortality amongst children who had been sent (as Lyonnais infants of all classes customarily were) to rural wet-nurses. So high was the death rate among the *enfants en nourrice* (between 1,500 and 2,200 a year) that the city suffered a real excess of deaths over births which sometimes reached 600 annually. But these victims of custom, over-crowding, ignorance, and economic necessity were more than replaced numerically by human traffic coming the other way, rural immigrants attracted to Lyon not only from its own *généralité* but from Dauphiné, Bugey, Switzerland, and Italy. There was also some emigration, mostly of males, with the overall result that most Lyonnais on the eve of the Revolution were Lyonnais by adoption not birth.[2]

Unlike the population, the land available to accommodate it did not increase much in the eighteenth century. Of the city's 364 hectares, four-sevenths were taken up by streets, squares, small farms, market gardens, church property, and land too steep for building, of which there was much in Lyon.[3] Some new space was won from the hills and the rivers, but only with great difficulty. In the early 1770s work began on Antoine Michel Perrache's proposal to move the confluence of the Saône and the Rhône southwards by making use of the difference between their levels. But a series of natural and financial disasters delayed any substantial levelling and draining work for twenty years, and then the first pieces of

---

[1] This discussion leans heavily on the monumental study by M. Garden, *Lyon et les Lyonnais au XVIIIe siècle* (Paris, 1970).

[2] Ibid. 25–140.

[3] Ibid. 7–8.

usable land went for flour-mills, not houses.[4] The project did nothing to ease the overcrowding of Lyon before the Revolution. Only at the north of the peninsula was there significant expansion. The most formidable obstacles here were the desire of the brother of the *prévôt des marchands* to protect his view, and the Abbess of Saint-Pierre's attempt to assert her community's rights over the whole area. Nevertheless, in 1772 the Saint-Clair Company succeeded in opening up what was to become the wealthiest residential *quartier* of Lyon by the time of the Revolution.[5] More important for the future was the wooden bridge over the Rhône built by Jean-Antoine Morand in 1774. It linked the sparsely settled Brotteaux area with the prosperous north-eastern *quartiers* of the peninsula, and opened the way for Lyon's expansion in the nineteenth century. But in the 1780s most of the land sold in the Brotteaux went to speculators and *cabaretiers*.[6]

Physical difficulties, financial instability, and vested interests thus combined to prevent Lyon from increasing its habitable area at anything like its rate of population growth. The results were high rents, tall houses, and cramped living-quarters. Narrow, dark, badly paved streets were the main features of the urban landscape, with relief provided by the hills, the rivers, two grand squares—Place des Terreaux and Place Bellecour—and architectural show-pieces such as Soufflot's elegant Loge du Change, the vast Hôtel-Dieu, and the pompous Hôtel de Ville. Overall, more than two-thirds of the buildings in Lyon had four stories or more. This was not only to make the most of limited space, but also because silk-weaving, from which half the population lived, directly or indirectly, depended on light. The weavers did not need much space to translate the pattern-makers' designs into elaborate cloth—perhaps 38 square metres for living and working, of which the loom took up half—but they could not afford to be overshadowed. This helps to explain why the weaving population steadily shifted towards the hillside *quartiers* where it was easier to build into the light.[7]

La Grande Fabrique

It was appropriate that the fabric of the city was shaped by the needs of the silk industry, for Lyon and silk were almost synonymous. According to municipal statistics, 24,000 men and 10,000 women worked in the

[4] R. Edgeworth, *Memoirs of Richard Lovell Edgeworth* (London, 1820), i. 320.

[5] L. Trénard, *Lyon, de l'Encyclopédie au préromantisme* (Paris, 1958), i. 16.

[6] Ibid. i. 19–20; Garden, *Lyon et les Lyonnais*, p. 9.

[7] Garden, *Lyon et les Lyonnais*, pp. 20, 168–9, 209.

Grande Fabrique or closely associated trades like braid-making and cloth-finishing. While the figures for female workers cannot be verified, those for males match Garden's samplings of marriage registers, which indicate that about 38 per cent of Lyon's artisans were silk-weavers.[8]

The industry's most notable characteristic was its capitalist structure, which differentiated it from the aggregations of more or less equal small-scale, self-employed merchant-artisans which were common in eighteenth-century French manufacturing. Its productive and distributive processes were controlled by about 400 very wealthy merchants known as *marchands-fabricants* but more accurately described in the registers of their guild as 'marchands de soie en gros' or 'marchands faisant fabriquer chez autrui'.[9] Their dominance was the fruit of a battle waged for more than a century against the small, independent merchant-weavers, 'maîtres-ouvriers en soie travaillant pour leur compte'. They won a great victory over the latter in 1712 by obtaining letters patent which obliged them to pay the very high patent fee of 200 *livres*. Combined with regulations introduced in 1731 which restricted master weavers to a maximum of four looms, this made it uneconomical to set up as a merchant-weaver without sufficient capital and connections to go into silk-trading in a big way, importing raw silk, and exporting the finished cloth.

The *marchands-fabricants* cemented their oligopoly by obtaining a permanent majority on the Fabrique's governing body and greatly raising the patent fee required to join their number.[10] Deprived of the chance to produce for sale on his own account, the master weaver had no choice but to take piece-work on terms dictated by the *marchand-fabricant* who supplied the raw silk and bought the finished product. His diminished status was clearly reflected in everyday language: the terms 'maître-fabricant en soie' and 'maître ouvrier' began to fall into disuse, and 'ouvrier en soie' or 'fabricant' was used for masters and *compagnons* alike.[11] But while the master weavers lost their financial and creative independence and became, in effect, wage-earners at average levels below that of day-labourers, they were not proletarianized in the sense of being concentrated in factories or deprived of ownership of the means of

---

[8] Archives Communales de Lyon (hereafter AC), I²4 *bis*, fo. 61; Garden, *Lyon et les Lyonnais*, pp. 318–19.

[9] AC I²4 *bis*, fo. 92.

[10] J. Godart, *L'Ouvrier en soie* (Lyon, 1899), 91–2, 181.

[11] Garden, *Lyon et les Lyonnais*, pp. 282–3.

production, for they owned their looms and contributed to work in small *ateliers*.

An important consequence of these changes was a remarkable unity of outlook and interest amongst masters, *compagnons*, and apprentices which made it extremely rare for *compagnons* to agitate against their masters.[12] Usually they joined in protests and insurrections without making independent demands. Apprentices and *compagnons* were masters in the making who, given a few years and a few hundred *livres* saved for the patent fee and working capital, could expect to end up on the same footing as the masters with whom they lived and worked, for the Fabrique did not require a *chef d'œuvre* but merely general competence from aspiring masters.[13] Masters and *compagnons* were bound together by resentment of the *marchands-fabricants,* each of whom could control the fortunes of several hundred *ouvriers en soie*. The weavers' dissatisfaction with their state of absolute dependence was increased by the recognition that the growth of the industry in the eighteenth century had not benefited them, but had rather brought about a relative decline in their material wealth.[14] Worse still, their work was of a specialized and debilitating kind which claimed its practitioners for life. After several years in the trade. silk-weavers were likely to be disqualified from other kinds of labour by the physical consequences, which included spinal disorders and hernias, of standing bent over their looms for the fifteen to eighteen hours of their working day.[15] But their main grievance was the difficulty of saving enough to see them through periods of unemployment, and their most frequent and bitter complaints concerned their chronic insecurity.[16]

The industry was extremely unstable. It had serious problems of supply caused by its dependence on the Levant and Italy for raw silk, and in particular on Piedmont for the type of silk needed to manufacture plain cloth, the only silk which, being to some extent immune to fashion changes, could safely be stockpiled.[17] Shortages caused by wars and crop failures could raise prices sufficiently to force many Lyonnais merchants out of the market, and this seems to have contributed to the severe

---

[12] Godart, *L'Ouvrier en soie,* p. 154.

[13] Ibid. 136, 155; Garden, *Lyon et les Lyonnais,* p. 286.

[14] See ibid. pp. 294–5, 298–9.

[15] *Mémoire de la ville de Lyon au Roi ... signé Servant, Terret, deputés de la ville de Lyon* (Paris, 1788), 8, 9. See also *Discours prononcé par M. Tolozan de Montfort ... le premier mars 1788* (Lyon, 1788), 6.

[16] Garden, *Lyon et les Lyonnais,* p. 301.

[17] *Discours prononcé par M. Tolozan de Montfort,* p. 7; Abbé Expilly, *Dictionnaire géographique, historique et politique des Gaules et de la France* (Paris, 1766), iv. 314.

unemployment of 1787.[18] Worse, the industry was extremely sensitive to even less predictable factors such as fashion and sudden fluctuations in demand. In the late 1770s, for example, the rustic simplicity and plain white materials made fashionable by Versailles set a style which soon spread to furnishings. English cotton and percales and printed wallpapers invaded Lyon's traditional markets. Where silk was still used it was mostly plain material trimmed with ribbon, but here Lyon had difficulty competing with cheap fabrics from abroad, and traditionalism in the Fabrique made it slow to adapt to the changed conditions.[19] Because the bulk of Lyon's production was exported, the trade was seriously damaged by wars, rebellions, and tariff changes such as occurred in Saxony, Prussia, the United Provinces, and England in the last quarter of the century. All these states either forbade imported silk cloth or placed higher duties on it. In addition, there was competition not only from other textiles such as English cottons, but from the nascent silk industries of the Italian states and Spain. By the 1780s some Spanish silks were 25 per cent cheaper than their Lyonnais equivalents.[20]

From the point of view of the Fabrique, a worse historical conjuncture could hardly be imagined than the 1770s and 1780s. Wars, disorders, and the decease of potentates might be expected from time to time, but philosopher-idols preaching rusticity, a queen playing milkmaids, and the mechanization of cotton-weaving could hardly have been. Between 1769 and 1783 the value of Lyonnais silks sold in France fell by a third, and that of silks sent abroad by almost the same proportion. The first serious blow was the loss of markets caused by the international conflicts of the early 1770s, the first partition of Poland, and the Russo-Turkish War. Silks prepared for the marriage of the Comte de Provence remained unsold, causing work in the industry virtually to cease between January and August 1771. Matters improved somewhat with the celebrations following Louis XVI's coronation, but in the 1780s, thanks to Rousseauism and neo-classicism, the Fabrique's most elaborate and profitable products were *démodé*.[21]

The weavers were put on the defensive. Temporary periods of high

---

[18] See *Réflexions d'un citoyen patriote, pour les ouvriers en soie de la ville de Lyon* (Lyon, 1789), 4.

[19] E. Pariset, *Histoire de la Fabrique lyonnaise* (Lyon, n.d.), 258.

[20] Trénard, *Lyon*, i. 23–4.

[21] See ibid. i. 24–5; Godart, *L'Ouvrier en soie*, pp. 227–30; E. Leroudier, *La Décadence de la Fabrique lyonnaise à la fin du XVIIIᵉ siècle* (Lyon, 1911), 12. See Pariset, *Histoire de la Fabrique*, pp. 213–15.

demand in 1779 and 1783 encouraged them to seek increased piece-rates for plain cloths, but they succeeded only in the former year, and they were unable to extract a general increase in rates for all types of cloth.[22] Nevertheless, the campaign for a *tarif*—a regularly adjusted general scale of fixed rates for all silk-workers—was not abandoned. It was revived during the most serious disturbances in Lyon since 1744, the two-*sous* revolt of 1786.

Trénard has shown that this movement, which was initiated by hat-makers and involved artisans and journeymen from trades as diverse as pastry-making and carpentry, was dominated by the masters and *compagnons* of the Fabrique. The troubles lasted from 7 August to 25 September, when a strike in the hat industry was broken. Although at the end of August the Consulat (the city corporation) was forced to accept the principle of a *tarif*, nothing lasting was won. A royal decree of 3 September not only forbade any new *tarif* but annulled even the obsolete *tarif* of 1779. Three hangings and the imprisonment of the weavers' spokesman, Denis Monnet, underlined the authorities' commitment to *laissez-faire*. With winter coming and unemployment on the rise, the disturbances ceased.[23] They had demonstrated both that the Fabrique was divided along clear-cut lines of economic interest and that the weavers were capable of sustained and formidable agitation. The merchants offered only charity to protect the workers against economic fluctuations. In reply the weavers articulated their claim to a guaranteed real income.[24] But the resumption of collective action was out of the question in 1787 and 1788, the worst years so far for the Grande Fabrique in the eighteenth century. Major outlets were closed by wars in eastern Europe and revolutionary disturbances in the Low Countries. Stockpiling was discouraged by high prices for raw silk. Fewer than two-thirds of the 15,000 looms in Lyon were occupied in 1788, and since at least two people worked each loom, contemporary estimates of 20,000 unemployed in the silk trade alone were probably not far from the mark.[25] Given the dependence of other trades such as braid-making on the demand for silk, unemployment overall was undoubtedly much higher.

---

[22] L. Trénard, 'La Crise sociale lyonnaise à la veille de la Révolution', *Revue d'histoire moderne et contemporaine*, 2 (1955), 21.

[23] Ibid. 25–45.

[24] *Doléances des maîtres-ouvriers fabricants en étoffes d'or, d'argent et de soie* (Lyon, 1789), 64.

[25] AC I²4 *bis*, fo. 2; *Mémoire de la ville de Lyon au Roi*, p. 4; Pariset, *Histoire de la Fabrique*, pp. 238–40; *Mémoire des électeurs fabricants d'étoffes en soie de la ville de Lyon* (Lyon, 1789), 18–19.

The Lyonnais economy was not well equipped to absorb this crisis in its principal industry. Not only were associated industries nearly ruined, such as embroidery and the manufacture of trimmings (gold and silver braid, ribbons, and lace),[26] but the activity of the building trades, and others dependent on the investment of wealth from the silk business, was drastically curtailed. There were no industries substantial enough to cushion the shocks delivered by the crisis of the Fabrique. Printing and finance, important in the sixteenth and seventeenth centuries, had declined into relative insignificance, and diversification of the city's economy had been impeded by the traditionalism of the Consulat, which was hostile to any developments which might compete with the Fabrique.[27] For nine years it resisted various attempts to establish cotton-printing factories on the land reclaimed by the Perrache enterprise. Only in 1787 was permission reluctantly given, and then it was more from fear of the consequences of unemployment than from a desire to found new industries. Furthermore, the Consulat refused to reduce duties on goods entering the new area (which Perrache had proposed as a bait for invest-ment) on the ground that this would disadvantage the old city.[28] The *banvins*, the *octrois*, and other indirect taxes and customs duties made Lyon unattractive to entrepreneurs, and there was more new industrial development in the smaller towns of the region and in the *faubourgs* than in the city itself. Substantial cotton-printing works at Tarare and Vernaison, a cotton-mill at Neuville, glassworks at Pierre-Bénite, and a chemical factory at la Guillotière were all established in the third quarter of the eighteenth century.[29]

The relative prosperity of three sizeable industries—leather-finishing, hat-making, and hosiery—partially compensated for the reverses of the rest. For the last two in particular, the 1780s were good years. According to the Consulat, hosiery occupied 3,777 men, women, and children in 1789. Technical advances were steadily improving the quality and efficiency of production, and the manufacture of silk stockings was said to have offered the master craftsmen 'une certaine aisance'.[30] Hatting

[26] The work-force in these trades dropped from 6,000 in 1782 to 3,000 in 1791: AC I²5, 46 *bis*, fo. 95. See also R. Verninac, *Description physique et politique du département du Rhône* (Lyon, an IX), 70–3.

[27] J.-P. Gutton, *La Société et les pauvres: L'exemple de la généralité de Lyon 1534–1789* (Lyon, 1970), 78; Verninac, *Description physique*, pp. 80–1; Expilly, *Dictionnaire*, iv. 315; P. Léon, 'La Région lyonnaise dans l'histoire économique et sociale de la France', *Revue historique*, 237 (1967), 41; Trénard, *Lyon*, i. 4.

[28] Trénard, *Lyon*, i. 33–5.

[29] Verninac, *Description physique*, pp. 85, 89–90, 96.

[30] AC I²4, 46 *bis*, fos. 70, 113, 139; Verninac, *Description physique*, p. 110.

prospered equally. Since the beginning of the eighteenth century it had been the city's most considerable industry after silk and hosiery, and the Consulat estimated that it employed 3,000 people in 1789—5,000 if associated workers are included.[31] But labour troubles were more frequent than in the silk industry.[32] A higher concentration of labour than in most other trades—up to a hundred men in a workshop—helped the hatters' *confrérie* to organize the *compagnons* against the masters who, by contrast with the master weavers, dominated the guild and the industry. The two-week strike in 1744 was supported by a strike fund. Fullers campaigned for wage increases in the 1760s, and in 1770, with food prices rising sharply, they and the less skilled *apprêteurs* stopped work for three months, demanding pay at Paris rates. They were sustained this time not only by a strike fund, but by jobs on the big building sites at Saint-Clair. During the weavers' unrest in 1786 there was yet another prolonged strike, culminating in a march through the city in support of wage rises for all hatters.[33] The prosperity of hatting was thus frequently interrupted by agitation amongst an increasingly unified and well-organized work-force.

Another major prop of Lyon's economy, its *commerce d'entrepôt*, was in serious trouble.[34] Situated at a river junction straddling the main roads from Paris to Italy and the south-west of France, and two days by coach from Geneva, Lyon had obvious advantages as a trading centre.[35] But by the last quarter of the century the fairs which had capitalized on these advantages had fallen into decline, and the fair at Beaucaire had eclipsed them.[36] At the same time, canal construction drained trade away from Lyon. A canal from Givors to Rive-de-Gier was completed in 1780 and Givors replaced Lyon as the most convenient port for goods being moved overland between the Rhône and the Loire.[37]

[31] Associated workers may have numbered as many as 2,000 (AC I²4, 46 *bis*, fos. 105, 111, 113).

[32] The following remarks on hatting are largely based on A. De Francesco, *Il sogno della repubblica: Il mondo del lavoro dall'Ancien Régime al 1848* (Milan, 1983), 79–85. See also the same author's 'Conflittualità sul lavoro in epoca pre-industriale: Le agitazioni degli operai cappellai lionesi (1770–1824)', *Annali della Fondazione Luigi Einaudi*, 13 (1979), 151–213.

[33] On the 1786 agitation, see also Trénard, 'La Crise sociale lyonnaise', pp. 27–8.

[34] 'Cahier du tiers-état de la Sénéchaussée de Lyon', in *Cahiers des États généraux*, ed. J. Mavidal and E. Laurent (Paris, 1868), iii. 613.

[35] *Almanach astronomique et historique de la ville de Lyon et des provinces de Lyonnais, Forez et Beaujolais pour l'année 1781* (Lyon, 1781), 223.

[36] Trénard, *Lyon*, i. 4.

[37] Ibid. i. 8–9.

These setbacks contributed to a general stagnation in the city's economic affairs on the eve of the Revolution. The conjunction of economic misfortunes created a sense of crisis and vulnerability reflected in Tolozan de Montfort's talk of 'l'abandon de nos manufactures', and in the *cahier* of the Third Estate which asserted that Lyon's industries were 'menacées d'une ruine totale'.[38] Other cities suffered periods of economic crisis after 1770, and most of those with large textile industries experienced continual difficulties from about 1776 to the Revolution.[39] Lyon was particularly hard-hit because of the extent of its specialization in a severely depressed industry whose problems were peculiarly numerous and intractable, and because it lacked compensating factors. It had few substantial, buoyant areas of trade and lacked the stable institutional base that anchored the economies of so many towns. For these reasons Lyon did not benefit greatly from the partial recovery of the French economy which occurred after 1787.[40] It is also worth noting that of the French provincial cities with a population of over 60,000—Bordeaux, Marseille, Nantes, Rouen, and Lyon—all but Lyon, and especially the first three, were insulated from the troubles of the economy after about 1770 by the continued expansion and prosperity of sea-borne commerce. Their boom years were not cut short, as Lyon's were, two decades before the Revolution. In Rouen, the linen trade shared the problems of the textile industries, especially after the Eden Treaty, but with its *parlement* to complement its ecclesiastical institutions, it possessed an element of economic stability that was missing in Lyon.

Lyon's pre-revolutionary crisis had its links with the general crisis of the old regime, the instability of the French economy, restricted sumptuary expenditure at court, and sharp rises in the costs of basic necessities after 1782.[41] But the sharpness of the social conflicts which accompanied it, the extent and intensity of discontent amongst the labouring population, and the scale of economic dislocation all reflect the city's principal peculiarity: its dependence on a single industry in which the tensions between the controllers of capital and the work-force were unusually marked.

[38] *Cahiers des États généraux*, iii. 615. See also M. de Montluel, *Quelques moyens proposés pour contribuer au rétablissement des manufactures et au bonheur des ouvriers de Lyon* (Lyon, 1789), 5; Trénard, *Lyon*, i. 86, 240–1.

[39] N. Hampson, *A Social History of the French Revolution* (London, 1962), 18.

[40] See Trénard, 'La Crise sociale lyonnaise', p. 6.

[41] Gutton, *La Société et les pauvres*, (Lyon,) p. 70.

POLITICS AND SOCIAL STRUCTURE: THE PROXIMITY OF
WEALTH, POWER, AND STATUS

In the politics of pre-revolutionary France the second city did not count
for much. It lacked the institutional weapons with which to defend itself
against the rapacity of the absolute monarchy, which regularly milked
the municipal treasury,[42] and it was incapable of playing a significant part
in the great eighteenth-century battles between Crown and *parlements*.
Nevertheless, Lyon possessed administrative bodies appropriate to the
seat of a *gouvernement* and an intendancy, as well as municipal, legal,
and ecclesiastical institutions which both defined the structure of status
amongst the local *notables* and provided the framework for such political
life as there was.

Lyon possessed neither *parlement* nor university, but it could boast a
see of great size and antiquity (if seldom the physical presence of the one
hundred and twenty-second archbishop, Yves-Alexandre de Marbeuf,
a resolute opponent of Jansenism and later of the Revolution). His
archiepiscopal province included the dioceses of Autun, Mâcon, Chalon-
sur-Saône, Langres, Dijon, and Saint-Claude as well as the diocese of
Lyon itself. This was extensive, though by no means the largest in
France,[43] and included parts of Dauphiné, Bresse, and Bugey as well as
the Lyonnais, Forez, and Beaujolais. After the archbishop, the principal
clerics were the twenty-two *chanoines-comtes* of Saint-Jean, distinguished
both by their wealth and their sixteen quarterings of nobility. There were
three other very wealthy chapters—Ainay, Saint-Paul, and Saint-Nizier.[44]
But while in the absence of a *parlement* or estates the senior clergy ranked
at the top of the local hierarchy of status along with the consular nobility
and the magistrates of the Cour des Monnaies, their political pretensions
far outran their actual influence, as was revealed by the ineffectual efforts
of the *chanoines-comtes* to intervene on behalf of the weavers in 1786.[45]

Lyon's legal aristocracy was to be found amongst the officers of the
Sénéchaussée—not much to boast of when smaller towns like Grenoble
had *parlements*—plus two commercial courts: the Cour des Monnaies,
which had jurisdiction extending from Bresse to Provence, and the unique
Cour de la Conservation, which had final jurisdiction in many areas of

---

[42] See the *Livre rouge de la municipalité de Lyon: Premier Cahier* (Lyon, 1790), a detailed
exposé of financial mismanagement under the old regime.
[43] M. Marion, *Dictionnaire des institutions de la France aux XVIIᵉ et XVIIIᵉ siècles* (Paris,
1923), 178.
[44] Expilly, *Dictionnaire*, iv. 286–7; Trénard, *Lyon*, i. 66.
[45] See Garden, *Lyon et les Lyonnais*, pp. 506–7, 588.

commercial litigation. It was the dignitaries of the powerful and prestigious commercial courts who endowed the Lyonnais magistrature with its éclat and a higher proportion of noblemen than that of any other provincial town. At a less exalted level, there were 52 *avocats*, 63 *procureurs*, and 40 *notaires*. They were amongst the wealthiest sections of the population, with average fortunes smaller only than nobles and office-holders and larger than *bourgeois* (in the limited contemporary legal sense of people living on *rentes* and income from property) and *négociants* (a term used for substantial merchants of whatever speciality). But there was no closed legal caste and there were few legal dynasties. It was unusual in Lyon for a legal office to remain in the same family for more than two generations, and only a third of legal practitioners had had fathers in the same occupation. The law in Lyon was a stepping-stone towards the world of the wealthy merchant families and sometimes towards the nobility.

The medical profession was the least important socially and economically of the groups dependent on the city's major institutions, in its case the Collège de Médecine and the Collège Royal de Chirurgie. The former dated from the sixteenth century and claimed to be one of France's oldest; the latter was constituted in 1756. Membership of each conferred the privileges of *bourgeois notables de Lyon*. Beyond the élite of the colleges, levels of wealth and status varied considerably, from physicians as wealthy as the richest merchants to surgeons (and not only the *chirurgiens-barbiers*) who were little better off than artisans.[46]

The other large concentrations of non-noble wealth belonged to financial and mercantile families. Garden's work on the tax-rolls of the *contribution mobilière* for 1791 in the three *cantons* of Lyon where professions were recorded (Nord-Est, Nord-Ouest, and Fédération) gives the average estimated rental value of taxpayers' dwellings as 150 *livres*. Possibly the gulf between rich and poor was greater in these *cantons* than elsewhere, and the proportion of nobles almost certainly was, but the areas are not so unrepresentative as to throw doubt on the main conclusions (except for the absence of professional men in significant numbers).[47]

By far the wealthiest were those who described themselves as bankers; then, in descending order, came silk-merchants, *agents de change*

---

[46] On the professions, see Expilly, *Dictionnaire*, iv. 295, 303–4; Garden, *Lyon et les Lyonnais*, pp. 202, 358, 383–6, 505; P. Dawson, *Provincial Magistrates and Revolutionary Politics in France 1789–1795* (Cambridge, Mass., 1972), 73; Trénard, *Lyon*, i. 62.

[47] These areas were remote from the courts and hospitals near which most lawyers and doctors lived.

(brokers), *négociants, commissionnaires* (commission agents), and *marchands-fabricants*. To these can be added the taxpayers classed as *bourgeois*, amongst whom were many retired business men and widows whose modest rents often concealed substantial assets.[48]

Garden's study of marriage patterns shows a very high degree of social cohesion amongst wealthy non-nobles. The vast majority of *négociants* were the sons of *négociants* or *bourgeois* (74 per cent), and most of them married the daughters of *négociants* or *bourgeois* (56 per cent). The other groups with which there were frequent family links were the liberal professions and *officiers* (12 per cent of fathers, 19 per cent of wives), and the merchants (7 per cent and 11 per cent). In sharp contrast to their numerical predominance in the general population, the artisan classes were represented by only 2.5 per cent of the fathers and 9 per cent of the wives. So it was a myth that industrious peasants and artisans could easily enter the business élite of Lyon.[49] The Tolozans and the Sériziats made it, with one generation moving from petty village commerce to metropolitan eminence and the next to the Lyonnais oligarchy, but few others did.

For all their wealth, the merchants of Lyon were separated from the local oligarchy by a large gulf, and it was not just a gulf of status. The image of Lyon as a centre of commercial wealth, an image reinforced by the paucity of ancient noble families there, masked the pre-eminence of noble fortunes until Garden showed that only the very richest non-nobles could match the assets of the nobility, who were taxed on an average assessed rental value that was 50 per cent higher than the silk-merchants, the wealthiest merchant group after the bankers. Both the size of noble marriage contracts and the extent of their real property far exceeded any other group's. What is more, the supremacy of established noble wealth was not under threat in the second half of the eighteenth century. Although the total wealth of the merchant community seems to have increased greatly between 1750 and 1790, this was largely due to the multiplication of merchant fortunes close to the average.

Maurice Wahl, the excellent nineteenth-century historian of Lyon, correctly described its pre-revolutionary consular milieu as 'un patriciat bourgeois'.[50] The mode of elevation to the Consulat was election as one

---

[48] This account of merchant wealth is based on Garden, *Lyon et les Lyonnais*, esp. pp. 198, 203–4, 258–374 except where otherwise stated.

[49] See e.g. A. Guillon de Montléon, *Mémoires pour servir à l'histoire de la ville de Lyon* (Paris, 1824), i. 29; P. Ballaguy, *Un Général de l'an II: Charles Sériziat 1756–1802* (Lyon, 1913), 1–6.

[50] M. Wahl, *Les Premières Années de la Révolution à Lyon* (Paris, n.d.), 7.

of four *échevins* (councillors) by an annual assembly of local *notables* which was dominated by the consular families. At the end of their two-year terms the *échevins* were ennobled, and it was from this process that most of Lyon's noble families derived their status. Of 182 *échevins* in the eighteenth century, 82 were men of commerce (mostly *négociants*, bankers, *marchands-fabricants*, or drapers) and 53 were *avocats* or office-holders. Because it was in effect a prerequisite for entry to the *échevinage* to have shouldered and survived the enormous financial burden of serving one of the two great hospitals as rector or treasurer, all the *échevins* were extremely rich. It very rarely happened that sufficient wealth accumulated in one generation, and consequently the consular nobility was drawn from a very narrow social stratum of established and exceptional wealth, so narrow indeed that the medical profession and even lawyers other than *avocats* were almost entirely excluded not only from the *échevinage*, but from the Assembly of Notables which elected it.[51]

The families of the consular milieu therefore constituted a group above and distinct from wealthy non-nobles. They were not strictly speaking a closed caste, but the chances of entering their ranks were small and their remoteness from the rest of the population was accentuated by their oligarchic role.[52] In so far as there were municipal politics in pre-revolutionary Lyon, their mysteries were reserved for the *échevinage* and a handful of magistrates and royal officials. The Consulat was the only body which had some formally recognized political independence. It controlled the city's finances and successfully defended its pre-eminence against the Church and the other potential sources of opposition, the Cour des Monnaies, the Bureau des Finances, and to a lesser extent the Sénéchaussée.

Early in the century the struggle took the form of disputes over precedent, but from the 1780s it turned more and more on the control of local finance. In their unsuccessful campaign against the Consulat's maladministration of the *octrois*, uncontrolled sumptuary expenditure, and self-enrichment from municipal funds, the office-holders and magistrates could reasonably claim to represent the interests of the city as a whole, but their skirmishing with the Consulat remained a limited conflict involving highly privileged groups with much more in common amongst themselves than with the bourgeoisie of commerce and the professions.

---

[51] See Garden, *Lyon et les Lyonnais*, pp. 198, 203, 358–63, 488–504.
[52] There is an excellent analysis of the politics of the Lyonnais élites in Garden, *Lyon et les Lyonnais*, pp. 488–526, on which the present discussion is largely based.

The barriers which prevented the merchant and professional classes from participating in municipal affairs could be passed by successful individuals, particularly *avocats* or *officiers*, but they nevertheless clearly defined their inferior status and the social distance between them and the oligarchy. Similar barriers surrounded the more exalted civic institutions. The hospital administrators of the Hôtel-Dieu and the Charité were recruited from and by the same stratum as the Consulat, and so were the *chevaliers de l'Arc* and the *chevaliers de l'Arquebuse* (pseudo-military societies). Lesser men could become junior officers of the *milice bourgeoise*, but little prestige and much inconvenience attached to this, for it involved rubbing shoulders with the *menu peuple* who made up not only the other ranks but a good proportion of the *sous-officiers*. The senior officers were drawn from the consular connection.

DISORIENTATION AND DIVISION AMONGST THE SOCIAL ÉLITES

While exceptional wealth, pre-eminent status, and local power were combined in the consular and magistratical élites, the propertied classes as a whole were fragmented and lacked unity of outlook. In broad outline, Lyonnais society resembled what has become the orthodox picture of pre-revolutionary French social structure,[53] with an integrated notability, of which the bourgeoisie was striving to become a part, and only one really clear dividing line, that between those who worked with their hands and those who did not. But there were tensions, ambiguities, disorientation, and uncertainty in the upper strata of Lyonnais society.

Perhaps because they were painfully aware of their predominantly commercial origins, the older families of the nobility insisted on their superiority to the *gens de commerce*. In 1780 an unequivocal assertion of this supremacy was made by Gesse de Poizieux, the *lieutenant-général* of the Sénéchaussée, when in the course of a legal battle with two obscure *négociants* he attempted to define the 'immense' distance dividing him from his opponents: 'l'un est le Chef de la Justice Royale d'une grande ville, les autres sont des gens de la lie du peuple, qui n'ont pas même le faible mérite de la fortune'. But there were too many mercantile branches in noble family trees for Gesse to get away with this. A *conseiller* of the Sénéchaussée, A.-J. Millanois, himself a noble, printed a reply to 'l'outrage que le sieur Gesse fait au commerce, de qualifier ceux qui

---

[53] A recent statement of this orthodoxy is W. Doyle, *Origins of the French Revolution* (Oxford, 1980).

exercent cette profession d'être des "gens de la lie du peuple"; c'est ainsi qu'il parle d'une profession aussi honorable qu'honorée dans sa Patrie : on se rappelle cependant que le sieur Gesse est, ainsi que moi, fils d'un négociant; il méconnaît sa source, et moi je m'en fais honneur'.[54] Most nobles, like Gesse, still did their best to forget their ties with the commercial world, but in the 1780s it was not easy. In 1788 a lampoon by a commoner, the *greffier* Billemaz, satirized two leading magistrates quarrelling about office: 'Je vois bien que vous êtes accoutumé à vendre; on a toujours du goût pour son premier métier.'[55]

Contempt for commerce strong enough to inspire Gesse's vainglorious outburst—and Garden provides many complementary examples[56]—is hard to reconcile with the image of a homogeneous propertied élite which has become fixed in the recent historiography of pre-revolutionary France.[57] There is no doubt that nobles and merchants shared many values and aspirations—above all to live nobly—and habits of investment in low-return, high-status landed property, *rentes,* and offices. But the case of Lyon highlights the main weakness in the notion of a unified pre-revolutionary élite: merchants may have been entranced by the noble condition, but the admiration was not reciprocated. Relations between nobles and rich bourgeois—even members of consular families—were uneasy and often rancorous, and they became, it seems, more and more distant. Far from increasing intercourse between wealthy commoners and nobles, the eighteenth century brought estrangement: 'de plus en plus au cours du XVIIIe siècle, bourgeois et négociants se retrouvaient entre eux, mais ne cotaient plus ou presque plus jamais les autres catégories de notables lyonnais'.[58]

It appears, too, that the propertied classes were divided on the crucial question of repression. In his stimulating analysis of the world of labour in eighteenth- and nineteenth-century Lyon, De Francesco notes that from the 1740s there developed a tendency in mercantile circles to criticize the traditional paternalism of the Consulat when faced with unrest in the regulated trades, and to demand instead more direct armed repression. The Consulat habitually distinguished between guild members, who,

[54] See Garden, *Lyon et les Lyonnais,* pp. 516–17, 534–5.

[55] F. Billemaz, *Le Grand Bailliage* (Lyon, 1788), 10.

[56] Garden, *Lyon et les Lyonnais,* pp. 534–8.

[57] e.g. Doyle, *Origins of the Revolution*; R. Darnton, 'A Bourgeois Puts his World in Order', in *The Great Cat Massacre and Other Episodes in French Cultural History* (London, 1984), 136–9.

[58] Garden, *Lyon et les Lyonnais,* p. 534.

however poor, formed an integral part of the social fabric, and the populace, day-labourers, *compagnons* (particularly when newcomers to the city), *étrangers* in general, apprentices, and *gens sans aveu*, who could conveniently be labelled *canaille* living outside the pale of ordered society.[59] Disorder was much more severely repressed when it involved the populace rather than the regulated trades, and when it affected both, punishment tended to fall most heavily on the former.[60] But in 1744, when for the first time the authorities were defied by the city's largest corporation—masters, apprentices, and wage-earners together—there was criticism (anonymous, but probably from the *marchands-fabricants*) of the Consulat's failure to respond with sufficient vigour.[61] De Francesco has shown that after the great majority of hatters ceased to be self-employed retailing artisans, paternalistic responses to their demands— from the mid-century mainly wage demands—could only be made at the expense of antagonizing the master hatters, who twice (in 1773 and 1785) furiously resisted wage settlements negotiated by the authorities. He has also found some incidents suggesting that the authorities were beginning to respond to the calls for vigorous repression of artisanal insubordination: the round-up of militant hatters in 1778 after an inn brawl in which they were not involved; and, most tellingly, the unprecedented display on the Place des Terreaux of the heads of the two hatters and one weaver executed for their roles in the labour troubles of 1786. But there was no clear break with the paternalistic pattern of response to labour agitation, and for some entrepreneurs in those areas of manufacturing which had departed most from the traditional corporate model this seems to have meant that the Consulat was failing in its prime task of maintaining social discipline.[62]

Despite these tensions, there is no indication before 1788 that interest in Lyonnais politics—which amounted to little more than perennial clan feuds amongst the notability—extended far beyond the leading families, even when the magistrature invited public support for its campaign against consular maladministration in the 1770s.[63] It took the political shocks caused by the financial crisis of the monarchy to broaden political

[59] See De Francesco, *Il sogno della repubblica*, pp. 37–50. The word 'populace' in French is more pejorative than in English.

[60] Ibid. 40–2.

[61] Garden, *Lyon et les Lyonnais*, p. 498.

[62] De Francesco, *Il sogno della repubblica*, pp. 79, 81–6, 101.

[63] Garden, *Lyon et les Lyonnais*, pp. 518–20. From the print runs of pamphlets published in the course of this debate, Garden estimates the 'classe politique' of Lyon at about 1780 to be between 600 and 700 people.

participation significantly, and, as with much of provincial France, it was the news in August 1788 that there were to be elections to form an Estates General for the first time in more than 170 years which finally touched off widespread, open expressions of resentment against the established local authorities. But while overt political activity was precipitated by the urgency of deciding who would speak for the second city in the moment-ous discussions at Versailles, late eighteenth-century social tensions help to account for its sudden emergence and rapid spread.

By early 1789 pamphlets were condemning the Consulat as unrep-resentative, usurping, outmoded, and deficient in both probity and com-petence.[64] Both its political and its social pretensions were brought into question, particularly when it claimed to speak on behalf of the Third Estate: 'Pourquoi cet empressement à vouloir représenter un corps [le Tiers] dont vous venez de sortir, et pour lequel vous avez peut-être plus de mépris que ceux qui depuis longtemps ont fait scission avec lui?'[65] Two of the *échevins'* most prominent critics were elected to the Estates General, another Millanois (Jean-Jacques, an *avocat*), and the printer and bookseller Jean-André Périsse-Duluc, whose choice as a guild delegate in February 1789 the Consulat had attempted to annul. And whereas the nobility's *cahier* glossed over the question of municipal reform, the Third Estate's vigorously attacked maladministration of local finances and proposed an elected municipal assembly of which at least half the members were to be commoners.[66] In early 1789 bourgeois Lyon still envisaged the continued existence of the Second Estate as an order, but the political crisis had nevertheless crystallized considerable latent antagonism towards the local élites.

The bourgeois, however, were themselves divided, and, as we shall see, this limited their capacity to press the political demands which began to be formulated in 1788 and 1789. 'Bourgeois' here refers to a broad group which was by no means revolutionary. Few concepts have been so relentlessly questioned as 'the revolutionary bourgeoisie', and its lim-itations are obvious in the case of Lyon. Class consciousness, unity of economic interests, and overt conflict with the nobility—not to mention any sense of revolutionary purpose—are as hard to find amongst the bourgeois of Lyon, ranging down from the *négoce* to well-off, independent

---

[64] Ibid. 520–6. See also below, Ch. 2, 'Initial Responses to the Revolution'.

[65] *Réponse au discours de M. le prévôt des marchands ... par un des commissaires de l'Assemblée du tiers état ...* (Lyon, [1789]), quoted in Garden, *Lyon et les Lyonnais*, p. 521.

[66] Wahl, *Les Premières Années*, p. 74; A. Latreille (ed.), *Histoire de Lyon* (Toulouse, 1975), 274–5.

artisan-retailers, as they have been in studies of other places.[67] But the speed with which their hostility to the Consulat emerged in 1789, and still more their pronounced consciousness of superiority to the labouring poor, suggests that in Lyon the middling groups loosely definable as bourgeois were acquiring a sense of class through friction with both the oligarchy and the populace. This is clearest in relationship to the world of manual labour, from which merchants and professional men were separated by a gulf which is quantifiable in terms of wealth and immanent in the language of social fear, disdain, and condescension.

According to Garden's analysis of the rolls of the 1791 *contribution mobilière*, the average assessed rental value of taxpayers' dwellings was 150 *livres*. Amongst the four lower occupational categories (day-labourers, female occupations, silk-weavers, and other artisans), the one with the highest average rental value—artisans (90 *livres*)—was far short of the general average, while the *marchands* and *négociants*, the least wealthy on average of the three upper categories (the others being nobles and *bourgeois* (in the restricted eighteenth-century sense[68])), had an average of 340 *livres*, well over double the general average. Alone amongst Garden's categories, the 'clerks and liberal professions' fell midway between the social extremes, with an average assessment of 145 *livres*. Few artisans had assessments much above the average, and the only group which straddled the wealth gap were those described by that most imprecise term 'marchand', many of whom, like most haberdashers and grocers, were little better off than artisans. Perhaps for that reason it was a merchant who left us one of the most striking pieces of evidence of the social gulf between bourgeois and artisans, a letter bitterly protesting against his nomination as a corporal in the *milice bourgeoise*, where artisans would be his equals. This, he was convinced, was nothing more than a base conspiracy with intent 'de le mortifier, d'altérer son crédit et son commerce'.[69]

Beyond the sense of distance from the labouring poor, there was little coherence in Lyonnais bourgeois culture on the eve of the Revolution. There were deep differences of outlook between the merchants and the intellectual circles of professional men and nobles where enlightened thought had made converts in the eighteenth century. The Académie des

---

[67] See C. Lucas, 'Nobles, Bourgeois and the Origins of the French Revolution', *Past and Present*, 60 (1973), 84–119.

[68] i.e., 'Primarily *rentiers*, who lived from annuities and land rents and did not work' (Darnton, *The Great Cat Massacre*, p. 112).

[69] Garden, *Lyon et les Lyonnais*, p. 524.

Sciences et des Belles-Lettres brought together the more cultivated of the *noblesse de robe*, some of the secular clergy, and, particularly after 1750, the élite of the professions. But it failed to interest many merchants, who were notorious for their indifference to matters beyond the narrowly practical. Even the Montgolfiers' balloon ascent from the Brotteaux in 1784 failed to interest the mercantile bourgeoisie sufficiently to produce many subscriptions in support of further aerostatic experiments, though the subscription lists are full of noble names. In Garden's words: 'On serait tenté de croire que l'élite marchande se tient volontairement en retrait par rapport à l'élite intellectuelle, qui ne l'accueille qu'avec réticence.'[70]

The cleavage deepened during the economic crisis of the 1780s. While the intellectuals reacted by proposing changes in the silk industry, the merchants remained conservative and corporatist in everything but their attitude to the exploitation of labour. They regarded certain conditions as essential to the survival of the Fabrique: close regulation of all aspects of production, including the labour force, combined with the maintenance of low wages and hence absolute freedom for themselves to determine piece-work rates. They were untouched by the new currents of economic thought which in 1788 inspired the academician and Inspector of Manufactures Roland de la Platière to write *Des causes de la décadence du commerce et de la dépopulation de la ville de Lyon*. This advocated de-regulation of the Fabrique and won him great unpopularity in commercial circles.[71] Another academician, the Abbé Bertholon, pointed out that starving the work-force and driving it to seek work elsewhere was as good a way as any of destroying the Fabrique.[72] But the silk-merchants remained true to the principle stated by Étienne Mayet: 'Pour assurer et maintenir la prospérité de nos manufactures, il est nécessaire que l'ouvrier ne s'enrichisse jamais, qu'il n'ait précisément que ce qu'il lui faut pour se bien nourrir et pour se bien vêtir.'[73] Until the end of the corporative regime and afterwards, they resolutely opposed the weavers' attempts to ensure themselves enough income while they were in work to accumulate reserves for protection against temporary indigence. In 1792 the *conventionnel* Louis Vitet, a physician who had been an academician in the 1780s, wrote from bitter experience after waiting in vain for a group of *négociants* who had promised to present plans for alleviating

[70] Ibid. 544.

[71] Godart, *L'Ouvrier en soie*, pp. 86–7; Pariset, *Histoire de la Fabrique*, pp. 225–31.

[72] Quoted in Godart, *L'Ouvrier en soie*, pp. 417–18.

[73] Quoted by Garden, *Lyon et les Lyonnais*, p. 309.

unemployment: 'N'attendez rien de négociants, ils aiment mieux mourir que de perdre leur cher argent ... ils sont dans l'impossibilité d'être éclairés ...'.[74]

It would be unreasonable to take Vitet's harsh judgement at face value, for clearly it was influenced by his suspicions of the silk-merchants' politics. It would also be wrong to assume that even if the silk-merchants were as callous as Vitet and the weavers claimed, the same was true of the propertied classes as a whole. Both Christian charity, through the parochial *œuvres de la Marmite,* and secular *bienfaisance* were said to have produced substantial sums for the Lyonnais poor, at least in times of severe unemployment such as 1787. The parish charities in particular, the only form of organized public activity engaged in by Lyonnais women before the Revolution, seem to have functioned smoothly and to have achieved the remarkable feat of recruiting from all elements of the notability, from consular circles and the great business families to the old nobility and the office-holding élites, in a way not to be found in any other form of association. By contrast, the efforts of the *intendant* and the Consulat to organize emergency charity in 1788 were bedevilled by the élites' clan conflicts. But after the Revolution had broadened the base of the notability and embraced the concept of fraternity, a secular charitable organization, the Société Philanthropique, was launched in October 1789. It attracted more than 1,600 subscribers at a minimum of 42 *livres* per head, plus substantial donations from the Consulat and the Crown, and it worked well enough to distribute bread to 8,821 families in 1790, as well as providing fuel and setting up weaving establishments to alleviate unemployment.[75]

The image of the Lyonnais bourgeoisie as indifferent to everything beyond the counting-house also needs qualification. In fact, much of bourgeois Lyon in the 1780s was in a state of intellectual ferment. Rosicrucianism, Martinist illuminism, Martinèsism, hermetism, Willer-mozism, and animal magnetism, amongst other doctrines, mostly mystical, fought for the allegiance of the flourishing masonic lodges.[76] The sixteen lodges which Garden has studied probably represented about half those founded between 1744 and the Revolution. Of their 1,100 identified members, merchants and *négociants* made up 61.3 per cent, but the social

---

[74] Letter of 12 Nov. 1792, in *Revue d'histoire de Lyon,* iv (1905), 312–13.

[75] Garden, *Lyon et les Lyonnais,* p. 533; Gutton, *La Société et les pauvres,* p. 55; Wahl, *Les Premières Années,* p. 115.

[76] See Trénard, *Lyon,* i. 77–8, 177–84; A. Joly, 'Pierre-Jacques Willermoz', *Albums du crocodile,* 6 (1938), 19.

composition varied considerably from lodge to lodge. La Bienfaisance was dominated by the military nobility descended from the *échevins* of the seventeenth century; others were largely composed of functionaries (Parfaite Réunion) or lesser merchants (Candeur and Parfait Silence).[77] The occupational specialization reflects the fragmentation of the Lyonnais bourgeoisie and, once again, the tendency of merchants and *négociants* to keep themselves apart.

Many lodges were little more than professional or dining clubs. Some were drinking societies so enthusiastic that they were denounced to the Grand-Orient of France.[78] But others were passionately serious, particularly those influenced by the founder of Lyonnais Masonry, the silk-factor J.-B. Willermoz. Willermoz was largely responsible for the strength of Martinist mysticism in Lyon and for stimulating an interest in the occult which led in turn to disunity, heterodoxy, arcane experimentation, and innovations in ritual, making Lyon a source of constant worry and occasional scandal for the Grand-Orient, and a perfect environment for Cagliostro, who took over the moribund lodge Sagesse, 'regenerated' it, and applied its resources towards his own upkeep. There was much that was bizarre but little that was original or profound in Lyonnais mysticism. Most of the ideas came from elsewhere. No doctrine achieved supremacy and no synthesis of ideas was achieved. But the confused, frenetic world of the Freemasons in pre-revolutionary Lyon seems to reflect the inability of sections of the bourgeoisie—and notably the medical profession, which was heavily involved in mystical Masonry—to reorient themselves after the weakening of old certainties by the impact of rationalism, economic crisis, and political decay.[79]

It is as difficult to assess the influence of the *philosophes* in Lyon as it is to know how deep Lyonnais mysticism went. The secularism of the Enlightenment clearly had some impact: fewer religious books were published and there was a decrease of more than a third in the recruitment of nuns.[80] But apart from a certain disenchantment with the regular clergy, there is little evidence that the Enlightenment made great inroads into traditional religious beliefs at any level of Lyonnais society, and there were few outspoken local exponents of rationalism.[81]

The Lyonnais praised the virtues of industry, probity, and discretion

---

[77] Trénard, *Lyon*, i. 62; Garden, *Lyon et les Lyonnais*, pp. 546–9.

[78] Ibid. p. 547.

[79] Trénard, *Lyon*, i. 184, 188, 207–12, 220.

[80] Latreille, *Histoire de Lyon*, p. 276.

[81] Garden, *Lyon et les Lyonnais*, pp. 471–86; Trénard, *Lyon*, i. 207–12.

in business; they were ambiguous about ostentation (it was good for silk and so to be encouraged by vast displays for visiting dignitaries, but they avoided it amongst themselves); they were obsessed by questions of precedence and protocol, and indulged in interminable feuds about them; they adored the theatre, and many showed an uncharacteristic fervour for Freemasonry; most practised their Catholicism unostentatiously and left conventionally pious wills. There is not much here to differentiate them from the inhabitants of a dozen other towns. But for contemporaries the Lyonnais mentality was characterized by one overriding peculiarity, an obsession with matters of trade: 'L'esprit du commerce est celui qui domine dans la ville de Lyon; aussi on ne voit peut-être nulle part autant d'industrie, autant de souplesse, ni autant d'attachement à l'ordre des affaires.'[82] It was one of Lyon's misfortunes that this reputation pursued it into a decade when trade and commerce, not to mention luxury and big cities (other than Paris), became suspect to a generation of revolutionaries inspired by Rousseau and the cult of republican Rome.

While it would be a mistake to take at face value the clichéd view of Lyon as a prosaic and self-absorbed mercantile community, it is not hard to believe that its inhabitants were preoccupied with the commercial affairs on which their city was so heavily and precariously dependent. They had good reason to be, given the peculiar severity of the city's economic crisis. And they had good reason to give them priority over other matters, even the political revolution. In their economic stagnation and their intellectual uncertainty, the bourgeois of late eighteenth-century Lyon thus seem singularly ill-fitted to play the historic role which some Marxist historians have written for the revolutionary bourgeoisie. They lacked the prosperity and the optimism which fuelled the ambition of their Marseillais and Bordelais counterparts.[83] Uncertain of themselves and of their city's future, they were ill-equipped to seize the political opportunities which arose during the spring and summer of 1789.

DEPENDENCE AND ISOLATION

Even had the economic circumstances been more favourable, Lyon would still have been poorly prepared to take a positive part in 1789. The eighteenth century had increased its dependence on the Crown as the

[82] Expilly, *Dictionnaire*, iv. 320. See also Trénard, *Lyon*, i. 85.
[83] See A. Forrest, *Society and Politics in Revolutionary Bordeaux* (Oxford, 1975); and W. Scott, *Terror and Repression in Revolutionary Marseilles* (London, 1973).

N

2. The *département* of Rhône-et-Loire

Consulat became less a defender of Lyon's privileges and independence than a mechanism of social advancement. Interference by the Villeroy family, hereditary governors of the city, and by the *intendants*, particularly after about 1750,[84] seems to have become accepted. This contrasts strikingly with Bordeaux, where there was great resentment at the transfer of decision-making to Paris.[85] In any case, few decisions of importance were taken locally at any time in the eighteenth century, and on major matters such as tariff policy Lyonnais opinion was not even consulted.[86] The Consulat retained general control of finance, public order, and routine administration, but these were hardly enough to feed a proud tradition of independence. The history of Lyon in the latter half of the eighteenth century is marked rather by a tendency to solicit royal intervention (both to resolve contentious issues and to restore the city's prosperity[87]), which is hardly surprising in view of the city's heavy dependence on the central government's tariff policy, the court's appetite for silk, and ministerial action to ensure that grain reached it in time of shortage.[88] The Lyonnais recognized this dependence: in the *cahier* of the Third Estate and in a spate of brochures on the silk industry in 1789 the dominant theme was how the King and his court had to revive the fashion for Lyonnais cloth if there was to be any hope for the Fabrique. The Eden Treaty, which was said to have contributed to the industry's ruin, drove home the point that a benevolently interested government was a pre-condition of prosperity.[89] Neither *ligueurs* nor *frondeurs* had seduced Lyon from its demonstrative loyalty to the Crown. Its economic interests demanded a similar loyalty as long as the monarchy lasted.

Frictions with the Crown caused by the defence of municipal and corporate privilege must be seen in the context of this overriding imperative. The city, like any other, had privileges to defend, and there was naturally sympathy for the *parlements* in their campaigns against ministerial despotism. But there was by no means such a firm consensus in

---

[84] See Garden, *Lyon et les Lyonnais*, pp. 494–5.

[85] Forrest, *Society and Politics*, pp. 384–5.

[86] See Trénard, *Lyon*, i. 30.

[87] See ibid. i. 18, 20.

[88] On the Fabrique's need for court patronage and protection, see AC I²46 *bis*, fos. 84 and 95. AN F¹¹1173–4, ds. 9 and 11, are full of pleas for special protection and assistance to ensure Lyon's food supplies (June–July 1789); AN F¹¹217, d. 8, contains similar material for 1792.

[89] Guillon de Montléon, *Mémoires*, ii. 20; E. Mayet, *Mémoire sur les manufactures de Lyon* (Paris, 1786), 70; *Cahiers des États généraux*, iii. 615. See also Trénard, *Lyon*, i. 30–1, 240–1.

support of the *parlements* as existed in the cities which housed them. Lyon had been deprived of both university and *parlement* as a matter of policy: Crown and Consulat alike feared that the status attached to such institutions would lure merchant families from their true vocation. So Lyon remained under the jurisdiction of the Parlement of Paris, which does not seem to have mattered to the consular élite and other noble office-holders and magistrates. They opposed, though not very vigorously, the royal attempts to replace the *parlements* with *Conseils supérieurs* in 1771 and *Grands Bailliages* in 1788.[90] Commercial Lyon, however, was not so willing to sacrifice its claim to a superior court in the interests of solidarity with the *parlementaires*, whose supporters in Lyon were disappointed by the rapid public acceptance of the Conseil Supérieur. Lyon did not have the tradition of solidarity with the *parlements* which caused conflict between other cities and the Crown. Causes of dispute and dissatisfaction there certainly were—above all the periodic royal raids on the municipal treasury of which the Third Estate complained in 1789[91]—but in the second half of the eighteenth century only Turgot's attempt to abolish the guilds could be regarded as a ministerial threat to Lyon's basic interests. And these decrees were never put into effect in Lyon. The reformed guild system which came in the wake of Turgot's fall was not regarded as obnoxious, except by the silk-workers.[92]

There is not even much evidence of overt anti-Parisian feeling, apart from resentment in the business community over the loss of Lyon's financial influence to the capital, and attempts by Parisian merchants to corner the silk trade in the 1750s. Metzger speculates that there may have been a sense of humiliation at being under the Paris Parlement's jurisdiction, and that the establishment of the Conseil Supérieur may have symbolized a kind of victory over Paris. But he can find no evidence for this.[93] The lack of a *parlement* may even have made for better relations with Paris, for provincial *parlements* often resented the latter's pretensions, while Lyon's courts had good relations with it.[94] Naturally, local sensibilities were often wounded by the mockery of metropolitan sophisticates, and there was doubt in Lyon about Parisian reliability in business[95] (a feeling artfully played upon by the Parisian Grimod de la

[90] See Garden, *Lyon et les Lyonnais*, p. 380; P. Metzger, *Le Conseil supérieur et le Grand Baillage de Lyon 1771–1774, 1788* (Lyon, 1913).

[91] *Cahiers des États généraux*, iii. 615.

[92] See Garden, *Lyon et les Lyonnais*, pp. 369–72.

[93] See Metzger, *Le Conseil supérieur*, pp. 25, 158.

[94] See ibid. 161.

[95] See Garden, *Lyon et les Lyonnais*, p. 537.

Reynière in his 'Tableau de Lyon'[96]). But in the absence of evidence to
the contrary, one must conclude that there was no strong sense of rivalry
between the two on the eve of the Revolution. In so far as there was a
Lyonnais sense of identity, it was of a less political kind than that in
Rennes, or Bordeaux, or Marseille. It expressed itself most obviously
through pride in the city's commerce. Variations on the formula, 'la
seconde ville par sa magnificence et sa population, la première par sa
situation, son industrie, ses richesses', were *de rigueur* in descriptions of
the city by Lyonnais and outsiders alike, followed inevitably by references
to Lyonnais industriousness and commercial probity.[97] Beyond that, the
Lyonnais wrote little in praise of their city or its institutions. Although
the *milice bourgeoise* served as a symbol of lost independence and as a
guarantee of remaining privileges, the decay into which it had fallen
diminished it as a focus of local patriotism. True, its existence had meant
that since the end of the sixteenth century Lyon had generally been
spared a royal garrison.[98] But even this 'privilège exclusif de se garder'
was eroded after the disturbances of 1786 by the establishment of barracks
just inside the city walls. To soothe Lyonnais feelings, however, it was
specified that there should be a barrier on the city side so that the entrance
should face the *faubourg* of Vaise rather than the city proper.[99]

If there is no indication of pronounced particularism in Lyon's relations
with the royal government, nor is there any sign in its relationship with
surrounding areas of a regional dominance sufficient to compensate for
its subjection to the capital, even though Lyon is well sited to dominate
the lands bordering the Rhône, the Saône, and their tributaries, the Ain
and the Gier. Between Mâcon and Valence there seems nothing to prevent
Lyon establishing its hegemony over the area marked out by the Massif
Central, the Alps, and the Jura. But in the eighteenth century a number
of factors prevented Lyon's region becoming an economic, political, or
psychological unity. It was divided administratively and by regional
antipathies, for the small *généralité* of Lyon lay to the west of the Rhône

---

[96] Grimod de la Reynière, *Peu de chose: Hommage à l'Académie de Lyon* (Lyon,
1788), 6.

[97] [P.-E. Béraud], *Sur le siège de Lyon et sur les malheurs qui l'ont suivi* n.p., n.d.), 3. See
also Expilly, *Dictionnaire*, iv. 275; Grimod de la Reynière, *Peu de chose*, pp. 6–7; Guillon
de Montléon, *Lyon tel qu'il étoit et tel qu'il est* (Paris, 1797), 8; Béraud, *Sur le siège de Lyon*,
pp. 6–7.

[98] See *Almanach* (1789), p. 97; Guillon de Montléon, *Mémoires*, i. 25; [Ricard-
Charbonnet], *Mémoires d'un Lyonnais de la fin du XVIIIe siècle* (Lyon, 1838), 54; Expilly,
Dictionnaire, iv. 302.

[99] AN F^{12}1441, d. 22, Arrêt du Conseil d'État du Roi, 3 Sept. 1786.

and the Saône, and its northern and western sections, the Forez and the Beaujolais, were traditionally hostile to the areas to the east—Bresse, Bugey, and Dauphiné. To the west, the Beaujolais and Forez mountains separated Lyon from the plain, and the appalling condition of the few roads made communications with this region extremely difficult, particularly in winter.[100] Rivers provided the best transport, and the Loire, flowing from south to north, oriented the plain through which it ran away from Lyon. By the 1780s, too, the town of Roanne had become the centre of a growing Forezien textile industry based on cottage weaving and determinedly independent of Lyon. In the last years of the old regime Roanne was seeking separation from the Lyonnais and the creation of *États* for the Forez.[101] All the major *communes* of the Forez resented Lyon's administrative predominance, and there were widespread demands in 1790 for the creation of a separate *département*.[102]

The more compact area which extended from the mountains' western slopes to the rivers had more links with Lyon. It provided immigrants, seasonal workers, and wet-nurses. Many Lyonnais owned property in the Beaujolais as well as in areas closer to Lyon. There were contacts also through Masonry.[103] This region was more accessible than the Forez, though still hilly for the most part: 'un amas de montagnes et de coteaux ... qui ne laissent d'espace qu'à des vallons ou des plaines d'une petite étendue.' Nevertheless, farms on the Rhône's banks provided fruit, cheese, vegetables, and wine; from further west came wheat and wine; and from the north, copper from the richest mines in France, not to mention great quantities of excellent wine.[104] But wine was the only essential commodity in which the *généralité* was self-sufficient. Seven-eighths of the area had poor soil, and the more fertile pockets could barely produce enough grain to sustain the rural population. As a result, the bulk of Lyon's needs had to be imported, principally from Burgundy and Dauphiné, and also from Bresse, Auvergne, Bourbonnais, and Franche-Comté.[105] Verninac, *préfet* for the Rhône in the year XII, estimated that

[100] See Léon, 'La Région lyonnaise', p. 40; C. Lucas, *The Structure of the Terror: The Example of Javogues and the Loire* (Oxford, 1973), 26–30.

[101] Trénard, *Lyon*, i. 34, 219.

[102] Lucas, *The Structure of Terror*, p. 51; J. Godechot, *Les Institutions de la France sous la Révolution et l'Empire* (Paris, 1968), 100.

[103] Garden, *Lyon et les Lyonnais*, pp. 362–3; Trénard, *Lyon*, i. 21, 78.

[104] Verninac, *Description physique*, pp. 7, 12–16, 33.

[105] Ibid. 51, 55; AN F^{11}1173–4, d. 9, letter of Tolozan de Montfort, 6 May 1789; AN F^{7}3637, d. 1, letter of the *préfet du Rhône*, 9 fruct., an XII; ibid., Rapport sur la consommation et les approvisionnements annuels de la ville de Lyon et de ses faubourgs.

the *département* produced only enough wheat for one-third of the year, even though the peasants mostly ate potatoes.[106] Burgundy was too far away and Dauphiné too ill-provided with roads to develop strong ties with Lyon, apart from a very unbalanced trade in products such as animal fodder, wine, wood, and coal.[107] Although a massive consumer of some primary products and a centre of administration, Lyon was to a large extent cut off from the surrounding countryside by poor communications. And, until the early nineteenth century, 'le monde rural semble peu attiré par le marché lyonnais, même dans les régions que les conditions physiques paraissent naturellement orienter vers la ville'.[108]

The economies of some larger towns were becoming increasingly influenced by Lyon, which provided an important outlet for Stéphanois arms and metal products from Rives; for hats from Mornant, Saint-Andéol, and Chazelles; for cotton goods from Vernaison, Neuville, and Tarare. It took some of the products of Beaujolais cotton-weavers (though Thizy and Amplepuis were still their main markets), and, of course, silk from the Forez, Vivarais, and Bas-Dauphiné. But it traded with its hinterland far less than with Paris, Switzerland, Italy, and Spain, and most of the industries just mentioned were just beginning to develop in the second half of the century.[109] In any case, they tended to compete with, rather than to complement, those of Lyon and so aggravated the tensions between the city and the countryside, especially after the collapse of wine prices made weaving even more necessary to the Beaujolais economy. This helps to explain why Beaujolais separatism was so strong, with Villefranche requesting an *Assemblée provinciale* in 1787 and *États* in 1789, and several *cahiers* arguing that the area had no natural commercial links with Lyon.[110]

Although an integrated regional economy centred on Lyon did not emerge until well into the nineteenth century, and Lyon did not in the eighteenth century control the commerce of the areas bordering on the Rhône valley, its administrative and economic power evoked hostility in nearby towns (such as Vienne and Mâcon), which feared exploitation and loss of independence, and in the capitals of adjacent regions (such as

---

[106] Verninac, *Description physique*, p. 55.

[107] Ibid. 57; on trade with Burgundy, see AN F¹¹1173–4, d. 9, letter of Tolozan de Montfort, 6 May 1789.

[108] Léon, 'La Région lyonnaise', p. 41.

[109] See Verninac, *Description physique*, pp. 64, 89–93; AC I²46 *bis*, fo. 107 (on the hat industry in the Lyon area); Godart, *L'Ouvrier en soie*, p. 222; Trénard, *Lyon*, i. 7, 33.

[110] See Trénard, *Lyon*, i. 7, 25–6, 28, 219, 329.

Dijon, Grenoble, Bourg, and Trévoux), which feared Lyon's encroach-
ment on their spheres of influence and resented its pressure on their food
supplies, especially as prices in Lyon were generally lower than in the
supplying areas.[111]

Squeezed between Forez and Dauphiné yet belonging to neither,
situated awkwardly at the margin of a *généralité* whose western and
northern parts wanted autonomy, relying for food, most raw materials,
and trade on a variety of distant and often hostile areas, and sharing few
interests or traditions with the surrounding countryside, Lyon had the
misfortune to be isolated and vulnerable as well as envied and feared.
Under these conditions it would have been unlikely to aspire to regional
leadership, even in prosperous times—for the region only existed as yet
in a vague geographical sense[112]—or to seek any sort of regional autonomy,
for its economic interests commanded the opposite. In these respects,
too, Lyon's situation differed from those of other large cities, particularly
those which were to become centres of revolt in 1793—from Caen, at the
heart of a rich agricultural region, from particularist Toulouse, and
above all from Bordeaux and Marseille, both ambitious to confirm their
leadership of regions which were already strongly under their influence.[113]

---

[111] See Léon, 'La Région lyonnaise', p. 43; Trénard, *Lyon,* i. 6–9; AN F[11]217, d. 8.
Département of Rhône-et-Loire to Minister of the Interior, 21 Aug. 1792.

[112] On this point see Léon, 'La Région lyonnaise', p. 43; Garden, *Lyon et les Lyonnais,*
pp. 44, 593.

[113] See A. Goodwin, 'The Federalist Movement in Caen in the Summer of 1793', *Bulletin
of the John Rylands Library,* 42 (1959–1960), 314–15; Forrest, *Society and Politics,* pp. 23,
61, 387; Scott, *Terror and Repression,* ch. 1, *passim.*

2

Disorder and Repression:
Dilemmas of the *patriotes* 1789–1790

The least documented year of the French revolution in Lyon is the first. Only a few individuals and some evanescent political groupings can be discerned through the confusion of what began as a period of cautious adjustment to the fall of the absolute monarchy but became by the summer a time of violent disorder. There is enough evidence, however, to establish that Lyon's response to the crisis was deeply ambivalent. On the one hand, important sectors of opinion endorsed the revolutionary stance of the National Assembly in June and July. On the other, the supporters of change declined to mount a direct challenge to the Consulat, and chose instead to enter into a collaborative arrangement with it, with the result that Lyon's local revolution, in the sense of a violent break with the established order, was deferred until 1790. The first of these developments suggests that despite the absence of any sign of political life in bourgeois Lyon under the old regime, the Third Estate was ready for radical change. The second is attributable largely to social fear.

Lyon could play little part in the political struggle of 1787–8 between the monarchy and the nobility of France, because it lacked the main institutional weapons—*parlements* and *États*—deployed by the first two orders elsewhere against the new royal judicial and taxation schemes. It could offer no rallying point for provincial feeling against the Crown, and in any case, as we have seen, what provincial feeling there was in Lyon's vicinity was rallying against Lyon. When in May 1788 Brienne tried to replace the fractious *parlements* with new provincial courts (*Grands Bailliages*), bourgeois political opinion seems generally to have favoured the new system; its promise of a *Grand Bailliage* for Lyon would have made the city a major judicial centre and spared its inhabitants the necessity of taking appeals to Paris. But Lyon's established élites remained characteristically supine, apart from a protest by the Sénéchaussée at the suspension of the *parlements* in May 1788 and the refusal of a *procureur du Roi*, Barou du Soleil, to join the new court, as a result of which he was briefly imprisoned.[1]

After the King's decision to call the Estates General, Lyon provided vocal support for the Third Estate's demands that it should have double its customary representation in the forthcoming assembly, and that votes should be by head and not by order, thus guaranteeing it effective control. When offered this unprecedented opportunity to share in power at a national level, the leaders of the Third Estate in Lyon were anxious to take it. But at the local level they made no attempt to mount a revolution in 1789.

The reasons for this hesitation are not hard to find. The battle for a new political order was being fought at Versailles and in Paris, where revolutionary opportunities were taken in an unequivocally revolutionary way.[2] There the stakes were high—the success or failure of a bid to transform the national government. But in the provinces *patriotes* had a choice: to support the Parisian revolution with action as well as words by overthrowing the local institutions of the old regime and establishing revolutionary militias with popular components, or to wait on events and accept the fruits of victory if it came. The former course might hasten desired changes but it might also endanger another objective: to preserve property and commerce from the claims of the people.

Lyon illustrates beautifully how local circumstances could produce a great disparity between expressed attitudes to the national crisis and the actual conduct of the revolution *en province*. On 17 July an Assembly of the Three Orders at Lyon issued an address to the King which joined the third and greatest flood of protests from the provinces in support of the claims of the Third Estate. In his discussion of these documents Lefebvre singled out Lyon's as one of the most uncompromising and quoted it as evidence that the protests of mid-July were 'nettement révolutionnaires': '[l'adresse] déclare personnellement responsables des malheurs présents et à venir les ministres et les conseillers du roi "de quelque fonction qu'ils puissent être"; si les États sont dissous, la perception des impôts cessera.'[3] For Lefebvre, Lyon's protest epitomized

[1] P. Metzger, *Le Conseil supérieur et le Grand Bailliage de Lyon (1771–1774, 1788)* (Lyon, 1913), 47, 157, 387–95, 409; M. Garden, *Lyon et les Lyonnais au XVIIIe siècle* (Paris 1970), 494–5; L. Trénard, *Lyon, de l'Encyclopédie au préromantisme* (Paris, 1958), i. 18, 20, 30; *Arrêté de la Sénéchaussée de Lyon, le 23 mai 1788* (Lyon, 1788); J. Egret, *La Pré-Révolution française* (Paris, 1962), 301.

[2] R. B. Rose, 'How to Make a Revolution: The Paris Districts in 1789', *Bulletin of the John Rylands University Library of Manchester*, 59 (1977), 426–57.

[3] See G. Lefebvre, *La Grande Peur de 1789*, 2nd edn. (Paris, 1970), 93–6.

the national revolutionary spirit of July.

But when it came to political action locally, to overthrowing the Consulat, imitating the many towns which established revolutionary municipalities, and forming a National Guard, the Lyonnais were much more circumspect. Certainly the political divisions amongst the propertied classes surfaced in a series of public debates, and public challenges were made to the Consulat's political pretensions, but there was no disorder.

In January and February pamphlets denounced the Consulat's claim that under the 1614 regulations governing the Estates General it had the right both to represent the Third Estate and to compose its *cahier*. When the government decided this question in their favour, the anti-consular forces began to campaign for the exclusion of the *échevins* from the electoral assemblies altogether. By the beginning of 1789 the Consulat's political pretensions were being openly denied, as were the puppet committees it set up to speak for the Third Estate. An electoral assembly of 200 consular nominees defended the *échevins'* rights but was denounced as irregular and unrepresentative by a meeting held in the monastery of the *Grands Carmes* from 12 to 19 January 1789. This meeting drew up a provisional *cahier* overtly hostile to the local nobility.[4] Little is known of the various assemblies which claimed to represent the Third Estate, such as the group of thirty 'citoyens patriotes' who met in January 'pour manifester le vœu de la justice, de la liberté et du sentiment'.[5] Amongst them was the *procureur* Didier Guillin, who also attended the assemblies at the Carmelite monastery near the Place des Terreaux where the *patriote* opposition seems to have been based.

The committed *patriotes* of early 1789 were not, it seems, very numerous, and they were certainly far from daring. Apart from pamphleteering and a few orderly meetings, politics in the spring were contained within the official channels provided by the election process and the drafting of the *cahiers* for the Estates General. That there was widespread dissatisfaction with the Consulat was shown clearly by the election of Périsse-Duluc and Millanois as *députés* to Versailles. (The other two *députés* were not known as critics of the Consulat but came from outside the consular milieu. One of them, Couderc, was a wealthy Protestant.) There were

[4] *Requête au Roi par les habitants de la ville de Lyon* [Dec 1788], (Lyon, 1789). See also *Adresse de remercimens au Roi à l'occasion de la décision portée par sa Majesté, en son Conseil, le 27 décembre 1788* (Lyon, 1789); A. Metzger (ed.), *Centenaire de 1789: Lyon en 1789* (Lyon, 1882), 12–17; Garden, *Lyon et les Lyonnais*, p. 521.

[5] [D. Guillin], *A Messieurs les officiers municipaux de la ville de Lyon* (Lyon, [1790]), 4.

demands in the Third Estate's *cahier* for local as well as national financial and administrative reform, but most of it dealt with less contentious matters—the need for more severe bankruptcy laws and for a sovereign court at Lyon; the possibility of revitalizing the *entrepôt* trade by establishing a *Bureau de transit;* the abolition of internal customs duties; the nationalization of municipal debts incurred by advances to the royal treasury; above all, economic protection.[6]

Once again, it must be stressed that this passivity is neither surprising nor indicative of indifference towards the National Assembly's revolution. It is merely further evidence that provincial responses to the crisis of 1789 were determined by local economic and social circumstances rather than by national conflicts between noble and bourgeois, or mercantile capitalist and feudal landowner.[7] Lynn Hunt's discussion of the variables affecting urban politics in 1789 is very helpful here. She identifies seven key factors:

(*a*) The size and restiveness of the urban masses;
(*b*) their availability for political mobilization;
(*c*) the degree to which popular discontent could be directed towards bourgeois goals;
(*d*) the importance of the merchant bourgeoisie relative to the professions;
(*e*) the strength of the old regime *notables*;
(*f*) their disposition towards the new political order;
(*g*) the local importance of administrative institutions.

Where (as Hunt found in Reims) the merchant classes were strong, most of the old notability were resigned to forming an alliance with them, and so, provided the more important *sections* of the artisan community were more or less under their conrol, a bourgeois municipal revolution could be made relatively easily, without risking widespread politicization of the lower orders. But where there was overt conflict between the old regime *notables* and the *patriote* bourgeoisie, where the merchants' economic position and their influence over the lower orders were weak, where the professional classes were either numerically and economically important or better placed to exert political influence than the merchants, and where the *menu peuple* was particularly restive and prone to violence, there was

---

[6] *Cahiers des États généraux*, ed. J. Mavidal and E. Laurent (Paris, 1868), iii 609, 613–15.

[7] L. Hunt, *Revolution and Urban Politics in Provincial France: Troyes and Reims 1786–90* (Stanford, 1978), 137.

likely to be rapid politicization, conflict amongst the propertied classes as well as between rich and poor, and a much less important political role for the merchants, at least in the short term.

The latter pattern corresponds roughly to Hunt's picture of Troyes in 1789, and it provides some suggestive parallels and contrasts with events in Lyon.[8] Troyes, like Lyon, was a silk town and consequently deep in an economic slump which diminished the influence of the merchants, who were in any case unable to establish a clientele amongst the semi-independent weavers as easily as their counterparts did in the woollen trade at Reims. In 1789 the Municipal Council came into conflict with the *patriotes*, and in the ensuing struggle the merchants and clothiers were obliged to turn for support not only to the liberal professions, which proceeded to take over the most important positions of local power, but to the artisans as well. Popular feeling was mobilized against the old élites, but it got out of control and politics in Troyes became a 'daily activity for almost everyone', by contrast with Reims where the 'concurrent bureaucratization and demobilization of politics', begun by the local revolutionary committee in 1789, merged successfully with the same policy pursued by the National Assembly in 1790–1.[9]

Lyon's experience was close to Troyes's in many respects but diverged from it in two crucial ways. As we have seen, there was only limited conflict between the old regime notability and the mercantile élite, despite the tensions that existed between them. And there is little evidence of attempts to mobilize either the professional classes or the artisans in support of bourgeois political aspirations. Like most large towns (including Reims and Troyes), Lyon formed a Committee of Electors (*Comité des électeurs-unis*) and a militia, but not until late in 1789 was there any attempt to use either of them to limit (much less abolish) the power of the Consulat. Several factors can be adduced to account for this. First, the fragmentation and disequilibrium of the bourgeoisie, combined with the grave economic difficulties of the past decade, left it ill-prepared to mount such a challenge. Secondly, there was no fundamental conflict of economic interest between the Second and Third Estates—as Jaurès pointed out long ago, the economic programme in the *cahier* of the *noblesse* of Lyon is almost impossible to distinguish from that of the *tiers*.[10]

[8] See Hunt, *Revolution and Urban Politics in Provincial France: Troyes and Reims 1786–90*, pp. 120–43.

[9] Ibid. 143.

[10] J. Jaurès, *Histoire socialiste: La Constituante* (Paris, 1901), 79–80.

Thirdly, the artisans exploited the passivity of the élites, took the initiative, and put them on the defensive.

In the meetings prior to the Estates General the weavers made it clear that they intended to use the political crisis to resume the campaign of 1786. Taking advantage of their numbers in the assembly of the Fabrique, the master weavers succeeded in excluding the merchants entirely from the delegation which drafted its *cahier*;[11] they howled down merchants who attempted to speak and chose thirty-four of their own number—'above all the most turbulent'—including several militants who had been under surveillance since 1786.[12] They accused the silk-merchants of paying rates that were less than half those proposed in the abortive *tarif* of 1786, and noted that their response to charitable collections on behalf of the indigent had been to lower piece-rates still further on the ground that charity was now available for those in genuine need.[13] They demanded a *tarif* that was subject to five-yearly revision so that rises in the cost of living could be allowed for, and eventually obtained an order in council requiring that a *tarif* be compiled, which, however, many merchants ignored. On 31 October 1789 the master weavers published their own comprehensive list of minimum rates and lobbied the Consulat to ratify it. The merchants, meanwhile, looked to the Consulat to protect their control of the labour market.[14] It was not, for them, the time to provoke a municipal revolution.

Organized agitation by the weavers remained a constant factor in Lyonnais politics from 1789 to early 1793.[15] For the whole of this period the size of the weaving population and the permanent threat of disorders on the scale of 1786—or, worse still, 1744 when Lyon had been virtually abandoned to the weavers for several days—provided a powerful rationale for solidarity amongst the propertied classes.

POPULAR MOBILIZATION, MUNICIPAL REVOLUTION, AND *PATRIOTE* ISOLATION

But it was the events of 1–14 July 1789 which made fully apparent the danger from below that had been created in Lyon by the revolutionary

---

[11] M. Wahl, *Les Premières Années de la Révolution à Lyon, 1788–1792* (Paris, n.d.), 55–7.

[12] AN BIII75, Actes de convocation et députation XXV, Lyon, fo. 686, the *prévôt des marchands* to the Director-General of Finances, 28 Feb. 1789.

[13] *Mémoire des électeurs fabricants d'étoffes en soie de la ville de Lyon* (Lyon, 1789), 4–5.

[14] See E. Pariset, *Histoire de la Fabrique lyonnaise* (Lyon, n.d.), 242–7.

[15] See D. Longfellow, 'Silk Weavers and the Social Struggle in Lyon during the French Revolution, 1789–1794', *French Historical Studies*, 12 (1981), 1–40.

crisis. On 1–2 July the city was illuminated to celebrate the news that the King had accepted the union of the orders (27 June). Taking this as a cue to act against the *octrois* (indirect taxes) which were popularly blamed for high prices, crowds attacked the *barrières* (customs posts) in the *faubourg* of la Guillotière and at Perrache. After two days of intermittent disorder, popular hostility turned against the *prévôt des marchands*. A tree which had been planted in his honour was cut down and his own guards were forced to throw it into the Rhône. Early on 4 July crowds invaded the Bureau des Portes near the Porte Saint-Clair, where they burnt the registers and other papers, then the Bureau des Fermes on the other side of the Pont de la Guillotière, and finally a bond-store containing wine, where they temporarily halted. Soldiers from the Swiss Sonnemburg regiment stationed in the *faubourg* of Vaise were unable to control renewed rioting the next day. Several Swiss were killed and their bodies followed the *prévôt*'s tree in the Rhône. Dragoons requisitioned from Vienne arrived on the 5th but were stoned and forced to retreat to la Croix-Rousse. On 7 July a Chambérien called Pierre Villarmé was hanged for his part in the disturbances, and a Tourangeau, André Gervais, was condemned to the galleys for nine years. (The choice of *étrangers séditieux* for punishment was probably due to fear of further antagonizing the local population.) It was another week before order and the *barrières* were fully restored.[16]

Thus, while the bourgeois of Paris were in the process of making a political revolution, a process which was completed by the taking of the Bastille, the bourgeois of Lyon were engaged in the more familiar task of protecting property from the lower orders. And while Paris was being mobilized to keep royal forces out of the city, royal troops were being brought into Lyon to restore order, a task which had proved beyond the *milice* and the *guet* (officers of the watch) for the third time in fifty years. In both Paris and Lyon the events of early July led to the formation of militias to defend bourgeois interests, but while in Paris it was, in the first instance, to defend them against the court, in Lyon it was to defend them against the people.

The defensive reaction amongst the wealthy of Lyon was more decisive than any of the initiatives which had come from the reformist bourgeoisie so far, and for good reasons. The July riots showed that outside impulses

---

[16] *CM*, i. 158–62 (1–16 July 1789); *Récit sanglant de ce qui s'est passé à Lyon, le 3 juillet, au sujet des réjouissances occasionnées par la réunion des trois ordres. Le 8 juillet 1789* (Lyon, 1789); Metzger, *Centenaire*, p. 65.

generated by the Revolution—news from Paris, rumours of change, and intimations of a new order—could trigger off dangerous upheavals. Secondly, they focused popular discontent on an issue which was capable of arousing the whole artisan population, the *octrois*. And they showed the rank and file of the *milice* to be unreliable in such circumstances: 'la milice de Lyon ... voyait d'un œil indifférent jeter les premiers fondements de l'anarchie'.[17] With the country in turmoil, there was no barrier against further massive breakdowns of public order, and so 'les citoyens honnêtes et de bonne volonté'[18] responded to the Consulat's invitation to form one.

A *corps de volontaires* had been suggested during the first week of July, and improvised units seem to have taken part in repressing the disturbances, although they were not given official status by the Consulat until 16 July.[19] There were seven companies of 120 *volontaires*, each ostensibly an auxiliary unit of one of the *milice* battalions and under the control of the *milice*'s senior officers. But in reality the *volontaires* were quite distinct from the old *garde bourgeoise* and replaced it rather than supplementing it as the first line of defence against popular disorder. Bourgeois dissatisfaction with the social heterogeneity of the *milice* was, as we have seen, not new. After the 1744 insurrection there had been a proposal for a true *garde bourgeoise*, selected so as to preserve its members from 'le prospectus désagréable du mélange avec l'artisan; dans ces fonctions honorables, il sera vis-à-vis de son semblable, par conséquent forcé à faire son devoir'.[20] But it took the Revolution to realize this aspiration.

On 17 July the Consulat's initiative was given the blessing of the Assembly of the Three Orders at the same meeting which endorsed the defiant address to the King drawn up the day before by 150 electors of the Third Estate, with its attack on the dismissal of Necker, its references to the King's evil counsellors, its denunciation of the 'aristocratie ministérielle', and its threat to withdraw taxes if the National Assembly were dissolved.[21] But the meeting was dominated by its president, the *premier échevin* Imbert-Colomès, acting for the *prévôt des marchands* Tolozan de

---

[17] *Mémoire pour les volontaires nationaux de la ville de Lyon* (Lyon, 1790), 3.

[18] J. Imbert-Colomès, *Lettre écrite à Bourg, le 29 février 1790, per M. Imbert-Colomès ci-devant chargé du commandement de la ville de Lyon, à MM. les officiers municipaux de Bourg* (Lyon, 1790), 3.

[19] Ibid.; *CM*, i. 161 (16 July 1789).

[20] Garden, *Lyon et les Lyonnais*, p. 524.

[21] *Procès-verbaux de l'Assemblée des trois ordres de la ville de Lyon ... le 17 juillet 1789* (Lyon, 1789), 13–19.

Montfort, who had fallen ill during a visit to Paris. He emphasized the threat of anarchy which was already afflicting the capital and which threatened in Lyon 'exciter le troisième Ordre contre les deux autres, et le porter à des excès inouïs'. After announcing the formation of the *volontaires* and promising that royal troops would remain to protect Lyon, Imbert-Colomès offered to relinquish the presidency, but his position was confirmed by acclamation and the meeting went on to accept his proposal that a committee of *commissaires* from the three orders be formed, each represented in the same proportion as in the National Assembly, to correspond and consult with the Consulat 'sur tout ce qui pourra intéresser le bon ordre, la tranquillité publique, et la prospérité générale de cette ville'. The meeting ended with a ringing endorsement of the Consulat's 'zèle, prévoyance, sagesse et activité'.[22] Although the consultative committee represented a formal concession to the forces of revolution, the Consulat emerged from the July crisis accredited by these same forces as the defender of property and order, and with a repressive force much better adapted to the purpose than the *milice bourgeoise*.

Quantitative evidence is lacking on the social composition of the *corps de volontaires*, but there is no reason to doubt that it was recruited as contemporaries agreed, mostly amongst the men of property, their sons, and their employees. To Mme Roland's anonymous attack on the *volontaires* in Brissot's *Le Patriote français* (she said they were mostly clerks in business houses or law clerks, and thus hardly citizens, 'cependant il se trouvoit aussi parmi eux quelques fils de commerçants'),[23] Imbert-Colomès replied that their units were 'formées de jeunes gens connus, de tout état, fils de citoyens très actifs'.[24] The *patriotes* attacked the *volontaires*' selective recruitment, their undemocratic methods of nominating officers, and particularly 'le dédain qu'ils marquoient aux ouvriers ou autres individus de la milice bourgeoise', a charge to which their superiors gave substance by arranging a dinner for officers of the Sonnemberg regiment with a subscription of 2 *louis d'or* intended 'd'éviter de se trouver confondu avec des gens qui'ils croyent au-dessous d'eux'.[25]

On the evening of 29 July 1789, as the Great Fear reached Burgundy and Dauphiné, Imbert-Colomès sent 300 *volontaires* 'donner la chasse

---

[22] *Procès-verbaux de l'Assemblée des trois ordres de la ville de Lyon ... le 17 juillet 1789*, 4–7, 19–22.

[23] *Le Patriote français*, 14 Feb. 1790.

[24] Imbert-Colomès, *Lettre écrite à Bourg*, 4.

[25] *Le Patriote français*, 14 Feb. 1790; *Adresse à MM. les volontaires ci-devant libres maintenant esclaves des officiers féodaux du quartier du Griffon* (Lyon, [1789]), 1.

aux brûleurs de châteaux' in those areas where wealthy Lyonnais had extensive land-holdings. Around Sallettes, Crémieu, and Trept the *volontaires* captured seventy-eight peasants ('brigands' loaded with booty and carrying poison, according to one Lyonnais account),[26] and on 4 August they were credited by the Commission Intermédiaire at Grenoble with preventing the sack of Crémieu itself.[27]

While they were away there were renewed disturbances in Lyon. Employees of the tax-farms were maltreated and threatened with the *lanterne* because they were carrying arms. There were threats to drive out the Swiss regiment and to deal with the prison of Pierre-Scize and its governor in the same way as the Parisians had dealt with the Bastille and de Launay. And on 30 July a detachment of *volontaires* returning to Lyon with prisoners had to fight its way through the *faubourg* of la Guillotière.[28] Almost unanimously the propertied classes rallied around the *volontaires*; even the *patriote* Chalier praised them as saviours who had preserved the city from the threat of pillage.[29] The electors of the three estates, who had continued to meet as the Comité de Électeurs-Unis, supported their use by the Consulat (including the expedition to Dauphiné), and in August strongly defended them against their critics.[30] On 15 October another *émeute* against the Swiss soldiers cemented the alliance between the senior officers of the *milice*, the Consulat, and the Comité. At meetings on the 16th and 20th it was agreed that the presence of the Swiss was vital and that the principal posts should be manned by *volontaires* (excepting four which were securely situated in wealthy areas—the Town Hall, the Arsenal, the powder-magazines, and the Loge du Change).[31] Thus it is doubtful whether Lyon really belongs, as Hunt has suggested, amongst the places where municipal power was shared between Revolutionary Committees and the old town councils.[32] There are no indications that its committees took such a positive role. Far from contesting the *échevins'* authority, they used their own prestige to bolster it.

Not much is known about the first challenge to this *entente* between the *notables* of the old regime and the first elected leaders thrown up by

---

[26] Anon., *Avis aux citoyens* (Lyon, 1789), 4–7.

[27] Ibid. 1.

[28] Metzger, *Centenaire*, pp. 49–56; Anon., *La Révolution du Lyonnois* (Lyon, 1789), 3, 5.

[29] *Courrier de Lyon*, 16 Feb. 1790, p. 323.

[30] *Avis aux citoyens, passim.*

[31] See Metzger, *Centenaire*, pp. 80–7.

[32] Hunt, *Revolution and Urban Politics*, pp. 135–7.

the new. *Patriote* opinion, already uneasy about the *volontaires*, seems to have become alarmed by the Consulat's efforts to retard the pace of change. In October public meetings called for reform of the *milice*, and pamphlets taxed the *milice* officers with unpatriotic reluctance to make way for elected successors.[33] The Consulat's promises to proceed with the formation of a National Guard began to look hollow when it refused to allow officers of the *milice* to attend a federation of National Guards at Valence, and even more insubstantial when, the year having ended with nothing done, the oath prescribed for National Guardsmen was administered to the *volontaires* (18 January 1790). Then, on 19 January, the Consulat established the highest possible tax qualification for active citizenship (3 *livres* in direct taxation, a third higher than in conservative Bordeaux), and required written proof of payment. The economic diffi-culties of the last few years had reduced tax assessments as well as the ability of many to meet them,[34] and according to a protest from the citizens of Porte-Froc, these provisions would have caused injustices 'soit à l'égard des propriétaires de maisons, par défaut de paiement de leurs locataires, soit à l'égard de la capitation, par le malheureux état des manufactures'.[35]

Bourgeois opinion was divided by the emergence of organized opposi-tion to the obstructionism of the local *notables*. Sufficient pressure was exerted on the officers of the *milice* to bring about their mass resignation in mid-January, forcing the Consulat to call elections for new ones. But the Consulat's opponents were also subjected to hostility, a fact to which we owe the only contemporary account of their campaign. Late in 1789 the *procureur* Didier Guillin had become involved with a group of *patriotes* whose objectives, he later claimed, were limited to the election of *milice* officers and a tax qualification for voters of 3 *livres* and 15 *sous*. If this is true, he and his associates—amongst whom he mentions the royal assayer Perret, an architect, and 'un négociant de la première classe'—were hardly rabid democrats, yet Guillin felt it necessary to defend himself against suspicions of demagoguery. He stressed that he attended only small gatherings of 'citoyens connus' (such as those held by the genteel

---

[33] *CM*, i. 181, 210 (22 Oct. 1789, 12 Jan. 1790); *Lettre à MM. les capitaines-pennons de la milice bourgeoise de Lyon non encore réformée* (Lyon, 1789); *Réimpression de l'Ancien Moniteur* (Paris, 1858) (henceforward *Moniteur*), iii. 390. See also Wahl, *Les Premières Années*, p. 323.

[34] *CM*, i. 213 (19 Jan. 1790); A. Forrest, *Society and Politics in Revolutionary Bordeaux* (Oxford, 1975), 50.

[35] *Courrier de Lyon*, 4 Feb. 1790, p. 243. See also Wahl, *Les Premières Années*, p. 132.

Société des Amis de la Constitution founded in December[36]), and avoided the larger meetings which were held in January. Guillin linked the defence of his political activities with that of his professional reputation, which was threatened by suggestions that he had been involved in agitation of any kind or in electioneering: 'j'ai toujours blâmé les démarches pour faire placer Pierre au lieu de Jacques, pour capter des suffrages'.[37] The character of an *honnête homme* was incompatible with participation in what an opponent of the *patriotes* called 'assemblées particulières, illégales, tumultueuses, composées de gens qui ne se connoissoient pas, ou qui se connoissoient à peine'[38]. To mix with the *canaille* was to risk social degradation, which for men in business or the professions was a strong disincentive to involvement in the *patriote* campaign as it began to pick up support beyond Guillin's 'gens connus'.[39]

But some bourgeois, notably Perret and the surgeon Michel Carret who presided at several of these meetings, persisted in their efforts to arouse opinion against the Consulat's increasingly obvious delaying tactics. With the election of National Guard officers due on 29 January, Imbert-Colomès attempted to sabotage the electoral process by refusing to specify the procedures for it, which provoked Perret to compose and circulate his own rules.[40] After the elections, however, Imbert-Colomès continued to use the *volontaires* to man the most important posts, and by early February this was causing friction with the newly elected National Guard officers.

On 7 February the Consulat's refusal to relinquish its *volontaires* produced a popular insurrection. Imbert-Colomès's policy was extra-ordinarily provocative and is hard to understand except as a strategy to burden the first revolutionary Municipalité with a legacy of violence. Elections to replace the Consulat were inevitable anyway, as was the disbandment of the *volontaires*. Yet on 5 February Imbert-Colomès insisted on sending an unusually large force of *volontaires* to relieve the National Guardsmen at the Arsenal, despite protests from four of the recently elected *capitains de bataillon*. One hundred and twenty *volontaires* reached the Rue de l'Arsenal which led southwards from Place Bellecour,

---

[36] *État des membres qui composent la Société des amis de la Constitution établie à Lyon le 12 décembre 1789, et affiliée à celle de Paris* (Lyon, 1791).

[37] [Guillin], *A Messieurs les officiers municipaux*, pp. 7, 1–6 *passim*.

[38] [M. Nolhac], *Lettre aux citoyens de Lyon* (Lyon, [1790]), 1, 8.

[39] According to Chalier, some of the meetings in January were attended by between 3,000 and 4,000 people (*Les Révolutions de Paris*, 30 Jan.–6 Feb. 1790, p. 45).

[40] Ibid. 45–6.

but the way was blocked by large crowds and they had to retreat under a bombardment of stones. The Arsenal was forced, and by the time Swiss soldiers were brought in, thousands of weapons had been removed and the armed crowds on the *quais* had grown so large that the Swiss could not get through. A second detachment of 200 Swiss arrived on the Place des Terreaux too late to prevent armed men from invading the Town Hall and firing on the soldiers, killing one and badly wounding another. Imbert-Colomès tried to raise the red flag of martial law but was forced to flee to his house. In the evening, crowds began breaking down his door and he had to make another retreat, this time over the roof-tops to the Swiss barracks and then to Bourg.[41]

There appear to have been no judicial proceedings against the insurgents, so the motives for popular involvement in the affair cannot be established with any hope of certainty. But it is not difficult to find plausible explanations. Both officers and men of the National Guard had felt insulted and suspicious at the use of *volontaires* in preference to them. And the posting of *volontaires* at the Arsenal, together with the preparations to accommodate two companies of Swiss there, naturally aroused suspicion of some counter-revolutionary purpose. Furthermore, Imbert-Colomès was personally unpopular: he had been held responsible for food shortages during the previous autumn and was rumoured to be a speculator.[42] Finally, as if to maximize the provocation, Imbert-Colomès's attempt to man the Arsenal with *volontaires* occurred early on a Sunday afternoon, with streets, cafés, and taverns crowded; no better time could have been picked to precipitate an *émeute*.

This was Lyon's municipal revolution. It achieved important changes, including some which could not have been welcome to the bourgeois, whom we know to have been involved in the campaign against the Consulat. One was the dispersal of weapons—mostly sabres but some muskets—amongst the population. Since 17 August 1789 the *milice* units had been required by consular ordinance to return their weapons to the Arsenal after each period of guard service. Now that the Arsenal had been ransacked, 'les citoyens aisés et la classe la plus honnête du peuple etoient sans armes'.[43] Martial law was not declared for fear of causing

---

[41] There is substantial agreement on points of fact amongst the printed accounts of these events: *CM*, i. 215–18 (17 Jan. 1790); *Mémoire pour les volontaires nationaux*, pp. 7–8; *Courrier de Lyon*, 9 Feb. 1790, pp. 274–5; Imbert-Colomès, *Lettre écrite à Bourg*, pp. 8–19; [Guillin], *A Messieurs les officiers municipaux*, p. 5. See also Wahl, *Les Premières Années*, pp. 126–218, and Trénard, *Lyon*, i. 225.

[42] J. Imbert-Colomès, *Aux citoyens de Lyon* (n.p., [1790]), 11–12.

[43] Id., *Lettre écrite à Bourg*, p. 13.

wholesale carnage, and the Swiss were withdrawn from the Place des Terreaux for the same reason. Keeping order on the night of 7 February was left to those National Guards who had been on duty in the morning and still had their weapons, assisted by a few spontaneously formed squads of vigilantes.[44] On 8 February the Swiss were withdrawn from the city entirely, and the Minister of War, La Tour du Pin, was warned against sending more troops. Two days later the *volontaire* units were disbanded.[45] The *journée* of 7 February thus defeated the efforts which the propertied classes had been making since 1789 to maintain a monopoly of armed force.

During the following week a series of public meetings demanded a reduction in the tax qualification for the right to vote, and on 17 February the remaining *échevins* halved it, so that instead of having one of the most restricted suffrages Lyon now had a relatively broad one.[46] Not only was the political dominance of the old élites destroyed by these developments, but that of the well-to-do in general was undermined. Before this change there were 4,106 *éligibles* (voters eligible for municipal or other office, who had to have paid three times the tax prescribed for active citizenship). Afterwards there were 7,677, and the total number of registered *actifs* was 15,981, perhaps half the males over 25.[47] While this was a lower proportion than in some other cities,[48] it was considerably higher than the Consulat had intended.

How far these outcomes were intended by the bourgeois opponents of the Consulat is difficult to judge.[49] The officers of those National Guard

[44] *Courrier de Lyon*, 9 Feb. 1790, p. 276.

[45] AC I²2, Consulat to La Tour du Pin, 10 Feb. 1790 (copy); *CM*, i. 240 (10 Feb. 1790).

[46] The Consulat agreed to accept receipts for direct taxes of 30 *sous* or more paid in either 1787 or 1788 (*CM*, i. 240 (17 Feb. 1790)).

[47] The *Liste des citoyens éligibles aux places municipales de la ville de Lyon* (Lyon, 1790) was compiled before the change. The names were counted by Garden (*Lyon et les Lyonnais*, pp. 192–3). The later figures are from AD 1L332–5, d. 1, District of Lyon (Ville) to Département of Rhône-et-Loire, 21 May 1791, and a list headed '1790. Sections de la ville de Lyon. Noms des sections. Actifs. Éligibles.' They should be taken as minima (Garden, *Lyon et les Lyonnais*, p. 177 n. 13).

[48] In Reims, for example, about 67% of adult males were 'active'; in Troyes, about the same % as in Lyon (Hunt, *Revolution and Urban Politics*, p. 115).

[49] The battalions posted to the Arsenal on 7 February were Bellecour and Port du Temple, amongst whose officers there were 6 *négociants*, 1 founder, 2 printers-cum-booksellers, the son of a *secrétaire du Roi*, a baker, a herniotomist, and a polisher. The professions of 3 have not been established. Of 87 captains of battalions in Lyon as a whole, the professions of 70 have been identified: 30 *négociants*, brokers, and commission agents; 18 merchants; 6 *bourgeois*; 5 professional men; 11 artisans (*CM*, i. 221–3, 228–30, 234–8, 243–4, 247–8, 267–8). Since professional identification was made using the *Liste des éligibles*, it seems likely that most of the remaining 17 were also artisans; 3 of the names, however,

units which refused to be relieved by *volontaires* on 5, 6, and 7 February were nearly all *négociants* or professional men. Even though the National Guard elections were based on a very broad suffrage (able-bodied males aged 18 to 60), they left it firmly under the control of the propertied classes in most *quartiers*. The initial dispute, then, set the bourgeois of the National Guard against the bourgeois of the *volontaires*. But the National Guard officers do not seem to have instigated or collaborated in the popular violence of 7 February. The officer in charge at the Arsenal was exonerated by the Consulat from any responsibility for the pillage, and although, according to Imbert-Colomès, some Guardsmen were involved in the disorders, they had no officers in charge of them.[50] It is not known who organized the campaign to broaden the suffrage which was mounted in the name of the passive citizens after 7 February. The *patriotes* might well have thought it in their interests to encourage it, and they were accused of doing so out of ambition,[51] but the only information about any of them for this period is that on 8 February Louis Vitet was engaged in preaching law and order in the poor *quartiers* at the invitation of the Consulat.[52] The *journée* seems to have been an autonomous popular outbreak, fuelled by the tension between the National Guard and *volontaires* and precipitated by fears that the Arsenal was being handed over to the counter-revolution, a danger which the crowds eliminated in a typical defensive reaction by seizing the arms themselves.

But no matter how much and how sincerely the *patriotes* protested their horror at 'la journée funeste du 7 février',[53] the logic of their position as partisans of the Revolution made them its main beneficiaries and, in some eyes, guilty by association with the objectives of the insurgents. In alliance with the Consulat and the old régime *notables*, part of bourgeois Lyon had done its best to use the city's political and military institutions as barriers against the threat from below. By the simple fact of supporting the rapid application of the National Assembly's decrees on the National Guards, and hence the replacement of the *corps de volontaires* with a socially more heterogeneous citizen militia, the *patriotes* isolated themselves from the rest of the propertied classes. Didier Guillin's account suggests that the division went very deep. Although he claimed to have

do not have an artisanal ring (de Montozan, Saint-Didier, and de Saint-Pierre), and 2 more were those of Lyon's leading banking families, Finguerlin and Schérer.

[50] Imbert-Colomès, *Lettre écrite à Bourg*, p. 14.
[51] [Nolhac], *Lettre aux citoyens*, p. 8.
[52] *CM*, i. 239 (10 Feb. 1790).
[53] [Guillin], *A Messieurs les officiers municipaux*, p. 8.

taken no part in the events of 7 February and to have been indifferent as to who stood guard at the Arsenal, he was believed by Coinde, a fellow-*procureur*, to have plotted the disbandment of the *volontaires*, of which Coinde had been officer during the incursion into Dauphiné. As Guillin left the law courts on 8 February some of Coinde's clerks, all *volontaires*, stoned him and chased him along the Rue de la Baleine. Next day they forced their way into his rooms and menaced him. When he wrote his long defence of his professional integrity and political independence he believed himself still to be in physical danger.[54]

The existence of such bitter animosity towards the *patriotes* does not mean that, as they themselves soon came to think, the bulk of the wealthy classes of Lyon were counter-revolutionary. The point of difference was that while accepting the revolutionary redefinition of some forms of property in land, the restructuring of economic life, and the relocation of national political power, few in mercantile Lyon cared to follow the *patriotes* in limiting the political prerogatives of property, and lowering some of its defences, for the sake of giving political meaning to the libertarian and egalitarian rhetoric of 1789. And the logic of the *patriotes'* position separated them still further from their social peers: they were so isolated that they had no alternative to an alliance with the lower social strata. Indeed, without the succession of popular interventions in local politics during the first two years of the Revolution, it is unlikely that the Lyonnais *patriotes* would have found any significant political role under the constitutional monarchy.

They did not get much immediate political advantage from the ending of the consular oligarchy. The February elections gave control of the new Municipal Council to an alliance of conservative merchants and members of the old political élites. Besides the mayor, Palerne de Savy (formerly *avocat-général* and *conseiller* in the Cour des Monnaies), and the *procureur* (town clerk) and his deputy (both lawyers), the Municipal Council consisted of two former *échevins*, eight *négociants*, three bourgeois, a banker, an *avocat*, a draper, a baker, a merchant, and the *custode-curé* of Sainte Croix. Of these, only two were known as *patriotes*, Jerôme Maisonneuve and Louis Berthelet.

The *notables* were of much less consequence under the local government legislation of the National Assembly. They joined the municipal officers to form the General Council of the *commune* when major matters of policy were being discussed—the budget, public works, direct taxes—

[54] Ibid. 2, 12–14; *Journal de Lyon*, 4 Jan. 1792, p. 120.

but the officers were the permanent administrators.[55] Even here, despite the opportunities for accumulating political support which had been provided by the campaign against the *volontaires*, there were only eight known *patriotes* including Perret, Carret, Vitet, and Roland. There were also fourteen artisans amongst those *notables* identified by occupation, a third of the total number. Of the rest, eighteen were merchants or *bourgeois*, and ten came from the professions or higher levels of the royal administration.[56] Political organization amongst the *patriotes*, and politicization amongst the artisans, had not proceeded far. Of nearly 16,000 active citizens, only 5,953 voted in the mayoral election on 23 February, 5,386 in the first round of voting for the Municipal Council, and 4,241 for the first of the *notables*.[57]

Despite the numerical predominance of the merchants, the composition of the General Council ensured that the ideological fragmentation of pre-revolutionary bourgeois society was carried over into municipal politics. The professional men, who included all the best-known *patriotes*, claimed to be defending the community against the narrow self-interest and obscurantism of the merchants as well as the remnants of the old regime. On behalf of the Council, the *procureur* Dupuis rehearsed the silk-weavers' grievances against the *merchands-fabricants* who had paid piece-work rates below the *tarif* approved by the National Assembly in 1789, reaffirmed the Council's decision to enforce the *tarif*, and condemned the 'disastrous experience' of free bargaining since 1786.[58] Roland, who regarded the Council's debates as an engine of popular enlightenment, attacked Palerne de Savy for closing meetings to the public,[59] and used the journal edited by his friend Champagneux to continue his campaign against the merchants, whom he lectured on their moral defects and social duties.[60] This earned him intense dislike:

Comptez sur la reconnaissance de tous les Marchands et Commerçants ... qui ... ont appris de vous que celui qui *entend mieux son commerce, n'est pas propre à raisonner du commerce. . . .* Inspecteur instruit, vous donnerez des leçons hardies à ces *Marchands* qui sont assez vains pour se croire de quelque importance

[55] J. Godechot, *Les Institutions de la France sous la Révolution et l'Empire* (Paris, 1968), 109–10.

[56] *CM*, ii. 1–2 (12 Apr. 1790); *Almanach de la ville de Lyon pour l'année 1791* (Lyon, n.d.), 154; *Liste des citoyens éligibles*; Wahl, *Les Premières Années*, pp. 192–3.

[57] AD 1L340, Formation de la municipalité de Lyon, 1790–2.

[58] *CM*, ii. 40 (1 May 1790).

[59] Ibid. 38–9 (1 May 1790).

[60] *Courrier de Lyon*, 6 Feb. 1790, pp. 255–66.

dans une place de Commerce, et que vous traitez avec le mépris qu'ils méritent.
Vous leur inculquerez que *l'Agriculture améliore les hommes*, comme le fumier de
vos écrits amende nos âmes, tandis que le *Commerce* corrompt les hommes...[61]

To judge by his wife's letters, Roland and his circle fully reciprocated
this animosity. Mme Roland considered Lyon 'une cloaque de tout ce
que l'ancien régime produisait de plus immonde'.[62] Her letters overflow
with contempt for the merchants and notables of Lyon—Palerne de Savy,
for example, 'un traitre fieffé, plein des préjugés du vieux régime, de la
morgue des robins, de l'insolence des gens du Roi'.[63] As if to remove any
doubts about the *patriotes*' assessment of Lyon, Chalier published his in
Les Révolutions de Paris:

Je n'ai pas du être peu surpris de retrouver Lyon, me patrie, plus ancrée dans
l'aristocratie que jamais ... La cabale de ceux qui occupent les places, qui y
aspirent, qui y devoient prétendre, et les adhérans, est en vérité inconcevable;
... Oh mon Dieu! où en sommes nous? quelle infâme ville que celle-ci! Ville
ingrate, ville perfide, que [*sic*] renferme plus que toute autre dans son sein les
ennemis de la plus heureuse, comme la plus étonnante des révolutions.[64]

When he wrote this, Chalier had just returned to Lyon after several
months in Paris, where the Revolution had produced in him a state
of exaltation which was to prove permanent.[65] He was a misplaced
revolutionary, just as Mme Roland, who found Lyonnais society crass
and boring,[66] was a misplaced Parisienne. Their dissatisfaction derived
in part from frustration at being so distant from the centre of national
politics. It was deepened by the feeling that revolutionary opportunities
seized in Paris had been missed in Lyon, as well as by the long complicity
between the leaders of the Third Estate and the old oligarchy. But it
was not new or merely political. It grew from, and fed on, the pre-
revolutionary antagonism and incomprehension between *hommes à talents*
and mercantile Lyon. For the *patriotes* the Revolution offered an opportunity to realize the ideal of civic humanism, the reconciliation of individual and community.[67] But in Lyon the way seemed blocked by the

[61] Du Vero (pseud.), *Lettre à Monsieur Roland de la Platière sur sa brochure intitulée:
Municipalité de Lyon. Du Vero, citoyen inactif Lyon ce 5 avril 1790* (Lyon, 1790), 3–4, 6.

[62] M. Roland, *Lettres de Madame Roland*, ed. C. Perroud (Paris, 1900), ii. 138 (to Bancal,
4 Aug. 1790).

[63] Ibid. 159 (to Bancal, 20 Aug. 1790).

[64] *Les Révolutions de Paris*, 3 Jan.–6 Feb. 1790, pp. 44–5.

[65] See M. Wahl, 'Joseph Chalier: Étude sur la Révolution française à Lyon', *Revue
historique*, 34 (1887), 1–30.

[66] Roland, *Lettres*, i. 91 (to Bosc, 24 Oct. 1787).

[67] P. Higonnet, *Class, Ideology, and the Rights of Nobles during the French Revolution*
(Oxford, 1981), 12.

inertia of the wealthy and influential, by their continued tolerance of 'cette vile canaille de gens qui s'imagine valoir davantage que ceux qu'elle opprimoit',[68] and by the philistinism which made them incapable (as Vitet later put it) 'de sentir le bien que le nouvel ordre de choses leur prépare'.[69]

It is tempting to relate the violence of these indictments to contradictions in the *patriotes'* own position. They believed that the solution to social conflict lay in enlightened self-interest expressed through philanthropy on the part of the rich and submission to the law and economic necessity by the poor.[70] But they also suspected the rich to be incapable of such far-sighted benevolence, and were frequently given reason to doubt the willingness of the *menu peuple* to submit either to law or to necessity. The behaviour of the rich in Lyon could be attributed to moral degeneration caused by commerce and attachment to the old regime on whose vicious appetite for *luxe* the city's commerce had been dependent. But popular protest presented a more difficult problem by bringing into question the ideological keystone of *patriotisme*, the myth of the Third Estate united in the revolutionary struggle for bourgeois liberties. *Patriotisme* made war on the abuses of the old regime, but it also stood for the inviolability of property and law as defined by the representatives of the *souverain*, who maintained relics such as the *octrois* which the *menu peuple* saw as intolerable abuses. Unable to resolve these contradictions, the *patriotes* buried them in an avalanche of rhetoric against the counter-revolution.

THE *OCTROI* RIOTS

In mid-1790 the *patriotes'* ideological problems re-emerged in the third, and so far the greatest, outbreak of revolutionary popular violence in Lyon. On paper the Third Estate was united against the *octrois*. They were denounced in the *cahier* of the Third Estate because they increased the cost of labour and decreased the competitiveness of Lyonnais silk.[71] But since they supplied most of the municipal income of Lyon, as of many other towns, the National Assembly continued them until other means of raising revenue could be found. There was a flood of pamphlets

---

[68] Chalier, *Les Révolutions*, p. 45.

[69] Letter of 12 Nov. 1792, in *Revue d'histoire de Lyon*, iv (1905), 313.

[70] See e.g. J. M. Roland's speech to the Société Philanthropique of Lyon in *Courrier de Lyon*, 6 Feb. 1790, p. 255.

[71] *Cahiers des États généraux*, iii. 615. See also Wahl, *Les Premières Années*, p. 226.

against them in the first half of 1790, with the *patriotes* prominent amongst the critics though always advocating submission to the law. Roland denounced internal tariffs on general principles as economically unsound and inequitable. Champagneux denounced them as having been established solely to exempt consular families from paying taxes necessitated by interest payments on a municipal debt inflated by their own extravagance. Projects proliferated for more equitable taxes on wealth.[72]

In August 1790, when the *menu peuple* translated these attacks into action, the pamphleteering was held responsible. The *patriotes'* view (endorsed by Wahl) was that counter-revolutionaries had set out to incite popular violence. Enemies of the *patriotes* (endorsed by Trénard) maintained that 'les boutefeux, les vrais moteurs de l'insurrection, étaient parmi les Notables'.[73] There is no convincing evidence to support either view. Royalist agents, including Imbert-Colomès, certainly saw counter-revolutionary possibilities in the popular hatred of the *octrois*, and some of the pamphlets which fanned it may have come from them.[74] The *patriotes* freely exploited the same issue, but they sedulously emphasized that the *octrois* had to be paid until the National Assembly decided otherwise.[75] Other factors encouraged direct action against the *barrières*, including the National Assembly's revocation of all *octrois* save municipal ones on 9 March and the indications that total abolition was not far away. But the mainspring of popular violence in the summer of 1790 was probably the same as in the summers of 1789 and 1786: *la vie chère* and the widespread belief that the *octrois* were largely responsible for it.

With the harvest still weeks away, the Municipalité tried to stabilize and conserve Lyon's supplies of grain by permitting only one kind of loaf (*pain national*) and fixing its price at 3 *sous* per pound. This was 50 per cent more than at the beginning of 1789, and the standardized bread was considered as unappetizing as it was expensive.[76] Late in June *taxations populaires* were attempted in various parts of the city, and early in July the discontent began to focus on the *octrois*. On 5 July a meeting in the weaving *quartier* of Port Saint-Paul resolved to seek the introduction of a substitute tax levied in proportion to the means of each citizen. In the neighbouring *quartier* of Pierre-Scize, another weaving area, a petition

---

[72] See Trénard, *Lyon*, i. 238–9.

[73] Ibid. i. 240; Wahl, *Les Premières Années*, pp. 174–81.

[74] Trénard, *Lyon* i. 239; Wahl, *Les Premières Années*, p. 183.

[75] e.g. J. B. Pressavin, *Avis aux citoyens de la ville de Lyon sur les octrois. Par M. Pressavin notable* (Lyon, 1790), 16-pp., *passim*.

[76] Wahl, *Les Premières Années*, pp. 22, 154.

was drawn up to this effect, and similar ones were produced in most *quartiers* by 7 July. When they were taken to the Town Hall next day, part of a large crowd on the Place des Terreaux broke into the council-chamber and shouted down Palerne de Savy with cries against the *barrières* and the *octrois*. The Municipalité tried to temporize by convoking the sectional assemblies for 10 July, but the announcement only increased the uproar and the session was adjourned.

Early the next morning a large crowd set out from Pierre-Scize towards the *faubourg* of Vaise, the main point of entry for food and wine from the north. A customs barge was seized and sailed downstream to the accompaniment of an impromptu band and gunshots. At various *barrières* the tax-collectors were chased away, and although the National Guard was said to have taken over their duties in some places, elsewhere goods were brought in freely. On 10 July the *sections* recommended the immediate abolition of the *octrois* and a proportionate reduction in prices, adding 'que s'il n'y étoit fait droit, ils ne pourroient pas se flatter de rentrer chez eux sans être égorgés; que la sûreté des officiers en dépendoit, que le sang des citoyens pourroit couler ...'. Crowds were gathering again on the Place des Terreaux and the municipal officers did not test the validity of these predictions. They suspended collection of the *octrois*.[77] Even when the National Assembly issued decrees ordering the immediate re-establishment of the *barrières* and sending troops to enforce them (13 and 17 July), the Municipalité did not dare to comply.[78]

As a result of the July riots, the nature and control of the instruments of repression became the central issue in both the social struggle between rich and poor and the political struggle between partisans and opponents of revolutionary change. This is illustrated by two incidents which took place in late July. During the troubles the National Guard had been used sparingly by its *commandant-général*, Dervieu du Villars, a veteran of the American war who made himself a popular hero by expressing his reluctance to fire on his fellow-citizens. On Sunday 25 July, the day after Dervieu resigned following criticism of his failure to put down the riots of the 9th, a procession of working men, including *compagnons* of various trades, set out for his country house with a drummer at their head in the hope of changing his mind. He was not at home. The next day, at about 4.00 p.m., some two thousand 'ouvriers de toutes professions' appeared

---

[77] *CM*, ii. 96, 104, 108, 111–12 (28 June, 6, 9, and 10 July 1790).

[78] The decrees were recorded ibid. ii. 118, 121 (18 and 21 July), but were not made public for a month.

'en ordre de marche reglée' on the Place des Terreaux demanding guarantees that the Municipalité would reinstate Dervieu. Palerne de Savy tried to make a speech and was nearly lynched. By about 6.00 p.m. the crowd covered the square, and sections of it moved off towards the Arsenal, disarming on the way the guards at the Hôtel de Ville and at Tolozan's house. At the Arsenal, National Guardsmen and constables of the watch were shot at, but this time the attackers were fought off and the area was cleared by the Swiss at 9.00 p.m.[79] The immediate threat of another 7 February was over, but the Municipalité did not risk re-establishing the *barrières* until 21 August, by which time, at its request, there were 4,600 regular troops in Lyon.[80]

The hope implicit in the popular overtures to Dervieu, that the National Guard might not be just another instrument of repression for the protection of the propertied classes, was expressed more clearly by an itinerant bookseller, Jean-Pierre Chabran, who told the officer who arrested him and his companions 'qu'ils n'étoient pas des anglois pour qu'on se mit sur le défensive qu'ils étoient des citoyens'.[81] By firing on the crowds, collaborating with the Swiss, and restoring the *barrières* the Guardsmen betrayed this hope and became objects of hatred, 'muscadins', a term which already meant[82] the opposite of the *sans-culotte* virtues—pride in manual work, satisfaction with a modest living, love of equality, and dedication to the Revolution—before *sans-culotte* had achieved its full politico-social meaning. On 26 July a National Guard officer arrested Françoise Buy, a silk-reeler from the Grande-Côte, 'laquelle tenoit au peuple assemblé des propos séditieux et lui conseilloit de tomber sur les suisses et les soldats citoyens qu'elle designoit sous le nom de muscadin'. A drummer who tried to rally the people after the attack on the Arsenal 'se vantoit d'avoir cassé un sabre des muscadins sur la place des Terreaux',

---

[79] This account of the events of 25–26 July 1790 is based on ibid. ii. 149–52 (26–7 July 1790); *Courrier de Lyon*, 28 July 1790, pp. 209–10; AD Bp3536, Sénéchaussée-criminel, June–July 1790; AD 2L90, Émeute du 26 juillet 1790; *Plaidoyer du compère Mathieu pour les habitants du canton de Pierre-Scize* (Paris, 1790), 4–5; Dervieu du Villars, *Lettre de M. Dervieux, commandant de la garde nationale de Lyon* (Lyon, 1790); Roland, *Lettres*, ii. 135 (to Bancal 4 Aug. 1790).

[80] AD 1L557, *Octrois*, municipal deliberation of 11 Aug. 1790 (not transcribed into the public record of proceedings); deliberations of the three administrative bodies sitting at Lyon, 11 Aug. 1790; Municipalité to the Lyonnais *députés* in the National Assembly, 29 July 1790. See also S. F. Scott, 'Problems of Law and Order during 1790, the "Peaceful" Year of the French Revolution', *American Historical Review*, 80 (1975), 883.

[81] AD Bp3536, Sénéchaussée-criminel, June–July 1790, from which subsequent material on those arrested during the *octroi* riots is also taken. I am indebted to Antonino De Francesco for drawing my attention to this dossier.

[82] See E. Littré, *Dictionnaire de la langue française* (Paris, 1863–74), iii. 672.

the *muscadin* in question being a National Guard sergeant.

Because its officers were elected by what amounted to adult male suffrage, and because its battalions were organized by *quartiers*, the National Guard was potentially the most popular of all the institutions created by the National Assembly, and as a result the *menu peuple* saw the uses to which it was put in July as a betrayal. About midnight on 26 July an unnamed basket-weaver made the point to a Guardsman who had responded to some abuse by saying that he was doing his duty: 'ce particulier lui répondit qu'il ne le faisoit pas puisqu' il soutenoit les suisses et il lui ajouta que s'il y avoit vingt-cinq personnes comme lui il mangeroit au déposant *tripes et boyaux*'. For the *menu peuple* the question now was whether the Revolution had produced a citizens' guard or a guard against the citizens.

The question was raised again on 28 July when the *quartier* of Pierre-Scize was entirely disarmed by order of the Municipalité because Swiss soldiers and National Guardsmen had been fired on as they passed along the *quai* opposite in the early evening of the 26th.[83] An officer and a sergeant of the Pierre-Scize battalion of the National Guard were accused of abetting the snipers by distributing cartridges, but, like several other residents of the *quartier* for whom warrants were issued, they could not be found. The disarmament was an exemplary punishment as well as a precaution. Eighteen hundred troops, including National Guardsmen from some of wealthier *quartiers*—'tous les clercs de palais, tous les commis de magasin, tous les coquins d'aristocrates, les huissiers, les dragons, les sapeurs de Vienne'[84]—conducted a house-to-house search for weapons, smashing doors, ripping up mattresses, overturning furniture, and tearing woven velvet from the looms. Eight hundred muskets were seized and a clear warning was given that the National Guard was not to be used in pursuit of popular objectives. By the vigour with which this operation was conducted the propertied classes showed that although the battle for a socially exclusive militia had been lost, they did not propose to let the National Guard be used to erode the preponderance of armed force which they still possessed.[85]

---

[83] The main accounts of this are in AD 2L90, émeute du 26 juillet 1790 (the Municipalité's version); *Courrier de Lyon*, 30 July 1790, p. 228.

[84] *Plaidoyer du compère Mathieu*, p. 3.

[85] See AD 2L90, petition of 20 Aug. 1790 to the Municipalité, protesting against the partial rearmament of Pierre-Scize: 'N'est-ce pas exposer les Suisses . . . que de leur assujettir à faire le service conjointement avec leurs lâches assassins?' There were 156 signatures, including the names of many prominent bourgeois families—Van Risamburgh, Monterrad, Gubian, Dussurgey.

They were equally determined to maintain (and if possible to increase) the contingent of regular troops stationed at Vaise, and it was this issue which translated most clearly into political terms the irreconcilable differences of interest and outlook between rich and poor. Popular hostility to any form of garrison found justification in Lyon's traditional *privilège de se garder*. Revolutionary nationalism provided another rationale for the desire to rid the city of *troupes étrangères*. There were more fundamental economic issues at stake. Besides the defence of property, the troops' most obvious role, re-emphasized in July 1789 and July 1790, was to protect the tax-collectors. And quite apart from their repressive function, the presence of regular troops was a direct economic threat to the people, for reasons clearly spelt out in a petition addressed to the National Assembly on 7 December 1791:

il s'agit de discuter si une garnison est utile et nécessaire ... Les riches et les négociants semblent se coaliser et faire tous leurs efforts auprès de tous les pouvoirs pour en démontrer la nécessité et l'utilité ... Elle occasioneroit la hausse des denrées ... les soldats logés et salariés par la nation, qui exerceroient les mêmes professions qu'eux [les Lyonnais] leur seroient toujours préférés pour l'ouvrage, pouvant s'en charger à meilleur prix n'ayant loyer ni imposition à payer.[86]

An incident during the *octroi* riots reveals the intensity of feeling aroused by the presence of the Swiss. André Lagier, a soldier of the Sonnemberg regiment, was unwise enough to go walking alone near the docks at Perrache. He was insulted by a small group 'de la dernière classe du peuple' and drew his knife. What followed took the form of a public execution. After Lagier had been condemned as an assassin of the people, a group of about ten men tried to hang him from one of the ropes used by the *trailles* crossing the Saône, then from a tree, and then (twice) from street lamps which broke. Finally, in front of a large crowd, he was subjected to a form of breaking on the wheel. Afterwards his corpse was treated in such a way that it was evident he was not killed just for using a knife. As night fell, the body was taken to the house of the *directeur des aides et octrois*, where it was suspended from a balcony with a candle tied to its head and harangued by the executioners: 'la multitude leur répondit par d'horribles applaudissements'. According to the defence at the trial

---

[86] AN F⁷6, Pétition des citoyens en trois cahiers de Lyon revêtue de dix mille cent quatre-vingt-dix signatures ... pour être jointe à celle précédement envoyée avec 3 400 signatures.

of one of those involved, Denis Saulnier, the crime was committed 'avec
la plus stupide ostentation' and was encouraged by great crowds: 'Saulnier
a cru ... que le salut de cette ville et la bonheur du peuple étoient
attachés a l'assassinat d'un Suisse pour forcer le régiment de Sonnemberg,
défenseur de la cité, à solliciter sa retraite.'[87] But whether political calculation was so important is doubtful. Symbolically, the execution of
Lagier, with its pseudo-trial followed by punishment, was an act of
popular justice against an agent of a system of repression which gave
protection and cheap labour to the rich while threatening the survival of
the poor.

THE POLITICS OF REPRESSION

From the well-to-do, by contrast, there came a flood of praise for the
Swiss, 'auxquels tous les bons citoyens ont la plus grande obligation
d'avoir conservé non seulement leur vie mais encore leur fortune',[88] and
pleas for the augmentation of the garrison. Throughout the disorders
the authorities had feared the consequences of an all-out confrontation
between the working population and the Guard: 'malgré le zèle des
individus qui la composent,' Périsse-Duluc told the National Assembly,
'elle ne pourroit résister aux citoyens inactifs qui remplissent nos manufactures, et qui sont quatre fois plus nombreux qu'elle'.[89] It was reported
that homes had been chalked to mark them out for pillage,[90] and a
spokeman for the *compagnon* hatters, Pierre Forgeron, was said to have
threatened that 'nous borderons une rue d'un bout à l'autre, nous tuerons
femmes et enfants et nous mettrons tout au pillage'.[91] The Municipalité
not only called in troops as an emergency measure, but petitioned for a
permanent garrison.[92] Fear of the masses outweighed fear of counter-
revolution, in strong contrast to Marseille, where the Municipalité of
1790, buoyed up by autonomist sentiment, led a vigorous movement of

---

[87] M. J. B. M. Roches, *Discours dans la cause de neuf hommes, accusés d'être les auteurs ou
participes des attentats horribles exercés, le 19 juillet 1790, pendant 6 heures, sur un soldat du
régiment Suisse, de Sonnemberg, en garnison à Lyon* (Lyon, 1791), 5–45.

[88] AD 2L90, petition of 20 Aug. 1790. See also *Journal de Lyon*, 18 Aug. 1790,
pp. 119–20.

[89] *Moniteur*, v. 153 (17 July 1790), speech of Périsse-Duluc, député from Rhône-et-
Loire. The Departmental Directoire expressed similar fears that the forces of order in Lyon
were insufficient given the numerical preponderance of passive citizens over active ones
(AD 1L557, extract from the minutes of the Directoire, 27 July 1791).

[90] *Courrier de Lyon*, 30 July 1790, p. 239.

[91] AD Bp3536, Sénéchaussée-criminel, interrogation of Forgeron, 4 Aug. 1790.

[92] *CM*, ii. 143 (14 Aug. 1790).

protest against the garrison and went so far as to acquiesce in the seizure of the three royal forts by the National Guard.[93]

But for the *patriotes* it was not so easy to turn to the Ministry of War for protection. They shared the general alarm provoked by the *octroi* riots—Champagneux considered that if the Arsenal had been forced, Lyon would have been pillaged.[94] Their interpretation of events, however, was predicated on their view of themselves as the natural leaders and spokesmen of the united Third Estate, except for those sections of it hopelessly corrupted by the old regime. Nothing was more important to their political thinking than the unity of the nation in defence of the Revolution, and so disorders which put it at risk and flouted the authority of the National Assembly could only be explained by counter-revolutionary agitation. Not for the last time the *patriotes* mobilized the counter-revolutionary menace to resolve their ideological problems: 'l'objet des ministres, du parti dominant et du plus grand nombre des membres de la municipalité, est de pousser le peuple ou de le laisser exciter, pour être autorisés a déployer la force ...'.[95] Mme Roland was certain that extra troops had been sent to Lyon not to preserve order, but to collaborate in foreign invasion.[96] For similar reasons her husband opposed the use of *troupes étrangères* within Lyon and insisted on the adequacy of the National Guard to defend the city.[97] The *patriotes* deplored the disarmament of Pierre-Scize, and to explain the firing against the National Guard and the Swiss they conjured up trouble-makers from Piedmont, Nîmes, and the Comtat, 'muscadins en bottines' who slipped into the *quartier* by boat to perpetrate the crimes for which the people had been unjustly punished.[98] One enthusiastic *patriote*, Antoine-Marie Bertrand (the son of the wealthy silk-merchant who employed Joseph Chalier), actually found an *agitateur étranger*, a well-dressed Parisian *rentier* called Pierre Devaux, in the act of inciting 'un peuple naturellement doux et bon à dire autour de lui, qu'il se foutait de l'assemblée

[93] Scott, 'Problems of Law and Order', pp. 881–2.

[94] *Courrier de Lyon*, 8 Aug. 1790, p. 294.

[95] Roland, *Lettres*, ii. 137 (to Bancal, 4 Aug. 1790). See also *Courrier de Lyon*, 28 July 1790, p. 211.

[96] Roland, *Lettres*, ii. 134 (to Bancal, 4 Aug. 1790).

[97] *CM*, ii. 176 (17 Sept. 1790).

[98] *Réponse des citoyens des 13* [sic] *sections à la lettre de M. Dervieux, commandant de la Garde nationale de Lyon* (Lyon, n.d.). This brochure bore the name of François Bret, later *procureur* of the Municipalité and at this time one of the better-known *patriotes*; 2,000 Lyonnais were said to have signed it. See also *Courrier de Lyon*, 28 July 1790, p. 211, and *Plaidoyer du compère Mathieu*, p. 4.

nationale et de son serment'.[99] But, as was to happen again during the Revolution, the hordes of counter-revolutionary agents whom the *patriotes* held responsible for the troubles of Lyon proved their cunning not only by fomenting disorder, but by evading detection. Apart from Devaux, those arrested during the *octroi* riots were local working men or women or petty merchants, and the two men hanged were not *étrangers séditieux* but Lyonnais.[100]

Given the *patriotes'* diagnosis of the disorders, the Municipalité's response to them could only seem worse than useless. Purging the National Guard of its popular elements was likely to produce a new version of the *volontaires* in national colours, just as the troop reinforcements provided more pawns for the counter-revolutionary game. But an alternative was not easy to find. The people, while 'naturally gentle and good', had been seduced from their natural goodness with remarkable ease. Civic education and good laws would do the trick eventually, of course, but in the short term the strategy of encouraging the people to respect the National Assembly and the *autorités constituées* was hardly practicable when local government was in the hands of *aristocrates*.

To make things worse, the departmental administration chosen in June 1790 by the second-degree electors of Rhône-et-Loire turned out to be even more 'aristocratic' than the Municipalité with which it shared the Town Hall. Since early 1789 the rural areas of the *département* had been waging a vigorous campaign to restrict the political influence of Lyon, and they won an important victory when the electors set the number of departmental councillors per *district* at six instead of varying it to allow for differences of population. (The legislation permitted a *district*'s representation to be varied between two and six.[101]) As a result, the Departmental General Council was dominated by Foréziens and Beaujolais,

---

[99] AD Bp3536, deposition by Bertrand, 31 July 1790.

[100] Those executed were Pierre Forgeron, a *compagnon* braid-maker, and Jean-Pierre Chabran, a pedlar of brochures. The professions of the others arrested were: Hatter, silk-weaver (4), *rentier*, maker of wooden heels, basket-maker, *compagnon* carpenter, maker of horsehair mattresses, fisherman, tailor, comb-maker, unemployed wig-maker, *compagnon* printer (2), silk-reeler. One was the son of a food-vendor at Saint-Georges, and another said he lived with his sister, a milliner. François Champion, a cloth-finisher, maintained that the bloodthirsty cries for which he was arrested on 26 July had been directed at his wife (AD Bp3536, Sénéchaussée-criminel, Note rélatifs aux accusés). While this evidence is of course by no means conclusive as to the composition of the insurgent crowds of July, it is consistent with several contemporary observations that the rioters were drawn from a broad range of working people (see *Journal de Lyon*, 18 Aug. 1790, p. 119, in addition to sources given in n. 79).

[101] Godechot, *Les Institutions de la France*, pp. 104–5.

small-town *notables* and former office-holders[102]—twelve *avocats*, a
notary, a banker, a *négociant*, a *conseiller du Roi*, a former *subdélégué* of
the *intendant*, two Sénéchaussée magistrates, a *chevalier d'honneur* of the
Cour des Monnaies.[103] The rest were landowners. Six of the ten members
of the Departmental Directoire came from outside Lyon, and the Lyonnais were all from the wealthiest social strata: the banker Finguerlin, the
avocat Dacier (both *administrateurs*), the former *lieutenant particulier* of
the Sénéchaussée, Chirat de Vernay[104] (who was *procureur-général syndic*),
and the president, Jean François Vitet, another *avocat*. Thus the new
Département, the principal local agency of the Crown, a body with
extensive police and administrative powers as well as the ear of the
ministries in Paris, was an amalgam of old regime *notables*, magistrates,
propriétaires, and *hauts bourgeois*, and it included not a single *patriote*.
From the *patriotes'* point of view the new Directoire of the *district* of
Lyon (Ville) was little better.[105]

One way out of the dilemma was, of course, to put *patriotes* into the
autorités constituées. But in mid-1790 their political base was so weak that
there could have seemed little chance of doing so. The Société des Amis
de la Constitution was said to have had forty members, all 'bourgeois
aisés',[106] at the time of its affiliation with the Paris Jacobins in the spring
of 1790, and by March 1791 the number had reached only 225.[107] It was
essentially a rich man's debating club,[108] its exclusiveness guaranteed by
high membership fees, and it was quite inadequate as a basis on which
to build control of the city. Caught between 'aristocratic' municipal and
departmental authorities and 'un peuple facile à tromper', the *patriotes*
felt doomed to watch impotently as Lyon became a centre of reaction and
misdirected popular violence. Champagneux lost heart and abandoned *Le*

---

[102] Main sources for departmental personnel: *Procès-verbaux du Conseil-général du département de Rhône-et-Loire*, ed. G. Guigue, 2 vols (Trévoux, 1895) (henceforward *Département*), i. 1–4; *Almanach astronomique et historique de la ville de Lyon et du département de
Rhône-et-Loire* (Lyon, 1791) (henceforward *Almanach*, p. xxix).

[103] A. Portallier, *Tableau général des victimes et martyrs de la Révolution en Lyonnais,
Forez et Beaujolais* (Saint-Étienne, 1911), article on Lacroix-Laval.

[104] Metzger, *Centenaire*, p. 379.

[105] See Wahl, *Les Premières Années*, p. 170; Roland, *Lettres*, ii. 139 (to Bancal, 8 Aug.
1790).

[106] *Journal de la Société populaire des amis de la Constitution*, 16 Jan. 1791, pp. 4–5.

[107] *État des membres qui composent la Société des amis de la Constitution*.

[108] The average tax assessment of the 65 members who can be located in the registers
of the *contribution mobilière* for 1791 was 433 *livres*, compared to Garden's estimate of
150 *livres* for taxpayers generally. On the tone of the club, see Wahl, *Les Premières
Années*, pp. 226–7.

Courrier de Lyon, while Mme Roland seems to have given up all hope of saving the city for the Revolution: 'Mon ami, la contre-révolution est commencée ici, c'est un pays perdu; il est incurable.'[109]

The *patriotes*' pessimism was justified, but not for the reasons they gave. They saw the lack of revolutionary fervour amongst the bourgeois as a virulent and probably incurable local disease, a symptom of the selfishness and *insouciance* of mercantile Lyon. But the lack of revolutionary *élan* which worried them so much was by no means peculiar to Lyon. For most of 1789, events in Lyon followed a common pattern of acquiescence in national revolution combined with avoidance of local conflict. Lyon was by no means the only city whose bourgeois were content to leave the old regime administrators in place until they were removed by decrees from Paris. And there was nothing unusual in the formation of *gardes bourgeoises* similar to the *volontaires* with more interest in protecting property than in defending the Revolution.

If the Revolution was in danger in Lyon it was not because the rich there had some innate predisposition against it, but because economic difficulties and social conflicts in the late 1780s made it hard for propertied élites to throw off the Consulat's tutelage and establish a new municipal order capable of commanding the confidence of the *honnêtes gens* and the obedience of the *menu peuple*. Particularly in the two largest trades, hatting and silk-weaving, and to a lesser extent in the printing and building trades, the traditional artisan's goal of being a middling, independent merchant-craftsman was becoming virtually unattainable. So there had emerged large masses of relatively undifferentiated workers who engaged intermittently in bitter and organized conflict, mainly over wages, with capitalist employers. After the destruction of the *compagnon* hatters' Mutual Aid Societies (*Bourses*) by the combined action of the Consulat and the merchant-hatters in the 1740s, the *compagnons*' frequent engagement in illegal forms of protest—strikes, clandestine *Bourses*, intimidation of non-Lyonnais workers, and threats against employers—had made them the most dangerous group amongst the labouring classes. Hatters were prominent in the popular violence unleashed by the Revolution, notably in the riots of July 1789 and, still more prominently, in those of July 1790, which as we have seen had distinct political overtones. Their disrespect for both the new Municipalité and the National Guard underlined the fact that the reorganization of local politics had not only

---

[109] *Courrier de Lyon*, 27 Sept. 1790, p. 212; Roland, *Lettres*, ii. 137, 139–40 (to Bosc, 4, 8 Aug. 1790).

failed to solve the problem of popular insubordination, but had given it a new radical edge.

While the silk-weavers were less prone to strikes and violence, they were potentially dangerous because of their sheer numbers, their capacity for organization, and their extreme hostility to the *marchands-fabricants*, expressed in repeated denunciations of the latters' dishonesty, callousness, and cupidity, and carried to its logical conclusion in the weavers' secession from the Fabrique in May 1790. By their political mobilization in 1789 they demonstrated their determination to mount an independent defence of their vital interests rather than its delegation to the leaders of the Third Estate, and throughout 1789 and 1790 they showed a formidable degree of solidarity. It is important to stress that their mentality was still that of guildsmen rather than proletarians. They favoured negotiation with the civic authorities rather than the direct action of the hatters, and they retained many of the attitudes of the traditional master craftsman: above all, pride in their skills, in their ownership of their looms, and in the partial independence they enjoyed through their control of the productive process at workshop level. Their main goal was a traditional one too: to obtain a just reward for their labour within a corporative framework and to regulate access to, and standards for, their trade. But in one important respect they had abandoned the outlook of the guildsman. Up to 1744 their aim had been to obtain a status of legal equality with the *marchands-fabricants* so that they could have the right (enjoyed by artisans in other trades) to market their product. Since then they had come to accept their changed status, and to see themselves as working men 'qui ne mettent plus en cause la supériorité des marchands, mais qui s'unissent pour arracher à l'égoisme des marchands des conditions de vie plus décentes'.[110] Above all, the campaign for a fixed *tarif* of piece-work rates shows that the weavers had abandoned hope of living as independent artisans, and accepted their conversion into *ouvriers*. Like the hatters, they saw that their prospects for a better life did not lie in rising to the status of their employers—the way up was blocked—but in collective struggle against them.

The weavers were remarkably successful in persuading the revolutionary authorities to grant the concessions which had been refused them in 1786. It is not possible to discover the precise reasons for this

---

[110] See Garden, *Lyon et les Lyonnais*, p. 580, and on labour protest generally, pp. 551–71, 580–3. The hatters' role in 1789–90 is described in A. De Francesco, 'Conflittualità sul lavoro in epoca pre-industriale: Le agitazioni degli operai cappellai lionesi (1770–1824)', *Annali della Fondazione Luigi Einaudi*, 13 (1979), 186–9.

generosity, but against the background of recurrent disorder in 1789 and
1790 a relevant consideration was likely to have been the desire to avoid
antagonizing such a large segment of the working population. Certainly
this line of thought had occurred to the weavers. When they lobbied the
National Assembly in August 1789 for the restoration of the *tarif*, they
argued that 'une liberté indéfinie ... donne de justes craintes d'un
soulèvement encore mieux fondé [que celui de 1786]'.[111] The *tarif* granted
by royal proclamation on 29 November 1789 was confirmed by the
Municipalité of Lyon on 27 April, and protests by the merchants were
overruled four days later. In June the political leverage acquired by
the weavers was confirmed by the Municipalité's endorsement of their
reformed corporation, and even more strikingly when, despite the abolition of the guilds (the Allarde law of March 1791) and the prohibition
of collective action by working men (the Le Chapelier law of June 1791),
the *tarif* was maintained in Lyon.[112] The existence of the *tarif* in principle
did not ensure its enforcement, of course: frequent complaints by weavers
indicate that many merchants refused to abide by it, and when the
industry was struck by another disastrous slump in 1792 they were able
to dictate their own terms for what work there was. What matters for the
present argument is that the conflicts in the silk industry were brought
into the political arena by the Revolution, and that in the bitter struggle
between merchants and weavers, 'the weavers alone had been able to take
advantage of the changing circumstances'.[113]

Thus, in the first years of the Revolution, social conflict in Lyon stood
as a barrier to the extension of the political influence of the mercantile
bourgeoisie over the *menu peuple*. Formidable new barriers were thrown
up by the first year of revolutionary disorder. On the one hand, there
were bourgeois fears, intensified by three great *émeutes* in four years, of
a general popular rising which would 'faire une omelette de la ville'.[114]
As a result, the question of public order, which to the wealthy simply
meant the effective organization of repression, came to dominate local
politics. On the other hand, the Revolution had placed new weapons in
the hands of the *menu peuple*, and the *octroi* riots showed that they were
learning to use them—the *section*, the concept of citizenship, and the
even more subversive concept of equality of rights. The threat implicit
in this was well illustrated by Jean-Pierre Chabran, who, declaring himself

---

[111] Longfellow, 'Silk-Weavers and the Social Struggle in Lyon', p. 15.
[112] See ibid. 15–18.
[113] Ibid. 18.
[114] This eloquent metaphor is used in *Plaidoyer du compère Mathieu*, p. 2.

a spokesman of the hatters (most imprudently in view of their leading role in the recent violence), reminded the National Guards of his citizenship as they arrested him on 26 July 1790. It seems not unlikely that his demonstration of political consciousness was a factor in the decision to hang him. In these circumstances it is not difficult to understand why most bourgeois rejected any thought of forming a political alliance with the people by championing popular grievances.

Bourgeois Lyon had entered the revolutionary period too divided and disoriented to provide the city with a stable political leadership, and its capacity to do so was further reduced after a year of revolution. Its most articulate elements, those most in sympathy with the new order, were at odds with the bulk of the *haute bourgeoisie*, and in any case social antagonisms were too pronounced for the mercantile élites smoothly to assume control of the new municipal institutions (as they did in places like Reims and Bordeaux), or to risk seeking leadership of a coalition with the professional classes, the artisans, and others of the lower orders (as happened in Troyes and Marseille), particularly after the struggle over the garrison had exposed so clearly the fundamental conflicts of interest between rich and poor. By mid-1791 it had become impossible for bourgeois politicians to assemble substantial support without alienating either most of the *haute bourgeoisie* or most of the *menu peuple*. Since the *patriotes* had come to see the latter as incomprehensibly perverse and the former as lamentably indifferent to the fate of the Revolution, they seemed to have come to an impasse in the autumn of 1790. But by the end of the year they had found a way out.

3

Clubiste Ascendancy
and Feuillantist Response

THE ADVENT OF THE CLUBS

Late in 1790 a predominantly artisanal democratic movement took the political initiative in Lyon. The significance of this has not usually been recognized,[1] partly because most accounts of the relationship between bourgeois radicalism and the popular movement have been based on the Parisian experience and on the period between the fall of the monarchy and Thermidor. Paris did not have a really strong, organized popular movement until 1792;[2] Lyon had one from the beginning of 1791. The particular conditions under which the struggle between rich and poor was conducted in Lyon, combined with the weakness of the *patriotes* there, meant that the *menu peuple* played a much greater role in radical politics than they did in Paris. But their success in forcing the pace of change increased the resistance to change amongst Lyon's social élites.

According to its journal, the Société Populaire des Amis de la Constitution brought true patriotism to a city which, at the dawn of Revolution,

s'est montrée froide et indifférente pour la chose publique ... A peine osoit-on y parler en faveur de la liberté naissante et contre le despotisme expirant. Cependant quelques *amis de la révolution* s'étoient réunis; mais ... [ils ne purent pas] contenir ces hommes *herminés* et *dorés* dont la ville étoit remplie [parce que] les fondateurs n'ont pas considéré que le patriotisme est en général, aussi rare parmi les riches, que commun dans la classe des ouvriers ... Il falloit donc une rivale à le [*sic*] Société de Lyon affiliée au club des Jacobins; elle est maintenant existante; sa naissance date de la fin d'août 1790. C'est à cette époque que quelques zélés patriotes se réunirent et jurèrent de s'appliquer autant qu'ils le pourroient à propager l'esprit dont ils étoient animés, et à renverser les débris de l'empire aristocratique ...[3]

---

[1] See B. Edmonds, 'A Study in Provincial Anti-Jacobinism: The Career of Denis Monnet', *French Historical Studies*, 13 (1983), 230, 246–7, 250–1.

[2] R. B. Rose, *The Making of the Sans-Culottes* (Manchester, 1983), chaps. 7 and 8.

[3] *Journal des Sociétés populaires des amis de la Constitution*, 16 Jan. 1791, pp. 1–2.

The first regular meeting of the Société Populaire was on 10 September 1790. By January of the following year its affiliated clubs claimed more than 3,000 members, and by April 1791 this number had risen to between 4,000 and 5,000.[4]

The establishment of the federated popular societies in Lyon has been attributed to Roland,[5] but there are no firm grounds for this. Of the actual founders only two are known, Éloi Labrude, a schoolmaster (who wrote the account just quoted), and François Billemaz, a clerk of court. There is no evidence that either of them was acting at the behest of the *patriotes* grouped around Roland, though they later gave them political support. The confusion may have arisen from the proprietorial enthusiasm with which 'un des plus fervents apôtres de notre liberté', Lanthénas, who was briefly a member of Roland's circle, announced the triumphs of Lyon's clubs to the world in *Le Patriote français*.[6] But it is uncertain whether the Rolandins were even members of the popular societies in 1790, and, while they commended them for their educative value, the enthusiasm was tempered by fear that they might become centres of demagoguery and usurp the powers of the *autorités constituées*.[7]

It was not difficult for bourgeois *patriotes* to support the stated objective: 'se rappeler sans cesse ses droits et ses devoirs, pour étudier les Loix et veiller à leur exécution'.[8] As Lanthénas argued, less was to be feared from the people if they were trained in the clubs to recognize the provocations used by counter-revolutionaries to foment disorder. Nevertheless, it seems very likely that some bourgeois politicians saw the clubs more as political tools than as instruments of popular democracy. It was axiomatic to men like Labrude, just as it was to Lanthénas, that sufficient education in the political ideas of the Revolution would dissuade the people from repeating the embarrassing excesses of July, and cement their allegiance to the National Assembly. Nor could it have been difficult to foresee that the clubs would be springboards for ambitious men like

[4] Ibid. 7; 10 Apr. 1791, p. 377.

[5] M. L. Kennedy, *The Jacobin Clubs in the French Revolution: The First Years* (Princeton, 1982), 26.

[6] 28 Feb. 1791, cited in F. A. Aulard (ed.), *La Société des Jacobins: Recueil de documents pour l'histoire du Club des Jacobins de Paris*, 6 vols. (Paris, 1889–97) (hereafter *Jacobins*), ii. 147–50.

[7] See J. Grandchamp, *Qu'est-ce que le Comité central des 31 clubs des sections de Lyon?* (Lyon, 1791), 7–14; J.-M. Roland, *Discours prononcé à la Société centrale par J.-M. Roland le 6 janvier 1791* (Lyon, 1791), 1.

[8] *Règlement pour la Société populaire des amis de la Constitution des XXXI sections de la ville de Lyon* (Lyon, 1790).

Billemaz whose careers had little chance while conservative *négociants* and old-regime *notables* monopolized local government office. Labrude stated plainly that the clubs were intended to do more than instruct 'cette partie du peuple qui a fait la Révolution et qui n'a aucune part aux élections, qui ne va point aux sections ni aux autres assemblées'. Part of the aim was to create organized support for the Revolution—'renverser les débris de l'empire aristocratique'—in other words, politically to mobilize the *menu peuple*: 'Que le petit bourgeois, que le simple artisan ait la faculté d'y entrer, et que sa part à la contribution soit si modique, qu'il puisse la fournir sans se gêner ... C'est dans les débats d'une société nombreuse, que l'artisan trouvera l'occasion de parler d'après lui-même, d'avoir un sentiment à lui.'[9] Labrude had no doubt, however, that this opinion would favour the *patriote* cause.

More significant than the intentions of the club's bourgeois founders and the political uses which the *patriotes* and others projected for them is the speed with which they accumulated support amongst the *menu peuple* and translated it into political influence. Similar organizations appeared elsewhere before and after September 1790. In Paris the Cordeliers Club was formed in April 1790 and a popular society was founded by Dansard in November. Attempts were made to found a federation of *clubs de quartier*, but they met with little success.[10] Similarly organized popular societies seem to have existed in other places, but there is insufficient information about them to permit comparison of their political role with that of their Lyonnais prototypes.[11] Contemporary commentators, however, regarded the political success of the Lyonnais clubs as quite exceptional. Lanthénas wanted them to be copied throughout France, and emphasized the remarkable improvement in the *patriotes*' political fortunes which followed their formation. For others the phenomenon was ominous: 'Apprenez que Lyon renferme 28 clubs, et que, lors des élections, ces clubs se divisent en sections qui manifestent les vœux et leurs choix. Elles font leurs scrutins comme si elles en avaient le droit, et les élus des clubs deviennent les élus du peuple. ... Craignez que tous ces *clubistes* n'imitent ceux de Lyon.'[12] Mallet du Pan was blunter still: 'A Lyon, les clubs des Amis de la Constitution se sont emparés de la

---

[9] *Journal des Sociétés populaires des amis de la Constitution*, 16 Jan. 1791, p. 6.

[10] Rose, *The Making of the Sans-Culottes*, pp. 98–9; Kennedy, *The Jacobin Clubs*, p. 27.

[11] See Kennedy, *The Jacobin Clubs*, ch. 1.

[12] *Avis aux Français sur les clubs* [March 1791], in Aulard, *Jacobins*, ii. 265–6.

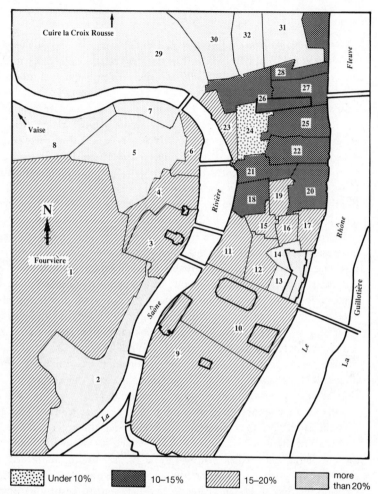

3. Approximate proportions of charity recipients in 1789, by *section*

liberté des suffrages, et décident les élections : de sort que l'Assemblée électorale, légitime, n'est que de pure forme.'[13]

The Lyonnais clubs were firmly rooted in the *quartiers*, and this played a large part in their early success. For the *menu peuple*, democracy meant direct democracy based in the *quartiers*, and this principle was the basis of the clubs' regulations of March 1791. The autonomy of each affiliated club was sedulously protected. There was a federal Club Central but it was designed as an instrument of the *clubs de quartier* rather than as an independent policy-making body. Not only was half of each club's delegation replaced monthly, but the *commissaires* from the *quartiers* were there, in theory, to present the clubs' views rather than their own: they were mandatories, not representatives. Decisions taken by the Club Central had to be ratified by a majority of the *sections*, and only in moments of great emergency could it initiate petitions independently.

By investing them with the powers of initiative and recall, the club movement acknowledged the supremacy of the *quartiers* and in return was able to draw on their remarkable political vitality, which survived into the revolutionary decade in spite of 'la volonté d'affirmer l'unité de l'ensemble de l'élite politique lyonnaise'.[14] For some bourgeois and *notables*, the old Lyon of the *quartiers* was obsolete, a political irrelevancy. There was no sense in maintaining 'des communautés séparées dont les individus [sont] unis par aucun intérêt, comme le sont les communautés rurales. Les habitants des quartiers n'y sont point liés comme les propriétaires des champs le sont au territoire où gisent leurs propriétés.'[15] But the conception of community as an association of property owners had not yet won out over the habits and traditions which led the Lyonnais to mobilize the *quartiers* whenever something was attempted by, for, or on behalf of the *menu peuple*. The *milice*, which had symbolized and in theory guaranteed Lyons' *privilège de se garder*, had been formed of twenty-eight *pennonages* bearing the *quartiers*' names. During the Revolution the Société Philanthropique, and before it the Institut de Bienfaisance pour les Mères-Nourrices, both based themselves in the *quartiers*, and in 1790 the Municipalité turned to the *quartiers* in an effort to defuse the *octroi* agitation. More significantly still, the *quartiers* were twice used

---

[13] *Mercure de France*, quoted in *Journal des Sociétés populaires des amis de la Constitution*, 30 Jan. 1791, pp. 69–70.
[14] Garden, *Lyon et les Lyonnais*, p. 526.
[15] Cited ibid.

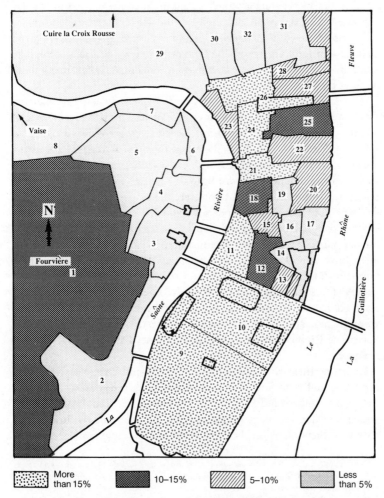

4. Approximate proportions of *citoyens éligibles* in 1790, by *section*

for popular political action during the first half of 1790, and the campaign against the *octrois* was conducted not in general meetings open to all citizens, but by separate assemblies held in different *quartiers* to endorse separate but similar petitions. Similarly, the weavers entrusted the choice of their spokesmen to meetings of delegates elected by each *quartier*, and in their plan for reorganizing the Grande Fabrique, decisions were to be made by a majority of the *quartiers* even though some had many more weavers than others.[16]

The administrative changes of 1789–91 not only left the *quartiers* intact, but encouraged their use as centres of local initiative, politics, and administration. In other big cities the old *quartiers* were abolished or renamed: Bordeaux and Marseille called them by numbers; Paris abandoned them and replaced them with sixty *districts* and then forty-eight *sections* whose boundaries bore little or no geographical relation to the old ones.[17] But the *sections* of Lyon were the old *quartiers* with new titles and new functions. The boundaries coincided exactly, except that four of the most populous were split into two divisions.[18] Even the names of the old *quartiers* were mostly retained until 1793, despite the gothic ring of la Juiverie, le Griffon, Pierre-Scize, and Porte-Froc. The National Guard battalions used the same names and boundaries as the *pennonages* (and in at least one case the same banners[19]). So did the primary electoral assemblies, the Société Fraternelle (successor to the Société Philanthropique), and more ephemeral organizations like the short-lived Société de Panificateurs and the Institution des Citoyennes Dévouées à la Patrie.[20]

By basing themselves in the *quartiers*, the popular societies were both exploiting and reinforcing a Lyonnais tradition, and they succeeded so well that to understand Lyon's political history between 1790 and 1794 means knowing something of the *quartiers*. There can be no close familiarity with them, however, because until the rise of the popular societies

---

[16] See above, Ch. 2; *Almanach astronomique et historique de la ville de Lyon et des provinces de Lyonnais, Forez et Beaujolais* (Lyon, 1789), 74–5, 97–100, 154–7; *Extrait des registres des délibérations des maîtres-ouvriers fabricants en étoffes . . . prises dans l'église cathédrale de Saint-Jean le 5 mai 1790* (Lyon, 1790), 7; *Doléances des maîtres-ouvriers fabricants en étoffes d'or, d'argent et de soie . . . addressées au Roi et à l'Assemblée nationale* (Lyon, 1789), 62.

[17] R. B. Rose, 'How to Make a Revolution: The Paris Districts in 1789', *Bulletin of the John Rylands University Library of Manchester*, 59 (Spring 1977), 427.

[18] Le Griffon, la Grande Côte, Bellecour, and Saint-Vincent (see C. Riffaterre, *Le Mouvement anti-jacobin et anti-parisier à Lyon et dans le Rhône-et-Loire en 1793* (Lyon, 1912–28), i. 101.

[19] *Journal des Sociétés populaires des amis de la Constitution*, 24 Mar. 1791, p. 316.

[20] *Almanach* (1792), 154–7.

they seldom rated a mention in print or in the kinds of documents which find their way into archives. They were beneath the notice of well-to-do Lyonnais and mostly ignored by eighteenth-century tourists, who usually recorded only the grander examples of urban improvement like Bellecour, the bridges, and Saint-Clair, otherwise regarding the city as little more than a gigantic manufactory. But it is worthwhile assembling what evidence there is, even if the result is only a patchy mosaic of impressions and chance remarks.

The *quartiers* were shaped by rivers and hills, and the hillside *quartiers* in particular were given a special character by the interaction of topography and social conditions. Because of their steep streets and their distance from the business districts and fashionable promenades of peninsular Lyon, the two hills did not attract the comfortable or the status-conscious, so those parts of them where buildings could be erected were shared, very unequally, by working people and the Church. But Michelet's metaphor of 'la colline qui travaille et la colline qui prie'.[21] is rather misleading for the eighteenth century. With the cathedral of Saint-Jean at its foot and eight religious establishments clinging to its sides, Fourvière certainly generated much prayer. Yet across the river on the slopes of 'the hill that works', la Croix-Rousse, there were more monasteries—thirteen—occupying much more land, and while increasing numbers of silk-workers were congregating on its lower slopes, there were nearly as many on the lower slopes of Fourvière.[22] Most of the hillside *quartiers* were weaving *quartiers*, separated by topography and vocation from the rest of Lyon.

The Saône was the other great topographical divider. Its right bank had been the commercial heart of Lyon from Roman times to the early eighteenth century,[23] and the austere cathedral, the old Palais des Gouverneurs, and numerous imposing Renaissance *hôtels* bore witness to its centuries of pre-eminence. But by the end of the eighteenth century the area's commercial strength had drained away. Even though the Loge du Change had been built there as recently as 1749, all the brokers (*agents de change, banque et marchandises*) listed in the *Almanach de Lyon* for 1789 had addresses on the other side of the Saône.[24] In 1787 the Provincial

---

[21] J. Michelet, *Le Banquet* (Paris, 1879), xvi. 159, quoted by Laferrère, *Lyon, ville industrielle* (Paris, 1960), 8.

[22] Garden, *Lyon et les Lyonnais*, pp. 8, 278; and Appendix I below.

[23] L. Trénard, *Lyon, de l'Encyclopédie au préromantisme* (Paris, 1958), i. 14; Laferrère, *Lyon*, pp. 6–8.

[24] *Almanach* (1789), 165.

Assembly requested the use of the Loge du Change on the ground that 'le commerce' had abandoned the area around the cathedral and had moved 'en entière aux Terreaux et sur le quai Saint-Clair'.[25] A nineteenth-century memoirist, Ricard-Charbonnet, recalled that in 1784 his father, a silk-merchant in the *quartier* of Saint-Georges, had been forced to move his business across the river: 'en 1784, le haut commerce se concentrant dans le cœur de la ville, mon père, qui voulait nous placer dans une sphère élevée, fut forcé d'aller s'établir dans un de ces quartiers où dominait son genre: il s'établit sur le beau quai du Rhône, dans le voisinage du Bon-Rencontre.'[26]

There were several reasons for the relocation of commerce. The development of the Terreaux *quartier* had followed swiftly on the building of the new Town Hall there in the seventeenth century, and its attraction was increased by the Saint-Clair project. Again, while the main roads from Burgundy, Bourbonnais, Aquitaine, and Languedoc used to meet near the cathedral, by the 1780s the *faubourg* of Vaise had become the customary stopping-place for those entering the city from the north, and work was proceeding on the Chaussée Perrache and the bridge towards the end of the peninsula which from 1792 were to carry the traffic from the south.[27] Another serious blow was the collapse of the bridge near the cathedral, which for some time left only the medieval Pont de Pierre, a traffic bottle-neck lined with precarious houses, and a temporary boat-bridge to link old Lyon with the central peninsula.[28] No new bridge over the Saône was built until 1796,[29] and the other means of crossing were hazardous: the *bêches* of the boatmen and the *trailles*, rope-guided ferries which were carried across diagonally by the fast current.[30] In the second half of the eighteenth century the isolation of the right bank of the Saône and its commercial decline went hand in hand. Only the *chanoines-comtes* of Saint-Jean, the archiepiscopal establishment, and the legal profession remained to give some social weight to the *quartiers* of Porte-Froc, Place Neuve, and le Change. Lawyers clustered around the bureaux of the *lieutenant-général de police* in the Place du Petit Change, the Cour des

[25] A. Kleinclausz, L. Dubois, et F. Dutacq, *Histoire de Lyon* (Lyon, n.d.), ii. 158.

[26] [Ricard-Charbonnet], *Mémoires d'un Lyonnais de la fin du XVIIIᵉ siècle: Précis de la vie de l'auteur* (Lyon, 1838), 5.

[27] Fuoc, *La Réaction thermidorienne à Lyon (1795)* (Lyon, 1957), 18; Laferrère, *Lyon*, p. 6.

[28] Trénard, *Lyon*, i. 14; Garden, *Lyon et les Lyonnais*, p. 10.

[29] Fuoc, *La Réaction thermidorienne*, p. 21.

[30] R. L. Edgeworth, *Memoirs of Richard Lovell Edgeworth, Esq.* (London, 1820), i. 268–9.

Monnaies, in the Rue Saint-Jean and Place Saint-Alban, the Tribunaux de la Douane, des Gabelles, and des Eaux et Forêts in the Place de la Douane and Place du Change, and the Parquet de la Conservation in the Place de la Baleine. Despite this, the percentage of active and eligible citizens in these *quartiers* was low compared to the wealthy *quartiers* of central Lyon.[31]

To the south and south-west of Porte-Froc stretched the *quartiers* of Saint-Georges and le Gourguillon. In 1790 the portions of these *quartiers* outside the old city walls were grouped into the *canton* of l'Ancienne Ville, and the portions inside were made part of the *canton* of la Métropole, along with Porte-Froc, Place Neuve, and part of le Change.[32] In the year II, there were 490 people dependent on agriculture in l'Ancienne Ville, the largest number in this category in any of the *cantons* of the *district* of Lyon-Ville apart from la Croix-Rousse.[33] In winter the bad condition of the roads often isolated the area from the rest of the city.[34] It was a source of provisions for Lyon, a favourite location for *bourgeois* country retreats,[35] and a place of working-class relaxation, which made it suspect to the authorities. Seditious meetings were said to have occurred at Saint-Just, near the city walls, during the disorders of 1786.[36] Le Gourguillon was socially diverse. It had the reputation of being one of the poorest parts of Lyon,[37] but while large numbers of its citizens were indigent, their proportion to its total population was relatively low by right-bank standards, and the proportion of active and eligible citizens was relatively high.

The six *quartiers* where the Société Philanthropique provided bread to feed a third or more of the population in 1790 were all on the right bank of the Saône.[38] In one of these *quartiers*—Saint-Georges, which lay between the eastern boundary of le Gourguillon and the river, stretching south some way beyond what had been the confluence of the Rhône and the Saône before the Perrache project pushed it downstream—the

---

[31] *Almanach* (1789), 143–5, 149, 160, 170, 175–8, 183–7; *Almanach* (1792), 162–70. See also Appendix III for sources not otherwise indicated.

[32] *Almanach* (1792), 65–6, and 54–69 *passim* for the boundaries of other *cantons*.

[33] 'Tableau général du dénombrement de la population effective de la ville de Lyon' (n., p., an II) (AD 1L482, d. 3).

[34] Delant, *Adresse à tous les bons patriotes* (Lyon, [1791]), 3.

[35] Garden, *Lyon et les Lyonnais*, p. 22.

[36] AN DXXIX *bis* 28, liasse 280, fo. 2, interrogation of Denis Monnet, 22 Nov. 1786.

[37] Delant, *Adresse*, p. 1.

[38] See Appendix I for sources for this and other statistical information on the *sections* given in this chapter.

proportion of the population in need of help was over one-half. Ever since the seventeenth century Saint-Georges had been known as 'une paroisse de la misère'.[39] The *canton* of la Montagne, also 'peuplé d'ouvriers et d'infortunés', began on the north side of the Pont de Pierre and included part of the *quartiers* of la Juiverie and le Change.[40] The former had a mixed population, with lawyers in the streets near the Loge du Change, silk-workers (though not so many as in the other right-bank *quartiers*),[41] and four religious houses perched beside the steep *montées* which zigzag up the north-eastern side of Fourvière. Overall it was one of the poorest parts of Lyon. Further north the social patterns encountered to the south of Porte-Froc recommenced: large contingents of silk-workers, with no other occupational groups of any significance save the scattering of silk-stocking-weavers and braid-makers typical of the right bank. Both Port Saint-Paul and Pierre-Scize, which adjoined Port Saint-Paul and followed the curve of the Saône as far as the *faubourg* of Vaise, were amongst the six most important silk-weaving *quartiers*. Pierre-Scize appears to have had very few even moderately rich inhabitants: only 5 per cent of the *capitations* paid there for 1788 were above the average for the whole city.[42] Like Saint-Georges to the south, it straddled a main road and lay beside the river which brought food and travellers, though in winter it was often isolated from the city by a spring which was prone to overflow.[43] Largely hidden from peninsular Lyon by the sharp westward curve of the river,[44] Pierre-Scize and Port Saint-Paul were distinct socio-geographic entities cut off from the rest of Lyon.

Directly across the Saône, the silk-weaving *quartier* of Saint-Vincent was relatively new and perceptibly better off than those on the right bank. In the four *quartiers* with the most silk workshops, there appears to have been a broadly similar ratio of workshops to the whole population, but in both Saint-Vincent (*canton* of le Nord-Ouest) and la Grande-Côte (le Nord-Est) the workshops could command much higher rents—in both

---

[39] J.-P. Gutton, *La Société et les pauvres: L'Exemple de la généralité de Lyon 1534–1789* (Lyon, 1970), 59.

[40] *Jugement du Tribunal du district de Lyon en faveur du citoyen Denis Monnet prononcé ensuite du plaidoyer du citoyen François Billemaz, homme de loi, défenseur officieux* (Lyon, 1791), 18.

[41] The Consulat estimated that the *quartier* housed 297 silk workshops in 1788. See Appendix II for sources for all information given here concerning Lyon's industry, except where otherwise indicated.

[42] Garden, *Lyon et les Lyonnais*, pp. 183, 185.

[43] *CM*, ii. 113 (10 July).

[44] *Lettres à ma fille sur mes promenades à Lyon* (Lyon, 1810), i. 65.

of them the sums paid by workshop masters were on average 60 per cent higher than in Saint-Georges and Pierre-Scize. It seems clear that the northern *quartiers* were not as poor as the western ones, but the proportion of active and eligible citizens was still extremely low.

La Grande-Côte was the weaving *quartier par excellence*. In the tax-rolls of 1791, 70 per cent of those listed as living in the *montée* of la Grande-Côte were silk-weavers, and there were few artisans in trades unconnected with silk. The *quartier* could support only a handful of retailers selling the most basic foodstuffs.[45] To the east of la Grande-Côte but still in the same *canton* (le Nord-Est), was the *quartier* of le Griffon, whose main street was one of the most important centres of the silk trade.[46] The northern part of le Griffon consisted of two distinct areas at different levels. The upper area, though wealthier than la Grande-Côte, was linked to it commercially and occupationally as well as topographically; the lower, which included Saint-Clair, was a place of grandiose *hôtels* like the architect Munet's with its 200 windows each flanked by Corinthian pilasters.[47]

Just to the south was the heart of eighteenth-century Lyon, les Terreaux, which housed the Town Hall and the only large theatre in a theatre-mad city. In the cafés of the Place des Terreaux the great merchants and financiers, 'toutes nos vieilles têtes mercantiles', gathered to discuss business.[48] It was said that merchants paid 'des prix fous'[49] for rooms in the area, and Garden's figures confirm this. In les Terreaux and Saint-Clair in 1791, 193 people were taxed on assessed rental values of between 500 and 1,000 *livres,* and 67 on values of over 1,000 *livres.* (By contrast, only 2 inhabitants of la Grande Côte were assessed at levels above 200 *livres.*) Of 42 brokers listed in the *Almanach de Lyon* of 1789, 23 gave addresses within the *quartiers* of le Griffon, les Terreaux, and their neighbour, le Plâtre.[50]

It is more difficult to make distinctions between *quartiers*, or groups of them, in the three most densely populated *cantons* which lay squeezed

---

[45] See Garden, *Lyon et les Lyonnais*, pp. 206, 208–10.

[46] Ibid. 696; M. Wahl, *Les Premières Années de la Révolution à Lyon, 1788–1792* (Paris, n.d.), 3.

[47] See Garden, *Lyon et les Lyonnais*, pp. 691–701, for an analysis of property values, rents, and occupational distribution in the *canton* of le Nord-Est; Trénard, *Lyon*, i. 17.

[48] E. Vingtrinier, *Le Théâtre à Lyon au XVIIIe siècle* (Lyon, 1879), 112–13, and *passim*; Grimod de la Reynière, *Peu de chose: Hommage à l'Académie de Lyon* (Neuchâtel, 1788), 54.

[49] Quoted in Kleinclausz *et al.*, *Histoire de Lyon*, ii. 230.

[50] Garden, *Lyon et les Lyonnais*, pp. 693, 696; *Almanach* (1789), 158.

between the two spacious squares of the peninsula and which contained in all perhaps 60,000 people.[51] As a broad generalization, the progression south along the peninsula from the Place des Terreaux to the northern end of Bellecour was from less populous *quartiers* to more populous ones, and from richer to poorer. But within the *quartiers* there were variations in wealth from street to street. This was particularly true of le Plâtre, partly occupied by very successful business men, especially along the Quai de Retz and near the Town Hall. The Rue Pizay, though it was still close to the Place des Terreaux, had fashionable residences on one side of the street only, and the next street down, the Rue de l'Arbre-Sec, consisted of smaller, poorer houses. In the *quartiers* further to the east, on the Saône side of the great abbey of Saint-Pierre, there were similar juxtapositions. The *quartier* of la Pêcherie was poor, especially the areas near the Quai de la Pêcherie, but even there the picture was varied by the presence of some splendid new houses.[52]

The two other central *cantons* contained significantly fewer houses in the highest of the categories established by Garden on the basis of the 1791 *contribution mobilière*, and, particularly in the *canton* of l'Hôtel-Dieu, considerably more in the lowest category. The five *quartiers* around l'Hôtel-Dieu and the nearby butchery were the poorest parts of central Lyon, and their main streets, Rue Confort and Rue Bourchanin, were amongst the most densely populated.[53] Three of these *quartiers*—Bon-Rencontre, l'Hôtel-Dieu, and Plat-d'Argent—appear to have had considerably higher proportions of their populations receiving bread from the Société Philanthropique in 1790 than any of the other *quartiers* between Bellecour and les Terreaux, and they also contained considerably lower proportions of *éligibles*.[54] These were silk-weaving and hatting areas—Place Confort, l'Hôtel-Dieu, and Bon-Rencontre accommodated well over a quarter of Lyon's silk-stocking-weavers. Together with the neighbouring Rue Thomassin and Rue Plat-d'Argent they also housed about a third of the braid-makers and half the hatters (1,258 *compagnons*

---

[51] According to an undated census, the *cantons* of l'Hôtel Commun, l'Halle aux Blés, and l'Hôtel-Dieu included 58,215 of the city's total population of 123,160 (excluding the *faubourgs*). (The figures were probably drawn up after the siege but before the administrative reorganization of the *cantons* in 1795.) (AD 1L482, d. 3, 'Tableau général du dénombrement de la population effective de la ville de Lyon'.)

[52] See Garden, *Lyon et les Lyonnais*, p. 24.

[53] Ibid. 168; L. Boitel (ed.), *Lyon ancien et moderne, par les collaborateurs de la Revue du Lyonnais*, (Lyon, 1838), 333–9.

[54] See Appendix I (AD 31L49, p. v, section de Thionville (Plat-d'Argent), 8 juin 1793).

employed in large workshops owned by 49 masters[55]). The high concentration of silk-workers and hatters made the area a suspect one from the authorities' point of view, particularly the Rue Noire, a centre of agitation in 1786.[56] These *quartiers* formed an enclave of poor artisans in the heart of Lyon.

Outside them there was less poverty and greater occupational diversity. Wealthy merchants had their houses near the Place des Cordeliers and Place Confort.[57] And running through the *quartiers* of Rue Tupin and Rue Thomassin was the Rue Mercière, the artery of the city's retail commerce.[58] Other streets were customarily associated with particular wares: Rue Pizay and Rue Neuve with silks, and Rue Longue with linen drapery.[59] Although there were a few hat-makers and silk-workers in these areas, there were not great concentrations of them to match those near the Hôtel-Dieu and to the north and west. But there were relatively larger numbers in the associated trades of silk hosiery and braid-making.[60] Statistics are rare for trades other than those connected with the Fabrique, but from the *Almanach de Lyon* it is clear that the central *quartiers* housed many doctors, retailers, and artisans in a variety of the less important trades—locksmiths, tailors, cabinet-makers, mercers, shoemakers, glaziers, café proprietors, pastry-cooks, confectioners, upholsterers, painters, and varnishers.[61] There was occupational variety amongst the poorer people also. In no other *canton* did the registers of the *contribution mobilière* list inactive citizens from such a wide range of occupations as in l'Hôtel-Commun and l'Halle aux Blés.[62]

River-workers and dock-labourers were numerous both in the central *quartiers* and to the south of Bellecour.[63] No doubt they formed a large proportion of the *affaneurs* who were given bread in Bellecour by the

---

[55] AC 1²46 *bis*, Rapport sur l'état de l'industrie et du commerce à Lyon de 1789 à l'an XIII (J. C. Déglize): 'Copie des deux tableaux des Relévés généraux de la situation des Manufactures d'étoffes, etc. (...) Tableau de la Visite Générale faite de l'ordre de Messieurs du Consulat (...) commencé le dix-huit octobre 1788 et fini le douze décembre suivant', fos. 60–1, 105–6, 113. See also Appendix II.

[56] AN DXXIX *bis* 28, liasse 280, interrogation of Denis Monnet, 22 Nov. 1786.

[57] Trénard, *Lyon*, i. 14.

[58] See Wahl, *Les Premières Années*, p. 3; Laferrère, *Lyon*, p. 6; L. Boitel (ed.), *Lyon vu de Fourvières: Esquisses physiques, morales et historiques* (Lyon, 1833), 193–4.

[59] A. Guillon de Montléon, *Lyon tel qu'il étoit et tel qu'il est* (Paris, 1797), 59; Wahl, *Les Premières Années*, p. 3.

[60] See Appendix II, and Garden, *Lyon et les Lyonnais*, p. 280.

[61] *Almanach* (1789), 192, 166–72, 198–201.

[62] AC G, Registre de la contribution mobilière de la ville de Lyon (1791), cantons de l'Hôtel-Dieu, de l'Halle-aux-Blés et de l'Hôtel-Commun.

[63] See ibid., canton de la Fédération.

Aumône Générale between 1786 and 1789,[64] as well as of the day-labourers and porters who, with servants, predominated amongst the inactive citizens of the *canton* of la Fédération in 1792.[65] There was a larger working population in this area than might be supposed from contemporary descriptions of the quiet streets between Bellecour and the abbey of Aînay, where exquisite *hôtels* sheltered much of the nobility of Lyon and those members of the *haute bourgeoisie* who could afford to live there.[66] As well as servants, grooms, and coachmen there were nearly 400 hatters and a sizeable group of silk-weavers.[67] And to the south of Aînay, on some of the land won from the rivers by the Perrache enterprise, a large cotton-printing works was built in 1787 by two Swiss, Picot and Fazy. The enterprise employed about 800 workers in 1788, many of whom lived on the premises.[68] So this centre of salon society, which housed the *intendant,* had the highest proportion of houses valued in 1791 at over 100,000 *livres,* by far the highest average *contribution mobilière* and the highest average valuation per house, had also the largest number of people receiving bread from the Aumône Générale.[69]

To the south was the half-finished Perrache area, 'ce foyer meurtrier de miasmes putrides'.[70] Here and along the bank of the Rhône lived the poorer citizens of the *canton* of la Fédération, many of them unemployed servants, cast-offs from the Rue Saint-Joseph and Rue de Sala.[71] The failure of the Perrache company had left a vast area of half-drained, uneven land, with avenues of poplars optimistically planted.[72] Only a few buildings stood amongst the brush and rubble, which gave it a reputation for murders and clandestine meetings. During the disturbances of 1786 weavers and hatters gathered there on at least three occasions,[73] and in July 1790 the murderers of Lagier were able to prolong his execution

[64] Gutton, *La Société et les pauvres,* pp. 44–5.

[65] This *canton* was divided into two *sections* in 1790, known firstly as la Fédération I and II and in 1793 as la Saône and le Rhône. They will be referred to here by their later names. See Riffaterre, *Le Mouvement anti-jacobin,* i. 101.

[66] Throughout the eighteenth century about half the nobles in Lyon lived in the area south of Bellecour (Garden, *Lyon et les Lyonnais,* p. 204). See also ibid. 109, 206 n. 55, 356; Kleinclausz *et al., Histoire de Lyon,* ii. 230; Trénard, *Lyon,* i. 17.

[67] 200 *chefs d'atelier*: see Appendix II.

[68] See *Discours prononcé par M. Tolozan de Montfort, prévôt des Marchands de Lyon* (Lyon, 1788), 5; Garden, *Lyon et les Lyonnais,* p. 167 n. 16.

[69] See Appendix I; Gutton, *La Société et les pauvres,* p. 55; Garden, *Lyon et les Lyonnais,* p. 182.

[70] Quoted in Wahl, *Les Premières Années,* p. 439.

[71] Garden, *Lyon et les Lyonnais,* p. 199.

[72] Trénard, *Lyon,* i. 18–19; Wahl, *Les Premières Années,* p. 12.

[73] Ibid. p. 52.

over several hours without attracting official attention. In the eyes of the authorities Perrache was a thieves' kitchen, an area to be searched routinely during periods of popular upheaval.[74]

The fear of disorder was associated with all the city's outlying areas, but most suspect were the *faubourgs* to the east and north. The inns of la Guillotière were the headquarters of the silk-workers during the insurrection of 1744, and of the saddlers in the 1760s.[75] Various *compagnonnages* met at the Mouton Couronné, an inn in Vaise, in 1778 and 1789. Both la Croix-Rousse and les Charpennes, an area on the edge of marshy ground to the north-west of les Brotteaux, were meeting-places for the silk-workers during the troubles of 1786, not only because they were remote but because they belonged respectively to Franc-Lyonnais and Dauphiné and were free of both Lyon's police and its wine *octrois*.[76] So, in practice, was la Guillotière, a favourite drinking-place for workers and a refuge for vagrants and criminals.[77] Its fixed population, mostly poor and primarily composed of agricultural labourers, fought doggedly for independence from Lyon throughout the eighteenth century.[78] Having won partial autonomy, la Guillotière petitioned to be included in the Dauphiné in 1788 and repeated the demand in its *cahier*.[79] Its dislike of Lyon was reciprocated by the Lyonnais, who regarded the *faubouriens* as 'un ramas de contrebandiers et de refugiés de tous pays ... une race presqu' étrangère ... sous le rapport des mœurs et de la civilisation'.[80] Vaise, too, was notorious for its smugglers, and fought a running battle against the city's *octrois*.[81]

Not all the *quartiers* were such clearly defined communities as the *faubourgs,* and Lyon was clearly not a collection of twenty-eight urban

[74] AN F¹¹217, d. 8, J.-F. Perret, *premier officier municipal,* to J.-M. Roland, Minister of the Interior, 20 Sept. 1792.

[75] Garden, *Lyon et les Lyonnais,* pp. 567, 586–7.

[76] See L. Trénard, 'La Crise sociale lyonnaise à la veille de la Révolution', *Revue d'histoire moderne et contemporaine,* 2 (1955), 22, 28; id., *Lyon,* i. 16, 52.

[77] See Guillon de Montléon, *Lyon tel qu'il étoit,* p. 117; J. Godart, *L'Ouvrier en soie* (Lyon, 1899), 375–6; R. Cobb, *Reactions to the French Revolution* (Oxford, 1972), 45–6; *Lettres à ma fille,* iv. 67.

[78] On la Guillotière's population see Garden, *Lyon et les Lyonnais,* pp. 42, 181–2, 256–8; on its separatism, see P. Ballaguy, 'La Guillotière contre Lyon', *Revue du Lyonnais,* 9 (jan.–mars 1934), 177–89.

[79] Ballaguy, 'La Guillotière', pp. 179–81.

[80] A. Guillon de Montléon, *Mémoires pour servir à l'histoire de la ville de Lyon pendant la Révolution* (Paris, 1824), ii. 23.

[81] C. Guillemain, 'Histoire de la commune de Vaise, faubourg de Lyon', *Albums du Crocodile,* 29 (1961), 18–19.

villages each 'a world in itself'.[82] Nor is it easy to tell how many *quartiers* had the parochialism and sense of community which Ricard-Charbonnet remembered from his youth in Saint-Georges.[83] But many of them had characteristics which made them distinct *quartiers* in more than just name. Most of those on the right bank of the Saône had fairly clear boundaries formed by topographical features—the curve of the river or the angles of the *montées* which stretched up the steep hillside. And most had distinct social characteristics—le Gourguillon, remote and semi-rural; poverty-stricken Saint-Georges strung out along the river; la Juiverie, artisanal and slightly more prosperous, perched on the northern slopes of Four-vière; and the weaving communities of Port Saint-Paul and Pierre-Scize, curving north-west out of sight of the central city. By contrast, the three *quartiers* around the law courts merged into each other, sharing the main streets and squares and a population 'composée en grande partie des ci-devant Avocats, Procureurs, Clercs, Greffiers, Huissiers, Sergens &c'.[84] Similarly, across the river on the flat peninsula of central Lyon, many *quartiers* lacked separately definable characteristics and merged into a large, fairly homogeneous commercial area. Here only a few enclaves of poverty and wealth had both social and topographical unity: aristocratic Aînay, south of Bellecour, and Saint-Clair; the poor *quartiers* clustered around L'Hôtel-Dieu; and the riverside communities of la Pêcherie and Port du Temple. But it was above all to the north that the boundaries of the *quartiers* were given meaning by their silk-weaving vocation and the strenuous climb needed to take you far behind the Place des Terreaux. If it can be said of any of the *quartiers* that they were 'worlds in themselves', it can be said of Saint-Vincent and la Grande-Côte. In much of Lyon, then, and particularly in its poorer parts, the *quartiers* were far more than mere administrative subdivisions: the physical shape and the social de-velopment of the city had formed them into communities with particular characteristics. In 1790 the Revolution gave them a new political focus.

CLUBISME AND ELECTORAL POLITICS

> La naissance du Comité [central] réveille le patriotisme, des
> sinistres complots furent déjoués, et la municipalité fut remontée
> au niveau de la révolution ...
> *Journal de Lyon*, 4 January 1792.

---

[82] R. Cobb, *The Police and the People* (Oxford, 1970), 122.

[83] Ricard-Charbonnet, *Mémoires d'un Lyonnais*, pp. 16–31.

[84] *Journal des Sociétés populaires des amis de la Constitution*, 24 Mar. 1791, pp. 316–17.

One of the great unintended changes made by the National Assembly was the creation of the *Assemblées primaires des sections,* which gave the *quartiers* a new identity and a sense of political purpose by turning them into political communities of a new kind and endowing them with enormous significance as the instruments of the sovereign people's electoral will. Much has been written lately of the continuities underlying the turbulence of the revolutionary decade in France, but the interlocked ideological and institutional changes which gave some force to the concept of popular sovereignty were fundamental breaks with the past, and in Lyon they transformed the nature of politics. By exploiting the proclamation of popular sovereignty which in 1789 the National Assembly had used for self-legitimization, only to spend the next two years legislating to limit its application in practice, sections of the *menu peuple* challenged the political dominance of property. It was in meeting this challenge—and not, as we were once taught, in the struggle against feudalism—that the bourgeoisie began to mobilize and to acquire a political class-consciousness.

The popular societies of Lyon made political activity routine and accessible to passive citizens—or rather, the better-off male ones. This brought about a sudden shift in the location of political power. Since the *clubs de quartier* were equal, each sending six delegates to the Club Central, the methods of electoral endorsement which they adopted gave a political advantage to just those parts of Lyon whose electoral weight had been limited by the laws governing the suffrage. Nearly 65 per cent of the *éligibles* (4,979) and 51 per cent of the active citizens in Lyon came from the twelve *sections* with high percentages of *éligibles* and/ or low percentages of indigents.[85] But the poorer *sections* outnumbered them at the Club Central, and even though they could not alter the conditions for eligibility to hold office, they could and did provide electoral support for the *patriotes* whom they saw as sympathetic to their interests, for artisans, and for residents of their *quartiers*. There can be little doubt that the clubs were responsible for the striking increases in the numbers of both *patriotes* and artisans who held municipal office between 1790 and 1792,[86] and for the increasing proportion of office-holders from the poorest *quartiers,* particularly the weaving *quartiers* on the right bank of the Saône and to the north of les Terreaux.

[85] See Appendix III.
[86] See Appendix V.

The popular societies were not, of course, exclusively composed of artisans and *boutiquiers*.[87] They accepted bourgeois members and generally chose bourgeois (including the surgeon Grandchamp and the *curé* Servier) to preside over the Club Central. They were certainly used to promote bourgeois careers. But the available evidence suggests that they had some claim to the adjective 'popular', in the poorer *sections* at least. Membership fees were left to the discretion of each club, and those we know of were low—an entry fee of 24 *sous* in one case (the same as the Cordeliers Club in Paris) and 30 *sous* in another, with monthly dues of between 8 and 12 *sous*, compared to the Paris Jacobins' 21 *livres* entry and 2 *livres* monthly, and the Lyon Jacobins' levy of 48 *livres* per member to meet costs in 1791.

In the club of Saint-Vincent, the only one whose records permit such calculations for 1791, the average assessed rental value of premises occupied by 102 members was 61.7 *livres*, nearly one-third lower than the average for artisans other than silk-weavers in the city as a whole. In Belle-Cordière the average was 105 *livres* for 111 members in the period August 1791–May 1793. In both cases there was a large majority of artisans amongst those whose occupations have been identified by Takashi Koi: 32 out of 38 members joining Saint-Vincent in 1792 were weavers.[88] Visitors considered the *clubistes* to be distinctly plebeian. Lanthénas's assertion that the popular societies 'renferment réellement le peuple de cette cité : le taux de l'admission le démontre assez', was echoed by other contemporary observers of various political persuasions, including J. F. Reichardt, the *Kapellmeister* of Friedrich-Wilhelm II, who was taken to visit one of them as part of his grand tour of the Revolution and found to his horror 'l'assistance composée en majorité de gens de la plus basse classe'.[89]

---

[87] A study of la Croisette, an atypical 'inter-class' *quartier* which combined a majority of artisans and tradespeople with pockets of bourgeois wealth, suggests that its club was founded by a relatively prosperous group—3 *rentiers*, 7 *commerçants*, 12 artisans—already politicized by the Revolution, but that it became rapidly more plebeian during 1791 (A. De Francesco, 'Le Quartier lyonnais de la Croisette, pendant les premiers années de la Révolution', *Bulletin du Centre d'histoire économique et sociale de la région lyonnaise*, 4 (1979), 40).

[88] T. Koi, 'Les "Chaliers" et les sans-culottes lyonnais', Thèse de doctorat, IIIᵉ cycle (Lyon, 1974), 157–60. In 1791, 79% of Saint-Vincent's identifiable members were silk-weavers. In Belle-Cordière 27.5% of identified *clubistes* were stocking-weavers, and 52% were artisans of other kinds. For Saint-Vincent, see AD 31L28.

[89] J. F. Reichardt, *Un Prussien en France en 1792: Strasbourg—Lyon—Paris. Lettres intimes de J. F. Reichardt*, ed. and trans. A. Laquiante (Paris, 1892), 147 (letter of 15 Feb. 1791). See also Guillon de Montléon, *Mémoires*, i. 450; *Journal des Sociétés populaires des amis de la Constitution*, 3 Mar. 1791, p. 230.

Within two months the clubs were helping the *patriotes* into municipal office. There are several contemporary references to their successful intervention in the municipal elections of November–December 1790, but we have no precise information on the methods they used. They were accused, as we have seen, of circulating lists[90] of favoured candidates, and three of the men named as being endorsed in this way—Billemaz, Dugenne, and Doret—won election, the first as a *juge de paix* for the *canton* of la Montagne and the other two as *notables*.[91] Probably the Club Central played a co-ordinating role, as it certainly did in 1791 and 1792, collating the preferences of the *clubs de quartier* and circulating a consolidated list.[92] Palerne de Savy relinquished the mayoralty to take a seat on the Tribunal de District, and the two former *échevins* resigned.[93] These and other resignations meant that several *patriote* replacements moved up from the ranks of the *notables* into the Municipal Council. The choice by lot of half those municipal officers and *notables* to be replaced by election also favoured the *patriotes*. In one way or another, all the *patriotes* amongst the *notables* of 1790 found their way into the Municipal Council, where their ally Maisonneuve remained. Louis Vitet became mayor, François Bret *procureur*, and Luc-Antoine de Rozière de Champagneux, Antoine Nivière-Chol, and Claude Arnaud-Tison municipal officers.

In despair only a few months before, the *patriotes* now found themselves in control of the Municipalité. Their alliance with the *menu peuple* was, like the Jacobin–*sans-culotte* alliance in Paris later on, a product of exceptional circumstances. It was based on shared hostility to the royal garrison, shared fears of counter-revolution, and not much else. But Vitet was a clever politician, and on this fragile foundation he was able to build nearly two years of relatively stable *patriote* government. He was rich and rather ugly, a physician with an interest in what would now be called community medicine, and he lived in the unfashionable *quartier* of Bon-Rencontre. According to a eulogy delivered at the Club Central in 1792 by Dubois-Crancé, his apartment was modest,[94] as befitted a true *patriote*,

[90] Their journal mentioned a list voted by the *clubs de quartier* in its issues of 30 Jan. 1791, but did not specifically relate it to elections.

[91] *Liste des neuf juges de paix que la Cabale fait circuler dans toutes les sections de la ville, avec les notes impartiales d'un PATRIOTE sur les postulants* (Lyon, 1790), 2–4; *Almanach* (1792), 71; *CM*, ii. 247 (12 Dec. 1790).

[92] See below, pp. 94–5, 131–2, 140–1.

[93] *CM*, ii. 227, 242 (18 Nov., 8 Dec. 1790).

[94] *Discours prononcé au Comité central de la ville de Lyon le 4 mars 1792. Par M. Dubois de Crancé* (Lyon, 1792), 10.

but that is hard to reconcile with his assessment for the *contribution mobilière*.[95] The fact that the Consulat called on him to help restore order in February 1790 suggests that he was already a man of influence amongst the people. He was also lucky. No sooner had the new Municipalité been installed than a grandiose counter-revolutionary plot was foiled.

It might almost have been composed by a revolutionary playwright as a propaganda piece. There were conspirators from both the First and Second Estates of the old order; plans, of course, to assemble thousands of counter-revolutionary troops in and around Lyon; tantalizing visions of the city becoming the new capital of France, of the *octrois* reduced, and the silk industry revived by a grateful court; and finally an attempt, based on this seductive prospect, to subvert the patriotism of the weavers by recruiting their best-known leader, who nevertheless stood firm and denounced the plot to the Municipalité. Both Imbert-Colomès and the *salon français* in Paris had concluded from the *octroi* riots that the poor of Lyon could easily be turned against the National Assembly by straightforward appeals to their material interests. A popular insurrection was planned for 10 December, and the royal troops in Lyon were expected to help the disaffected nobility of the Vivarais, Beaujolais, and Auvergne to secure the Midi for the counter-revolution.[96]

Louis XVI had enough sense to reject this fantasy out of hand, and so had the weavers who were approached by the plotters. One of the latter, Guillaume de Pingon, a former *chanoine-comte de Lyon*, went to Denis Monnet, who had been involved in the strike of 1786 and was now a *maître-garde* of the Fabrique, and proposed that he should persuade his followers to join the rebellion. Monnet and two other weavers played along with the conspirators and then denounced them to the Municipalité.[97] Four men were arrested and the grand strategy—which had hardly existed outside their heads—came to nothing. This greatly enhanced the Lyonnais *patriotes'* reputation for revolutionary vigilance, and the whole affair nicely illustrated their rhetoric about the need for collaboration between the people and its magistrates in defence of the Revolution. But it did Lyon's reputation a great deal of damage. Since nothing was believed in so fervently in revolutionary circles as the existence of countless labyrinthine counter-revolutionary plots, of which disappointingly few were actually uncovered, the 'Lyon Plan' became

---

[95] See Appendix V.

[96] On the 'Lyon Plan', see G. Lefebvre, *La Révolution française*, 2nd edn. (Paris, 1957), 152; J. Chaumié, *Le Reseau d'Antraigues et la contre-révolution* (Paris, 1965), 54–8.

[97] AN DXXIX *bis* 28, liasse 277, d. 16, interrogation of D. Monnet, 8 Dec. 1790.

nationally notorious as the 'Conspiration de Lyon'. It has remained one of the very few episodes in Lyonnais history from 1790 to 1793 considered worthy of notice in general histories of the Revolution, particularly neo-Jacobin ones.

Vitet's second piece of good luck was that the *octrois* were abolished by the National Assembly in February 1791. This left the Municipalité free to concentrate its political energies on campaigns which would win it popular approval without too much risk of bringing on popular violence. And when things went wrong it had a perfect scapegoat in the Departmental Directoire, which resolutely defended both its pre-eminence in the local government hierarchy and the letter of the administrative laws. The main focus of conflict was the apparatus of repression. The Directoire insisted that the maintenance of order in the *département* as a whole required a large garrison based in Lyon. The Municipalité replied that this was only a ploy to usurp its own powers of police, and campaigned for the withdrawal of the la Marck regiment which had been brought to Lyon after the *octroi* riots.[98] With rumours constantly recurring of plots to use counter-revolutionary troops against the city, which the Directoire stubbornly refused to credit, the Municipalité was able to exploit the issue throughout 1791 and so to demonstrate painlessly its devotion to the people's cause. When the rumours multiplied in September 1791, the Municipalité attempted to convoke the *sections* to discuss the issue but it was blocked by the Département. Then two petitions bearing about 13,600 signatures were drawn up and sent to the National Assembly, only to be rejected on the ground that Lyon was trying to resurrect one of its *ci-devant* privileges. Far from removing the troops, the National Assembly told their commander to call for more.[99]

Simultaneously, battle raged over the organization and control of the National Guard. The Municipalité disputed the staff officers' claim that they could requisition the Guard at will and, further, determine the order of service—which battalion would occupy which post—giving them effective control of the Arsenal, the powder magazine, and the Town Hall. In June 1791 the staff officers established élite grenadier and *chasseur* companies with distinctive red and green insignia.[100] The Municipalité objected; inevitably, the Département defended the staff officers and demanded that the *sections* be consulted, a blunder as it turned out, for

[98] See Wahl, *Les Premières Années*, pp. 417–22.
[99] AN F⁹6, Extrait du procès verbal de l'Assemblée nationale du 29 novembre 1791.
[100] Wahl, *Les Premières Années*, pp. 374–9.

on 17 June a considerable majority of voters opposed the *corps d'élite* and favoured the Municipalité's proposal to allocate posts to the National Guard units in strict rotation. The grenadier units were by now almost as unpopular as the garrison, and thirteen clubs, nearly all in poor *quartiers*, publicly supported the Municipalité.[101] Once again rich and poor seem to have taken opposing positions. Voting records have survived for only five *sections*, three of them wealthy and none of them poor. All five voted in effect for the staff officers and against direct democracy by refusing to consider the propositions put to them.[102] In the end, the law of 29 September–14 October resolved the dispute in favour of the staff officers by permitting the establishment of grenadier companies in each battalion of the Guard.

The Civil Constitution of the Clergy provided other occasions for duelling between Municipalité and Département. Vitet accused the Directoire of encouraging non-juring clergy to congregate in Lyon by failing to implement the laws against them, and claimed that 3,000 non-jurors were in hiding there by the end of 1791.[103] The problem, however, went deeper than Vitet acknowledged. Encouraged by a barrage of propaganda from the dispossessed Archbishop de Marbeuf, and still more by the papal brief 'Quot aliquantum' of March 1791, resistance to church reforms boiled over into riots both in that month and in the spring of the following year. *Patriote* crowds harassed worshippers as they gathered for mass read by non-jurors; a few refractory priests were arrested; the Municipalité locked up chapels and monastery buildings where illegal masses were said to have been held; yet the underground church survived, led by Marbeuf's *vicaire-général*, Linsolas.[104] Nevertheless, the religious issue did not dominate the political struggle in Lyon. It injected more bitterness into already bitter partisanship, but it left the political landscape largely unaltered. Had the clergy been more openly and unanimously opposed to the new ecclesiastical regime, things might have been different, as they were in parts of rural Rhône-et-Loire where the Département gave what support it could to non-jurors in the name of freedom of speech. Again, for all its complaints against the Département's lack of

---

[101] Place Neuve, La Juiverie, Pierre-Scize, Port Saint-Paul, Le Gourguillon, L'Hôtel-Dieu, Belle-Cordière, Plat-d'Argent, La Grande-Côte, Saint-Vincent, La Pêcherie, Saint-Nizier, Les Terreaux (ibid. 379.)

[102] Port du Temple, Rue Tupin, Saint-Nizier, le Plâtre, le Griffon (AD 1L818, 20 June 1791).

[103] L. Vitet, *Adresse à l'Assemblée nationale* (Lyon, [1792]), 4.

[104] AD 2L90; *CM*, ii. 365, 501, 524 (24 Mar., 8 and 25 July 1791).

rigour, the Municipalité's own approach to the religious problem was itself comparatively gentle. Four priests, including Linsolas, were imprisoned for distributing Marbeuf's inflammatory writings; there were the church closures, but only after repeated street disturbances; the nonjuring priests of the Hôtel-Dieu and the Charité were given two months to reconsider before being replaced; and the strongest measures, which combined the expulsion of non-juring priests not normally resident in Lyon with the imprisonment of any non-jurors who were denounced by twenty citizens, were not ordered until the panicky days of August 1792, which also saw attempts to rid Lyon of all strangers who did not have legitimate business there.[105] Persecution of non-jurors was far more rigorous in many other places.[106]

Unfortunately (but not surprisingly, in view of their increasingly venomous and dangerous politics), no detailed records survive of the Club Central and all but three of its affiliated *clubs de quartier*. But it seems clear that most *clubistes* regarded the *patriote* Municipalité as their creation, and the defence of its interests against the Département as synonymous with theirs. All the indications are that the clubs' views on the great local political issues of this period were in accord with the Municipalité's. And they expected, and seem to have got, action from the Municipalité on various popular grievances. In the first two months after the *patriote* victory, at least eight deputations from the Club Central were received at the Town Hall, and many of their complaints were acted upon. The Municipalité attended to such matters as the construction of a public gallery in the Town Hall; the protection of the water supply to the *quartier* of Saint-Georges which was threatened by the sale of nationalized church property on the slopes above; the enforcement of legislation suppressing the privileged status of *bourgeois*; and the repair of the parish pump at Pierre-Scize.[107] Club delegations were treated with considerable respect, even when their missions were superfluous. For example, the Municipal Council received 'avec plaisir' a deputation from Saint-Pierre requesting (on the ground of danger to national security), the suppression of masquerades during *carnaval*, even though the necessary steps had already

[105] *CM*, ii. 366, 397–8 (25 Mar., 26 Apr. 1791); ibid. 352, 419, 426 (10 Mar., 12 May, 19 May 1791); *CM*, iii. 242, 247 (7, 11 Aug. 1792).

[106] See P. de la Gorce, *Histoire réligieuse de la Révolution française* (Paris, 1922), vi, chaps. 9–12.

[107] *Journal des Sociétés populaires des amis de la Constitution*, 20 Jan. 1791, 27 Jan. 1791, 30 Jan. 1791, 3 Feb. 1791, 10 Feb. 1791, 13 Feb. 1791, 17 Feb. 1791, 20 Feb. 1791; *Journal de Lyon*, 2 Apr. 1791, 4 Apr. 1791.

been taken in response to earlier representations by the clubs.[108] Food prices and quality were, of course, the *clubistes'* main preoccupation: various malpractices by butchers; the excessive price of municipal flour; the need for a *Bureau de panification* elected by the *sections* to prevent the baking of bad bread. Once again Vitet was lucky—bread prices fell from 2 *sous* 3 *deniers* per pound in January to 1 *sou* 11 *deniers* in July, and it proved possible to keep them fairly stable until spring 1792.[109]

When the clubs' regulations were finalized on 4 March they provided for petitions and deputations only in emergencies, and the regular dispatch of delegations to the Town Hall seems to have stopped. In any case, the clubs had to avoid seeming to dictate to the *autorités constituées*, particularly during the reaction against popular democratic organizations which developed in the spring and intensified after the Champ de Mars 'massacre' of 17 July. The National Assembly consistently opposed such activity, restricted it by a decree of 10 May, and tried to strangle it entirely by one of 9 October 1791 against collective petitions or deputations in the name of clubs, societies, or associations. But Lyon's clubs still maintained a view of themselves as moulders of municipal policy. According to a petition of August 1791, for example, the reduction of bread prices in July 'n'a été rendu qu'à la sollicitation et à la prévoyance des Clubs pour favoriser nos concitoyens ...'.[110] And they continued to strengthen the *patriote* majority on the Municipal Council.

The ticket determined at the Club Central for the 1791 elections seems to have been followed by the voters, though creative counting by *patriote* sectional officials cannot be ruled out. In l'Hôtel-Dieu all but 7 votes out of 136 went to Champagneux, who was standing for the post of deputy *procureur*; 308 out of 309 went to Vitet in the mayoral election; and between 164 and 178 votes went to 10 candidates for the same number of places on the Municipal Council. No other candidate received more than 10 votes.[111] Overall, the elections left the *patriotes* safely in power, and increased the representation both of the poorer *quartiers* and of artisans.

They also continued the trend which had begun in 1790 for the representation of professional men to increase at the expense of merchants. (This is in striking contrast with the other great provincial towns, where merchants held (and in Bordeaux substantially strengthened)

---

[108] AD 34L4, 25 Jan. 1791.
[109] Wahl, *Les Premières Années*, pp. 344, 413, 526.
[110] AD 34L4, club of Saint-Pierre, minutes, 21 Aug. 1791.
[111] AD 31L41, 13 Nov., 6, 20 Dec. 1791.

their grip on municipal politics during the first two years of the constitutional monarchy.[112]) The effect of the municipal revolution in Lyon, combined with the advent of the clubs, had thus been drastically to limit the local political influence of the wealthiest section of the bourgeoisie. Mercantile Lyon was obliged to look on impotently while its critics amongst the educated élites collaborated with popular democrats to create a version of democracy which for the first time permitted men below the level of the bourgeoisie to carry out sustained and organized intervention in the city's affairs. Channels had been established through which the *menu peuple* could apply political pressure in an organized way, the social basis of political participation had been deliberately widened, and, at the municipal level, a damaging blow had been struck at the constitutional link between property and political influence.

It is important to stress that the clubs only partially realized the subversive potential of popular democracy. Even the very low dues they demanded were too much for the poor and the unemployed to pay. Women were denied membership, though some clubs allowed them to attend meetings, and a short-lived women's society (meant strictly for educational purposes and as an antidote to feminine religious fanaticism) was formed in August 1791.[113] Of those Lyonnais not disqualified by gender or poverty, only a small minority became *clubistes*. La Croix-Rousse had 92 members by 1 May 1791, and Belle-Cordière, one of the more active clubs, had 178 by November of the same year. Even if Belle-Cordière's numbers were close to the average for the thirty-one *sections*, the total for the city could not have been as high as the 6,000 claimed by the *Journal de Lyon* in July.[114] Active *clubistes* were fewer still: attendance and the frequency of meetings varied according to the political temperature,[115] and the surviving minute-books show that numbers quite frequently declined below the quorum of thirty. And despite all their efforts, the clubs did not get large numbers of voters to the polls. In the first round of voting for the municipal officers in 1791, only 2,604 ballots were cast, 1,000 fewer than the year before.[116]

As with pre-industrial popular movements generally, the clubs' ability

[112] See A. Forrest, *Society and Politics in Revolutionary Bordeaux* (Oxford, 1975), 38; W. Scott, *Terror and Repression in Revolutionary Marseilles* (London, 1973), 25–6.

[113] *Institution des citoyennes dévouées à la patrie* (Lyon, 1791), 1–8.

[114] AD 34L1, club of Rue Belle-Cordière, minutes, 9 Nov. 1791; 34L3, club of La Croix-Rousse, minutes, Jan.–Apr. 1791.

[115] Koi, 'Les "Chaliers" et les sans-culottes lyonnais', p. 60.

[116] *CM*, ii. 654 (24 Nov. 1791), 235 (26 Nov. 1790).

to mobilize the *menu peuple* was limited by contradictions inherent in
what Kaplow succinctly calls 'the political alliance between the master
artisans and independent shopkeepers (proprietors) on the one hand, and
the labouring poor (wage-earners, or more generally, non-proprietors) on
the other'.[117] These contradictions did not manifest themselves openly in
the Lyonnais clubs, but they stood in the way of any coherent economic
or social programme being developed within the popular societies. Apart
from food prices, the fundamental economic concerns of the wage-earners
and even (until late 1792) the silk-weavers seem to have been largely
neglected by the clubs. When they did arise they involved questions on
which the *clubistes'* interests were deeply divided. Many wage-earners,
for example, would have concurred with the address published in the
Journal des Sociétés populaires des amis de la Constitution 'pour demander
l'abolition de toutes les Maîtrises, jurandes et corporations qui entravent
l'industrie et l'exercice des Arts'.[118] There had long been deep resentment
in various trades against 'les horreurs journalières que commettent ici les
Maîtres-gardes des corporations et les suppôts de l'ancien palais'.[119] But
to the masters, defenders of their corporative traditions, and—for rather
different reasons—to the weavers, whose corporation and *maîtres-gardes*
had won them such important victories in 1789 and 1790, the destruction
of the guilds was a very mixed blessing. It was probably just as well for
their alliance with the Rolandins that the clubs steered away from such
issues, but the fact that they confined themselves so narrowly to political
questions undoubtedly made them less relevant to the concerns of the
mass of Lyonnais.

They nevertheless remained dominant in Lyonnais politics throughout
1791 and 1792, and it is a reasonable conjecture that the reduced interest
in the 1791 elections reflected this, at least in part. Vitet gathered 93
per cent of the vote in the mayoral election—a slightly larger percentage
than the year before—and the electoral dominance of the other *patriotes*
was not much less pronounced.[120] With the results a foregone conclusion,
there was little point in voting except for the enthusiasts of *patriotisme*.

While it remains true that the *clubistes* were in a minority, it is also
true that the clubs' significance cannot be measured simply in terms of
votes cast or members recruited. It lies rather in their continuous existence

---

[117] J. Kaplow, *The Names of Kings: The Parisian Laboring Poor in the Eighteenth Century*
(New York, 1972), 164.

[118] *Journal des Sociétés populaires des amis de la Constitution*, 23 Jan. 1791, p. 34.

[119] Ibid. See Garden, *Lyon et les Lyonnais*, pp. 559–61.

[120] Wahl, *Les Premières Années*, pp. 287–8, 449–50.

over two and a half years as a framework for popular political participation and a radical alternative to constitutional politics. As long as they existed, the political hegemony of the propertied classes could not be complete, and this in itself placed them at risk, as was made clear by the National Assembly's efforts to repress organized political activity outside the Constitution.[121] But in 1791 the growing strength of the Parisian democrats prevented the full application of its repressive measures, and apart from the necessity already mentioned to avoid seeming to influence the local authorities, the Lyonnais clubs were not much affected by them.

VARENNES AND POLITICAL POLARIZATION

For all its rapid growth and its electoral effectiveness, the club movement had serious internal weaknesses. Because of Lyon's social geography, any political organization based on the *quartiers* ran the risk of polarization along the same lines as Lyonnais society, and this began to happen after June 1791, when Louis XVI's attempt to escape from France was foiled at Varennes and the continuing coexistence of the Bourbons and the Revolution became a matter of open debate. The resultant marriage of social resentment and republican feeling is nicely illustrated in an open letter to the club of Bellecour (Louis-le-Grand) from the club of Port Saint-Paul, signed by Billemaz and the weavers' leader Monnet, secretary and president respectively, rejecting a call for charity:

Il y a donc infortunés par-tout, et jusque dans le quartier de l'opulence, cela nous fait bien de la peine, nous voudrions pouvoir les soulager tous. Mais y avez-vous bien réfléchi? Louis-le-Grand demander des secours pécuniaires au Port Saint-Paul, boné deus [*sic*]! ... Si nous ne sommes pas riches en numéraire, nous le sommes en bon conseils ... Faites fondre la statue équestre de Louis XIV qui est dans votre arrondissement, vous détruirez un monument du despotisme, et vous aurez de quoi soulager vos nécessiteux.[122]

Long before Varennes, social tensions amongst the clubs had coloured discussion of their nature and function. The club of Saint-Pierre, for example, seems to have proposed the deletion of the adjective 'popular' from their official title, provoking La Croix-Rousse to affirm

que le mot populaire tient essentiellement à la nature de nos Sociétés et que les [*sic*] supprimer seroit une operation à la fois dangereuse et inutile. ... que nos

---

[121] Rose, *The Making of the Sans-Culottes*, p. 141.
[122] *Journal de Lyon*, 10 Aug. 1791, p. 57. Monnet signed as president, Billiemas [*sic*] as secretary.

Sections ne peuvent être comparées aux sociétés des amis de la Constitution répandues dans les différentes villes du Royaume et que le mot Peuple, trop rarement apprécié à sa juste valeur porte avec lui l'idée de la majesté suprême. Dans un pays libre il n'y a que des citoyens et ceux-là sont le peuple; sous le règne des Tyrans au contraire, il n'y a point de peuple il n'y a que des esclaves.[123]

The *clubistes* of La Croix-Rousse also rejected Saint-Pierre's proposal to limit membership to active citizens, declaring:

qu'un des principaux objets de notre institution est de nous pénétrer de l'esprit des lois sublimes qui gouvernent le peuple français, et comment parviendrons-nous à ce but si nous excluons la classe indigente? celle qui a le plus benoin d'instruction ... qu'il doit suffire pour être admis d'avoir de bonnes mœurs et de faire le service de garde nationale, que n'étant pas une assemblée primaire on ne doit pas se régler sur l'activité.

Dans notre bourg plusieurs personnes ont fait le service sans payer l'imposition prescritte [*sic*], or puisqu'ils deffendent [*sic*] la patrie, ne doivent-ils pas être reçu parmi nous? Ne devons-nous pas chercher à les consoler de la nullité politique que la loi a prononcé contr' eux?

Et dans ce temp [*sic*] où nos manufactures languissent le vœu des citoyens non-actifs est certainement bien digne d'être pris en considération.[124]

Exploiting in this way the contradiction between popular sovereignty and the property qualification for voting, the democrats of the clubs were able to defeat the more conservative proposals of Saint-Pierre. But later there were allegations that in certain wealthier *quartiers* the poorer members were being deliberately forced out of the clubs. Informed 'que le Club de rue Neuve avoit fait des dépenses considérables pour ses agréments dans le dessein sans doute de forcer nos frères dont la fortune est dans leur travail journalier à des dépenses au dessus de leurs forces ou à se retirer de la Société', La Croix-Rousse argued that 'une forte contribution de ses membres tendroit à sa dissolution en expulsant la classe la plus laborieuse et la moins fortunée qui est celle des ouvriers'. Declaring 'qu'il est tems [*sic*] que la société soit ramenée à ses vrais principes', the assembly proposed that in future no club should be able to ask for more than 24 *sous* as an entry fee and 10 to 12 *sous* per month to cover both its own expenses and those of the Club Central.[125]

Undoubtedly, the shock waves generated by the flight to Varennes

[123] AD 34L3, La Croix-Rousse, minutes, 27 Feb. 1791. A similar accusation was later made against the club of Rue Neuve (*Memoire justificatif des citoyens de la Société populaire des amis de la Constitution de la section de rue Neuve* (Lyon, 1791), 9).

[124] AD 34L3, La Croix-Rousse, minutes, 20 Feb. 1791.

[125] Ibid. 9 Oct. 1791.

encouraged these attempts by the well-to-do to take over at least some of the clubs. At the news of the King's attempted escape there was an outburst of strong republican sentiment,[126] and the Club Central underlined the fact that the whole constitutional settlement had been brought into question by petitioning the Assembly to declare a republic. Rue Neuve opposed this decision, together with at least one other club in wealthy central Lyon, Les Terreaux, which denounced the Club Central for acting without proper consultation. Rue Neuve soon became the storm-centre of the conflict. One of its more controversial members, Perez, who had been president of the Club Central when it proposed a republic, was personally blamed for Rue Neuve's divisions by the Feuillantists who took it over in the late summer. According to them, he was 'l'homme de plus intriguant, le plus séditieux, le plus profondément pervers qui existe peut-être dans tout le Département',[127] a former con-vulsionist who had been dismissed from a series of ecclesiastical posts, most recently by Vitet from the seminary of Saint-Irenée. His tactic, they said, had been to arouse 'hommes simples' against persons of 'lumières et probité'; thanks to him, 'Alors s'établit une ligne de démarcation entre ce qu'il appelloit les gros et les petits; alors furent dénoncés comme *aristocrates* toux ceux qui jouissoient d'une aisance honnête ...'.[128] If this account is correct, Perez had provoked a counter-attack before Varennes, resulting in his credentials as a delegate to the Club Central being withdrawn. Despite this, it was alleged, he was elected president and used his position to engineer the 'insidious' motion against the monarchy.[129] The divisions in Rue Neuve deepened. Brawls broke out at meetings, and a group of secessionists left to set up a new club in the Rue Gentil, which the Club Central recognised.[130] Rue Neuve was then disaffiliated, and the affair became a *cause célèbre*.

The political debate started by Varennes may have been the catalyst for this schism, but the struggle which followed was rooted in social conflict. It is clear from Rue Neuve's published defence that the case against it was not just the accusation of Feuillantism, but the betrayal of

---

[126] *Discours prononcé par un citoyen de la Société populaire des amis de la Constitution de la section de l'Hôtel-Dieu* (Lyon, 1791).

[127] *Mémoire du club de rue Neuve, 18 septembre 1791* (Lyon, 1791), 1.

[128] *Mémoire justificatif ... de rue Neuve*, p.2; M.-A. Pelzin, *Observations, réclamations, motions, pétitions, justifications de la Société populaire des amis de la Constitution de Lyon, de la section des Terreaux. Par le citoyen Pelzin. Lues dans la séance publique du Comité central, le jeudi 22 septembre 1791* (Lyon, 1791), 10.

[129] *Mémoire justificatif ... de rue Neuve*, pp. 2–3.

[130] Ibid. 1, 8.

its popular character by the rich and the 'gens d'esprit' who had taken it over and used their corrupt sophistication to baffle honest artisans:

au lieu de nous rendre savants il sembloit qu'on ne cherchoit qu'à nous rendre méchants. Depuis que les négociants et les riches s'étoient introduits parmi nous, au lieu de nous parler des Décrets, ils nous faisoient employer tout le temps à disputer les uns contre les autres sur des affaires personnelles ... depuis longtemps leur éloquence et leurs plaisanteries nous avons réduits au silence et en une espèce de captivité ... [ils] conduisoient à leur gré le club de rue Neuve, paroissoient avoir notre Centre en horreur ...[131]

Rue Neuve replied with a list of those members, mostly artisans and shopkeepers, who attended regularly since the schism.[132] But when Perez announced that he wished to transfer to Pierre-Scize, to join 'l'élite des patriotes', the *négociant* Rousset launched a counter-attack loaded with social insinuations: 'le citoyen Perez choississoit de préférence le club de Pierre-Scize, parce-que les habitants de ce *Faubourg* étoient plus faciles à séduire que les autres', as had been shown in 1790 when '[ils] voulurent soutenir l'insurrection de quelques brigands prêts à piller et à incendier la ville'. Rousset was also said to have claimed 'que l'intention du citoyen Perez etoit d'exciter une seconde sédition dans ce faubourg'.[133] In fact, Perez went to live in la Croix-Rousse. The club there had also split, and the faction Perez joined referred to its rival as 'le club des gens comme il faut'.[134]

The campaign against the republicans had considerable success in the wealthier parts of Lyon. On 21 August the Club Central lamented the loss of six of 'ses enfants',[135] and a total of eleven clubs were later said to have refused to collaborate in selecting candidates for the national elections. Apart from La Croix-Rousse, the clubs known to have split or campaigned against abuses at the Club Central were all in well-to-do areas—in addition to the ones so far mentioned, they were Rue Tupin, Porte-Froc, Port du Temple, and Le Plâtre.[136] The dissenters exploited the damaging charge that the Club Central, dominated by ambitious demogogues, 'discoureurs énergumènes ... membres éternels du comité central, candidats municipes pour le Saint-Martin prochain',[137] was riding

[131] *Mémoire justificatif ... de rue Neuve*, p. 10.
[132] *Adresse du club de rue Neuve le 2 octobre 1791* (Lyon, 1791).
[133] *Mémoire justificatif ... de rue Neuve*, pp. 9, 15.
[134] AD 34L3, club of La Croix-Rousse, minutes, 4 Sept. 1791.
[135] AD 34L4, letter to the club of Rue Neuve.
[136] Ibid., letter to the club of Place Saint-Pierre, 5 Feb. 1792; 34L3, club of La Croix-Rousse, minutes, 29 Dec. 1791; *Le Surveillant, par une Société de patriotes*, 31 Aug. 1791.
[137] *Mémoire justificatif ... de rue Neuve*, p. 7.

roughshod over the society's rules and the rights of the *clubs de quartier*. Threats to their autonomy could be relied upon to arouse the *sections* (clubs), always (as Port du Temple declared) 'jalouses de leurs droits'.[138] The club of Les Terreaux complained that speeches had been printed by the Club Central and other costs incurred without permission from the sectional clubs. Worse, its spokesman alleged, dissent was stilled by abuse and murderous threats, and instead of discussing only proposals submitted by the *sections* (as the *clubs de quartier* were now frequently called), the delegates freely debated 'une multitude d'opinions particulières'.[139] Port du Temple proposed the regeneration of the Club Central and sought agreement on a new set of regulations. Saint-Pierre complained that one of its deputations to the Club Central had been met with shouts and whistles, and its delegates' subsequent withdrawal with ironic cheers.[140] A delegate from Le Plâtre was also booed and manhandled when he began to read out a letter from Lyon's *députés* at the National Assembly condemning excesses committed by the clubs in the name of patriotism.[141]

The reality behind these highly partisan accounts was probably that various radicals were entrenching themselves at the Club Central in defiance of the clubs' regulations, and using its rostrum to accumulate personal followings—men like Perez, Cusset (later a Montagnard *député*), and the leaders of the very active radical club of Rue Belle-Cordière, Bussat, Gravier, Dubessey, and Pilot. How much this was resented in the more popular *quartiers* is unclear, but there are signs of flagging enthusiasm in the first half of 1792, perhaps because the initiative had been taken from them by the Club Central, whose meetings were now generally open to the public (too often for La Croix-Rousse) and were held more than three times weekly (too often for La Croisette);[142] perhaps because the clubs' façade of fraternal unity had been destroyed; perhaps because they had become overtly factionalized, so that continued involvement with them meant making dangerous commitments. Weekly readings of the National Assembly's decrees and the joys of revolutionary fraternity may have lost their pristine appeal, particularly now that the Assembly

---

[138] *La Société populaire de la section de Port du Temple à toutes les autres Sociétés populaires des amis de la Constitution de Lyon, Salut* (Lyon, 1791), 2.

[139] *Observations ... de la section des Terreaux*, p. 3. See also *Le Surveillant*, 10 Sept. 1791, p. 13.

[140] *La Société populaire ... de Port du Temple*, pp. 1–2; AD 34L1, club of Rue Belle-Cordière, minutes, 23 Oct. 1791; AC I²4, club of La Croisette, minutes, 25 Jan. 1792.

[141] *Le Surveillant*, 10 Sept. 1791, p. 14.

[142] AD 34L3, minutes, 17 Aug. 1791; AC I²4, minutes, 15 Jan. 1792.

was producing such unappetizing legislation as the Le Chapelier law and the September laws against the popular societies, not to mention the rejection of the great petition against the garrison. Attendances were often low, even at Rue Belle-Cordière where only fifty-six voters were recorded on 17 April 1792.[143] At La Croix-Rousse, meetings were held only about once weekly between February and June. Belle-Cordière and La Croisette complained respectively of the difficulty of extracting dues and of high incidental expenses incurred by the Club Central for such things as printing, which the *clubs de quartier* had to help pay, 'attendu qu'une grande partie des membres peuvent à peine fournir aux frais les plus urgents'. La Croix-Rousse argued that public sessions (which were held by individual clubs as well as the Club Central for the instruction of non-members) reduced the attendance at its regular meetings. La Croisette frequently had trouble maintaining a quorum, and in August 1792 discussed a proposal to find a smaller room because 'depuis longtemps, les sociétaires s'éloigne [*sic*] des séances'.[144]

The process of political polarization along the lines of social tension made the *patriotes* of the Municipalité more dependent on the popular societies by obliging them to cut their links with the former Jacobin Club. In March 1791 eleven members of the Municipal Council had belonged to the Société des Amis de la Constitution, familiarly called the Club du Concert. Even then, the Concert's relations with the popular societies were somewhat strained. The clubs resented the fact that the Concert was recognized as the Paris Jacobins' affiliate in Lyon, which prevented the Club Central's affiliation with *la société mère*,[145] and anyway there was too much contrast between the affluence of the Concert and the deliberately plebeian orientation of the clubs for them to collaborate harmoniously. A motion was passed in the Club Central banning members of the Concert from its presidency,[146] and lengthy but inconclusive debates occurred in the *clubs de quartier* as to whether they should be admitted even as ordinary members. In July the Concert abandoned its Jacobin affiliation and aligned itself with the Feuillantists; and on the 20th it congratulated Lafayette for his actions in the massacre at the Champ de Mars. This provoked furious attacks from the popular societies

[143] AD 34L1.

[144] Ibid. 1 Jan. 1792; AC I²4, club of La Croisette, minutes, 8 Jan., 22 Apr., 7 and 13 June, 19 Aug. 1792; AD 34L3, club of La Croix-Rousse, minutes, 7 Feb., 6 Mar. 1792.

[145] See the article by Lanthénas in the *Patriote français*, 28 Feb. 1791, reprinted in Aulard, *Jacobins*, ii. 148–50.

[146] *Journal de Lyon*, 9 May 1791, p. 3.

and their advocate Laussel, the editor of the *Journal de Lyon,* according to whom 'une société qui présente une masse imposante de plus de six mille citoyens, dont la plupart sont artistes ou artisans, tient fortement à la liberté', while the Concert's membership, 'les lâches, élévés dans la molesse, accoutumés au luxe, corrompues jusqu' à la moële des os, ne peuvent subsister que par la faveur d'un maître, et non par le travail, comme les citoyens des nos sections'.[147] La Croix-Rousse, which had previously rejected proposals to exclude members of the Concert, now advocated a purge of aristocrats and resolved not to admit members of any other club.[148] The *patriotes* had no choice but to cut their links with the Concert and to rest their political fortunes entirely on the popular societies.[149] The union which Vitet and Roland had been trying to establish within the ranks of the old Third Estate had been unmistakably shattered.

THE POLITICS OF THE PROPERTIED CLASSES

Although the *patriotes* were able to retain control of the Municipalité of Lyon, their position was thus quite vulnerable. Why, then, was there no sustained effort by more conservative elements to displace them? Why did the mercantile classes not struggle for a share of local office proportionate to their economic importance? Throughout 1791 and 1792 they seem to have withdrawn from municipal affairs. The disengagement began with the simultaneous resignation of a banker, two former *échevins,* a *bourgeois,* and a *négociant.* It continued when several of the councillors who had been chosen by lot to be replaced by election refused to stay on in place of those who had resigned.[150] The elections, as we have already noted, saw low total votes and large majorities for the *patriote* candidates.

One of the reasons for this was the prevalence of attitudes towards municipal politics ranging from indifference to disdain. The Prussian *Kapellmeister* Reichardt, who moved amongst the merchant élite in early 1792, was much struck by this, and deeply disappointed by the Lyonnais refusal to behave in a manner appropriate to participants in a sublime

---

[147] Ibid. 25 July 1791, p. 2. See Wahl, *Les Premières Années,* p. 399.

[148] AD 34L3, minutes, 27 Mar., 9 Oct. 1791.

[149] Vitet was referred to as an ex-member of the Concert in the *Journal de Lyon,* 21 Dec. 1791, p. 3.

[150] *CM,* i. 224 (16 Nov. 1790). See also Wahl, *Les Premières Années,* p. 288. According to the *Journal de Lyon,* 14 Dec. 1791, 12 Lyonnais refused municipal offices to which they had been elected during the year.

world-historical event: 'Du tapage au théâtre, quelques mauvaises pièces patriotiques sont ici, à peu près, les seuls indices d'une révolution politique. La bourgeoisie est trop riche et trop absorbée par ses affaires propres pour vouloir autre chose que la tranquillité à l'interieur et la paix à l'extérieur.'[151] Reichardt found that by and large the propertied classes of Lyon did not share his passionate desire to be involved in the inauguration of liberty. They had initially been happy enough to take the municipal offices created by the new regime, but they were not prepared to canvass for votes in order to retain them. Very probably the old bourgeois disdain for the masses remained a barrier now that effective participation in municipal politics involved frequenting the clubs. As we have already seen, social antagonisms and, in particular, the militancy of the hatters and weavers made it hard for the merchants to translate their economic influence into political leadership by using patronage and establishing a popular clientele. If they wanted office they had to compete with the *patriotes* and the clubs' candidates for artisan votes, but this was to risk the kind of *dérogeance* which, it seems, haunted the wholesale clothier Jean-Pierre Granier, one of the municipal officers who withdrew from politics late in 1790. This 'fort ancien roturier', a pamphleteer alleged, 'trouvant la démocratie de fort mauvais ton, pour n'être pas confondu avec *la canaille et les va-nus-pieds,* a mieux aimé être le singe de la noblesse'.[152]

Perhaps most importantly, anyone who contemplated displacing the *patriotes* from office had to consider the dangers of popular disorder which a more conservative Municipalité might bring with it. Vitet had some influence and prestige amongst the *menu peuple,* and there had been no serious riots during his mayoralty. Deprived of their *patriote* Municipalité, the people and the clubs might turn to more radical methods still, and to violence.

Municipal office also had disadvantages which can hardly have been overlooked by practical-minded men. It was dangerous: Vitet's two immediate predecessors had only narrowly survived their periods of office. It was also unpaid, and the paid judicial offices and District and Departmental Directoires provided much more attractive alternatives for the ambitious. Again, while there was a slight economic recovery in 1790 and 1791, things were still difficult for business men, who cannot have found attractive the prospect of devoting their time to the troubles of a

---

[151] Reichardt, *Un Prussien en France,* p. 187.
[152] *Opinions impartiales des officiers municipaux sortis par le voie du sort* (Lyon, 1790).

nearly bankrupt city.[153] In Lyon, as in France as a whole, active involvement in revolutionary politics was much less common among business men than among men of the professions, who were better placed and better equipped to take advantage of the opportunities for advancement provided when the state apparatus was thrown open to bourgeois talent, and a political environment was created which favoured men trained in law and the rhetoric of classical humanism. Where there were large numbers of lawyers, former office-holders, clergy, and administrative personnel—in other words, in Paris and in the cities which had housed *parlements* under the old regime—the potential for extensive bourgeois involvement in revolutionary politics existed right from the beginning, and it was bourgeois from the professional classes who generally took the leading role.[154] In manufacturing towns, too, the mercantile élites were often able to take over local politics; but if—as in Lyon—local circumstances prevented this, they had to make do with the other means which the National Assembly provided to look after their interests.

It is vital to remember, however, that these means were formidable and multifarious, beginning with the constitutional equation of property with national political power. Despite the reduced property qualification which followed the insurrection of 7 February 1790, the two-stage electoral process and the rural vote ensured that the *députés* sent by Rhône-et-Loire to the Constituent and the Legislative Assemblies were men of wealth and conservative views. Millanois and Périsse-Duluc may have been opponents of the Consulat, but this did not translate into radicalism in national affairs. Their colleagues, the banker Guillaume Couderc and the silk-merchant René-Louis Goudard, showed still less revolutionary zeal, and Rhône-et-Loire's *députés* to the Legislative Assembly were so far to the right that Vitet declined to take the place amongst them which was offered to him by the electoral college.[155] On both the great issues of 1791, the garrison and the grenadiers, the Legislative Assembly supported the Departmental Directoire. In addition, its economic policy was generally favourable to Lyonnais interests. As was to be expected in a centre of international trade, the *assignats* were only grudgingly accepted, and there was considerable alarm at the effects on credit of their instability

---

[153] See Wahl, *Les Premières Années*, pp. 403–5.

[154] Bordeaux and Grenoble are the best examples. This argument was partly suggested by the work of L. Hunt, *Revolution and Urban Politics in Provincial France: Troyes and Reims 1786–90* (Stanford, 1978), 137.

[155] Wahl, *Les Premières Années*, pp. 74–6, 424; M. Roland, *Lettres de Madame Roland*, ed. C. Perraud (Paris, 1900), ii. 376 (letter of 9 Sept. 1791 to J. M. Roland).

and rapid depreciation.[156] But while the *laissez-faire* legislation of 1790–1 went against the Fabrique's deep-seated belief in the silk industry's need for regulation, it had some compensations for the merchants.[157] The Le Chapelier law made it more difficult for the weavers to organize, and the removal of the *octrois* had long been desired in the interests of reducing labour costs. Still more important, fuller tariff protection was provided for the industry in August 1791 than had existed since the Eden Treaty of 1786.

The thoroughly conservative policy of the Département was another source of reassurance for the propertied classes. Given the electoral laws and the conservatism of the rural *districts* of Rhône-et-Loire, the prospect of the Département becoming a seat of radicalism was remote. And the electors of the *district* of Lyon-Ville themselves made sure that their representatives on the General Council were of similar political outlook to the rest. The Département was victorious in nearly all its skirmishes with the Municipalité until May 1792, and it underlined its authority by prosecuting Champagneux and Chalier—and suspending the latter from office—for abuses of power, and by sequestering the municipal treasury.[158] In the Directoire of Rhône-et-Loire there existed a powerful defence against municipal radicalism, just as the legislators of 1790 had intended.

The third source of reassurance was the National Guard. The July riots of 1790 had demonstrated that the social geography of Lyon presented considerable advantages for the defenders of property, and that the selective use of National Guard battalions could be effective in serious emergencies. Certainly, the involvement of Guardsmen in the insurrection of Pierre-Scize was a cause for alarm. But, like most of the poorer and more turbulent parts of Lyon, this *quartier* was remote from the centre of the city and the Arsenal. From Pierre-Scize the only way to the Saône bridges was along the Rue Pierre-Scize, which could easily be blocked off. If need be, most of Lyon's dangerous *quartiers* could also be isolated, provided sufficient National Guard battalions could be found to do the job.

The successful defence of the Arsenal on 26 July gave reason for confidence on this point. Early in the day the *négociant* Jean-Baptiste Odobé, *capitaine en chef* of the Bellecour battalion, 'prit la précaution

---

[156] See e.g. *Opinion de la Chambre de commerce de Lyon sur la motion faite le 27 août 1790 ... pour la liquidation de la dette exigible de l'État* (Lyon, 1790).

[157] See E. Pariset, *Histoire de la Fabrique lyonnaise* (Lyon, n.d.), 256–61.

[158] Wahl, *Les Premières Années,* pp. 478–84, 521.

d'inviter les meilleurs citoyens à se tenir prêts à porter en cas de besoin, des secours à l'arsenal'. They did so at the first sign of trouble, reinforcing the designated guard detachment of the day which was drawn from the plebeian *section* of Rue Belle-Cordière. After the first attacks had been beaten off, National Guards from Port du Temple joined in a defensive action which the literary *Journal de Lyon* eulogized as 'un de ces faits que nous aimons à consigner dans nos feuilles'.[159] By contrast with 1744, 1786, July 1789, and February 1790, a civilian force proved able to repel a serious threat from below, and as long as the Guard's officer corps was composed of men like the *chefs de légion* chosen in March 1792, there was reason to hope that similar emergencies could be safely met. Of the twelve *chefs de légion* who had been elected by officers with the rank of lieutenant and above, two had links with the *échevinage* (Justin Badger and Riverieulx de Jarlay), one was a former *commissaire à terrier* (Dalin), two were ex-army officers (Bollioud and Vernon), one was a wholesale mercer, one was a *négociant,* and one was a farrier (André Pichard, Dupin, and Falconet).[160]

If the propertied classes of Lyon were too nervous of popular disorder for any but the most deeply committed *patriotes* amongst them to want a local revolution, they nevertheless adapted readily to the one made by the National Assembly. They approved of the Constitution, and found weapons in its legislation well suited to protecting and promoting their essential interests. What they disliked was Jacobinism and the prospect of war, not the new national political system.[161] The radical changes brought about by the *journées* of 1790 and exploited by the *patriotes* and the *clubistes* had shifted the social location of power to an extent and by means which the properties classes found dangerous and unacceptable. In response, bourgeois Lyon joined the former *notables* in a sustained defensive action.

Other cities had experienced disorders as great as Lyon's during the first two years of the Revolution, but few had experienced greater, and

---

[159] *Journal de Lyon,* 15 Aug. 1790, pp. 119–20. (This was edited by Mathon de la Cour, a noble and former member of the Academy of Lyon. Unlike the *Journal de Lyon* edited by Carrier and Laussel, it was generally apolitical.)

[160] AD 1L818, *Extrait ... du procès-verbal de la nomination des chefs ... des 4 légions de la Garde nationale de Lyon, 9 mars 1792* (Lyon, 1792); *Liste des citoyens éligibles aux places municipales de la ville de Lyon* (Lyon, 1790); G. Bussière, *Une famille anglaise d'ouvriers en soie à Lyon (1753–1793)* (Lyon, 1908), *passim*; A. Portallier, *Tableau général des victimes et martyrs de la Révolution en Lyonnais, Forez et Beaujolais* (Saint-Étienne, 1911), article on Badger.

[161] See Reichardt, *Un Prussien en France,* p. 160.

none was faced with popular radicals so well organized as those of the Lyonnais clubs. Nowhere, except perhaps in Marseille and Toulon, were persons of property so insecure or so dependent on the safeguards provided by the Constitution of 1791, on the Département, the District, and the National Guard, and on the political principle which the Feuillantist journal *Le Surveillant* succinctly defined in July 1791: 'Le Peuple est Souverain; mais l'exercice de la Souveraineté lui serait funeste.'[162] All this cemented the attachment of the Lyonnais propertied classes to the political structures established by the National Assembly, and made them hostile to any hint of change.

In late 1791, for example, when petitions for the suppression of the royal veto were received by the Legislative Assembly, a shrill warning came from mercantile Lyon that even to contemplate altering 'les bases de la Constitution' threatened ruin to the nation's credit.[163] After Varennes, similar fears fuelled the dissension in the popular societies. The local victories of the clubs might be tolerated by the propertied classes, but not a direct challenge to the Constitution. Provoked to counter-attack, they inflicted some damage on the club movement by organizing opposition to the Club Central in the wealthier *quartiers*, but the radical majority remained too strong for them, and they seem to have withdrawn from club politics during the brief calm that followed the King's resumption of his place as constitutional monarch. Nevertheless, for the first time they had shown signs of recognizing that under the conditions created by the Revolution it would be necessary to use the weapons of democratic politics in self-defence.

RUMOURS OF COUNTER-REVOLUTION

> Toute la surveillance doit se porter à Lyon ...
>
> De Hesse at the Paris Jacobins, 6 April 1792

It was easy for the *patriotes* to suggest that the Feuillantism of the Lyonnais social élites was nothing more than a mask for counter-revolution, and the claim was repeated by Jacobins in Lyon and Paris with increasing certainty and frequency between 1790 and 1793. But there is no historical basis for it unless we accept unquestioningly the Jacobins' definition of counter-revolution, which was, in effect, dissent

---

[162] *Le Surveillant par une Société de patriotes: Prospectus* (1791), 2.
[163] *Pétition à l'Assemblée nationale par plusieurs negocians, fabricans et autres citoyens de la ville de Lyon, le 18 décembre 1791* (Lyon, 1791), 6.

from their programme for defending a revolution whose essential nature they redefined in the face of rapidly changing circumstances, particularly those dictated by their need for the support of a radicalizing Parisian popular movement. There were few amongst the well-to-do in Lyon who saw any reason to criticize Lafayette for shooting down demonstrators in the Champ de Mars, or to jeopardize the Constitution by deposing the King. This refusal to keep up with the march of the Jacobins' revolution might make them counter-revolutionary in the Jacobin sense, but there is no evidence that they became so in the sense of dissenting from the broad lines of the verdict which the National Assembly had pronounced on the old regime.

Many of them would undoubtedly have liked to have had some laws unmade, particularly the law providing for the direct election of municipal officials. Many would have been much happier if the 'les sociétés soi-disant patriotiques'[164] (as *Le Surveillant* called them) could be effectively suppressed. On these points, cultivated society made its collective feelings clear at its favourite political forum, the Théâtre des Célestins, where the hit of winter 1791–2 was *Le Club des bonnes gens*. The performances of this topical piece offered wonderful opportunities for heaping ridicule on the *clubistes*—particularly the women (talking endlessly, lecturing husbands on revolutionary principles)—and on the *patriote* Municipalité as well. On one wild evening in February 1792 the municipal officer Perret appealed for calm, repeating constantly the word 'on'. 'auquel le parterre faisait écho en répétant à son tour on! on! ... on formulait des motions pour *ou* contre; l'un, faisant allusion à le piteuse harangue de l'officier municipal disait: "Je fais la motion que le discours de M. Perret de la municipalité soit imprimé!" Un autre: "J'appelle de la municipalité au département".'[165] Sometimes the demonstrations had a more reactionary flavour, like the shouts of 'Vive la Nation!' when the brigands made their entrance during *La Forêt-Noire*, and the prolonged royalist outbursts which greeted performances of the suggestively named *Richard Cœur-de-Lion*.[166] But nothing closer to a counter-revolutionary manifestation occurred in Lyon during the eighteen months after the exposure of the 'Conspiration de Lyon'.

The Abbé Fauchet nevertheless gave official status to Lyon's reputation as a capital of aristocratic intrigue in his report to the Legislative Assembly

---

[164] *Le Surveillant*, 10 Sept. 1791, p. 14.
[165] Reichardt, *Un Prussien en France*, p. 166.
[166] Ibid. 62.

on 17 April 1792. Fauchet depicted Lyon as 'un ferment toujours plus actif de la contre-révolution', and accepted as literal truth the Lyonnais *patriotes'* conviction that the Département's lack of revolutionary commitment was attracting a flood of dangerous strangers—aristocrats by blood or conviction, refractory priests, counter-revolutionary organizers, recruiting agents from Coblenz. (Some arrests were actually made in the last category.)[167]

Just as it suited the Municipalité to discredit the Département by advertising the consequences of its laxity, it suited *patriotes* in nearby towns like Mâcon and Bourg, always resentful of Lyon's economic and administrative influence, to embellish the 'second city's' counter-revolutionary image.[168] Lyon became notorious throughout the Midi as the preferred destination of fleeing aristocrats—which it may well have been, since it was big enough to get lost in and conveniently close to the *émigré* havens of Switzerland and Northern Italy. Reichardt encountered many ex-nobles and wealthy landowners who thought life was much less dangerous in Lyon than on their estates.[169] But very few certifiable enemies of the Revolution were actually discovered, despite the Municipalité's strenuous efforts—a failure which, of course, only strengthened the suspicions in Paris, Mâcon, Vienne, Clermont, and elsewhere that the city was under the thumb of the aristocrats. It seems likely that if Lyon did contain numbers of refugee aristocrats and priests, they were there more for concealment than to set up a base for counter-revolution, at least until the summer of 1793. As the Municipalité itself pointed out, belying its own alarmist talk about agitators, Lyon was a more peaceful town than most for the best part of 1791 and 1792.[170] But however little proof there was one way or the other, Lyon's reputation with *patriotes* elsewhere was indelibly black by the end of the constitutional monarchy, and the wildest absurdities could be put about to blacken it further.[171] Lyon was expected to put on a counter-revolution, and in the absence of

---

[167] The report of Fauchet is reproduced in A. Metzger and J. Vaesen (eds.), *Lyon en 1792: Notes et documents* (Lyon, n.d.). It is largely a restatement of the charges in *Adresse du Conseil-général de la commune de Lyon, lue à l'Assemblée nationale dans la séance du 13 février 1792* (Lyon, 1792), *passim.*

[168] AC I²2, fo. 12, letter of the Municipalité of Mâcon, 8 Aug. 1792; Walh, *Les Premières Années*, p. 473.

[169] Reichardt, *Un Prussien en France*, p. 161.

[170] *CM*, iii. 251 (12 Aug. 1792).

[171] The Jacobin Prince de Hesse denounced to the Paris Jacobins a *coup de main* that was planned for Lyon using 18,000–20,000 troops, 'sans les troupes auxiliaires' (Aulard, *Jacobins*, iii. 469–70 (6 April 1792)).

any more concrete evidence, the conspicuous lack of revolutionary fervour amongst its élites helped to make the prediction plausible. Later the prediction was fulfilled, but the rebellion of 1793 certainly cannot be used as proof that the *patriotes* were right about Lyon in 1791 and 1792. It took a complex interaction between national and local conflicts in the year following Fauchet's report to create the pre-conditions for revolt against what the Jacobin revolution was becoming. And the very prediction of counter-revolution was to play a large part in its fulfilment.

4

The Great Upheaval

The clubs' ascendancy was reaffirmed in the first important election of
1792 when, in May, their candidate Joseph Julliard was voted *commandant-général* of the National Guard. Julliard was a silk-weaver who
was so poor that he qualified only because of his long army service. This
made his election a direct challenge to one of the main bastions of
property, and the Feuillantists reacted predictably to it. A widely circulated exposé denounced it as a threat to the social order engineered by
'une Société qui, par son organisation, influe sur toutes les élections
qui émanent directement des Assemblées primaires'.[1] Pointing out that
Juillard relied on his daily toil for his living, the pamphleteer maintained
that his election transgressed the most basic political principles. Could it
be, he asked, that 'le premier Agent d'une partie essentielle de la force
publique, sur la tête duquel repose une si grande responsabilité, ne doit
avoir d'autres garants que les suffrages qui l'ont élevé à cette place de
confiance?'[2]

On this occasion, however, the panic proved groundless. The new
commandant-général, who fled when informed of his election and had to
be retrieved,[3] proved no match for the *chefs de légion* and the departmental
and district administrators. They repeatedly overruled both his orders
and those of the Municipalité. On 17 May the *chefs de légion* defied him
by posting grenadiers to the Town Hall, nearly provoking a riot on the
Place des Terreaux. The next day more grenadiers were placed in charge
of the Arsenal, where they insulted and shouted down members of the
Municipal Council who ordered them to retire.

Together with the *chefs de légion* and the Département, the grenadiers
were now firmly established in *patriote* opinion as 'aristocratique', if not

---

[1] *Exposé de tout ce qui s'est passé relativement à l'organisation de la Garde nationale du
district de la ville de Lyon* (Lyon, [1792], 3–5).
[2] Ibid. 28.
[3] Ibid. 5.

outright counter-revolutionary. According to the Municipalité the *chefs de légion*, chosen 'par des électeurs très aristocratiques', had imbued them with 'un esprit de parti'.[4] According to their defenders, the grenadiers embodied the best traditions of the *milice bourgeoise*; they were being viciously slandered as 'les enemis de la chose publique, disons le mot que la multitude a consacré, des *aristocrates*, et par conséquent des *contre-révolutionnaires* liés avec ceux d'outre-Rhin'.[5] In response to accusations of social exclusiveness, it was asserted that height was the only criterion of acceptance in a grenadier company, but the exposé gave the game away: they were '*les hommes de bonne volonté* qu'on seroit toujours sûr de trouver au besoin', by contrast with 'l'ouvrier paisible, qui doit tout son temps à son honnête famille'.[6] There is insufficient evidence for rigorous social analysis of the grenadiers, but although there seems to have been an influx of artisans into some companies during the democratization of the National Guard in 1792,[7] the *patriotes* probably had reason to regard most of them as *volontaires* reborn, in social as well as political terms.

Again there was deadlock between those who did not trust a democratic National Guard to defend property and those who did not trust a bourgeois National Guard to defend the Revolution. But two new elements entered the situation in the spring of 1792, and during the summer they were to transform it. One was that the *patriotes* could now look to Paris for help with some degree of confidence. Previously, all the interventions by the National and Legislative Assemblies in Lyon's affairs had served the interests of the propertied élites. That the Assemblies took on such a role is not at all surprising, since sanctity of property was the main pillar of the new order they were creating. But the crucial significance of this role needs underlining. The histories of provincial cities during the Revolution tend to be overshadowed by the events of 1793, when for a time France seemed on the verge of war between Paris and the 'federalist' provinces. Yet the struggle over 'federalism' was an aberration,[8] while

---

[4] AN F⁹6, Vitet and four municipal officers to Servan, Minister of War, 14 May 1792.

[5] *Exposé de tout ce qui s'est passé*, p. 32.

[6] Ibid. 7, 35. On the social character of the grenadier battalions, see also G. Bussière, *Une famille anglaise d'ouvriers en soie à Lyon (1753–1793)* (Lyon, 1908), 68–9; J. F. Reichardt, *Un Prussien en France en 1792: Lettres intimes de J. F. Reichardt*, trans. A. Laquivante (Paris, 1892), 142 (letter of 13 Feb. 1792).

[7] A. De Francesco, 'Le Quartier lyonnais de la Croisette pendant les premières années de la Révolution (1790–1793)', *Bulletin du Centre d'histoire économique et sociale de la région lyonnaise*, 4 (1979), 39.

[8] B. Edmonds, '"Federalism" and Urban Revolt in France in 1793', *Journal of Modern History*, 55 (1983), 22–53.

the social struggle was a permanent condition. There were undoubtedly tensions between local élites and the national government, but the interests of the propertied classes everywhere—and particularly where the social struggle was acute—lay in supporting the national legislative and executive powers which until 1792 were firmly committed to maintaining the constitutional and coercive arrangements necessary to meet the threat from below. So long as the national legislatures remained firmly committed to preserving these arrangements, the Lyonnais élites showed no sign of any concern to defend, and still less to increase, municipal or regional independence from Paris.

But since the flight to Varennes, the political situation in the capital had changed drastically, with the reaction against republican agitation, the Feuillantists' withdrawal from the Paris Jacobin Club, and the massacre of republicans at the Champ de Mars by Lafayette's National Guard. Under the astute leadership of Robespierre, the core of Jacobins not only survived the loss of the majority of the Club's members, but within two months they had replenished their membership and re-established a large network of affiliated clubs. By the time the newly elected Legislative Assembly met on 1 October, the Jacobins were in a strong position to pursue what had become their principal activities: consolidating their leadership of revolutionary democratic opinion, defending popular political interests as they conceived them, and elaborating strategies against counter-revolution. They embarked on the first by admitting passive citizens as members and by throwing their sessions open to the public; on the second by succcessfully opposing attempts to make the Constitution more conservative; and on the third by preaching vigilance against conspiracies of *émigrés*, refractory clergy, and the court. To accelerate Jacobin victory on these fronts, the Brissotin group proposed a war of liberation against the tyrants of Europe with the aim of provoking a show-down between an aroused people and the counter-revolution. Once their successful advocacy of this policy had brought them to ministerial office (10 March) and the Assembly to a declaration of war on Austria (20 April), a change in government policy towards Lyon was clearly likely. It became inevitable when the Ministry of the Interior was given to the most prominent of the early *patriotes* at Lyon, Jean-Marie Roland.

Roland had been sent to Paris in February 1791 to seek financial aid on behalf of the Municipalité of Lyon,[9] and he had rapidly acquired

[9] *CM*, ii. 325 (11 Feb. 1792).

influence amongst the Brissotins, considerably assisted by the enthusiasm of several of them for his wife's salon.[10] His first ministry only lasted thirteen weeks, but in the course of it he obtained the removal of most of the regular troops from Lyon, authorized the Municipalité to determine the allocation of posts amongst the National Guard units, and on 10 June re-established the Municipalité's control over the funds which the Départment had sequestered in the course of a long financial dispute.[11] From now on, Parisian politics and Lyonnais politics were intimately linked and bourgeois Lyon became a prime target for intervention from the capital on behalf of the *patriotes*.

At the same time, an ideological reorientation was occurring amongst the democratic left in Lyon, and its leadership was passing into the hands of elements who were more deeply hostile to the Lyonnais élites than Roland had ever been. Until 1792 the relevance of social conflict to politics had been obscured by conventions of rhetoric which were observed by the members of the contending *autorités constituées*. According to the *patriotes*, the grenadiers were manipulated into aristocratic errors by ill-intentioned officers. The people, on the other hand, were said by the *patriotes*' critics to have been led into excesses by ambitious demagogues and criminals bent on pillage. No one questioned the commonality of interest between well-intentioned rich and virtuous poor. But now Joseph Chalier redefined Lyonnais politics in social terms:

Lyon fut toujours partagée entre un grand nombre de riches privilégiés et oppresseurs, et un beaucoup plus grand nombre de pauvres, écrasés par le poids des charges, avilis par celui de l'humiliation. Les premiers s'indignèrent de ce que d'autres osoient avec eux contempler *la déclaration des droits de l'homme et du citoyen*; la haine de l'égalité fut la source des troubles de Lyon; ces troubles commencèrent avec la révolution; ils ont continué, ils existent encore par le dessein et l'espoir de rétablir l'ancien régime.[12]

Not Coblenz, not the civil list, not the priests or the nobility, but the inherent *incivisme* of the rich explained the deep-seated aristocratic tendencies of Lyon. Chalier went beyond the generalized hostility which the *patriotes* had long felt for commercial Lyon. He declared that the political struggle between the Département, 'coalisé avec le pouvoir

[10] See M. J. Sydenham, *The Girondins* (London, 1961), 86–91.
[11] See M. Wahl, *Les Premières Années de la Révolution à Lyon, 1788–1792* (Paris, n.d.), 485–525.
[12] *Adresse de Joseph Chalier officier municipal de la ville de Lyon à l'Assemblée nationale* (Paris, 1792), 2.

exécutif', and the Municipalité, sustained by 'la confiance du peuple',[13] grew out of the long-standing conflict in Lyon between rich and poor. And whereas Roland thought that the rich could be won over to the Revolution and to their social responsibilities by appeals to enlightened self-interest, Chalier suggested no possibility of their redemption.

What led Chalier to these convictions is by no means clear. His later career as a Jacobin demagogue and advocate of terror aroused both idolatry and vilification, and these have tainted most accounts of his life. It is not possible to establish more than a few basic facts about his early years. He was born near Briançon in 1747 and migrated at an early age to Lyon, where he dabbled in painting and philosophy and did some teaching. Then he entered the silk trade and prospered, representing his firm in the Levant, Italy, Spain, and Portugal. Several biographies claim that he was expelled from Lisbon in 1783 and from Sicily in 1790 for expressing opinions against despotism, and he was certainly an early convert to the Revolution. He rushed to Paris to greet its dawn, acquiring pieces of the Bastille which, when lecturing on liberty, he would produce for his listeners to kiss. Chalier's article of February 1790, which denounced the 'aristocratic spirit' of Lyon in the pages of *Les Révolutions de Paris*, began his crusade to raise his adopted city 'à la hauteur de la Révolution'. It also made him extremely unpopular in the mercantile circles that he had previously frequented, and this may have increased, though it did not cause, his hostility towards them. He was one of the few *patriotes* amongst the *notables* elected in February 1790, but he resigned his post. By November 1791, however, he was popular enough to be the third municipal officer elected, and during the next year he became the most prominent of the agitators who used the Club Central to mobilize the *menu peuple* in defence of the Revolution, which Chalier believed the rich were betraying. The accounts of his rambling performances at the rostrum are mostly from hostile sources, but his friends and enemies were agreed that, while bizarre, ('Roland, Roland, ta tête branle ... Clavière aux doigts crochus, à bas, à bas tes vilains ongles'), his speeches were effective in communicating his urgent sense of the need for direct, and possibly violent, popular political intervention.[14]

Here was the beginning of schism amongst the *patriotes*, but for several months the noise of battle against the Departmental Directoire hid their

[13] Ibid. 2, 5.
[14] See M. Wahl, 'Joseph Chalier: Étude sur la Révolution française à Lyon', *Revue historique*, 34 (1887), 1–10. This is the only reliable biographical study of Chalier.

differences, with Chalier leading the charge. His pursuit of fictitious counter-revolutionary conspiracies led him to break into private premises, whose owners then had him prosecuted. This was more than enough excuse for the Directoire to suspend him from municipal office (25 January 1792). To seek both personal vindication and redress of the Municipalité's grievances against the Directoire, Chalier went to Paris, only to encounter difficulties and delays which hardened his intransigence and fed his chronic suspiciousness. He was tormented by the Legislative Assembly's slowness in acting on his complaints, and soon also by the Lyonnais *patriotes*' passivity:

Il s'agit de prendre un parti vigoureux, ou nous sommes immolés, car le crime triomphe, l'aristocratie lève la tête ici plus que jamais, parce que l'Assemblée nationale est gangrenée à la très grande majorité ... les quatre-vingt-trois départements sont contre moi, juges [*sic*] de la lutte effroyable ... Parlez à la municipalité, ferme, dites lui qu'il n'est plus temps de s'amuser à raisonner, qu'il faut agir. Qu'elle envoye des députés par le conseil général de la commune, ou que les citoyens sortent de leur léthargie; que les sociétés populaires se montrent avec énergie, car l'audace et la perfidie du Directoire sont à leur comble ... tout est mis en usage [contre moi], justement par les Thuileries [*sic*] pour cela; elles en voudront à bout, parce que le peuple n'est ni assez instruit, ni assez uni, ni assez résolu, il a eu des chaînes, il en aura. La révolution ayant été manquée et ensuite paralysée par Lafayette elle ne peut aller plus avant sans une commotion générale et elle est impossible, il y a trop de factions ... je mourrai de chagrin, non par rapport à moi, mais à l'aspect de tant de brigandages et de trahisons de toute espèce, parlez aux vrais patriotes ...[15]

Like many democrats in the political turmoil of spring 1792, Chalier was wary of the Brissotins' ambitions and saw in Robespierre the brightest hope of turning the aristocratic tide. He recommended the latter's *Défenseur de la Constitution* to the *patriotes* of Lyon as 'vrayment [*sic*] beau et dans les plus grands principes'.[16]

As he expected, his affair dragged on, and it was only after 10 August, when the Paris *sections* and the provincial *fédérés* overthrew the monarchy, that the Legislative Assembly, abandoned by the royalists, finally reinstated him in office 'avec honneur' and destituted the Departmental Directoire.[17] He returned to Lyon in triumph, committed to duplicating there the 'commotion générale' which had been so effectual in Paris, and

---

[15] Letter of Chalier to Delorme, the *premier juge de commerce* at Lyon, 13 May 1792, reproduced in *Revue du Lyonnais*, 11 (1855), 429–30.
[16] Chalier to Delorme, 18 May 1792, ibid. 432–3.
[17] Wahl, 'Joseph Chalier', pp. 9–10.

to mounting a popular campaign against the aristocratic rich which went far beyond anything his colleagues on the Municipalité were willing to contemplate.

The situation into which Chalier irrupted was superficially secure for the Rolandins. As late as 16 August Billemaz could complacently celebrate the clubs' alliance with the Municipalité: 'par notre union nous l'avons emporté sur l'aristocratie, et nous avons eu une municipalité patriote; nous l'avons ensuite soutenue de tout notre pouvoir; nous avons été fermes, surveillants et sages avec elle; et voilà, pourquoi Lyon a joui d'une paix et d'une tranquillité constante: il ne falloit rien moins pour tenir en échec dans Lyon le parti formidable de l'aristocratie.'[18] But since the *patriotes*' re-election in November–December 1791, things had become considerably more precarious. Their conservative opponents retained a hold on the *État Major* of the National Guard and on the Departmental and District Councils, and the Feuillantist feelings which were freely voiced in Lyonnais bourgeois circles produced one of the most fervent declarations of support for the King to come in from the provinces after the first invasion of the Tuileries, bearing many leading merchant names—Roccofort, Courajod, de Gérando, Dujast, Personnaz—amongst the 2,000 signatures.[19] In the context of the Parisian democratic agitation for sectional *permanence* and for the admission of of male passive citizens to political life, the forcing of the Tuileries placed the constitutional settlement under the gravest threat so far, and there could be no certainty that this would not provoke the counter-revolutionary alliance between bourgeoisie and aristocracy of which Pétion had warned in February.[20]

At the same time, there was an obvious risk that extremists like Chalier might win over the militants in the *sections*. Cusset, the future Montagnard *député* who had been president of the Club Central in 1791, was the most prominent. He and others who were to become leading Jacobins later in the year—Turin, Vital, Pilot, and Gravier—were members of the Belle-Cordière Club. Gravier was amongst its preferred candidates for the municipal elections, and its president in December 1791. The others were all elected to represent the club in various capacities during the six

[18] F. Billemaz, *Discours prononcé au Comité central ... le jeudi 26 août l'an IV* (Lyon, 1792), 1–2.

[19] AN F¹ᶜIII, Rhône 6, d. 3; Reinhard, *La Chute de la royauté: 10 août 1792* (Paris, 1969), 545–7; Garden, *Lyon et les Lyonnais*, pp. 196–7, 229 and n.

[20] See N. Hampson, *A Social History of the French Revolution* (London, 1963), 143.

months before the fall of the monarchy.[21] Both Cusset and Gaillard, another prominent radical and a member of the neighbouring club of Plat-d'Argent, were sufficiently well known outside their *quartiers* to win support from the *faubourg* of la Croix-Rousse when (for reasons unknown) they came under attack in the Club Central in June 1792.[22] There is no evidence that these men were actively opposing the Rolandins before August 1792 or that the latter's support was being seriously eroded even in the more radical *sections*. Cusset and Gravier appear side by side with Roland and Pressavin on Belle-Cordière's list for the 1791 municipal elections, and on 24 May 1792 the same club decided to print an address by Roland rather than one by Robespierre.[23] In national affairs it remained moderate enough to request the deletion of certain articles of a petition printed by the Club Central in June: '[l'article] qui demande le licenciement des troupes de ligne et qu'elles soyent changés [*sic*] en légions des nations &c ... l'art. 2 qui dit que vous déclarier [*sic*] déchu du commandement des armées l'ex-marquis Lafayette l'art. 15 qui dit que les patriottes [*sic*] de l'assemblée nationale se mettent d'un côté et les aristocrates d'un autre'.[24],

But if in mid-1792 the threat to the Rolandins remained potential rather than actual, Varennes had certainly increased it. Some radicals established personal followings—the Chalonnais ex-noble Riard, for example, who led a secession from the Porte-Froc Club in June 1792.[25] Many clubs, and particularly the Club Central, were now strongly influenced by opponents of the status quo. A taste of things to come could be seen in the election of two radical *clubistes* amongst the four new *chefs de légion* in August 1792. The results in those *sections* for which records have been found strongly suggest that both benefited from organized support in the clubs. In l'Hôtel-Dieu, 234 votes out of 243 cast went to Emery, a violent radical; and in Port Saint-Paul, 139 votes out of 152 went to Riard.[26] At the same time, while the Municipalité's radicalism remained

---

[21] AD 34L1, minutes of Belle-Cordière Club, 1 July, 8 Dec. 1791, and 1 Jan.–25 Aug. 1792, *passim*. (After a call to the Municipalité for pikes on 25 July there was no meeting until 10 Aug.)

[22] AD 34L1, 7 June 1792; AD 34L3, minutes of the club of La Croix-Rousse, 17 June 1792.

[23] Ibid., minutes of Belle-Cordière Club, 11 Nov. 1791, 24 May 1792.

[24] Ibid. 6 June 1792.

[25] AD 31L25, Habert, president of Porte Froc to the president of La Pêcherie, 26 June 1792.

[26] AD 31L41, minutes of the *section* of l'Hôtel-Dieu, and AD 31L20, Port Saint-Paul, both 9 Aug. 1792. At battalion level, however, the existing officers suspect to the *patriotes* were nearly all re-elected (see *Journal de Lyon*, 23 Aug. 1792; Wahl, *Les Premières Années*, pp. 569–70).

confined to its noisy war of attrition with the Département, some clubs continued to question the Constitution long after the main surge of post-Varennes republicanism had subsided, and later, in the wake of the first invasion of the Tuileries, criticisms of the Constitution were once again boldly expressed. La Croix-Rousse's resolution that 'notre société déclare qu'elle suivra provisoirement toutes les loix et qu'elle poursuivra sans relâche le Redressement de celles qui seroient contraires aux principes d'éternelle vérité qui sont les droits de l'homme', was openly revisionist, as were the clubs' declamations against the royal veto.[27] The Municipalité, on the other hand, while not hesitating to challenge and even to disobey the superior administrations, had always sought to justify its actions in terms of written law. Its argument *vis-à-vis* the National Guard, for instance, turned on the interpretation of certain articles of the decree of 29 September–14 October 1791, and there was no suggestion from the Rolandin *patriotes* that there was any need to amend it, still less that there was a fundamental defect in the Constitution as a whole. But until August there was no public airing of these differences between the *clubistes* and the Municipalité.

Only on the eve of the monarchy's overthrow did unmistakable signs begin to show that the Municipalité and the clubs were no longer marching in step. On 25 July 1792 the Club Central established a *Comité de surveillance*—the Comité des Trois Cents—consisting of ten delegates from each *section*. Nothing more is known of it except that it was too much for the moderate club of La Croisette, which expressed indignation on hearing from that of Place Confort 'que le comité de Surveillance, autrement des trois cent [*sic*] avait pris des arrêtés contraire [*sic*] au bien public sans avoir consulté les section [*sic*]', and declared 'qu'elle n'a point coopérer dans cette sourde mésure car ses membres se sont retirer [*sic*] du dit comité [*sic*] avec toute l'indignation qui appartient à des hommes qui ne veulent que le mort des tirans [*sic*], et d'exterminer tous les traîtres qui cherchent par des menes [*sic*] insidieuse à nous faire entre gorgé [*sic*]'.[28]

The Municipalité, meanwhile, was responding to the national crisis with extreme caution. Four times it deferred discussion of the monarchy's

<hr />

[27] AD 34L3, minutes of the club of La Croix-Rousse, 20 Nov. 1791; AD 34L1, minutes of Belle-Cordière Club, 26 July 1792; AC I²4, 45, minutes of the club of La Croisette, 26 June 1792.

[28] AC I²4, 45 (29 Aug. 1792). On 25 July the Belle-Cordière Club chose Gravier, Villard, Pelletier, Ferrand, Vital, Pilot, Cusset, Turin, and Grand as its delegates to the Committee of Three Hundred (AD 34L1).

future, and even on 12 August it committed itself only partially by voting for the provisional suspension of the King.[29] Roland's return to the Ministry of the Interior necessitated continued caution, as well as ostentatious respect for his legalistic approach to administration. His familiarity with Lyonnais affairs made deviation from his principles difficult, and he lost no time in announcing the latter to his former colleagues: 'aujourd' hui que les prêtres fanatiques ou suspects n'ont plus d'asile, que les mauvais citoyens sont arrêtés et punis, nous retomberions bientôt dans l'anarchie et dans la guerre civile la plus cruelle si des individus se permettront d'user de violence, et de mettre leur volonté à la place des loix'.[30] For Roland, the Revolution was over, and his position was already declared in the great debate over the legitimacy of further revolutionary and popular violence which was soon to divide France.

Roland's return to national office thus had the incidental effect of limiting the Municipalité's freedom of action. The destitution of the Directoires and *procureurs-généraux* of the Département and the District, followed by elections which produced *patriote* replacements,[31] limited it further by undermining Vitet's favourite tactic of deflecting discontent towards the higher administrations. This came at a time when popular anger was being fanned simultaneously by political, military, and economic crises. Invasion by Piedmont seemed imminent, and the threat was not significantly reduced until late September when General Montesquiou took control of Savoy. There were renewed fears of counter-revolution and rumours of a plot to seize the Arsenal on 22 July.[32] At the same time, the effects of war, lack of confidence in the *assignat*, and, by a harsh coincidence, mourning in the courts of Russia, Sweden and Austria, began to have a crippling effect on the silk industry after two and a half years of relative stability. According to the Lyonnais authorities, 30,000 people were out of work by winter.[33] Inflation was also causing distress. In September and October there were meetings in several

---

[29] *CM*, iii. 236–349 (5–12 Aug. 1792).

[30] AN F[11]217, d. 8, Roland to Chalier, 29 Aug. 1792 (copy).

[31] See Wahl, *Les Premières Années*, pp. 566–8.

[32] AC I[2]2, no. 120. AN F[1]A, 431, d. 11, Vitet *et al.* to Roland, 1 June 1792. A public meeting in Pierre-Scize on 10 Sept. blamed popular discontent specifically on fear of famine, inflation, and unemployment (address to the municipalité: AC F[14]).

[33] 'Nous apprenons depuis quelques jours ... que les ateliers des manufactures en soie cessent en grande partie d'être occupés' (*Journal de Lyon*, 11 Aug. 1792). See also AN F[1a], Rhône 8, d. 1, *Pétition faite à la barre de la Convention nationale par B. J. Frossard et Chalon députés extraordinairement par les 3 corps administratifs de Lyon ... novembre 1792* (n.d., n.p.) 3–4; AN AF*III12, deliberations of the Commerce Committee of the Convention, 2 Dec. 1792.

weaving *quartiers*, and the clubs of La Grande-Côte, Saint-Georges, Belle-Cordière, and La Croisette lent their weight to the weavers' demands for compensation for the decline in the value of the *assignats* with which they had been paid since 1790.[34]

The situation was aggravated by serious food shortages in August–September. Lyon was particularly vulnerable in this respect, because its reputation as a den of hoarders (and, more recently, of counter-revolutionaries) gave the *communes* through which its grain had to pass all the excuse they needed to hold up or intercept consignments. In Tournus, a Lyonnais merchant was murdered as a speculator late in August; 1,200 bags of flour were held up in Auxerre; a boat-load of wheat for Lyon was pillaged in Trévoux. On 27 August the Municipalité complained that no corn was arriving by way of the Saône, and attributed this to the rumours of Lyonnais hoarding which were rife in all the river ports and supply centres from Verdun to Trévoux. These problems were intensified by a relatively poor harvest in Dauphiné, crop failures in the Levant, and high demand in northern Italy. As a result the price of wheat rose sharply from 50 *livres* per *ânée* (306 pounds) delivered to Lyon on 24 August, to 72 *livres* on 13 December. To maintain adequate supplies, the Municipalité was obliged to import foreign wheat through Marseille at a cost of 85 *livres* per *ânée* in mid-December. Despite the payment of indemnities to bakers, the price of bread rose from 3 *sous* per pound in late September to 4 *sous* 3 *deniers* in December.[35]

In these circumstances, there would have been popular demands for economic controls and repressive measures against counter-revolutionaries and economic criminals—hoarders, speculators, and pro-fiteers—with or without the encouragement of Chalier. But there can be little doubt that Chalier's return accelerated the articulation of these demands and ensured that they were linked to a radical political pro-gramme strongly influenced by Robespierre. It is also clear that the mayor and municipal officers could not compromise with either the popular economic demands or Chalier's political programme, tied as they were to the policies of a Minister of the Interior whose *laissez-faire* principles

[34] AN F[11]217, d. 8, Municipalité of Lyon to Roland, 24 Sept. 1792; AN AF*II12, Commerce Committee, 17 Nov. 1792; AN F[7]3686[6], d. 9, Municipalité of Lyon to Vitet, 9 Oct. 1792; AD 34L1, minutes of Belle-Cordière Club, 23 Sept. 1793.

[35] AN F[11]217, d. 8, Directoire of Rhône-et-Loire to Roland, 27 Aug. 1792; Municipalité of Lyon to Roland, 27 Aug. and 24 Sept. 1792; Council of Rhône-et-Loire, 21 Aug. 1792; AC F[4], Livre d'annotations sur l'approvisionnement des grains, fos. 3, 20, 23; Wahl, *Les Premières Années*, p. 611.

were inflexible and whose personal relations with Robespierre were soon to deterioriate beyond repair. Thus the Parisian excursions of Chalier and Roland contributed to the division of the Lyonnais *patriotes*, so poisoning relations between their respective Lyonnais admirers that mutual comprehension was entirely lost. Worse still for Lyon's prospects of tranquillity, they involved Lyon directly in the emerging conflict between Gironde and Montagne.

THE *JOURNÉES* OF SEPTEMBER AND OCTOBER

> Trois ans de tranquillité que la municipalité avait procuré à Lyon
> ... ont été perdus en un seul jour.
>
> Louis Vitet, 11 September 1792

Chalier's campaign for the 'general upheaval' that was needed to regenerate Lyon began, probably, in the fourth week of August. On the 25th, Vitet sent Roland a warning of the likely consequences:

avant hier Monsieur Chalier monta à la tribune du Club Central et dit qu'il faut environner la municipalité, le nouveau district et le nouveau département et pendant ce temps faire jouir le peuple de toute sa souveraineté en tranchant la tête aux prêtres réfractaires et à tous les aristocrates: ce n'est qu'en voyant ruisseler de tout côte [*sic*] le sang impur que vous acquerrez tranquillité, sûreté et bonheur; il a tellement exalté les têtes du peuple qu'on ne peut plus le contenir et que dans peu il se passera des scènes d'horreur.[36]

On the 24th, the day after Chalier's speech and probably in response to it, the primary assembly of la Juiverie, presided over by the print-corrector Manlius Dodieu, declared itself permanent and circulated a pamphlet which contained threats of popular justice and exhorted the other *sections* to follow its lead. This was the first attempt in Lyon to assert popular sovereignty directly through the sectional assemblies, and it marked the beginning of a new wave of popular militancy which, while drawing inspiration from the Club Central, seems to have been largely independent of the club movement.

The Rolandin Municipalité denounced Dodieu's initiative, and on 30 August a warrant was issued for his arrest. For the first time since their accession to municipal power in 1790, the Rolandins now found themselves in open conflict with radical popular opinion. They also found

[36] AN F⁷3686⁶, d. 8.

themselves confronting a clamour for action to meet popular demands. On 27 August, ninety-six members of the Club Central called for stronger measures against suspect priests and strangers, and on 10 September a public meeting in Pierre-Scize demanded remedies for inflation, famine, and unemployment.[37] But the Municipalité was in no position to act on any of these fronts.

In the prevailing atmosphere of panic over food supplies, invasion, and counter-revolution, and in the absence of placatory initiatives from the authorities, some kind of defensive reaction from the *menu peuple* was inevitable. When it came it was a typical pre-emptive blow against groups identified as hostile to the popular cause. Some officers of the Fifth Cavalry regiment (formerly the Royal-Pologne) were in prison at the time on suspicion of intending to emigrate, perfect symbols of the counter-revolutionary threat and of the hated regular army. Early in the afternoon of 9 September, inspired by the example of the Parisian prison massacre and probably also by the usual heavy Sunday drinking at Vaise and les Brotteaux, large crowds invaded Pierre-Scize and killed eight of the officers and three refractory priests with axes and crowbars.[38]

Committed as they were to the proposition that the people was innately good, but finding the crowds at the prison indifferent to Vitet's calls for order, the Rolandins resorted, as was their habit, to a conspiracy theory according to which the killings were all the work of *étrangers*, though the presence at the prison of 150 women armed with pikes made this even less plausible than usual. After Thermidor, when Vitet was reproached with his failure to prevent the massacre, he shifted the blame to Chalier and the Club Central's agitators, and jettisoned the *étrangers* in favour of a crowd which had come from the direction of Port du Temple, led by three veterans of the National Guard. He also alleged that the principal *massacreurs* had been given refuge and fêted at the Club Central.[39] There is no direct evidence of this, but it seems certain that Chalier's speech helped to provoke the killings and it is possible that the Club Central's Comité de Surveillance played some role in initiating them, perhaps by

[37] Ibid., d. 9, Copie d'une lettre adressée au président de l'Assemblée primaire de la section de Place Neuve . . . signée a l'original DODIEU président de la section de la Juiverie'; AC I²20, d. 188, warrant for the arrest of Dodieu, signed Ampère, *juge de paix*, 30 Aug. 1792; AC F¹⁴.

[38] The main accounts of the massacre of 9 Sept. are in AN F⁷3686⁶, d. 7, Vitet and municipal officers of Lyon to Roland, 10 and 11 Sept. 1792; AC I²2, 133, report by Arnaud, *sous-lieutenant*, 24 Aug. 1792; L. Vitet, *Vitet député du département du Rhône à ses concitoyens sur le massacre des prisonniers de Pierre-Scize* (n.d., [1795?]), esp. 4–8, 11, 13.

[39] Ibid. 5, 13.

the decision taken late in August which caused La Croisette's delegates
to withdraw.[40] Whether or not they were organized in the Club Central
or the Comité des Trois Cents, the massacres were heartily approved by
one club, Belle-Cordière, where 'les citoyens déclarent unanimement
prendre sous leurs protection et sauve garde [sic] ceux à que l'on pourroient [sic] faire quelques inculpations ou poursuites quelconque les
membres de la susditte assemblée ont pretté [sic] serment de verser leur
sang pour soutenir et protteger [sic] qui ont si bien travailler [sic] le 9 du
présent mois'.[41] There are no indications of direct disapproval of the
massacre in any of the clubs, but those which, like La Croisette, had
repeatedly stressed the need for order and unity are unlikely to have shared
Belle-Cordière's enthusiasm. The club movement was now squarely
confronted with the great national debate over the legitimacy of further
revolutionary violence.

There were no arrests on 9 September, because the National Guard
refrained from intervening until 9.00 p.m. when it was all over. A few
battalions were then rounded up to make the long march through Port
Saint-Paul and Pierre–Scize to clear the prisons.

Thus began the longest period of popular disorder in Lyon since 1786.
On 14 September food shops in various *quartiers* were raided and the
contents sold at prices fixed by 'le tribunal féminin'. During the next few
days a wave of *taxations* spread throughout the city: 'C'est le peuple, le
peuple presque tout entier qui force les magasins, pour faire délivrer tous
les comestibles, toutes les femmes à peu de chose près se sont mises en
avant pour se les faire déliverer.'[42] Prices for fifty-nine items, from wood,
wine, and candles to mocha coffee and *bleu de Gex* were listed on printed
proclamations distributed by 'commissaires de police femelles'.[43] The
inclusion of luxury goods suggests that it was not only the poor who
considered prices to have increased beyond reasonable bounds. Small
traders rather than wholesalers suffered the first and, relatively speaking,
the greatest losses (113 grocery shops were pillaged between 17 and 19 September),[44] indicating that the intention was not principally to deal with

---

[40] See above, n. 28.

[41] AD 34L1, 15 Sept. 1792.

[42] AN F[11]217, d. 8, Municipalité of Lyon to Roland, 19 Sept. 1792.

[43] AN F[7]3686[6], d. 7, *les Citoyennes de Lyon* (undated printed placard, sent by Laussel to Roland, 18 Sept. 1792).

[44] Ibid., d. 8, Roland to the president of the Convention, 7 Dec. 1792; *Journal de Lyon*, 19 Sept. 1792; AN F[11]217, d. 8, Municipalité of Lyon to Roland, 18 Nov. 1792. Wholesalers lost heavily too: cheese valued at 21,000 *livres* was seized from one warehouse and sold off in a single day (AN F[7]3686[6], d. 9, widow Ziegler to Roland, 11 Jan. 1793).

hoarders and monopolists, but (as the declaration which accompanied the price-list stated) to counteract the effects of currency depreciation. It was a massive and, to some extent, organized protest against *la vie chère*, based on traditional notions of economic justice, probably with encouragement, direct or indirect, from some of the radical *clubistes*. Payment of the just prices was insisted upon, and the insurgent women formed 'une société délibérante' and armed themselves with pikes to check 'excesses' on the night of 19 September.[45] The declaration stressed that the *taxations* were not acts of violence but considered measures founded on the sovereignty of the people and its right 'se procurer sa subsistance sans être dans le cas d'employer de ces moyens violens que nécessitent les calamités publiques venues à leur période'.

The authorities' attempts to stop the *taxations* by a show of force were worse than useless. The National Guard battalion of le Plâtre was stoned while trying to restore order near the Place des Terreaux on 17 September. Then a grenadier shot someone in the crowd and was hacked to death. There were cries of 'à bas les grenadiers! et les houpettes!' According to Bonnemant, a *commissaire observateur* for the Ministry of the Interior, a pitched battle would have followed had not the grenadiers removed their insignia and placed cleaning-rods in their gun-barrels.[46] Very few Guardsmen reported for duty the next day, and in any case the Municipalité was reluctant to use them, both because their loyalty was uncertain and because popular feeling might be further antagonized. According to Perret, who had been acting mayor since Vitet had been elected to the Convention in September, 'le pillage deviendroit général et la ville seroit peut-être incendiée', if the Municipalité had resorted to force. The fears of 1744, 1786, 1789, and 1790 had returned to haunt the *patriotes* just as they had haunted Palerne de Savy and the *échevins*: 'nous perdrions la ville et la grande majorité des citoyens riches auroient été massacrées'.[47]

The Municipal Council tried to bring the situation under control by taking advantage of its partnership with the clubs. It accepted the Club Central's demands that sectional *commissaires* should be appointed to keep order and that a house-to-house search should be conducted jointly by the *clubistes* and the National Guard. It also made concessions, lowering the price of bread by 2 *sous* per pound and fixing the price of butter,

---

[45] *Journal de Lyon*, 20 Sept. 1792.

[46] AN F^{11}217, d. 8, president of the Département of Rhône-et-Loire to Roland, 19 Sept. 1792, and Bonnemant to Roland, 18 Sept. 1792.

[47] Ibid., Municipalité of Lyon to Roland, 18 Sept. 1792, Perret to Roland, 20 Sept. 1792, and Laussel to Roland, 16 Sept. 1792; *Journal de Lyon*, 19 Sept. 1792.

eggs, and meat. 'Sans faire un va-tout de la cité', Perret told Vitet, 'j'ai pensé que sans approuver le peuple, il falloit constamment le suivre et lui rappeller ses vrais intérêts.'[48] But his policy seems to have had little effect. The *taxations* continued for a week and the fact that they did not recur before the end of September was probably because the shops and markets were empty, peasants and wholesalers having understandably declined to bring in more supplies. The successive arrival of two boat-loads of wheat and three *représentants en mission* (Vitet, Boissy d'Anglas, and Legendre) may also have helped to prevent further outbreaks and to bolster the Municipalité's authority. On 9 October the revocation of the price controls produced disillusionment but no violence.[49]

Even though the *taxations* petered out, the local authorities had nearly lost control of the city. They had bowed to popular violence and they continued to suffer public humiliation by self-appointed popular spokes-men, notably the lawyer Bussat, one of the radicals of Belle-Cordière. A *commissaire de police* appointed by the Municipalité, he was temporarily suspended on suspicion of drawing up the declaration which had accompanied the price-lists. In October he led a crowd to the Place de Roanne and forced Perret to release a 'charlatan de place' who had been arrested during the disorders. Three days later, Eustache, a *juge de paix* from Trévoux who frequented the Croix-Rousse Club and the Club Central, burst into the General Council of the *commune* at the head of a delegation demanding arms for all Lyonnais volunteers. He harangued the councillors 'avec un ton et une audace inconcevable [*sic*], prescrivant au Conseil de délibérer sur le champ, *qu'il étoit temps que le peuple souverain fut obéi*'.[50] About 20 October, in the Club Centrale and in the *quartier* of Pierre-Scize, demands were voiced for the public display of the guillotine, after the example of Toulon and Marseille; and on the 26th a crowd broke into the Town Hall where the device still lay in its packing cases. It was removed and set up on the Place des Terreaux.

[48] Ibid., Le Conseil général de la commune de Lyon en permanence, 17 septembre 1792, Municipalité of Lyon to Roland, 18 Sept. 1792, and Perret to Roland, 20 Sept. 1792.

[49] AN F[11]217, d. 8, Municipalité of Lyon to Roland, 22, 24, 27 Sept. 1792; *Moniteur*, xiv. 163, letter of Boissy d'Anglas, 9 Oct. 1792; AC F[12], Adresse des citoyens de la section de Saint-Georges au citoyen Roland'; *Journal de Lyon*, 25 Sept. 1792. Vitet, Boissy d'Anglas, and Legendre were in Lyon until 30 Oct. (*Journal de Lyon*, 3 Oct. 1792). A second mission with Alquier in place of Legendre was in Lyon for most of November (*Journal de Lyon*, 6 Nov. 1792; letter of Vitet, Boissy, and Alquier, 24 Nov. 1792, in F. M. Aulard (ed.), *Receuil des actes du Comité de salut public* (Paris, 1889–1933) (hereafter *Actes*), i. 264).

[50] Ibid., Municipalité of Lyon to Roland, 9 Oct. 1792; F[7]3686[6], d. 7, Municipalité to the *représentants enmission* in Lyon, 9 Oct. 1792.

Later in the day, seven prisoners were taken from Roanne prison and two—a forger and a baker—were killed. The National Guard was again called out too late, and again 'beaucoup de bons citoyens effrayés restent enfermés chez eux et par la [*sic*] diminuent beaucoup notre force armée'.[51]

By this time the position of the Rolandins had deteriorated so much that they could not hope to restore the status quo ante. Both they and the *réprésentants en mission* seem to have realized this: 'Nos municipes patriotes jusqu'à présent chéris du peuple sont devenus l'object du mépris et des menaces', wrote the Rolandin Villieux to the minister on 28 October. The *réprésentants en mission* were still more pessimistic: 'La ville de Lyon ne présente plus qu'une société entièrement désorganisée, les fonctionnaires publics n'y sont plus écoutés, la loi n'est plus respectée, et des ennemis du bien public y établissent l'anarchie.'[52]

This was a crisis not only of public order but of ideology. The two years of Rolandin rule in Lyon had been based on a misunderstanding, on the assumption that bourgeois *patriotes* and the *menu peuple* shared the same view of the Revolution. This illusion had been a necessary condition of *patriote* victory in 1789 and it remained a characteristic of *patriote* ideology under the constitutional monarchy. But while in Paris the debate over the *marc d'or* and the 'little tricoloured terror' after the Champ de Mars massacre had partially dispelled it, in Lyon the *entente* between the clubs and the Municipalité had protected it from the challenge of social realities. By acting as intermediaries and channels of communication between the people and 'its' magistrates—a relationship whose nature was conveniently obscured by the ambiguous possessive—the clubs had enabled two ideas of sovereignty to coexist, one based on the concept of representation, the other on direct democracy, the direct exercise of its authority by the sovereign people. This changed during the autumn of 1792. According to Jean-Baptiste Goubet, a silk-weaver from the *quartier* of Saint-Georges who was arrested during the September troubles: 'la municipalité n'avoit pas le droit de fixer le prix des marchandises on devoit s'en rapporter à la taxe qu'avoient fait les citoyennes.'[53] By provoking such direct and unequivocal expressions of

---

[51] For the *journée* of 26 Oct., see AN F⁷3686⁶, letters to Roland from the Municipalité and the *procureur-général-syndic* of the Département, 24 and 27 Oct. 1792, from Bonnard, administrator of the District of Lyon-ville, and Arnaud-Tison, municipal officer, both 26 Oct. 1792, and from Hidins, 28 Oct. 1792; *Journal de Lyon*, 27 Oct. 1792.

[52] AN F⁷3686⁶, *représentants en mission* in Lyon to Roland, n.d.; Villieux to Roland, 28 Oct. 1792.

[53] AC I²2, d. 139, register of interrogations by the *commissaires des sections*, 24 Sept. 1792.

popular sovereignty—the principle specifically invoked in the placard *Les Citoyennes de Lyon*—the September troubles showed it to be irreconcilable with Rolandin conceptions of representative democracy. Encouraged by the fall of the monarchy and the economic crisis, the *menu peuple* had defined their sovereignty much more broadly than the Rolandins could accept, and rejected the restrictions imposed on it by legislation. Ephemeral though the direct action of September was, it generated currents of popular radicalism which broke the Rolandins' grip on the club movement and the Municipalité.

At the same time, the *taxations* exposed the contradiction between Rolandin and popular economics. Roland had been greatly irritated by the fixing of food prices, and had even threatened to cut off financial aid to Lyon if the agitators responsible for the troubles were not apprehended.[54] His own local reputation as 'l'homme du peuple, le plus ardent défenseur de ses droits',[55] was protected by his distance from Lyon—the authors of some protests over the removal of price controls were sufficiently misled by it to apply to his ministry for their reimposition.[56] But his allies on the spot were exposed: they were denounced for delivering the poor into the hands of speculators and accused of conniving with hoarders and ex-nobles. It was becoming hard for the Rolandins to persist with the assumption that the benevolence of their intentions and the rationality of their view of society would be universally accepted under conditions of political liberty. From the heights of the Ministry of the Interior Roland could still persist: 'Lorsque le peuple verra que ses Magistrats s'occupent fructueusement de son intérêt le plus pressant et le plus cher, il sera tranquil et supportera bien plus patiemment les calamités de circonstance qu'il sait bien qu'on ne peut empêcher.'[57] But the municipal officers' confidence had totally collapsed: 'la persuasion, seule arme qui nous reste ... est bien foible pour ne pas dire nulle'.[58] What Vitet had called 'trois [*sic*] ans de tranquillité que la municipalité avoit procuré a Lyon'[59] had encouraged them to see themselves as natural

---

[54] AN F¹¹217, d. 8, Roland to the mayor of Lyon, n.d.; F⁶3686⁶, d. 7, Roland to the Directoire of Rhône-et-Loire, 15 Oct. 1792 (copies).

[55] AC I²2, d. 108, club of La Pêcherie, minutes, 9 Dec. 1792.

[56] AC F12, Adresse des citoyens de la section de Saint-Georges au citoyen Roland, n.d.; F⁷3686⁶, d. 7, citizen Georges to Roland. (Both strongly defended the use of 'une petite violence du peuple' in September.)

[57] AN F¹¹217, d. 8, Roland to the Directoire of Rhône-et-Loire, 25 Oct. 1792; see also Roland to the Municipalité of Lyon, 20 0ct. 1792 (copies).

[58] AN F⁷3686⁶, d. 7, Municipalité to Roland, 26 Oct. 1792.

[59] Ibid., Vitet to Roland, 11 Sept. 1792.

leaders and spokesmen of the common people. After September they could do so no more.

The Rolandins' problems were not just local. One of the products of the Parisian revolution of 10 August was a new centralism designed to intensify the war effort and to make certain that the provinces were 'à l'hauteur de la Révolution'. The Rolandins had long been hoping that the capital would intervene to fortify them against their enemies to the right, but the help that finally came in September 1792 was help for their new enemies on the left. Between 9 and 22 September four *commissaires du pouvoir exécutif* spent various periods in Lyon. They were members of, and chosen by, the Paris Commune, 'hommes du 10 août' dispatched with Roland's reluctant consent to requisition suitable National Guard units in the Midi for the defence of Paris. To achieve this they were given extensive and extremely vague powers (one of them, Chartrey, interpreted his as 'pouvoirs sans bornes'), and their peremptory way with the local authorities provoked bitter complaints from Vitet.[60] They brought a new element of uncertainty into local politics and further undermined the Municipalité's authority. Both as men of 10 August and as proponents of revolutionary improvisation to meet the war crisis— they called for pikes to be issued to unarmed *patriotes*, for sectional permanence, and for the designation of *commissaires de section*—the *commissaires* were natural allies of the Chaliers, Dodieus, and Bussats, and natural enemies of the *modérantisme* for which the Municipalité now stood. There were other intruders from whom the Municipality might have hoped for better things—Roland's *commissaires observateurs*. Two of these were moderates, the 'orateur du faubourg Saint-Antoine', Gonchon, and the ex-*constituant* Bonnemant. But the third, François Auguste Laussel, 'l'ange tutélaire' as he described himself, 'arrivé tout exprès pour consoler le peuple',[61] outdid even the *commissaires du pouvoir exécutif*, denouncing the Municipalité's incompetence to the Club Central with the virulence he had earlier directed (while editor of the *Journal de Lyon* in 1791) against the District, the District Tribunals, and the Département.

---

[60] See P. Caron, *La Première Terreur (1792): Les Missions du Conseil exécutif provisiore et de la Commune de Paris* (Paris, 1950), 24, 33–4, 40, 172, 182; AN F^{11}217, d. 8, Vitet to Roland, 14 Sept. 1792.

[61] AN F^{11}217, d. 8, Laussel to Roland, 16 Sept. 1792; AN F^{7}3686^6, d. 7, Laussel to Roland, 22 Sept. 1792.

An oratorian *abbé* turned constitutional priest, he had been ejected by his intended flock from the parish of Saint-Bonnet-le-Troncy in the Monts dy Lyonnais (where, he later claimed, bullet-riddled presbytery shutters testified to the risks he had run for the Revolution). He had made his way to Paris in July with the *fédérés* of Rhône-et-Loire. Roland withdrew his commission on 10 October, on the ground that he was not acting 'avec le mesure qui lui a été recommandée'.[62] But by then Laussel was already well entrenched as a spokesman of Lyonnais Jacobinism.

THE END OF THE ROLANDIN MUNICIPALITÉ

Within little more than a month of Billemaz's speech celebrating the triumphant union of the people and their magistrates, the Rolandin Municipalité thus found itself besieged by opponents who had substantial popular support in Lyon, who could count on assistance from their Parisian counterparts, and who were unhindered by ideology, legalistic scruples, or constraints of office from endorsing popular demands for drastic new measures. Ironically, the Municipalité's predicament was closely analogous to the Feuillantists' in 1791. Their interests and their ideology committed them to parliamentarianism, legislative supremacy, and representative government. They were beneficiaries of 1789 faced with a rising tide of demands for a new revolution based on price controls, direct democracy, and the repression of political and economic criminals, a revolution armed with new instruments of executive power, exceptional laws, suspension of individual liberties, and purges of the civil and military administrations, a revolution which demanded the subordination of everything to its own defence. It was not, of course, only in Lyon that 'the events of August and September [1792] seemed to divide those who were prepared to condone, if not to advocate violence from those determined to maintain order and protect lives and property even of counter-revolutionaries',[63] and not only there that the latter were on the defensive. But in Lyon their position was particularly precarious because the Club Central had turned against the Rolandins. Now its electoral machinery was in the hands of radicals grouped around Chalier who thus found themselves in a position to take control of the city.

---

[62] *Département*, ii. 157–8 (14 Oct. 1792). On Laussel and his mission, see Caron, *La Première Terreur*, p. 197; Wahl, *Les Premières Années*, pp. 342–3, 370; S. de la Chapelle, *Notice sur l'abbé Laussel* (Lyon, 1882), 2–14.

[63] Hampson, *French Revolution*, p. 171.

This they duly did in elections held under the Convention's decree of 28 October which ordered that, because of the recent troubles, Lyon's Municipalité should be renewed a month early and *in toto*. Unimpeded by the conservative rural electors who had limited their success at the elections to the Convention, the radicals suffered only one serious setback, Chalier's defeat in the mayoral election by the Rolandin Nivière-Chol.[64] Laussel was elected *procureur*, and an ex-president of the Club Central, Bertholon, was chosen as his deputy. On the Municipal Council the extremists won a clear majority, and the District Tribunal of Lyon-Ville became a stronghold of the most extreme radicals, including Chalier (president), Bussat, Dodieu, Dubessey (a lawyer), Gaillard (an actor, *clubiste*, and authentic *héros du 10 août*—he had been wounded in the thigh during the fighting at the Tuileries), and the *dessinateur* Fernex. Rousseau Hidins, who described himself as a man of letters and who was soon to publish a project to nationalize the grain trade, became *commissaire national*, and a silk-weaver, Berliez, clerk of the court.[65] Just as striking as the radicalism of these bodies was the Municipalité's social composition, which made these elections an unprecedented victory for the plebeians over the propertied classes. Half the members of the new Council were artisans or small shopkeepers, and half occupied premises with rental values assessed in 1791 at 100 *livres* or less, as did two-thirds of the *notables* for whom tax records have been discovered; 19 of the 25 *notables* identified by occupation were artisans, 8 of them silk-weavers. In the previous Municipalité the 10 members of the Council for whom records have been found had an average rental assessment of 607 livres, and the lowest was 150. Amongst those whose assessments have not been identified, there were 2 stocking-weavers, 1 silk-weaver, 1 shoemaker, and 1 haberdasher, all of whom were probably in the lower ranges of the tax-scale, but there can be no doubt that the last Rolandin Municipal Council had been dominated by men of property or that this dominance was overthrown by the elections of 1792. At the same time, there was a great increase in the proportion of councillors from the poorest *sections* of Lyon. This proportion had doubled between the first elected Municipalité (February 1790) and the third (November–December 1792). Now it more

---

[64] *CM*, iii. 353–4 (5 Nov. 1792): Nivière-Chol, 5,127 votes; Chalier, 3,578.

[65] Ibid. iv. 18 (13 Dec. 1792). On various members of the Tribunal, see A. F. Delandine, *tableau des prisons de Lyon* (Lyon, 1797); AN F[11]217, d. 8, Municipalité of Lyon to Roland, 9 Oct. 1792; F[7]3686[6], d. 7, Hidins to Roland, 28 Oct. 1792; R. Hidins, *Hidins au genre humain* (Lyon, 1792); 'Tableau de réforme' (probably by Chalier), and another list of office-holders signed by Guillard, Fonds Coste 609.

than doubled again, to almost half the councillors. Only 7 of them came from the 12 more prosperous *sections*, as against 14 in the previous Municipal Council and 15 in the first.[66]

Amongst the propertied classes the election results were regarded as a further manifestation of the criminal conspiracy which had begun with the September massacres. According to one of Roland's correspondents, Rébrié, men 'présomptueux par ignorance, ambitieux par intérét, trompent le peuple pour se faire élire aux places'. They were 'Solons et licurges modernes, la plupart illettrés, plusieurs ayant le pain de l'aumône', who had usurped positions for which they were transparently unfitted and which they no doubt had sought with a view to plundering public funds.[67] This letter, like many of those which flowed into Roland's office from Lyon as the election results became known, radiates an intense class feeling, a feeling summarized a little later in a statement attributed to a certain David, who was said to have held that 'un ouvrier n'étoit pas fait pour tenir les rênes d'une administration. Que l'ouvrier ne devoit que ramper et non pas se mêler des affaires politiques pour s'enricher et voler la publique.'[68] The authenticity of this remark is questionable, of course, and David's denouncer is not identifiable by profession. But the point is that the very presence of the poor and uncultivated on the Municipal Council was regarded across a wide spectrum of bourgeois political opinion as not only undesirable, but illegitimate and suggestive of conspiracy and criminal intent. Rébrié might have been a monarchist rubbing Roland's nose in the consequences of unbridled democracy, but Fleury Villieux, who expressed similar views,[69] was one of the minister's sympathizers, as was François Billemaz, the clubs' founder, who was no less contemptuous: 'leur moindre défaut est l'ineptie et l'ignorance absolue, ils sont bons pour l'exécution ... [tous] ont été fabriqués dans le même atelier, par Chalier, sur les vingt officiers municipaux on compte quatorze scélérats, tous coupe-têtes, je ne parle pas d'incapacité'.[70] Mixed in here are the feelings of resentment of a popular leader who has been outpaced by more radical rivals, as well as the no doubt genuine horror of bloodshed and disorder which underlay Rolandin and Girondin resistance to the

---

[66] See Appendices IV and V.

[67] AN F^{1a} Rhône 8, d. 1, Rébrié to Roland, 11 Dec. 1792.

[68] AD 42L72, d. 49 (Claude David), denunciation by Estelle, n.d. The statement was said to have been made before the insurrection of 29 May 1793.

[69] AN F^{7}3686^6, d. 7, Villieux to Roland, 28 Oct. 1792. See also d. 8, Patrin to Vitet, 23 Nov. 1792, Verne to Roland, 16 Jan. 1793.

[70] Ibid., d. 8, Billemaz to Roland, 29 Nov. 1792.

new wave of revolutionary violence. The fact remains that Billemaz, who in August was breathing fire in the Club Central against mercantile egoists, *insouciants*, and aristocrats, was now attacking the new incumbents of municipal office in language ('ignorance ... incompetence') loaded with class insinuation and highly reminiscent of the Feuillantist tirades against the *clubistes* during the constitutional monarchy.

Chalier's great upheaval, combined with the substantial democratization of French politics under the Republic, provided the basis for an unprecedented degree of political unity amongst the Lyonnais bourgeoisie. If, as Lucas argues, the French Revolution was not made by, but was rather the making of, the bourgeoisie[71]—and the case of Lyon seems broadly consistent with such a view—then the crisis of August–December 1792 was important in this process of class formation. We can argue further that the social consequences of the democratization forced on the bourgeoisie in 1792 played a much more obvious role in the development of a bourgeois class-consciousness, at least in Lyon, than the struggle with the nobility in 1788–9. The Lyonnais bourgeoisie perceived some of its socio-political interests during the struggle over the formation of the Estates General, and announced the fact by committing itself verbally to the cause of the revolutionary nation. But acting on this commitment at home seemed less crucial than maintaining an *entente* with the old élites against the threat from below. The process of self-discovery was more profound and less equivocal in 1792, and it was generated by the social trauma of democratization. It continued into 1793, as the propertied classes, no longer divided by legally sanctioned status distinctions, united to contain and turn back the *menu peuple*'s invasion of constituted authority.[72]

In this context it should be added that the social significance of the political struggle in 1792–3 would in no way be limited by the discovery that the artisans on the new Municipal Council were better off than they appear to have been on the evidence we have. It is not my intention to suggest that revolutionary Lyon was the scene of a war between the propertied and the property-less. Many of the Jacobin artisans in Lyon were far from poor; many probably had disposable capital. This was

---

[71] Lucas, 'Nobles, Bourgeois and the Origins of the French Revolution', *Past and Present*, 60 (1973), 126.

[72] Control of the Town Hall was all the more important after the decree of 11 August had given the Municipalités full control of police and *sûreté générale*, a power which had previously been shared with the Départements (A. Cobban, *Aspects of the French Revolution* (London, 1969), 123–4).

no proto-proletarian movement, though some of the most hysterical contemporary reactions to it might suggest as much. What was at issue was the exclusive right of the unequivocally bourgeois, the men of property, the professions, and commerce, to manipulate the levers of power. Some of those who challenged this exclusive right might, by some crude economic criteria of class, be termed bourgeois; but in terms of the class identification that was being forged out of the pre-revolutionary status system, alloyed with the revolutionary assertion of the homogeneity of real property and the identification of personal worth with bourgeois talent, those who inhabited the inferior and insecure world of manual labour and petty commerce stood outside the socio-political world of the bourgeoisie.

The municipal revolution of 1792, at least as drastic socially as that of 1790, thus exposed the common ground between the moderate *patriotes* of 1790–2 and the more conservative elements amongst the Lyonnais social élites—not that the latter were ever to forgive the Rolandins their 'democratic' sins.[73] With the extremists installed in the Municipalité, there was a common enemy.

Not just the political structure but the social foundations of the society established by the revolution were thought to be in danger. It is not surprising to find this point of view coming from members of the mercantile élite like the silk-merchants Laugier and Girard, who denounced Chalier's supporters to Roland as ambitious demagogues creating disorder by fostering the illusion that sovereignty resided in 'la classe des malheureux', inciting the poor against the rich by promising a redistribution of property, and advocating the proscription of all who came into the interchangeable categories of 'rich', 'aristocratic', or 'moderate'.[74] It is more significant that Vitet took a similar view, with political nuances, in a series of letters begun in his capacity as *représentant en mission* four days after Laugier and Girard's, and in the wake of Roland's disastrous involvement in the affair of the *armoire de fer*:

La faction Robespierre que le *Club central* partageoit et soutenoit contre tous les citoyens amis de la paix, des propriétiés et des sûretés [*sic*] des personnes va désormais commander en souverain à toutes les autorités constituées. Ne comptez

[73] See J. Chassagnon, *Offrande à Chalier* (Lyon, 1793), in which the Vitets and Nivière-Chols are given heavy responsibility for preparing the way for Jacobin excesses, while Chalier is partially excused on the ground of mental instability.

[74] AN F⁷3686⁶, d. 9, letter to Roland, 6 Nov. 1792. Similar fears were expressed in the letters to Roland (already cited) from Rébrié (11 Dec. 1792), Verne (16 Jan. 1793), and the Municipalité of Lyon (24 Sept. 1793).

plus sur le rétablissement de l'ordre, surtout dans un moment où les ouvriers n'ont ni travail, ni pain, où l'oisivéte de ces hommes favorise si bien les projets des agitateurs ... ils provoqueront le désordre, la violation des propriétés et peut-être des sûretés individuelles.[75]

An undated letter in the same series repeated the warning that after the *représentants* left, 'les agitateurs commenceront à exciter les affamés contre les riches',[76] and suggested that the only hope was to use ministerial funds to pay a good journalist to found a republican popular society which could combat the Robespierrists, or to buy off the 'enragés coup-têt' [*sic*]. The last of these letters, dated 15 November, after Vitet had seen 'the list for the election of municipal officers' (presumably the Club Central's list) predicted, correctly, that 'si [ces personnes] son élues, c'en est fait de la tranquillité de Lyon'.[77]

The democracy Vitet and Billemaz had envisaged when they established their connection with the popular movement had been a democracy led by men like themselves and guided by their principles. The clubs had now far exceeded the limits which their bourgeois allies had set for them. They had been intended to act both as channels through which Rolandin ideas could flow out amongst the people and as a political force to carry out the functions which the propertied classes had failed to perform: defending the revolution and maintaining the *patriotes* in office. But the conservatives had seen more clearly when they denounced the club movement as subversive of the social order. Now the Rolandins were forced into a position which was fundamentally indistinguishable from that of the Feuillantists a year before: 'La scène a changé; les lois qui n'étaient favorables, avant le 10 août, qu'à nos enemis, sont maintenant la sauvegarde de la liberté.'[78] This was the end of the Lyonnais *patriotes*' attempt actively to associate the people in the construction of the new order. The clubs which they had encouraged had opened the way to power for the unpropertied and for men of violence whose respect for property and for the rule of law was at best doubtful. The only refuge from the resulting dangers was rigid constitutionalism. This, however, did nothing to solve their local political difficulties, since the power which the extremists had acquired was constitutionally no less legitimate than

---

[75] 'Lettres de Vitet à Roland (10 au 15 novembre 1792)', in *Revue d'histoire de Lyon*, iv (1905), 311 (letter of 10 Nov.).
[76] 'Lettres de Vitet à Roland (10 au 15 novembre 1792)', in *Revue d'histoire de Lyon*, iv (1905), 314 (undated letter).
[77] Ibid. 316 (letter of 15 Nov.).
[78] AN F⁷3686⁶, d. 7, Villieux to Roland, 28 Oct. 1792.

the power they themselves had exercised during the previous two years. The Rolandins could do nothing but wait on developments, but the developments of early 1793 were to offer no way out of this dilemma.

As a whole, the Lyonnais propertied classes were more seriously threatened than at any earlier moment of the revolution. Plebeians seemed on the verge of completing the usurpation begun by the clubs in 1790, and renegades from their own ranks were breaking the common front against popular violence which politicians of all persuasions had previously maintained. It was above all the Jacobins' legitimization of popular violence which obsessed the minds of those who denounced them to Roland. Chalier, the *patriote* who had praised the *volontaires*' defence of property during the riots of July 1789, was now openly inciting insurrection, for reasons which the moderates seem to have been genuinely unable to comprehend. In a city so deeply divided, where the fear of pillage and massacre was never far from the surface and had been reinforced several times by spectacular *émeutes* during the previous three years, Chalier's behaviour seemed madness and automatically evoked suspicions that his aim was to overthrow the social order itself by a general assault on property. Nothing could have been better calculated to provoke a counter-attack from those men of property who had previously avoided local political affairs. Unfortunately for Lyon, this enhanced consciousness of the threat from below reinforced its élites' antagonism to popular involvement in politics just when national policy was being reshaped by radical democrats in Paris who regarded popular political involvement as essential to the defence of the Revolution.

5

A Precarious Victory:
The Jacobins in Power,
December 1792–May 1793

THE BASES OF JACOBIN POWER

For all the terror it inspired, the Jacobin victory was precarious, as the election results show. Against Nivière-Chol's 5,129 votes, Chalier managed only 3,478, 844 more than he had received as a municipal officer two years earlier.[1] This was despite the enlargement of the electorate by the enfranchisement of most previously 'passive' male citizens—the group Chalier's enemies saw as an easy target for his demogoguery—and despite an overall increase of about 250 per cent in the vote at the mayoral election compared to 1791 (from 3,578 to 9,012). Several reasons might be advanced for this remarkably large vote (which can be contrasted with the 3,497 votes cast in Bordeaux,[2] a city three-quarters Lyon's size, at about this time) and the candidates' shares of it. The election was a real contest after two years of foregone conclusions. And one of the candidates was notorious not only for his radicalism, but for instability and frequent rages against aristocrats and *insouciants* in Lyon, groups which he clearly believed to include a large part of the population. Finally, to quote one of the few general histories to take real account of the Revolution in provincial towns, there was a 'sudden rallying to [Nivière-Chol's] support of voters who shared his concern for order but not necessarily his republicanism'.[3] The last three factors all seem likely to have been important, though we should not assume that those who did not share the new

[1] For the election results cited here, see *CM*, iii. 353–83 (5 Nov.–10 Dec. 1792). Chalier's vote in Nov. 1790 is recorded in AD 1L340 (26 Nov. 1790).

[2] A. Forrest, *Society and Politics in Revolutionary Bordeaux* (Oxford, 1975), 40. Forrest appears to attribute the low vote to the electoral laws which limited voting powers to active citizens. But this distinction had been ended by the revolution of Aug. 1792.

[3] N. Hampson, *A Social History of the French Revolution* (London, 1963), 172. The reference is to a later election in Feb. 1793, when Nivière-Chol again won a substantial victory against a Jacobin candidate. But the reasoning applies equally well to Nov.–Dec. 1792.

mayor's republicanism were necessarily dedicated opponents of it.

The essential point is that the rallying was not just sudden but brief, and it did not persist into the tedious series of elections for other municipal posts. As well as a general fear of disorder, this suggests a widespread panic at the prospect of Chalier as mayor, a panic which brought to the polls many usually apathetic voters who then stayed away while lesser posts were contested by lesser-known candidates. Decreasing turn-outs at the polls after the mayoral elections were nothing new in Lyonnais politics, and complacency after Nivière-Chol's big win might have played a part this time, as well as the absence of well-known alternatives to the radical candidates now that the leaders of the Rolandin group had withdrawn or gone into national politics. But at the time, and in later anti-Jacobin histories, fear was seen as the deciding factor[4] and may well explain why so few of those who voted against Chalier supported the lawyer Bernard de Charpieux in his contest with Laussel for the vital post of *procureur*. Laussel's violent radicalism while editor of the *Journal de Lyon* can hardly have been forgotten, and only a little more than half of Nivière-Chol's vote would have been enough to keep him out of office. But those who turned out again and again to vote for moderates risked antagonizing Chalier's supporters, who were, as we shall see, well organized and assiduous at the primary assemblies. Appearing there to vote for Nivière-Chol was one thing, but attending day after day as a known person of property and moderation might have become quite dangerous. For whatever reason, most of the Jacobin candidates needed only 2,000 or 3,000 votes to win. Ironically, two Rolandin members of the previous Municipalité, Jean Sallier and Toussaint Gleyze, received more votes than the most successful Jacobin candidate for the Municipal Council.[5]

So these elections revealed a substantial reservoir of opposition to Chalier, but one which was not systematically tapped. Organization and a sense of purpose made the difference between the Jacobins and their opponents. Since August the propertied classes had lost their constitution,

---

[4] AN F⁷3686⁶, d. 7, Villieux to Roland, 28 Oct. 1792. See also A. Guillon de Montléon, *Mémoires pour servir à l'histoire de la ville de Lyon pendant la Révolution* (Paris, 1824), i. 94; J. F. Reichardt, *Un Prussien en France en 1792: Lettres intimes de J. F. Reichardt*, trans. A. Laquiante (Paris, 1892), 187; AN F¹ᵃIII, Rhône 8, d. 2, Vitet, Alquier, and Boissy d'Anglas to the Convention, 10 Nov. 1792. The numbers voting in 1791 were: for mayor (21 Dec.) 3,573; for municipal officers (20 Nov.) 2,604; for *notables* (10 Dec.) 2,272. The corresponding numbers in 1792 were: (5 Nov.) 9,012; (18 Nov.) 7,288; (26 Nov.) 6,088. Clearly, an important election like that for mayor could reverse the downward trend. But in 1792 the decline continued in the vote for *procureur* (28 Nov., 5,080 votes).

[5] Gleyze: 4,285 votes; Sallier: 3,421; Noël (a Jacobin): 3,401.

the monarch who had symbolized its conservative guarantees, the departmental administrators who had restrained municipal radicalism, and the
État Major which had struggled to keep the National Guard safe from
democracy. They had also lost the Vitet regime which, for all its democratic and republican tendencies and its compromises with the popular
movement, had at least maintained order for two years and had persuaded
the clubs to acknowledge its authority. To erect new defences for property
amidst the uncertainties of the early Republic needed a degree of political
involvement and organization which could not spring up overnight.

Yet the very success of the Jacobins in marshalling their vote disguised
a serious weakness in their position: their heavy dependence on organized
support in a few poorer *sections*. Their most important stronghold was
l'Hôtel-Dieu, where 581 votes went to Chalier on 4 November and 41 to
Nivière-Chol. On 28 November 449 votes out of 503 went to Laussel,
and on 30 November 530 out of 537 went to Bertholon. In the election
for twenty municipal officers, twenty candidates (many of whom were
eventually elected to one office or another, and most of whom can be
associated with the extremists) received more than 300 votes, while no
other candidate received more than twenty-two. A similar pattern
occurred in the other *section* for which records have been found, Port
Saint-Paul, for elections on 15 and 22 November.[6] There is no direct
evidence to show that the candidates endorsed by the Club Central were
the ones that these *sections* supported, but there can be little doubt that,
as in the past, its choices had a great deal of influence on the results. It
had followed its usual practice of asking the *clubs de quartier* for nom-
inations, and Vitet's letter of 15 November suggests that it published as
usual a composite list.[7]

L'Hôtel-Dieu and Port Saint-Paul together provided 25 per cent of
Laussel's vote in an election which he won narrowly by 2,766 votes out
of 5,080, and 17 per cent of Louis Emery's (he was elected a *notable* with
4,891 votes, more than any other candidate). Without all of the returns
we cannot say which *sections* provided the rest of the Jacobins' support
on these occasions. But the geography of radicalism was probably similar
to that of a referendum held in October 1792 on whether to pay municipal
officers. More than half the votes in favour of municipal salaries (1,093
out of 1,914) came from four *sections*—Saint-Vincent II, Pierre-Scize,

---

[6] AD 31L20 and 41, minutes of Port Saint-Paul and l'Hôtel-Dieu.
[7] La Croisette recorded requests for the nomination of suitable candidates on 1 and
21 Nov. (AC I²4, 45).

l'Hôtel-Dieu, and Belle-Cordière, all of them hatting or weaving areas. All but one of the relatively poor *sections* on the Saône's right bank produced a clear majority for municipal salaries; so did the northern weaving areas, and all five of the *sections* in the vicinity of l'Hôtel-Dieu. Elsewhere, in the more prosperous *quartiers*, only one *section* passed the proposal by a clear margin, and three others did so narrowly.[8] So the Jacobins' electoral success rested on modest foundations.

There is some reason to believe that they were even more modest than the recorded figures show. Allegations of fraud were to be expected in the overheated political climate, but even before the Jacobin victories the club of La Croisette had complained that it was possible for anyone at all to cast a vote in some *sections*, and that the primary assemblies were not organized in conformity with the law.[9] Later there were allegations of wholesale electoral fraud: 'Les scrutins de plusieurs sections en sont une preuve. Ils formoient le bureau, en écartoient les amis de l'ordre et des loix, fournissoient le bulletin de ceux qui n'y paroissoient pas à l'assemblée et ajoutoient des noms supposés.'[10] Unfortunately, there is no more specific direct evidence than this. But if l'Hôtel-Dieu's returns are not fraudulent, they record a prodigy of political mobilization which deserves wide recognition. They require us to believe that in a working-class area with a population of about 3,500, never less than 300 and mostly between 500 and 600 voters appeared in the long series of electoral assemblies held between 1 November and 16 December—622 on 4 November, for example, when the thirty-one other *sections* could muster only 8,085 between them—and that 359 voters attended this *section*'s assembly for the referendum on 21 October, while in twelve other *sections* there were fewer than 50.[11] Even granted that the clubs had politicized the artisan population and inured them to the rigours of the extra-ordinarily tedious municipal voting process (which by itself probably contributed a lot to electoral apathy), this display of mass political commitment is suspiciously inconsistent with voting patterns elsewhere in Lyon.

Victory went to the Jacobins because they won consistently high votes

[8] *CM*, iv. 10 (8 Dec. 1792); AN F⁷3686⁶, d. 7, Municipalité of Lyon to Vitet, 9 Oct. 1792; AN DIII216, d. 4, Extrait des registres de la municipalité de Lyon, 29 octobre 1792.
[9] AC I²4, 45 (14 Oct. 1792).
[10] Coste MS 634, anonymous letter to the *représentants en mission* in Lyon, Mar. 1793; *Copie de la lettre écrite par les administrateurs du Conseil général du département de Rhône-et-Loire ... à la Convention nationale* (Lyon, 1793).
[11] AD 31L41, fos. 6–18, minutes of l'Hôtel-Dieu, 1 Nov.–16 Dec. 1792; AN DIII216, d. 4, Extrait des registres de la municipalité de Lyon, 29 octobre 1792.

for a large number of their candidates in a long series of primary assemblies in certain of the poorer *quartiers*. They were able to achieve this because they controlled the Club Central, the only body capable of coordinating political activity in Lyon, and they were no doubt helped by the endorsement of the city's only newspaper. But their victory was obtained without widespread support, and their political survival depended on both the continued loyalty of their working-class strongholds and their opponents' failure to mobilize the vote in the numerous unfriendly *sections*.

Nevertheless, even if the radicals of l'Hôtel-Dieu did display typical Jacobin fondness for a priori assessments of the people's will as well as a large measure of revolutionary contempt for both legality and arithmetic, the achievement of November–December 1792 should not be underestimated. With the help of the seasoned militants of the Club Central, l'Hôtel Dieu, Belle-Cordière, and Pierre-Scize, the clubs had now completed the remaking of the Municipalité into a body whose social composition reflected that of the city as a whole. In the sense that poor men were now well represented on the General Council of the Municipalité, the promise of political equality implied by the rhetoric of 1789 was closer to reality in Lyon than it had ever been before, and closer perhaps than it has been since. Around l'Hôtel-Dieu, on the right bank of the Saône, and on the slopes of la Croix-Rousse, those *quartiers* which formed distinct working-class communities had developed a solid radical tradition.[12] Their commitment to the working man's right to hold office was expressed by the October vote for substantial municipal salaries (4,000 *livres* for the mayor, 2,000 *livres* for councillors) as well as by the elections.

The Jacobins grouped around Chalier appropriated this victory of the popular democrats by using the club network and their own reputations as friends of the people to obtain key offices at the municipal, district, and departmental levels,[13] and by so doing they anticipated the national political victories of the Montagnard–*sans-culotte* alliance. But here, paradoxically, lay their greatest weakness, because the only way Jacobins could control the forces threatening to expose the contradictions between their aims and their popular allies—contradictions necessarily heightened

[12] See Appendix VI.

[13] In a manuscript headed *Tableau de réforme*, probably written by Chalier, the president (Grandchamp), an administrator (Achard) and 4 councillors of the Département are listed as *patriotes*, together with 2 district administrators (Thonion and Macabéo). (Coste MS 609.)

by the very fact that they now held local office—was by using weapons which only the national government could command. When the new Municipalité took office in December, Montagnard control of the national government was more than five months away.

JACOBIN DILEMMAS

Although in the autumn of 1792 the renewal of Rhône-et-Loire's Departmental Council moved it to the left, the political distance between it and the Municipalité of Lyon was not narrowed. The institutional friction ground on, pre-ordained by electoral legislation which ensured that one body reflected the views of rural *notables* and the other those of a predominantly artisanal urban population. In the General Council of the Département there were five lawyers, four merchants (one an ex-noble and member of the first elected Municipalité, Gabriel-Claude Servan), three surgeons, two *rentiers*, a landowner, a silk-weaver, and one other artisan. One of the lawyers, Borde, had signed a declaration of loyalty to the King in July 1792 while *procureur-syndic* of the District of Lyon-Campagne. The *secrétaire-général*, as he had been since 1790, was Antoine Gonon de Saint-Fresne, another ex-noble.[14] Little though these men had in common with the moderate republicans who sat alongside them, they were more than willing to join with them in containing Lyon's Municipalité. For the Jacobins, the Département remained a dangerous obstacle.

At least the hostility of an 'aristocratic' Département made sense in terms of Jacobin ideology. A more fundamental problem of office was to play out the Jacobin role of embodying the people's will when the people willed the end of shortages and lower food prices, practically impossible goals while the popular will elsewhere, at Trévoux, Marseille, Arles, and all along the Rhône, was implacably against movements of food towards Lyon, and while the currency was rapidly depreciating. The Lyonnais Jacobins' greatest misfortune was to have won power in the people's name at a time when anyone in power at Lyon was bound to be deeply unpopular, to bear the brunt of popular dissatisfaction over rising prices but to be unable to do much about them. The great misfortune of the Lyonnais was that the Jacobins quickly resolved this ideological dilemma

[14] *Département*, ii. 88, 445–9 (20 Aug., 14–17 Nov. 1792); AD 42L12, Commission de Justice Populaire, interrogations of J.-F. Dubost and Antoine Gonon; AD 42L86, d. 115, interrogation of Servan; AD 1L986, d. Borde; AN F¹ᶜIII, Rhône 6, d. 3, Les Directoires des districts de Lyon au Roi citoyen (16 July 1792).

by understanding their unpopularity to mean that, as so many good *patriotes* had suspected for so long, Lyon was unfitted for liberty.

Defining all their opponents indiscriminately as enemies of the people, irrespective of the rate at which opposition grew or which social groups it began to embrace, was one of many mistakes which rapidly converted the Jacobins' victory into a disaster. But their position was probably impossible anyway. The conditions which produced the Montagnard–*sans-culotte* alliance in Paris during the winter and spring of 1792–3 did not exist in the provinces, and the Lyonnais extremists were not the only ones to suffer as a consequence.[15] In the capital the alliance was made possible by the Montagnards' ability to produce legislation which the *sans-culottes* wanted, and by the *sans-culottes*' ability to intimidate the Convention. Well before the *maximum* of 4 May was decreed, the threat of popular disorder in the capital was sufficient to produce enormous subsidies and administrative and political effort to keep the price of bread at 3 *sous* a pound, for which the Paris Commune could take the credit. The Montagnards' success depended on their ability to time such concessions so as to dampen down or exploit surges of unrest in Paris, and the range of measures to placate the *sans-culottes* was wide—purges, the Revolutionary Tribunal, legislation against hoarders, the *maximum*, the Revolutionary Army, and so on. But the Montagnards and the Convention were in a much better position to respond quickly and appropriately to popular feeling in the capital than they were to news of provincial troubles. And angry crowds in the Tuileries *section* (as on the night of 25 February 1793) provided a much stronger incentive to do so than reports of disturbances from places two or three days away. Rousseau Hidins and Manlius Dodieu might propose elaborate systems of price limitation, and the Club Central's scheme for state controls over the grain trade might be pondered by the Municipalité, but these were matters of national policy, and the Jacobins had to wait on events.

For all the rhetoric on the theme of 'les besoins les plus pressants du peuple', the Municipalité was slow to take an obvious step within its power—submitting an address on *subsistances* to the Convention. Chalier seems to have proposed an address in the Club Central on 6 December, but it was not accepted by the Municipalité until 25 March.[16] Meanwhile the clubs were demanding immediate action. On 2 January, for example,

---

[15] I first developed this argument in 'A Jacobin Débâcle: The Losing of Lyon in Spring, 1793', *History*, 69 (1984), 1–14.

[16] AN F^{1a} Rhône 8, d. 1, no. 93; *CM*, iv. 154 (25 Mar. 1793).

La Croisette called on the Municipalité to establish a *tarif* for all commodities brought into Lyon, particularly wood and coal.[17] Eleven weeks later, Rue Belle-Cordière expressed impatience at the delays with the address to the Convention, and threatened to have one of its own printed.[18] But frequent discussions with deputations of the clubs were inconclusive.[19] The Municipalité could do no more than continue its predecessor's policy of subsidizing bread prices, and the first *maximum* on grain prices (decreed 4 May) came too late to help it.

Subsidies were provided only with the greatest difficulty. Municipal income in 1792 had been 80,177 *livres* and expenses 385,679 *livres*, and income from the *sous additionels* had trickled in only very slowly in 1793. There were supplementary resources: the Ministry of the Interior had advanced a total of 400,000 *livres* in the last quarter of 1792, and there was a loan fund of 1,450,000 *livres*, all for the purchase of wheat. In November the cost of providing municipal flour cheaply enough to keep the price of bread at 5 *sous* per pound was estimated at 3,000 *livres* per day. Yet on 20 February the price per pound was fixed at 4 *sous*, and between 4 November and 20 March the price of wheat in Burgundy rose from 69 to 80 *livres* per *ânnée*. To make matters worse, the decree authorizing the loan of November 1792 had stipulated that grain be bought only at Marseille or abroad, which involved such difficulties of supply and transport that the Municipalité was able to spend only about three-quarters of the fund by 22 March. By 12 May, high prices and the impossibility of getting sufficient wheat to Lyon had raised the threat of famine. Only a week's supply of grain remained, and there were not enough funds to continue the bread subsidy.[20]

According to Riffaterre: 'la municipalité jacobine réussit à maintenir le pain à un prix relativement bas par trois moyens'—subsidies, appropriating a proportion of the wheat passing through Lyon, and establishing municipal ovens.[21] Yet the ovens ran at such a loss that on 16 April their use was discontinued after only a month, and the decision of 20 February to purchase compulsorily a percentage of all the wheat passing down the

---

[17] AC I²4, d. 45, fo. 31, club of La Croisette, 2 Jan. 1793.

[18] AD 34L1, club of Rue Belle-Cordière, 10 Mar. 1793.

[19] *CM*, iv. 81, 132, 147 (27 Jan., 4 Mar., 19 Mar. 1793).

[20] Ibid. 115, 157, 227 (20 Feb., 27 Mar., 28 Apr. 1793); AC F⁴, fos. 9, 28, 32, 35, 39, 40, 41, *Rapport du Bureau d'administration de l'emprunt de trois millions pour l'approvisionnement de la ville de Lyon* (Lyon, 22 mars 1793), 2, 6; *Pétition faite à la barre de la Convention nationale par B. J. Frossard et Chalon* (n.p., n.d. [Lyon, 1792]).

[21] Riffaterre, *Le Mouvement anti-jacobin et anti-parisien à Lyon et dans le Rhône-et-Loire en 1793* (Lyon, 1912–28), i. 338.

Rhône—impolitic for a city whose own supplies were coming the other way—was revoked on 30 April.[22] These were not effective measures but signs of desperation, for Lyon's administrators simply lacked the power to satisfy popular demands. On 21 May the decision had to be taken to replace the indemnity paid to bakers with a selective indemnity paid to the poor, just as the moderate Municipalité of Bordeaux had done in March.[23] It is difficult to see in what sense the price of bread was 'relatively' low. On 1 April it was raised to 4 *sous* 6 *deniers* for a one-pound loaf. In the same month the Paris Commune had fixed the price of a four-pound loaf at 12 *sous*; and the price in Bordeaux, only 2 *sous* 9 *deniers* on 7 March, did not reach 4 *sous* 6 *deniers* until 24 April. In both Paris and Bordeaux the pound (*livre de marc*) contained 2.25 *onces* more than the *livre de Lyon*.[24]

Not the least of the Jacobins' misfortunes was to hold power when the *assignat* was depreciating particularly rapidly. From January 1791 to January 1793 the value in terms of gold coin of 100 *livres* in *assignats* fell by a little less than one-third (from 92 *livres écus* to 62). It fell by nearly a third again in the next four months (to 42 *livres écus* in May 1793).[25]

Both the Municipalité and the clubs were aware that prices in Lyon were exorbitant. The former, just as its predecessor had done, worried that the situation might be exploited by agitators.[26] The latter bombarded the Town Hall with complaints about the quality and price of bread and demands for more effective action. It cannot be quantified, but clearly there was bitter frustration at the extremists' failure:

on ne sait par quelle fatalité nous ne pouvons pas manger d'aussi beau pain qu'à Paris ... à présent que le peuple est souverain et que nous avons des officiers municipaux sans-culottes en qui nous mettons notre confiance nous ne savons par quel malheur plus l'on augmente le pain plus ces fripons le font mauvais quelle infamie ... un boulanger de la rue Gentil qui s'appelle Chabou ... a demandé à notre brave municipalité la permission de ne plus faire du pain mais de lui permettre de faire des belles brioches ... notre bonne municipalité lui à

[22] *CM*, iv. 115, 178, 200, 233 (20 Feb., 2 Apr., 16 Apr., 30 Apr. 1793).

[23] Ibid. 261 (21 May 1793); Forrest, *Society and Politics*, p. 297.

[24] *CM*, iv. 172 (26 Mar. 1793); G. Rudé, *Paris and London in the Eighteenth Century* (London, 1970), 175; Forrest, *Society and Politics*, p. 300; M. Marion, *Dictionnaire des institutions de la France aux XVIIᵉ et XVIIIᵉ siècles* (Paris, 1923), 375.

[25] S. Charléty, *Département du Rhône: Documents relatifs à la vente des biens nationaux* (Lyon, 1906), 613–15.

[26] See *CM*, iv. 198, 212 (14, 22 Apr. 1793); Coste MSS 4126, 553, letter of Achard and Gaillard, 11 Feb. 1793, Lacombe-Saint-Michel to Basire, 20 Feb. 1793.

permis de ne plus faire que des brioches et par ce moyen les aristocrates en mange d'avantage à leur déjeuner ...[27]

As well as bread the *sans-culottes* expected justice, or in Lefebvrean terms, the execution of their punitive will. But in early 1793 it was nearly as difficult for would-be terrorists in the provinces to take effective repressive measures against counter-revolutionaries and economic criminals as it was to find cheap grain. Provincial Jacobins could improvise repressive machinery, and many did, but with a hostile Département, and the Convention not yet committed to large-scale terror, such initiatives were likely to be overruled. The result was that while in this field of policy the Lyonnais Jacobins showed real enthusiasm and persistence, their repressive efforts only succeeded in increasing the opposition to them. A policy of *attentisme* might have been more prudent in the circumstances; but that would have further alienated the *sans-culottes*. And in any case the Lyonnais Jacobins were psychologically incapable of *attentisme*. Chalier set their tone, a man (as the Montagnard *député* Lacombe Saint-Michel noted with considerable understatement) 'à la vérité dit-on fort exalté, peut-être imprudent'.[28] They lived in agonies of anxiety, convinced that only the immediate application of *grandes mesures* could save Lyon and the Republic from ruin. For *grandes mesures* they looked to the Paris Jacobin Club and the Convention—or rather the Montagnard *députés* who comprehended the people's will. Here lay both the great strength and the great weakness of the orthodox Jacobinism practised by the Lyonnais Municipalité. It assumed that there was an essential unity of purpose amongst true republicans, that there existed universal and eternal principles of political virtue on which alone justice and liberty could be built, and that the enunciation of these principles was pre-eminently the task of the Paris Jacobins and the Montagne. This meant that the Jacobins marched in step more often than their opponents, but in the provinces being in step with Paris frequently meant being out of step with the local community. The centralist and unitary characteristics of Jacobinism suited it for the task of running a revolutionary war, but left little room for tactical manœuvring when local circumstances were different from Paris.

It is true that in some places, like Marseille, provincial militants took

---

[27] Coste MS 601, petition of Dubreuil to the *députés* of the Convention at Lyon, [March 1793]. See also *CM*, iv. 22 (14 Dec. 1792); AC I²2, d. 106 *bis*, club of La Pêcherie to the Municipalité of Lyon, 26 Dec. 1792; AD 34L1, club of Rue Belle-Cordière, 28 Apr. 1793; *CM*, iv. 97, 214 (10 Feb., 24 Apr. 1793).

[28] Coste MS 553, Lacombe-Saint-Michel to Basire, 20 Feb. 1793.

their own exceptional measures without reference to the *société mère* or the Convention, a form of revolutionary action often referred to as Jacobin federalism.[29] But the Lyonnais Jacobins were not strong enough for this, and in any case their inclination was to follow the lead of Paris, the fount of patriotism from which they drew their inspiration and their hope. They responded like puppets to Parisian impulses, publishing the Paris Jacobins' denunciation of Roland in December, organizing a petition for the immediate execution of Louis le Dernier in January, and demanding the expulsion from the *clubs de quartier* of all those who failed to sign or otherwise gave evidence of sympathy for the *appelants*.[30] The result was more friction between the *clubs de quartier* and the Club Central. Roland was an easy target for the Parisian Jacobins, with his *laissez-faire* economics, provincial background, and intellectual wife, but in Lyon he still had a following as a critic of the *octrois*, a democrat, and an early defender of the popular societies. The club of La Pêcherie refused to accept that 'l'homme du peuple, le plus ardent défenseur de ses droits' should be regarded 'comme suspect aux vrais amis de la liberté'. It denounced the Paris Jacobins' letter as 'une dénonciation vague et qui a tous les caractères de la calomnie'. By reprinting it the Club Central had exceeded its powers and was threatening to bring about 'la chute de nos sociétés'.[31] La Croisette also expressed dissatisfaction with the attack on Roland, though a resolution to this effect was later deleted from the minutes.[32] At some time before 6 January La Pêcherie split into two opposing factions, and when the Club Central requested its affiliates to recognize only the original club, La Croisette refused to commit itself.[33] The Club Central then attempted to purge La Croisette of moderates, and there followed another schism which proved contagious.

THE BEGINNINGS OF ORGANIZED ANTI-JACOBINISM IN THE POPULAR SOCIETIES

La Croisette lay virtually at the centre of peninsular Lyon, between the turbulent *quartiers* near the hospital and the wealthier commercial areas

---

[29] The best accounts of the varieties of provincial revolutionary militancy are to be found in R. Cobb, *Les Armées révolutionnaires: Instrument de la Terreur dans les départements, avril 1793–floréal, an II*, 2 vols. (Paris, 1961–3), and *The Police and the People* (Oxford, 1970).

[30] See Edmonds, 'The Losing of Lyon', pp. 11–14.

[31] AC I²2, no. 108, extract from the minutes of the club of La Pêcherie, 9 Dec. 1792.

[32] Ibid. 45, club of La Croisette, 9 Dec. 1792.

[33] Ibid. 6 Jan. 1793.

of Saint-Nizier, Rue Buisson, and Rue Tupin. The membership of its club seems to have been socially mixed.[34] Of 129 members in 1793, 88 have been identified by Koi as active citizens in 1791. (This does not mean that the others were all passive citizens, only that they cannot be located in the poorly kept tax records for a year during which some of them may not have been residents of the *section*.) Of these, nearly 7 per cent were weavers and about 50 per cent were artisans.[35] The club had often been rather conservative: in February 1792, for example, it had requested that in an address proposed by the Club Central the phrase 'Roi des François' be replaced by 'Sire' or 'Majesté'.[36] But in June it called for the suspension of the royal veto during the war, and advocated the reinstatement of the Brissotin ministers unless the King could provide adequate reasons for their dismissal. By November 1792 the club was divided. Opponents of the Jacobins seem to have had the upper hand: Bernard de Charpieux was preferred to Laussel as *procureur*, and the Club Central was criticized for permitting 'incendiary motions', though this was deleted from the minutes.[37] It is impossible to determine which group of club members was responsible for the anti-Jacobin thrust of late 1792. Two of the wealthier ones, the *notaires* Bonneveau and Fromental, were active at about this time, and Fromental was president in December. But La Croisette still supported the payment of municipal officers (6 January) and controls on grain prices (2 January 1793). On the other hand, it rejected a proposal from Le Change to discuss means of increasing piece-work rates for weavers.[38]

Early in February the Jacobin *clubistes* of Lyon stepped up their campaign against the moderates with a domiciliary visit by *commissaires* of the Club Central. There were about 300 arrests, but nearly all the victims were quickly released for lack of evidence, and the main outcome was increased political polarization. As the *officier municipal* Emery admitted: 'de tout ce choc qui n'a fait peur qu'aux mauvais riches il n'en est malheureusement rien résulté d'efficace pour le bien générale, tant s'en faut, car cela n'a fait qu'augmenter le nombre des mécontents, car ces messieurs saisissent en merveille tout ce qu'ils croient être utile à leurs

---

[34] See the exemplary study by A. De Francesco, 'Le Quartier lyonnais de la Croisette pendant les premières années de la Révolution (1790–1793)', *Bulletin du Centre d'histoire économique et sociale de la région lyonnaise*, 4 (1979), 21–64.

[35] T. Koi, 'Les "Chaliers" et les sans-culottes lyonnais', Thèse de doctorat, IIIᵉ cycle (Lyon, 1974), 159–60.

[36] AC I²4, 45 (7 Feb. 1792).

[37] Ibid. 19 Nov. 1792.

[38] Ibid. 9, 17 Dec. 1792; 2, 6 Jan. 1793.

causes'.[39] A protest meeting in the *section* of Port du Temple was denounced as illegal by the Municipalité, which used the incident as a pretext for deploying cannon around the Town Hall. Suspecting an insurrection, Nivière-Chol called on National Guard units and some regular troops to protect the cannon.

The moderates' fears seemed to be confirmed by the news that a secret meeting of *section* delegates had been held at the Club Central on 6 February. Nivière-Chol believed, probably rightly, that the meeting had been to organize a Revolutionary Tribunal, and rumours multiplied: one of la Grande-Côte's battalions had been illegally requisitioned; the Club Central had distributed cartridges; the guillotine was being readied for action. The Jacobins claimed that these were fabrications and libels against the people, while Nivière-Chol and his supporters maintained that the city had been narrowly saved from a massacre. One estimate put the number of Lyonnais marked for execution at 6,000, another at 20,000. From this point on, fear and distrust divided the Lyonnais more deeply than ever into proponents and opponents of Jacobin terror. Nivière-Chol, ill and demoralized and unable to work with the Conseil Général, which now began to denounce him openly, conceded the bankruptcy of Rolandin politics by resigning on 9 February. He was soon followed by the remaining moderate municipal officers.[40]

The reaction of the club of La Croisette was to demand stricter controls over the operations of the Club Central and to disavow 'l'assemblée clandestine tenue au Comité Central mercredi dernier 6 courant'.[41] By 17 February there were schisms in several clubs,[42] but it is not clear in how many nor whether the cause was disagreement amongst the old *clubistes* or an influx of new members. The next day saw the first violent

---

[39] Coste MS 547, letter of Emery, 12 Feb. 1793.

[40] The evidence on the troubles of early February comes mainly from partisan accounts: the letter of Emery just cited; Coste MS 4126, Achard and Gaillard to Javogues, 11 Feb. 1793; AD 36L57, District Tribunal, Lyon-Ville, statement of charges against Palerne de Savy (he was suspected of corresponding with *émigrés*), 2 Feb. 1793; AN AFII, plaq. 343, fos. 24, 27, anonymous letter to Vitet, 7 Feb. 1793, and letter of Nivière-Chol, 7 Feb. 1793; Coste MS 598, De la Tour to the *commissaires* at Lyon, [March, 1793]; J. Guerre, *Histoire de la Révolution de Lyon*, in *Registre du Secrétariat général des sections de la ville de Lyon 2 août–11 octobre, 1793*, ed. G. Guigue (Lyon, 1907) (hereafter *Secrétariat*), 364–5; *Adresse de Nivière-Chol à ses concitoyens* (Lyon, [1793]). The official accounts are also obviously biased: *Extraits du registre des délibérations du Directoire du département de Rhône-et-Loire* (Lyon, 6 Feb. 1793). *CM*, iv. 87 (6 Feb. 1793).

[41] AC I²4, 45, club of La Croisette, 10 Feb. 1793.

[42] Ibid. 17 Feb. 1793. La Croisette called for unity within the clubs which had split, but the names of only two of these are known, La Pêcherie and La Grande-Côte (see *Journal de Lyon*, 21 Feb. 1793, p. 166).

anti-Jacobin incident, triggering events which split the club movement completely: Nivière-Chol was re-elected mayor with 75 per cent of the vote but refused the post.[43] Crowds of his supporters invaded the Hôtel de Ville, and one municipal officer and the wife of another were attacked.[44] During the night the Club Central was raided, its bust of Jean-Jacques desecrated, its members beaten, and its furnishings taken to the Brotteaux and burnt.[45] The anti-Jacobin offensive continued with the victory of the naturalist and physician J.-E. Gilibert in the mayoral election of 27 February. But Laussel had taken the precaution of gaoling him on the 26th 'comme moteur d'insurrection'. After some days of increasingly uncomfortable solitary confinement, Gilibert relinquished the mayoralty and was allowed better conditions.[46] On 9 March new elections made Bertrand mayor, but again there were allegations that the Jacobins had used intimidation and fraud, and at least three *sections* (les Terreaux, la Pêcherie, and Port du Temple) refused to take part in the last of the ballots.[47]

In a pre-election vote, the club of La Croisette strongly favoured Gilibert.[48] It questioned the Club Central's right to nominate a final list of candidates and asserted the independence of the sectional clubs.[49] Relations between the two still existed on 3 March, but by the 10th a group of 'vrais sans-culottes' had seceded and formed a new club (Lepeletier) which affiliated with the Club Central.[50] Communication between

---

[43] Nivière-Chol received 8,097 of the 10,746 votes cast. His main opponent was the silk-weaver Fillion (*CM*, iv. 110 (18 Feb. 1793)).

[44] Ibid. iv. 104–5 (18 Feb. 1793).

[45] See *Rapport et projet de décret sur les troubles arrivés à Lyon ... Par J. L. Tallien* (Paris, 1793), 7, for the Municipalité's view of this affair; and C. Genet-Bronze, M. Pelzin, and J. Badger, *Rapport et pétition sur les troubles arrivés à Lyon, présentés et lus à la barre de la Convention nationale, le lundi 15 avril, 1793* (Lyon, 1793), 7, for the anti-Jacobin version. Both accounts agree on the main events but not on the intentions of the rioters.

[46] *CM*, iv. 126, 131, 133 (27 Feb., 4, 5 Mar. 1793), J.-E. Gilibert, *Jean-Emmanuel Gilibert à ses concitoyens* (Lyon, 1793), 1–2.

[47] *CM*, iv. 137 (9 Mar. 1793); AN DIII216, d. 4, primary assembly of Port du Temple, 9 Mar. 1793. See *Journal de Lyon*, 24 Feb. 1793, p. 175; 25 Feb. 1793, p. 177; 9 Mar. 1793, p. 209. Once again l'Hôtel-Dieu performed incredible feats for the Jacobins, producing 595 votes for Bertrand out of the 650 cast on 25 February, 702 out of 749 on the 27th, and 831 out of 846 on 8 March, almost a quarter of the *section*'s entire population, and 12.8% of the total vote cast (or rather recorded) in Lyon for the Jacobin candidate. (In all, 6,481 votes went to Bertrand out of a total vote of 9,986.) (*CM*, iv. 138 (9 Mar. 1792); AD 31L41, l'Hôtel-Dieu, 25, 27 Feb., 28 Mar. 1793.)

[48] Gilibert: 38; Emery: 5; Fillion: 11 (AC I²4, 45, club of La Croisette, 23 Feb. 1793).

[49] Ibid.

[50] AD 31L1, club of Rue Belle-Cordière, 10 Mar. 1793.

the latter and the original club of La Croisette appears to have ceased about this time.

Riffaterre misleadingly implies that organized anti-Jacobinism did not begin until May, when the Municipalité took action against the moderate clubs.[51] But some clubs had been resisting the Club Central from late 1792, and there was an alliance of anti-Jacobin clubs by the beginning of April. Soon after the secession of the *sans-culottes*, new members joined La Croisette in large numbers: thirty-one between 13 March and 13 April, against only five in the previous four months.[52] Outside the *section*, support for the anti-Jacobins of La Croisette also grew quickly, particularly in the central peninsula area and the more prosperous *sections* of the Saône's right bank.[53] Fourteen clubs were aligned with la croisette by 10 10 April, so the Club Central's transformation into the Club des Jacobins de Lyon in early April did not cause (as Riffaterre thought),[54] but only accelerated, the fragmentation of the clubs. In fact, the Lyonnais Jacobins implied that it was the trouble in the popular societies which had created the need for a Jacobin Club: 'Amis,' they told the Montagnard *représentants en mission* in Lyon in mid-March, 'cinquante chauds défenseurs de la liberté des nations désirent instamment de se réunir dans un lieu commun pour y Jacobiner. Vous savez que toutes nos Sociétés sont sans caractère d'esprit public ... le défaut de l'organisation est ici la source de la fermentation sourde qui menace même vos jours.'[55] Undoubtedly the Jacobins' move encouraged several *clubs de quartier*[56] to join La Croisette.[57] Le Plâtre proposed the printing of 1,000 copies of an address

---

[51] Riffaterre, *Le Mouvement anti-jacobin et anti-parisien à Lyon*, i. 57; *CM*, iv. 247 (11 May 1793).

[52] AC I²4, d. 45, club of La Croisette, minutes, Nov.–Apr., *passim*.

[53] Central peninsula: Place Saint-Pierre, Rue Tupin, Le Plâtre, Saint-Nizier, Rue Terraille, Rue Buisson. (La Fédération (Bellecour) and La Pêcherie had also broken with the Club Central, but they are not mentioned as corresponding with La Croisette.) Right bank (Saône): Place Neuve, Porte-Froc, Le Change, Saint-Georges. Hôtel-Dieu area: Bon-Rencontre, Place Confort. (Ibid. 13, 17, 20, 26 Mar., 1, 3, 10 Apr. 1793.)

[54] See Riffaterre, *Le Mouvement anti-jacobin et anti-parisien à Lyon*, i. 57; *CM*, iv. 177 (31 Mar. 1793); AC I²4, d. 45, club of La Croisette, 10 Apr. 1793.

[55] Coste MS 600, Achard and Gaillard to the *commissaires* of the Convention at Lyon, 17 Mar. 1793.

[56] Rue Terraille and Saint-Georges, the first of the poor weaving areas to join the anti-Jacobin movement, referred specifically to the Jacobin Club when they first fraternized with La Croisette (ibid. 26 Mar., 1 Apr. 1793).

[57] Place Neuve and Saint-Georges proposed a new 'point de ralliement où on enverrait des commissaires comme cy-devant' (ibid. 10 Apr. 1793). But La Croisette seems to have retained its co-ordinating role until it was forcibly dissolved in mid-May (AC I²20, d. 230, interrogation of J.-F. Dubost, president of the club of La Croisette by the Committee of Public Safety of Rhône-et-Loire, [May, 1793]).

to the clubs and *sections* 'pour les mettre en garde contre l'établissement qui projettent des ennemis de la République d'un Club en cette ville à l'instar de celui des Jacobins de Paris'.[58] The long-standing tension between the Club Central and the *clubs particuliers* had been increased to breaking-point by the élitism and ideological rigidity of the Robespierrist Jacobins, and their disregard for the independence which the *quartiers* had guarded jealously since 1790.

Ideology rescued the Jacobins from the embarrassment of widespread resistance to their programme, if not from the practical political consequences. Since the Revolution was by definition popularly willed, it was inconceivable that the people might not will the measures laid down by the Montagne to meet the crisis of early 1793. Opposition to them indicated a morbid condition in the body politic, and excision of the affected parts was a matter of patriotic duty. As Furet has shown,[59] this was the Jacobins' characteristic method of legitimizing their policies. But for it to work, there had to be fairly broad acquiescence to these policies, particularly amongst those groups—peasants, artisans, and *petit bourgeois*—which could not easily be written off as *suppôts du despotisme* or *esclaves déjà regrettant leurs fers*. In the big provincial cities, and in Lyon above all, the Jacobins were much less successful in obtaining this acquiescence than has been recognized in the neo-Jacobin histories of the nineteenth and twentieth centuries—and even in some recent criticisms of them, so seductive is the image of a France united in desperate struggle against the old Europe in 1793.[60] Very little can be understood about the civil war at Lyon unless it is accepted that Jacobinism was a disastrous failure there, and that one of the most important reasons for this was the existence of a well-established popular movement with its own claims, unchallenged by the *patriotes* before 1793, to express the people's will.

There was a certain logic in the line of action the Lyonnais Jacobins chose,[61] and it is misleading to suggest[62] that they failed because they

---

[58] AC I²4, d. 45 (10 Mar. 1793). The other clubs collaborating with La Croisette by this date were Rue Tupin, Saint-Nizier, Place Saint-Pierre, and La Pêcherie.

[59] See F. Furet, 'La Révolution française est terminée', in *Penser la Révolution française* (Paris, 1978).

[60] See Edmonds, 'The Losing of Lyon', pp. 1–2, 14.

[61] Much of the material in this paragraph, and certain passages elsewhere in this chapter, originally appeared in the present author's 'The Rise and Fall of Popular Democracy in Lyon, 1789–1795', *Bulletin of the John Rylands University Library of Manchester*, 67 (1984). Thanks are due to the editor of the *Bulletin* for permission to use it.

[62] As A. de Francesco does in 'Montagnardi e sanculotti in provincia', *Studi storici*, 19 (1978), 602.

misunderstood the Lyonnais popular movement. In fact, they had good reason for believing that the club network was not a suitable tool for Montagnard purposes. It was too loose and ill-disciplined, and too many clubs retained Rolandin sympathies from the partnership with Vitet in 1791–2. The Jacobins concluded, quite reasonably, that in a national crisis which required quick and decisive action, this squabbling, unwieldy organization would be of little use. And *sections* of the club movement shared their views. Several *clubs de quartier*, mostly in the poorer parts of Lyon, endorsed the new Jacobin Club. Certainly Belle-Cordière and La Croix-Rousse did, as well as the clubs which split away from the existing ones in la Pêcherie, la Grande-Côte, and la Croisette.[63] The clubs and the politicized elements of the *petit peuple* did not turn away from the extremists *en masse*: they divided, and some stayed with Chalier. But from the point of view of their ability to control Lyon with a limited base of support, the Jacobins could not afford to antagonize so many of the *clubs de quartier*.

It is very difficult to estimate how far and how fast opinion amongst the *menu peuple* became anti-Jacobin. By early May fifteen clubs were corresponding amicably with La Croisette and six of them had formally affiliated with it. Of the six affiliates, one was in a poor weaving area (Saint-Georges) and none of the others, with the exception of Rue Buisson, was in the richer parts of Lyon.[64] Most of the nine corresponding clubs were in prosperous *quartiers*, but they also included three in weaving areas, La Grande-Côte, Rue Terraille, and Port Saint-Paul.[65] These may, of course, have been taken over by bourgeois elements. But De Francesco's intensive study of La Croisette—the only club for which detailed records exist for this period—shows an influx of artisans into the anti-Jacobin ranks. Between the secession of the *sans-culottes* shortly before 10 March and the closure of the club on 14 May, 72 new members joined it. Of the 56 he could identify by occupation, De Francesco found that 'only 12 belonged to the world of businessmen and rentiers while the remainder were all connected with artisanal activity properly speaking: noteworthy

---

[63] AD 34L1, club of Rue Belle-Cordière, 11 Apr. 1793; 34L3, club of La Croix-Rousse, 24 Apr. 1793; AC I²4, 45, club of La Croisette, 13 Mar. 1793. All but 4 of 31 members of Lepeletier Club were artisans, mostly poor, or wage-earners, and on average they were poorer than those of their rival club (De Francesco, 'Le Quartier lyonnais de la Croisette', pp. 54–7).

[64] The others were Place Neuve, La Pêcherie, Le Gourguillon, and Le Change (AC I²4, 45, club of La Croisette, 5–7 May 1793).

[65] The others were Rue Tupin, Rue Thomassin, Port du Temple, La Fédération, Les Terreaux, Le Plâtre.

amongst them silk-weavers, tanners, tailors, cobblers, shopkeepers, food retailers and textile workers in general'.[66] To judge by the subsequent history of the anti-Jacobin movement in Lyon, the proportion of artisans in La Croisette was by no means atypical.[67]

By March an awareness seems to have been emerging that Jacobin policies could be imposed only at the expense of popular economic and social interests. De Francesco has pointed out that workers in luxury trades—silk above all—were economically threatened by the war of confiscation and terror which the Jacobins seemed to intend against those who employed them and bought their products, and some statements made by weavers to the *représentants en mission* in Lyon in the early spring would seem to support this view.[68] Possibly, rumours of confiscatory taxes and the *partage des biens* spread fear amongst artisans and *boutiquiers* as well as merchants and *rentiers*, though if the Jacobins were clear on one point it was that their foes were the counter-revolutionary rich. While some of the better-off artisans may have seen themselves as potential targets, it seems unlikely that many weavers or others of the *petit peuple* became anti-Jacobin on this score.

But it was not just the indirect effects of the Jacobin campaign against the rich which endangered the textile-workers' livelihood: there was a basic contradiction between the Jacobin cult of austerity, which reviled *luxe*, and the *raison d'être* of their industry, which was *luxe*. Lyonnais plans to revive their trade by dressing the *conventionnels* in satin and velvet[69] were pipe-dreams under a regime which was busy modelling itself on the Roman Republic, with its semi-official *couturier*, David, imagining civic uniforms in the severest warrior style. The clubs were well aware of the problem. At least two of them requested the Club Central not to debate motions discouraging luxury: 'au contraire l'on devroit inviter tous les citoyens de se parer autant qu'il se pouvroit des étoffes de soie'.[70] But the Jacobins of Rue Belle-Cordière were unmoved: 'Le luxe et la boté [*sic*] d'un vrai Républicain doit être aux armes.'[71]

Again, Jacobinism's fundamental rationale—the pre-eminent necessity of defending the Revolution against internal and external enemies—

---

[66] De Francesco, 'Montagnardi e sanculotti', p. 623.

[67] See below, Chaps. 6–8.

[68] De Francesco, 'Montagnardi e sanculotti', pp. 616, 625.

[69] AC F[14], Municipalité of Lyon to Frossard and Chalon (its agents in Paris), 13 Dec. 1792.

[70] AC I[2]4, 45, club of La Croisette, 13 Feb. 1793. The same motion had been passed by the club of Rue Tupin.

[71] AD 34L1, club of Rue Belle-Cordière, 10 Mar. 1793.

turned its provincial supporters into agents of the war machine. This could make for difficulties with the *menu peuple*, as was most apparent in towns like Toulon where a large part of the population was involved in war production, and where a Jacobin administration reimposed work discipline at the Arsenal and presided over substantial reductions in real wages. The result was that the *sans-culottes* had largely abandoned the Jacobins in the spring of 1793.[72] Lyon was not heavily involved in weapon manufacture, but it was an important supply centre for the Armée des Alpes, and the necessity for this does not seem to have been at all obvious to the *menu peuple*. On 12 May the Municipalité noted the currency of rumours that all the supplies arriving at Lyon were being taken for the Armée des Alpes and the Armée du Midi, and for the inhabitants of the Midi as well. On 24 May a warehouse containing butter for the Armée des Alpes was broken into by a crowd of women and the contents sold off. The Jacobin Mayor Bertrand and an agent of the Ministry of the Interior, Gonchon ('l'orateur du faubourg Saint-Antoine'), harangued the crowd for three hours but to no effect. Gonchon reported that although he had seen the mayor 'faire les plus grands efforts pour éclairer le peuple et dissiper l'attroupement', all Bertrand's arguments were disputed. Rumours were circulating that the *magistrats sans-culottes* had connived at butter-hoarding under the absurd pretext that it was for the army, when everyone knew (so Gonchon was told) that soldiers' rations did not include butter and that the vats used were unsuitable for prolonged storage. It was also said that a method had been found to use butter as a substitute for tallow.[73] In Paris, as we have seen, these contradictions between Jacobin policy and popular interests could be smoothed over by well-timed concessions and cheap bread. In Lyon they were blatant and irremediable.

In this sense, provincial Jacobins everywhere were in a precarious position, and one that could only get worse without substantial direct support from Paris. But in Lyon there was a serious additional difficulty. Amongst the legacies of the clubs and their alliance with the Rolandins had been the politicization of many artisans and the making of many minor political careers, as well as relationships of clientage between some

---

[72] See M. Crook, 'Federalism and the French Revolution: The Revolt of Toulon in 1793', *History*, 65 (1980), 387–8.

[73] AC F[14], fo. 41, Municipalité of Lyon to the Convention, 12 May 1793; AN AFII43, plaq. 339, no. 28, statement by Gonchon, extracted from the minutes of the Département of Rhône-et-Loire, 25 May 1793; *CM*, iv. 268 (25 May 1793); AN F[1c]III, Rhône 8, d. 3, no. 32, Gonchon to Garat, 31 June 1793.

popular activists and bourgeois politicians. The Jacobins have become so firmly established in historical literature as partners and patrons of the popular democrats, and their opponents as enemies of the *sans-culottes*, that the significance of this Rolandin connection with the Lyonnais clubs has been overlooked. For politically involved artisans with strong Rolandin links, the choice between Jacobins and Rolandins was far from clear-cut. Amongst them was Denis Monnet,[74] the weavers' leader, who had been prominent in the affairs of his *section*, Port Saint-Paul, since the municipal revolution of 1790. He was elected a captain in the National Guard in January 1790 and president of his sectional assembly in May, in which capacity he advocated the immediate abolition of the *octrois* and harsh penalties for opponents of the Civil Constitution of the Clergy. By this time he was clearly an advanced *patriote*. His involvement in the exposure of the 'Conspiration de Lyon' made him famous enough for the popular society of Saint-Vincent to eulogize him as a champion of both the silk-weavers' rights and the nation's liberty. With support in the Port Saint-Paul Club (he was president of it in August 1791), Monnet was well placed to share the fruits of Rolandin victory, and in November 1791 he was elected a *notable*. But he also shared the Rolandins' enemies, including Laussel, who denounced him and his Rolandin patron, the *juge de paix* Billemaz, as embezzlers. And when the Rolandins went into political eclipse, Monnet followed them. He did not win re-election as a *notable*, and although he had regularly been chosen as president of his *section* over a period of more than two years, he seems to have played no official role in it between August 1792 and March 1793.

But Port Saint-Paul's enthusiasm for the Jacobins waned during March 1793 as the anti-Jacobin feeling began to spread from La Pêcherie and La Croisette to other clubs and *sections*. Monnet re-emerged as president of the sectional assembly, and in the mayoral elections necessitated by Nivière-Chol's resignation the anti-Jacobin candidates received a much higher share of the vote in Port Saint-Paul than they had done in November 1792. It cannot be established that the votes for the anti-Jacobins (or indeed for Monnet) came from the *menu peuple*, though Koi has shown that those who were active in the *section* in early 1793 were predominantly poor and predominantly weavers. All that can be said with confidence is that opinion amongst the politically active in a poor *quartier*

[74] See the present writer's 'A Study in Popular Anti-Jacobinism: The Career of Denis Monnet', *French Historical Studies*, 13 (1983), 16–22. The argument here and in the next paragraph is based on research summarized in this article.

which had previously been consistently radical was now drifting away from the Jacobins, and this coincided with Monnet's return to his accustomed role as *section* president. Again, it cannot be assumed that Monnet *led* his fellow-*sectionnaires* to embrace the anti-Jacobin cause. The point is that he was available to lend that cause his experience as a sectional official and his established reputation as a *patriote* and popular activist. It seems likely that he facilitated, even if he did not engineer, Port Saint-Paul's increasing involvement in anti-Jacobin activity. So the Jacobins' difficulties were increased by the fact that the political struggle in Lyon was not at all as they liked to see it—a straightforward struggle of the counter-revolutionary rich against a people *un et indivisible*. Part of it was happening within an organized popular movement which had been established long enough to develop alternatives to the Jacobins in terms of leadership and outlook, and which was deeply divided over which direction to take.

The Sectional Movement

Just as the schisms in the clubs were deepening, the sacking of the Club Central presented a more direct challenge to the Municipalité. According to the Jacobins, this rape of the Temple of Liberty was the work of a cross-section of Lyonnais high society and their hirelings: 'de tous les gens comme il faut, dames à pelisse et à grand manteau, muscadins ... de commis de marchands, de clercs de procureurs, de perruquiers, de domestiques, d'hommes riches et de ces gens qui se vendent au plus offrant ... en veste courte, armés de gros batons, de pistolets et de haches, ils annoncent par leur langage que c'étoit d'hommes très instruits.'[75] This was demonology rather than social analysis, but the Jacobins had reason to believe that the propertied classes were beginning to mobilize against them. The violence of 18 February had a clear message. Its target was the body which, by placing municipal power in the hands of the Jacobins and their plebeian allies, had undermined the hegemony of property promised by the Revolution of 1789–91. The *gens comme il faut* now felt sufficiently threatened to counter-attack, and they showed their readiness to use extra-constitutional means of containing their antagonists. Simultaneously, and for the first time, they took up the challenge of the democratic revolution of 1792. If the rights of property were to be secured in the circumstances created since August 1792, they had to accept,

---

[75] Coste MSS 547, 553, deposition by Jullien, 18 Feb. 1793; Lacombe-Saint-Michel to Basire, 20 Feb. 1793 (reporting information given by the Municipalité).

temporarily at least, the political rules devised by the radical democrats who now dominated the Convention. They had to accept that their claim to political power could only be legitimized as an expression of popular sovereignty, and they sought to do so by adapting to their own purposes the theory and practice of sectional permanence which had been developed by the Parisian democrats. In the process they became more politicized and more united.

Despite the ideological justifications which were soon elaborated, the campaign for permanence was essentially a tactical move to weaken the Municipalité's authority. The sectional assemblies could provide a focus of opposition and could claim a political authority ('c'est là qu'un peuple libre émet son vœu'[76]) which the squabbling clubs could not. Sectional permanence was the weapon of men out of power—at least when they felt they had the support of the majority of those likely to attend the *sections*: of the Parisian radicals under the monarchy, of provincial extremists like Dodieu in Lyon and the Club National in Bordeaux[77] in the second half of 1792, and then of moderates in the cities in early 1793.[78] By the same token, those in power quickly rationalized their opposition to permanence. Ignoring the example of the Parisian *sections*, Achard argued that 'il seroit contradictoire aux droits du peuple et aux loix, que le peuple fût en permanence avec ses magistrats'.[79]

Since only the Paris *sections* could legally sit *en permanence*, subterfuges had to be adopted in Lyon to try to evade the laws which limited the functions of sectional assemblies. The first device was to continue the primary assemblies as 'popular assemblies', which were represented as being legally quite distinct from the electoral bodies.[80] This was done on 18 February. According to Jean Gilibert *l'aîné* (a retired *négociant* and brother of the moderate candidate for the mayoralty), the 559 citizens who met as the primary assembly of le Plâtre were simply exercising the right of free speech when, after voting had closed, they moved to another place and became 'popular'. Permanent popular assemblies were formed that night in ten other *sections*, seven of them in the central peninsular

---

[76] AN AA53, d. 1487, no. 29, Copie de la pétition présentée aux commissaires de la Convention nationale envoyés à Lyon. Par les citoyens de la même ville (9 May 1793).

[77] See Forrest, *Society and Politics*, pp. 75–6.

[78] The earliest example of this was in Marseille. See W. Scott, *Terror and Repression in Revolutionary Marseilles* (London, 1973), 70–83.

[79] *CM*, iv. 266 (23 May 1793).

[80] Coste MS 612, proceedings against Jean Gilibert in connection with the troubles of 18–19 Feb. 1793, no. 2, Discours de J. Gilibert l'aîné en assemblée.

area where the moderate clubs were strongest.[81] All of them were ordered to dissolve by the Municipalité. Copies of Jean Gilibert's speech proposing that the permanent assemblies should publish their deliberations were sent to several *sections*.[82] The *sections*' right and duty were to assemble 'pour surveiller la chose publique, ou le corps politique, pendant sa maladie', but, said Gilibert, 'les méchants réunis pour faire le mal voulaient empêcher les bons de s'assembler pour faire le bien'.[83]

The Municipalité was thus faced with two opposition movements, one based on the *sections*, the other on the clubs, and both drawing most of their support from the commercial area of central Lyon. While not identical, the movements had much in common, and Herriot's assertion that the sectional movement and the clubs were at odds is misleading,[84] for some of the moderate *clubistes* quickly threw their weight behind the demands for permanent assemblies.[85] What was worse, there was little the Municipalité could legally do to destroy this opposition. While the District Tribunal was controlled by its sympathizers, this was not true of the Tribunal de Police Correctionnelle (composed of six *juges de paix*) or of the Tribunal Criminel (most of whose members came from outside Lyon).[86] According to Chalier, criminals and conspirators were being allowed to escape by counter-revolutionary judges.[87] The *juges de paix* released most of those accused of crimes related to the February disturbances,[88] and the rest were eventually acquitted by a court in Mâcon to which their cases had been referred by decree of the Convention.[89] With their enemies invading the clubs and the *sections* and entrenched in the National Guard, the Jacobins lived in constant fear: 'Je sais que ma

[81] Ibid., and *CM*, iv. 104 (18 Feb. 1793). The central peninsular *sections* concerned were Saint-Nizier, la Pêcherie, Rue Neuve, le Griffon (both divisions—only one of these was a wealthy area), Place Saint-Pierre, and les Terreaux. The others were: Saint-Vincent, la Juiverie, Place Neuve.

[82] Coste MS 612, proceedings against J. Gilibert, no. 7, interrogation of Gilibert, 27 Feb. 1793.

[83] Ibid., no. 2, Discours ... Proposals for dealing with 'les méchants' by petitioning higher authorities to dismiss the Municipalité were said to have been discussed in le Change, Place Neuve, and other *sections* (AC, I²3, d. 51, unsigned statement, 18 Feb. 1793); Coste MS 610, proceedings against Simon-Jean Adam, *avoué*, for inciting rebellion on 18 Feb. 1793 (no. 2, statement by Adam, 28 Feb. 1793).

[84] E. Herriot, *Lyon n'est plus* (Paris, 1938–40), i. 167.

[85] AC I²4, 45, d. 45, club of La Croisette, 3 Mar. 1973.

[86] On the composition and functions of these bodies, see J. Godechot, *Les Institutions de la France sous la Révolution et l'Empire*, 2nd edn. (Paris, 1968), 149–52.

[87] Coste MS 551, letter of Chalier, 18 Feb. 1793.

[88] Ibid. 552, minutes of the District Tribunal of Lyon, fo. 5, 20 Feb. 1793.

[89] See *CM*, iv. 198 (14 Apr. 1793); *Journal de Lyon*, 12 May 1793, pp. 327–8.

tête est à prix,' Hidins warned the *représentants en mission* at Lyon in March, 'ainsi que celles de Chalier, Gaillard et le vôtre.'[90] Chalier felt so threatened by the lawyers with whom he had to deal as president of the District Tribunal that he suspended the court's sittings: 'la bazoche que je ne perd pas de vu dans ses dédales a juré de m'exterminer'.[91] The need for extraordinary institutions to preserve the Revolution seemed self-evident, and after twice being requested to do so by the Jacobins, the Municipalité petitioned the Convention for a Revolutionary Tribunal, for which the Jacobin Club was already preparing by inviting its affiliated clubs to nominate judges.[92] C.-F. Dubost, president of the club of La Croisette, denounced the project to the moderate *député* Chasset, who was instrumental in obtaining the decree of 15 May which forbade the establishment of Revolutionary Tribunals unless specifically authorized by the Convention.[93]

CHARACTERISTICS OF LYONNAIS JACOBINISM

The *sans-culottes* of the Lepeletier Club urged defiance, declaring 'que les lois étant insuffisantes il était de leur sagesse d'établir le tribunal, malgré la Convention'.[94] Judges were elected by certain Jacobin sectional clubs, and on 9 May they assembled on the Place Bellecour for a patriotic feast, probably to inaugurate the tribunal. But all they achieved, apart from drinking a lot of wine (two bottles per man according to a hostile source), was to demolish an obelisk of feudal appearance.[95] The Jacobin

[90] Coste MS 582, undated. See also *CM*, iv. 132 (9 Mar. 1793); Coste MS 547.

[91] Coste MS 547, Chalier to the Committee of General Security, 19 Feb. 1793. See also ibid. 549, minutes of the District Tribunal of Lyon, 19 Feb. 1793.

[92] *CM*, iv. 185, 197, 239 (7, 13 Apr., 6 May 1793); AD 31L24, Jacobin Club to club of Place Saint-Pierre, 3 May 1793.

[93] *Moniteur*, xv. 392; AC I²20, d. 229, Dubost to Chasset, 6 May 1793; CM, iv. 259 (18 May 1793). S. Charléty confused this Dubost with J.-F. Dubost, president of the Département of Rhône-et-Loire in mid-May. C.-F. was a retired *caladois* merchant, aged 61; J.-F., aged 38, a broker, born in Lyon. Both lived in the Rue Grenette, at nos. 99 and 111 (S. Charléty, 'La Journée du 29 mai 1793 à Lyon', *La Révolution française*, 39 5 (Nov. 1900), 411; AD 41L12, fo. 23, Commission of Popular Justice, interrogation of J.-F. Dubost, 8 brumaire, an II; AC I²20, d. 230, interrogation of C.-F. Dubost, Committee of Public Safety of Lyon, 17 May 1793.

[94] AC I²4, d. 45, club of La Croisette, 8 May 1793, reporting their rival club's response to a deputation protesting at the preparations for a Revolutionary Tribunal.

[95] On the attempts to organize the Tribunal, see *Journal de Lyon*, 7 May 1793, p. 303; 9 May 1793, p. 310; AD 34L1, club of Rue Belle-Cordière, 4 May 1793; 36L7, interrogation of Gesse by Chevassu, *juge de paix*, 9 June 1793; Fromageot, *négociant*, letter of 10 May 1793, cited in Herriot, *Lyon n'est plus*, i. 326.

authorities did not take any steps to carry things further and the jurors do not seem to have met again. This little fiasco is significant as a manifestation of the popular 'federalist' impulses which were conspicuously neglected by the authorities at Lyon. Unlike their counterparts at Marseille, they were not prepared to press on with unauthorized revolutionary measures, no matter how much the local political situation and their *sans-culotte* supporters might seem to demand them. On the contrary, they kept to the line dictated by the political circumstances of the Montagnards, whose relations with the Plain were touchy in early May and threatened to get touchier still if the rash of unauthorized Jacobin-controlled tribunals in the provinces freshened memories of the September massacres and gave flesh to the spectre of popular anarchy which the Girondins were trying to exploit. It was typical of the Municipalité that when Robespierre attacked its emissary Théophile Leclerc for his excessively bloodthirsty language, Leclerc was stripped of his powers and replaced.[96]

Clearly, Richard Cobb's account of the Lyonnais Jacobin resistance to Parisian dominance in the year II should not be read back into early 1793[97] when their attitude to Parisian direction was quite compliant. They accepted the right of the Montagne and the *société mère* to formulate policy, and the necessity to follow it. This not only limited their flexibility, but made it impossible for them to play the roles they had assigned themselves in 1792—spokesmen of the *sans-culottes* and interpreters of the popular will. De Francesco makes the point in terms of the familiar antithesis between popular revolutionary spontaneity and Jacobin authoritarianism.[98] The Jacobins had ridden a wave of protest to municipal power, but they now sought to restrain, control, and direct it to Montagnard political ends. Having failed to realize popular hopes in the matter of *subsistances,* they were now trying to defer the implementation of the popular justice which they had been advocating since August 1792 until the situation in Paris was favourable.

The orthodoxy of the Lyonnais Jacobins needs emphasis in another context. Beginning with the third volume of Jaurès's *Histoire socialiste,* there have been repeated suggestions that they were proto-socialists or, at the least, super-*enragés* in social policy. Jaurès himself seems to have

---

[96] R. B. Rose, *The Enragés: Socialists of the French Revolution* (Melbourne, 1965), 51–2.
[97] Cobb, *Les Armées révolutionnaires,* ii. 788–95.
[98] See De Francesco, 'Montagnardi e sanculotti', pp. 594–626. I owe much to discussions with A. De Francesco, as well as to the articles cited here, for clarifying and strengthening my understanding of Lyonnais Jacobinism.

considered that the bitterness of the social struggle in Lyon and the intransigence of the Jacobins' advocacy of the poor against the rich produced a more 'advanced' social programme in Lyon than in Paris. In the 1930s Herriot endorsed this view, but his *Lyon n'est plus* failed to convince Georges Lefebvre that the Lyonnais had transcended the limitations of Jacobin social thinking.[99] More recently Takashi Koi has revived the Jaurès view, and, in the process, has renamed the Lyonnais Jacobins 'les Chaliers', whom he apparently regards as having been genuine mouthpieces of the *sans-culottes* and advocates of a 'social war' against the rich.[100]

It is true that, mainly before their accession to municipal power, the Jacobins foreshadowed a social revolution founded on virtue, a time when 'le simple, le vertueux cultivateur sera au-dessus de l'égoïste riche ou opulent, le règne de l'égalité se répandra sur toutes les sphères terrestres'. (But the author of this, Achard, proceeded to make the customary bourgeois qualifications of equality: 'que les vertus et les talens soient seuls récompensés, honorés'.[101]) It is true that Chalier put more emphasis than Robespierre did on the need for popular initiatives in defence of the Revolution,[102] and it seems to be true, too, that for a time 'Lyonnais working men loved him as the man who shared their sufferings, felt their rage, lent to their passions his bizarre but ardent voice'.[103] It is beyond question that he and the more violent of his followers used language against the rich—enemies simultaneously of the Revolution and the poor, the *secte mercantile contre-révolutionnaire*—which anticipates the language of class struggle. But Lefebvre's scepticism still seems justified. Like the *sans-culottes*, Chalier probably wanted, as Riffaterre suggests, 'une certaine égalite des biens'.[104] Yet the only evidence linking him with any more fundamental questioning of property rights than that of the *sans-culottes* consists of assertions by his enemies (who accused him of preaching the agrarian law and the redistribution of property), the pleas of his

[99] Herriot, *Lyon n'est plus*, i. 279, citing J. Jaurès, *Histoire socialiste: La Convention* (Paris, 1901), 1070; G. Lefebvre, review of E. Herriot, *Lyon n'est plus*, *AHRF*, 18 (1946), 78.

[100] See T. Koi, 'Les "Chaliers"', *passim*. There is some useful criticism of Koi's work in De Francesco, 'Le Quartier lyonnais de la Croisette', pp. 45–7.

[101] Coste MS 534, 'Discours prononcé au Comité central le 27 août l'an 1er de la République française par devant MM. les commissaires de la Convention nationale' (Achard).

[102] See Koi, 'Les "Chaliers"', pp. 177–8.

[103] M. Wahl, 'Joseph Chalier: Étude sur la Révolution française a Lyon', *Revue historique*, 34 (1887), 13–14.

[104] See Riffaterre, *Le Mouvement anti-jacobin et anti-parisien à Lyon*, i. 309 n. 3, 349.

official defender, Moulin, in July 1793 (who sought to deflect accusations that Chalier was an ambitious demagogue by depicting him as an over-enthusiastic humanitarian), and the ritual eulogies of 'le patron des pauvres' in the year II, by which time he had become a revolutionary martyr:

> Voulant en tout la Sainte Egalité
> Au riche il fit toujours la guerre ...

There were people in Lyon with radical social views, like a certain Bonafous who suggested to Roland, of all people, a *maximum des fortunes* (but a high *maximum*, prohibiting businesses with a capital of over 500,000 *livres*), and François-Joseph L'Ange, who proposed in his *Remède à tout* a kind of state socialism organised around a network of *greniers d'abondance*.[105] But these cannot be linked with the Jacobins—indeed, L'Ange was a pronounced anti-Jacobin and was executed for it.

It is sometimes difficult to find sufficient consistency in the Jacobins' thinking to speak of them as having a social policy at all. For instance, they tended to regard charity with contempt, while Rolandins like Nivi-ère-Chol thought a rational generosity would be sufficient to palliate poverty until the natural justice and harmony of the *laissez-faire* system abolished it forever.[106] The Rolandins had supported the formation of Fraternal Societies in late 1792, while for the Jacobin Dodieu such institutions were tools used by the merchant aristocracy to appease popular anger.[107] Late in December 1792 the Jacobin Municipalité tried to limit the Fraternal Societies' activities, and replaced the word 'Charité' on the façade of the l'Hôtel-Dieu with 'Fraternité'.[108] But there was little more to this than gestures. Laussel adopted a soldier's son to save him from the orphanages, 'ces institutions ... infectées par leur nature des vices de l'ancien régime',[109] but the Municipalité continued to support charities such as the *Œuvre de la Marmite*, channelled funds though the Fraternal Societies, and never revoked the assent it gave to their plan for a cotton-mill to occupy the workless.[110] If the Municipalité or its sup-

---

[105] See F. Rude, 'Du nouveau sur le socialisme de L'Ange: La Découverte du "Remède à tout" ', *Cahiers d'histoire*, 15 (1970), 223–42, *passim*.

[106] See Nivière-Chol's inaugural address, *CM*, iv. 3 (5 Dec. 1792); L. Vitet, F.-A. Boissy d'Anglas, C.-J.-M. Alquier, 'Les Députés et commissaires de la Convention nationale aux citoyens de Lyon' (Lyon, 1792) (proposing workshops funded by charitable subscriptions to relieve unemployment):

[107] M. Dodieu, *Mémoire à consulter* (Lyon, 1792), 1.

[108] *CM*, iv. 41, 74, 77 (24 Dec. 1792, 20, 24 Jan. 1793).

[109] Ibid. 95 (9 Feb. 1793).

[110] Ibid. 16–17, 59, 86 (12 Dec. 1792, 4 Jan., 4 Feb. 1793).

porters had theoretical objections to charity, they were overcome by the realities of politics and administration in a city beset by unemployment and want.

There was more consistent enthusiasm for taxes on the rich, but not, apparently, with the aim of introducing any permanent social changes, for the taxes were to operate on an *ad hoc* basis rather than permanently.[111] As with many Jacobin proposals against wealth, it is difficult to disentangle punitive political aims from redistributive social ones. But it is somewhat misleading to state that for the Jacobins 'les propriétaires sont toujours aristocrates'.[112] Several of them were rich. ('[Le] citoyen Bertrand a des culottes', the *Journal de Lyon* observed, 'sans celles qu'il attend encore de son père.'[113]) They believed that the Lyonnais merchant classes and their satellites were crypto-royalists: 'Nos marchands, négociants, agents de change sont toujours les mêmes: des âmes de boue, des hommes corrompus regrettant leurs fers et les abus qui les saturoient ...'.[114] But their target was not so much wealth as its abuse by those who used it to exploit the people and strangle the Revolution. This is clear from the Municipalité's declaration in favour of the *maximum*—a diatribe not against the wealthy in general, but against 'Le vorace accapareur, l'agioteur infernal, l'avare toujours tremblant, le propriétaire avide, le négociant égoïste et especulant sans cesse ...'.[115] This was not far from the moral economy of the *sans-culottes* expressed by Imberton of la Grande-Côte in a petition to the *représentants* in March: 'la loi ordonne de respecter les propriétés, elle est juste mais la fortune acquise par le mensonge, l'agiotage, la friponnerie, le vol, le brigandage n'est pas une propriété, la confisquant au profit de la nation seroit un acte de justice.'[116] Laussel's contrast between 'le coffre inutile de l'avare' and 'le salaire sacré du manœuvrier', to which Riffaterre appears to have attached great significance,[117] was merely question-begging rhetoric, not part of a campaign against excessive wealth. Bonafous and the Parisian *sans-culottes* came closer to this by indicating that controls on wealth should be applied at some level. The Lyonnais Jacobins of early 1793 went no further than vague ethical statements about illicit riches, and there is no trace of an

[111] See below, 'Attempted Rescue: the Missions of Spring 1793'.
[112] Riffaterre, *Le Mouvement anti-jacobin et anti-parisien à Lyon*, i. 335.
[113] *Journal de Lyon*, 1 May 1793, p. 283.
[114] Coste MS 606, Noël, Bertrand, Gravier, and Laussel to the Convention, 9 Feb. 1793.
[115] *CM*, iv. 156 (25 Mar. 1793).
[116] Coste MS 601.
[117] Riffaterre, *Le Mouvement anti-jacobin et anti-parisien à Lyon*, i. 337, citing *CM*, iv. 4 (5 Dec. 1792).

attempt by them to indicate how deserved and ill-gotten gains could be distinguished from one another.

There can be no doubting the Jacobins' deep suspicion of the politics of the rich. They believed that the rich had engineered Nivière-Chol's election.[118] They suspected that there were links between Roland's 'cercle social' and 'les Cercles Lyonnais aristocrates des Terreaux et de Bellecour' where 'se fabriquoient jadis les Échevins'. But the last remark suggests that there is no need to seek a class struggle to explain the Lyonnais Jacobins' belief in a plot to establish 'l'aristocratie des Riches'.[119] They did not fear a new kind of *bourgeois* class rule, but the restoration by counter-revolution of something like the old noble oligarchy.

Such attitudes largely explain their desire to tax the trouble-makers of 18 February[120] (the money would be used to meet the cost of billeting volunteers for the army) and 'les gros propriétaires et capitalistes' (to support the families of *défenseurs de la patrie* or to pay for the construction of fighting ships).[121] These were primarily responses to the military and political crisis, not measures of social reform. The only project apparently designed to redistribute wealth was a tax on the rich to finance the indemnity paid to bakers, but again it was a temporary measure to meet the problems created by high food prices,[122] and in any case the same plan had been suggested to the *députés* of Rhône-et-Loire several weeks earlier by the moderates Nivière-Chol and van Risamburgh.[123] The Jacobins may have looked on the wealthy with greater suspicion than the moderates did; they may also have been readier to contemplate drastic emergency measures against them. But to see Jacobin talk of sacrificing 'les biens des "aristocrats" aux besoins des pauvres' as evidence of 'conceptions sociales bien différentes'[124] to the moderates, is to confuse political aims with social ones.[125]

[118] *CM*, iv. 96 (9 Feb. 1793).

[119] Coste MS 578, Mémoire présenté aux citoyens députés commissaires de la Convention nationale à Lyon (by the Municipalité, [March, 1793]).

[120] *CM*, iv. 116 (20 Feb. 1793).

[121] AD 2L10, fo. 3, District of Lyon-Ville, minutes of 9 Apr. (suggesting a tax on *rentes* above 2,000 livres a year and on rich merchants); 34L1, club of Rue Belle-Cordière, 17 Mar. 1793.

[122] *CM*, iv. 101 (15 Feb. 1793).

[123] AN AFII43, plaq. 343, no. 19, letter of 5 Jan. 1793.

[124] Riffaterre, *Le Mouvement anti-jacobin et anti-parisien à Lyon*, i. 348–9.

[125] Riffaterre makes the error of using proposals (e.g. for 'manufactures nationales') that were made after the siege of Lyon to support his view of the Jacobins' earlier ideas. By then, circumstances had drastically changed: Lyon was a proscribed city, many of its merchants and manufacturers had been imprisoned or killed, and its commerce was in ruins (ibid. i. 343–7).

Only with their plans for controlling grain prices did the Lyonnais extremists produce a clear response to the social unrest of the previous six years. As Riffaterre observes, this was to be no temporary expedient, but a permanent solution to the problem of want and a step towards true equality.[126] Here they almost certainly intended a fundamental break with the *laissez-faire* system, and in the area of *subsistances* at least, they attempted to conceive measures to meet the combined problems of shortage, inflation, and unemployment. But this does not put them ahead of their time, or suggest that they were particularly sensitive to Lyon's peculiar social problems, such as those of the silk-workers, whose aims they supported but did nothing effective to achieve.[127] They were at pains to show that price control was not an attack on private property in general, but an attempt to reconcile it with *le droit à l'existence*: 'Le blé étant une partie inhérente à l'existance de l'espèce humaine, le cultivateur qui la récolte n'est que le fermier de tous, et tout ce qui excède sa propriété, c'est-à-dire les subsistances qui assurent son existence, est un dépôt sacré qui appartient à tous les individus en lui accordant une juste et préalable indemnité, pour le prix de ses sueurs ...'.[128] In making this one clear exception to the sanctity of private property they spoke on behalf of small consumers and as members of a community whose size and situation brought problems of food supply which the policy of free trade in grain had proved quite incapable of meeting. But while they had a programme of undoubted popular appeal here, they had no means of implementing it. If it had come earlier, the decree of the *maximum* (4 May) might have done something to prevent the disillusionment caused by the Jacobins' inability to effect the price controls which they had been advocating since August 1792. As it was, their five months in municipal office were barren of both achievement and coherent policies in social and economic areas.

ATTEMPTED RESCUE: THE MISSIONS OF SPRING 1793

It was the same with their political programme, which was clear enough—the elimination of moderates and aristocrats—but depended for its implementation and legitimization on the Convention's acquiescence and the collaboration of the *représentants en mission*. Here at least the prospects began to look brighter in the early spring, as the *commissaires* from Paris

---

[126] Ibid. i. 340–1. See *CM*, iv. 153–5 (25 Mar. 1793).
[127] *CM*, iv. 354 (25 Mar. 1793). On this point, see Edmonds, 'A Study in Popular Anti-Jacobinism', pp. 239–40.
[128] *CM*, iv. 354 (25 Mar. 1793).

began laying the foundations for what was to become the revolutionary government of France in the year II. Armed with enormous prestige as *représentants du peuple souverain* and with very wide powers, most of the *commissaires* were Montagnards prepared to take whatever steps were necessary to entrench advanced *patriotes* in the provinces. They carried the parliamentary war against the Girondins into the *départements* where the Girondins' support was believed to lie, purging the administrators and leaving them in ideologically pure hands.

But a fundamental difficulty arose here. Jacobinism was essentially a composite of responses to events in Paris. You became a bona fide Jacobin by jumping the right way in a series of national crises. But the test did not work well in the provinces, where adherence to Parisian initiatives might be nothing more than prudent conformity. Who knew what might lurk behind the mask of provincial patriotism? In these circumstances, *patriotes* with Parisian credentials, like Chalier and Achard, esteemed by Robespierre, and Gaillard, whose broken thigh from 10 August was suitable accreditation, were particularly precious—still more so if they were in a city notorious for royalism and mercantile insouciance. Since Jacobinism placed a high priority on conformity, it was natural for the Montagnards to use ideological purity as the criterion for deciding whom to back in Lyonnais politics. But because the immediate aim of Jacobin policy was war on the people's enemies, endorsing the ideologically pure meant licensing them to eradicate their opponents. In Lyon these were becoming very numerous by the spring of 1793.

Basire, Rovère, and Legendre, the first *commissaires* despatched to Lyon in 1793, arrived about 3 March. Their mission was decreed on 26 February and was to restore order using 'all the measures of general security' they thought necessary.[129] Charléty is probably right to suggest that their main intention was to prop up the Jacobins,[130] who were certainly in need of help at the beginning of March. The Municipalité felt so insecure that on 25 February it had requested 100 regular troops and a cavalry regiment to maintain order during the elections, and kept them in the city until 12 March. Its sense of dependency on the Montagne is patently obvious. It sought help from the *Députés* Saliceti, Delcher, and Lacombe-Saint-Michel who were passing through Lyon, but they refused as their missions were not concerned with Lyon. Fillion and

---

[129] '*CM*,' iv. 129, 131 (1, 3 Mar. 1793).
[130] Charléty, 'La Journée du 29 mai', p. 393.

Gravier were sent to address the Convention: 'y réclamer la vengeance des lois outragées'.[131]

The appearance of Basire and his colleagues coincided with Gilibert's resignation (indeed, it was Basire who brought the resignation letter to the General Council), and was soon followed by Bertrand's election. On the day of that election the *commissaires* made their attitude towards the sectional movement clear by abruptly rejecting a petition for the convocation of the primary assemblies which had been signed by 559 'respectable citizens' on 9 March.[132] On 22 March, after some prodding, the *commissaires* authorized the payment of the municipal officers which had been prevented by the Département.[133] Next, on 9 March, they ordered the arrest of J.-L. Fain, acting editor of the *Journal de Lyon* which had become increasingly anti-Jacobin since he had taken it over in February.[134] The last in this series of exceptional measures was the creation, at Basire's suggestion, of a Committee of Public Safety, funded by the Département and composed of Jacobins from the District of Lyon-Ville, the Département, and the Municipalité.[135] Its powers were undefined, but they included the arrest of suspects—at least 143 of them by 29 May.[136]

The *commissaires'* activities aroused great resentment; they listened to the lies of the Jacobins, said the *Journal de Lyon*, but ignored the *sections*.[137] They brushed aside complaints of lack of due notice for the mayoral elections of 9 March, and when confronted with evidence that Gilibert's resignation had been obtained under duress, Basire replied that 'son corps était enchaîné, mais que sa volonté était libre'.[138] Their *sans-culotte* bodyguard, Rocher, caused particular offence: 'Vous trois se donnent les airs d'avoir un scélérat de moustafa avec ses moustaches et son air assassin ce coup-tête vous suit comme licteur oui sans doute

---

[131] *CM*, iv. 107, 120, 131, 141 (18, 25 Feb., 3, 4 Mar. 1793).

[132] Coste MS 587, Pétition aux citoyens législateurs et commissaires . . . ce 9 mars 1793. On the *commissaires'* behaviour, see Genet-Bronze, Pelzin, and Badger, *Rapport et pétition*, p. 13; *Journal de Lyon*, 12 Mar. 1793, p. 210; *Pétition adressée aux citoyens législateurs . . . avec la réponse des commissaires en députation auprès d'aux* (n.p., n.d.).

[133] *CM*, iv. 133, 139, 148, 150 (3, 11, 19, 22 Mar. 1793).

[134] AN AA53, d. 1487, no. 31, Carrier, journalist (and editor of the *Journal de Lyon*), to the president of the Convention, 20 Apr. 1793; AD 42L12, fo. 1, interrogation of J.-L. Fain, 4 brumaire, an II.

[135] District: Thonion, Macabéo; Département: Achard, Maillan; Municipalité: Roch, Noël, Richard (*CM*, iv. 188, 194 (8, 12 Apr. 1793).

[136] AC I²3, d. 38.

[137] *Journal de Lyon*, 12 Mar. 1793, pp. 211–12.

[138] Ibid. 210.

comme chez les Romains . . .'.[139] Even Chépy, an agent of the Ministry of Foreign Affairs who had no sympathy for the Lyonnais moderates, reported that Rocher's conduct had been 'peu mésurée, quoique patriote'.[140] More than thirty years later, the memory of this 'spadassin', of 'la *sauvagerie* de ses moustaches', his 'costume grotesque', huge sabre, and multiple pistols still aroused the fury of the abbé Guillon de Montléon.[141]

These visitations from Paris allowed the anti-Jacobins to play on the belief that Lyon was being systematically misrepresented. Tallien's report on the events of 18 and 19 February, delivered to the Convention on the 25th, had simply put the case for the Municipalité,[142] and was based upon the assumptions which the *patriotes* had routinely made about Lyon since 1790. ('Vous savez, citoyens, que la ville de Lyon à toujours été le refuge des contre-révolutionnaires.') Tallien proceeded to enumerate various reasons for mistrusting the second city—its size, its distance from Paris (the fount of patriotism), its proximity to the frontiers (convenient for foreign agitators), its reputation as a haven for priests and *ci-devants*. The events of 18 and 19 February had struck 'une étincelle contre-révolutionnaire' which might easily ignite insurrection elsewhere.[143] Tallien's account of Lyon was denounced as calumny by the Municipalité's opponents, and the decree which followed it as 'le terrible décret d'incivisme et de réprobation contre une ville entière'. 'On nous peindra en état de contre-révolution. Le préjugé est contre nous.'[144] That the Montagnards had doubts about Lyon is quite understandable. But their urge to denounce conspiracy made the path from doubt to certainty a short one where signs of counter-revolution were perceived. The resulting denunciations were good integrative politics in Paris, but they also helped to unite the disparate forces of Lyonnais anti-Jacobinism.

With its actions formally approved by the Convention's decree of 25 February, and with the public endorsement of the *commissaires*, the Municipalité's political position in mid-April seemed stronger than at any time since its election. But in fact, when the *commissaires* left on 20 April nothing had been done to overcome its fundamental weaknesses.

---

[139] Coste MS 596, anonymous letter to Legendre [March, 1793].

[140] Quoted by Herriot, *Lyon n'est plus*, i. 337.

[141] Guillon de Montléon, *Mémoires*, i. 203.

[142] Tallien's sole source was the Municipalité's account of developments in Lyon since Dec. 1792 (Tallien, *Rapport et Projet*, p. 4).

[143] Ibid. 7.

[144] *Journal de Lyon*, 3 Mar. 1793, p. 186; 12 Mar. 1793, pp. 211–12.

And it had been damaged by the revelation that Laussel, soon after denouncing his *substitut* Bertholon for negligently releasing persons arrested on 18 and 19 February, had himself been selling residence certificates to suspected *émigrés* and releasing prisoners in return for substantial bribes. The *commissaires* arrested and destituted him on 13 March and sent him before the Revolutionary Tribunal of Paris.[145] It was easy for the *Journal de Lyon* to insinuate that several municipal officers had been involved in Laussel's dealings.[146]

But more damaging still was the Jacobins' increasingly obvious isolation. 'L'oligarchie municipale' and its adherents, wrote Fain, had set themselves above the city and apart from it. Chalier, Laussel, and Gaillard, he maintained, had personally encouraged the calumny against Lyon. Fain turned the Jacobin version of Lyonnais politics on its head, so that the pure *patriotes* to whom the Montagnards had committed themselves became not saviours but betrayers. And curiously, within their different framework of values, the Jacobins conceded the point. Aliens in a world of mercantile egoism and incomprehensible popular apathy, they saw themselves as 'le petit nombre de patriotes purs et incorruptibles que le vent de la Révolution a jetté [*sic*] par une espèce de miracle au milieu de cette Sodome'. They were missionaries beset by the 'égoïsme et insouciance' of 'cette ville impure'.[147] Mme Roland had been saying much the same thing in 1790, but the conviction had been reinforced since then by hard political experience, and the bitterness deepened by Lyon's refusal to be woven into the seamless cloth of revolutionary conformity. It was unfortunate for the Lyonnais that the local Jacobins should be suffering their bitter disillusionment with the people they aspired to lead just when the national government was falling into the hands of men who were all too ready to believe diagnoses of anti-Jacobinism in terms of the corruption and selfishness of the big provincial cities. It was also unfortunate for Lyon that the mobilization of the anti-Jacobins provided all the evidence the Montagnards needed to justify intervention in its affairs.

The Jacobins seem by now to have become convinced that only drastic intervention from Paris could save Lyon for the Revolution. At the very

---

[145] *CM*, iv. 142, 155 (14, 15 Mar. 1793); *Actes*, ii. 1386–8, letter of the *commissaires* at Lyon, 17 Mar. 1793; *Journal de Lyon*, 15 Mar. 1793, p. 223.

[146] *Journal de Lyon*, 15 Mar. 1793, p. 224.

[147] Coste MS 578, Mémoire présenté aux citoyens députés commissaires de la Convention nationale à Lyon, [March, 1793]; MS 600, Achard and Gaillard to the *commissaires*, 17 Mar. 1793.

least they wanted a purge of the higher administrations—preferably a suspension of them all, as well as of all the judicial bodies other than the District Tribunal. The grenadiers of the National Guard should be suppressed, and a special tax imposed on the rich for the benefit of the war effort. Chalier thought the measures that had been taken so far by Basire, Rovère, and Legendre were totally inadequate: 'Oh mon cher Legendre, qu'avez vous fait? Vous avez servi nos ennemis d'un plat de leur façon . . . pas une seule vaste mesure n'a encore été prise . . . Réveillez-vous, sortez de votre léthargie, il en est temps . . . je ne vais pas vous voir parce que je viens d'être poursuivi par deux soldats sabre en main, en face de vos appartements.'[148] The *patriotes* began to fear that the *commissaires* had been bought by plutocrats 'tels que Finguerlin et autres'.[149] Chalier denounced their moderation to the Paris Jacobins, and according to the *Journal de Lyon* they were reprimanded for it by Robespierre *jeune*.[150]

Unexpectedly, the Jacobins' position was strengthened by the arrival of four new *commissaires* charged with responsibility for the Armée des Alpes and hence with the security of Lyon's military establishments (the Arsenal, a military hospital, the stores, and a commissariat) which were vital to the army's supply system.[151] Nioche, Gauthier, Albitte, and Dubois-Crancé arrived on 10 May.[152] To Dubois-Crancé in particular, deeply concerned with military problems, Lyon was a strategic danger: 'Je connaissais cette ville pour un foyer continuel de l'aristocratie; je sentais que de sa tranquillité dependait le sort des frontières.'[153] Like their predecessors, all four *conventionnels* saw Lyonnais politics in the crudest terms. The Municipalité alone was *patriote* and must be given the means of intimidating its enemies. So they threw their weight behind a Jacobin proposal for a Revolutionary Army which, following the lead of the Département of l'Hérault, a joint session of the three local authorities had approved on 9 April. On the 26th the Municipalité announced a project for a corps of 4,050 men, but failed to specify its objectives precisely or to indicate by whom it would be controlled. In any case, it could not be financed without funds from the Convention which would

---

[148] Letter of 9 Mar., quoted in Charléty, 'La Journée du 29 mai', p. 397.

[149] Coste MS 582, Hidins to the *commissaires*, [March, 1793].

[150] *Journal de Lyon*, 1 May 1793, pp. 281–2.

[151] *Actes*, iv. 424, Dubois-Crancé and Albitte to the Committee of Public Safety (henceforward CPS), 2 June 1793.

[152] *Journal de Lyon*, 12 May 1793, p. 322.

[153] E.-L.-A. Dubois-Crancé, *Discours sur le siège de Lyon* (Paris, [an II]). See also *Actes*, iv. 421, Dubois-Crancé and Albitte to the Convention, 2 June 1793.

have to be channelled through the Département.[154] It was therefore easy for the Département to bypass the Municipalité with its own proposal, very like that of l'Hérault which already had the Convention's approval. This was to be funded by a tax on the rich levied by the Département, and the force of 5,000 men was to be controlled by the Département under the general supervision of the Executive Council in Paris.[155]

The *commissaires* attended a joint session on 14 May which transformed the situation. There were to be 6,400 men instead of 5,000, and the tax was to raise 6 million *livres* instead of 5; instead of being levied throughout the *département*, both men and taxes were to come from the *district* of Lyon-Ville exclusively. The soldiers were to be conscripted by the *Comités de surveillance* and the Committee of Public Safety of Rhône-et-Loire; and the first two battalions (1,500 men) were to be sent to the Vendée while the rest stayed in Lyon. The same authorities would decide who would pay the tax, and how much, and payment had to be made within twenty-four hours. They would also disarm those whom they considered unfit for service in the National Guard and give the arms thus acquired to the revolutionary force, which would be controlled jointly by the *commissaires* and the Committee of Public Safety.[156] Albitte and Dubois-Crancé accepted joint responsibility for the measures and were the first to sign the minutes.[157] In the interests of the war effort, they had licensed the Lyonnais Jacobins to repress their opponents by force and made it clear that they regarded the latter as *ipso facto* enemies of the Convention. This meant that, in Lyon, opposition to the local Jacobins and opposition to the Montagne became one and the same thing. By equating local conflicts with national ones, the Montagnard *commissaires* defined the anti-Jacobin movement in Lyon as subversive, and gave all those involved in it reason to fear a Montagnard triumph in the Convention.

ANTI-JACOBINISM IN THE *SECTIONS*

A combination of Parisian and local developments prevented the Jacobins from exploiting the opportunities provided by the *commissaires*.

[154] *CM*, iv. 192, 218 (10, 26 Apr. 1793).

[155] *Département*, ii. 266–8 (3 May 1793).

[156] *CM*, iv. 250–3 (14 May 1793).

[157] *Actes*, iv. 421–2. Dubois-Crancé and Albitte to the Convention, 2 June 1793. They later denied having presided over the assembly or dictating measures to it, but admitted making some 'propositions que l'arrêté renferme'. They claimed that the decisions were all conditional on the Convention's approval, but this is not mentioned in the minutes (see *Actes*, iv. 459–60, Dubois-Crancé and Albitte to CPS, 5 June 1793).

Paradoxically, the greatest difficulties arose from the law of 21 March which created *Comités de surveillance* to control the activities of aliens. This was a measure proposed by the Montagne (although it won the support of some moderates, probably because of the deteriorating military situation),[158] and like many such measures its benefits in Paris were counterbalanced by severe disadvantages in the provinces. In cities such as Marseille and Lyon it played into the hands of a developing anti-Jacobin sectional movement whose adherents argued that by empowering the sectional assemblies to supervise the work of the committees, article 11 of the decree authorized the former to meet regularly, if not *en permanence*.[159] Foreseeing this danger, the Municipalité set up Revolutionary Committees in each *section*, specified municipal officers and *notables* to preside over them, and gave them the functions prescribed by the decree. But the decree had made the committees elective, and on 10 May the Département forced the Municipalité to arrange elections for the 19th.[160] The sectional movement had been dormant since the meeting which drew up the petition of 9 March, apart from a petition delivered to the Convention on 15 April reiterating the demand for permanence.[161] But opposition to the Jacobins had been kept alive in the moderate clubs,[162] which were operating in more than half of the *sections* by the end of the first week in May. La Croisette became more active during the next week, sending deputations to the various authorities of Lyon and to the other *districts* of the *département*.[163] It invoked the example of Marseille (where the *sections* had already destroyed the clubs and the Jacobin Municipalité) while endorsing only legal methods of protest.[164]

Behind these tactics lay the awareness that events in Lyon would turn on events in Paris. On 10 March an attempt to expel the Girondins from the Convention had failed miserably, but after the desertion of Dumouriez on 5 April, support for a purge grew rapidly in the *sans-culotte sections*

---

[158] See M. J. Sydenham, *The Girondins* (London, 1961), 159.

[159] *Moniteur*, xv. 751, 762.

[160] *CM*, iv. 173, 175, 245 (29–30 Mar. 1793).

[161] Genet-Bronze, Pelzin, and Badger, *Rapport et Pétition*.

[162] Affiliates of La Croisette: Place Neuve, La Pêcherie, Saint-Georges, Le Gourguillon, Le Change, Rue Buisson. Corresponding clubs: Rue Thomassin, Rue Terraille, Port du Temple, La Fédération (Bellecour), Les Terreaux, La Grande-Côte, Le Plâtre, Port Saint-Paul, Rue Rupin (see AC I²4, 45, club of La Croisette, 5–7 May 1793).

[163] Ibid. 8, 10, 12, 14 May 1793; *Département*, ii. 275 (8 May 1793).

[164] AC I²4, 45, club of La Croisette, 10–14 May 1793, and d. 46, La Société populaire de la Croisette à tous ses concitoyens (copy signed by Achard).

of the capital. The Lyonnais Municipalité quickly endorsed the campaign.[165] On 10 May, when 'guerre aux anarchistes' joined 'guerre aux tyrans' in La Croisette's *profession de foi*, 'respect à la représentation nationale' was added to 'respect aux lois et aux autorités constitués'.[166] As the denunciation to Chasset of the project for a Revolutionary Tribunal indicates, the club still held hopes that intervention from Paris might save the situation for the moderates. But late in the day on which the *commissaires* approved the new Revolutionary Army, the club of La Croisette was raided by members of the Committee of Public Safety of Rhône-et-Loire, and its president and secretary were arrested 'pour mesure de salut public'.[167] It does not appear to have met again.

Despite the reverses of mid-May, the Municipalité's opponents were still in a strong position. The Girondins were counter-attacking both in the Convention and in the *sections* of Paris, and the decree of 15 May showed that they could still offer valuable aid to the Lyonnais moderates, for it not only forbade the Revolutionary Tribunal, but placed the operations of the proposed Revolutionary Army under the joint direction of the three local authorities so long as it remained inside the *département* of Rhône-et-Loire. Outside the *département*, it would be under the orders of *représentants en mission* or the Provisional Executive Council.[168] So the local Committee of Public Safety could no longer count on full control of the force. This may explain why so little appears to have been done to organize it. Requisitions for the payment of the special tax and for compulsory service were sent out, but there appear to have been few enrolments.[169] Once again, the benefit conferred on the Jacobins by the intervention of the *commissaires* proved less than anticipated.

Another weakness of the Municipalité was the National Guard. Its officer corps had not been renewed since July 1792, when candidates distrusted by the *patriotes* had been elected to most of the vacant posi-

---

[165] On the Parisian situation, see Rose, *The Enragés*, p. 20; A. Goodwin, *The French Revolution*, 4th edn. (London, 1966), 134.

[166] AC I²4, 45, club of La Croisette, 10 May 1793.

[167] Ibid. I²20, d. 230, CPS (Rhône-et-Loire), interrogation of C.-F. Dubost, 15 May 1793.

[168] *CM*, iv. 259 (18 May 1793); *Moniteur*, xv. 392.

[169] AN AA53, d. 1487, Puisne to the president of the Convention, 19 May 1793; Coste MS 618, requisition of Veillas to join the revolutionary army, 20 May 1793. By 17 May, only 17 volunteers had joined from the *section* of Porte-Froc. During the rebellion of Lyon it was claimed by the 'federalists' that the Municipalité had assembled 300–400 men by 29 May (AD 31L39 (17 May 1793); *Les Citoyens de la ville de Lyon à leurs frères de la République française* (Lyon, n.d.), 7).

tions.[170] Jacobin suspicions of the Guard were confirmed on 18 February, when the Club Central was attacked while a detachment from Rue Neuve looked on.[171] More ominous still was the behaviour of forty grenadiers who surrounded the Arsenal with cannon, shouting that they would not leave until the prisoners taken the previous night had been released. It took a joint delegation of the three local authorities, accompanied by a detachment of dragoons, to change their minds.[172] Not unnaturally, the Municipalité preferred the army to keep order in Lyon, but as the *Journal de Lyon* gleefully observed, this was hard to reconcile with the *patriotes'* earlier encouragement of popular hostility to the garrison: 'c'étoit alors le département qui vouloit *ceindre la cité d'un double cordon de troupes de ligne*. Les démagogues de la municipalité s'y opposoient fortement.'[173] The Jacobins' political insecurity exposed the superficiality of their commitment to popular causes. Their request for 1,200 regular troops to control the city in mid-February could easily be seen as evidence of the Municipalité's hostility towards its own constituents, and its implication in the conspiracy to depict Lyon as a city on the verge of counter-revolution.[174] Worse still, it underlined the precariousness of the Jacobins' position.

The Committee of Public Safety in Lyon now feared the worst: 'Le peuple ici est en grande détresse du décret dont il est fait mention sur la lettre de cet infâme Chasset. L'aristocratie se remue en tous sens, et lève un front audacieux qui fait craindre sous peu de jours des mouvements de notre Département.'[175] To an anti-Jacobin observer, however, the decree of the 15th 'a fait le meilleur effet possible'.[176] Riffaterre criticized the Municipalité for failing to use caution and to play for time in these unfavourable circumstances, 'nécessité pressente pour des gens qui s'attendaient à une insurrection parisienne au profit de leur parti'.[177] But

---

[170] *Journal de Lyon*, 23 Aug. 1792, pp. 341–2; *CM*, iv. 82, 238, 247 (30 Jan., 3, 12 May 1793).

[171] Coste MSS 609, 612, 560, statement by Baille, commander of Rue Neuve (n.d.); charges against Baille and J.-F. Roux, corporal, 20 and 27 Feb. 1793; denunciation by Ferlay (n.d.).

[172] *CM*, iv. 109–12 (18–19 Feb. 1793); Coste MSS 610, 550, charges against Bonnavel, tailor, commander of a grenadier detachment at the Arsenal on 19 Feb.; declaration by the deputation of the three *autorités constituées*, 19 Feb. 1793.

[173] *Journal de Lyon*, 24 Feb. 1793, p. 176.

[174] *CM*, iv. 109 (18 Feb. 1793); Genet-Bronze, Pelzin, and Badger, *Rapport et Pétition* p. 8.

[175] AN F^{1a}III, Rhône 8, d. 2, no. 13, CPS (Rhône-et-Loire) to CPS, 18 May 1793.

[176] AN AA53, d. 1487, letter of Puisne, 19 May 1793.

[177] Riffaterre, *Le Mouvement anti-jacobin et anti-parisien à Lyon*, i. 64.

while the Lyonnais Jacobins certainly had hopes that the moderates in the Convention would be crushed,[178] they could not be sure that the Parisian *sans-culottes* would strike as quickly and effectively as they did. Since they were obsessed by the danger of counter-revolution in Lyon, they continued their efforts to intimidate their opponents by using the only more or less effective weapon at their disposal, the Committee of Public Safety. And since the decree of the 15th was followed by the establishment of the Girondin Commission of Twelve on the 20th, any hope that events in Paris would soon turn decisively in the Montagnards' favour might well have seemed faint towards the end of May.[179] In a letter written in gaol on 7 June Chalier's pessimism was no doubt increased by the overthrow of the Lyonnais Jacobins. But it suggests that he took to gaol on 30 May a very gloomy assessment of the situation in Paris: 'Hélas! tout est perdu. La Convention elle-même ne peut sauver la patrie. Que dis-je? C'est elle-même qui la précipite dans le gouffre de tous les maux imaginables.' Traitors in Paris, he believed, 'tiennent tout, gouvernent tout'.[180] The Municipalité's opponents, on the other hand, having received one instalment of aid from the Convention, might reasonably hope for more.

They could also count on support from the Departmental Directoire, which repeatedly criticized the Municipalité for its failure to respect the administrative hierarchy.[181] Particularly after the formation of the Committee of Public Safety of Rhône-et-Loire, which in practice acted in concert with the Municipalité, the distinction between municipal and departmental authority had become more blurred than ever, again raising the prospect of Lyon giving the law to the rest of the Département. Furthermore, two of the Jacobin sympathizers on the Directoire were now dividing their time between the Département and the Committee of Public Safety, while the other, the president, Grandchamp, resigned on 12 May because of his health, pressure of work, and 'mille autres raisons'.[182]

---

[178] *CM*, iv. 181 (5 Apr. 1793).

[179] News of the Commission's abolition could not have reached Lyon before 29 May. Two full days were needed for reports of events in Paris to reach Lyon, even by special couriers of the Ministry of the Interior (e.g. Chasset's letter of 15 May announcing the decree prohibiting the establishment of a Revolutionary Tribunal in Lyon was not received there until 18 May: AN F¹ᶜIII, Rhône 8, d. 3, no. 50).

[180] Letters of 7 and 8 June 1793, in L. Bernascon and B. Lauras, *La Vie, la mort et le triomphe de Chalier* (Paris, [1793]), 11, 16.

[181] AN M669, d. 4, nos. 1 and 7, extracts from the Département's minutes, 6, 21 Feb. 1793; *CM*, iv. 237 (2 May 1793).

[182] *Département*, ii. 279 (12 May 1793).

The anti-Jacobin majority in the Directoire was made more determined by attacks on Meynis, the *procureur-général-syndic*, at the joint session of 14 May, and by fears that members of the Département might find themselves before the projected tribunal.[183] Why the District of Lyon-Ville came to oppose the Municipalité is less clear. Its president, Angelot, formerly considered a Jacobin, commended the club of La Croisette on 10 May and delegations from the latter were welcomed by the District Directoire.[184] At all events, throughout the May conflicts the District seems to have been content to follow the Département.

After the election of the *Comités de surveillance* on 19 and 20 May, the Municipalité's struggle with the Département centred on sectional permanence. On 23 May the Municipalité ruled that sectional assemblies could only discuss matters concerning residence certificates, and then only with its permission. It further declared that the functions of the *Comités de surveillance* were limited to keeping registers of visitors to the city, and that the Revolutionary Committees it had created should attend to broader questions of public order.[185] Two days later, however, the Département published an order contradicting the Municipalité on every major point. The *sections'* permanence was authorized as necessary to their committees' proper functioning, and the latter were given the functions of the Municipality's Revolutionary Committees.[186] Now the *sections* could work in the open with a plausible claim to legality.[187] The *permanents* were also fortified by the precedents of 'Paris, Bordeaux, Aix et Nîmes',[188] and the *Journal de Lyon* praised the example of Marseille, though emphasizing the virtues of legal sectional permanence rather than rebellion.[189]

There is nothing to suggest that at this stage the *sectionnaires* intended to use methods other than peaceful and legal ones. The Municipalité, however, maintained that until it had obtained clarification of the law, sectional permanence was illegal and sectional assemblies could only meet with its permission and under the conditions it prescribed. On these grounds it continued to arrest sectional officials who failed to comply

[183] *Département*, ii. 275, 279 (8, 12 May 1793); *CM*, iv. 255 (14 May 1793).

[184] AC I²4, d. 45, minutes of 8, 12 May 1793.

[185] *CM*, iv. 267 (23 May 1793).

[186] *Département*, ii. 296–7 (25 May 1793).

[187] AD IL375, *Extrait des procès-verbaux de la section de Saint-Georges, les 28 mai et 3 juin 1793* (Lyon, [1793]).

[188] *Extrait des registres de la section de la Convention* [meeting of 27 May, printed 1 June] (Lyon, 1793), 1.

[189] *Journal de Lyon*, 9 May 1793, p. 310; 10 May 1793, pp. 313–15.

with its regulations, and to dissolve their assemblies. It is in this context that a declaration made by the *section* of la Convention (le Griffon) on 27 May should be interpreted: 'Le moment est venu d'oser dire la vérité, et de résister, avec la Loi, à une oppression qui est la violation la plus audacieuse de toutes les Loix.' This declaration was a defence of the 'droits des Sections', and it was 'pour en obtenir l'exercice dans toute sa plénitude' that the *sections* of la Convention, Rue Neuve, Port du Temple, and no doubt others defied the Municipalité's regulations on 26 and 27 May.[190]

The *sectionnaires*' position was further strengthened the next day, when the Département called out the National Guard, overriding the Municipalité's formal refusal to do so[191] on several grounds: attacks and threats against some of the sectional assemblies; the *taxation* of the army's butter store on the 24th; and the Municipalité's own declaration on the 25th that it could no longer be held responsible for the maintenance of order.[192] This was a direct challenge to the Municipalité, not only because it encroached on its powers but because for some time its policy had been to requisition only 'quelques bataillons privilégiés' and to sound the tocsin only in *sections* friendly to it.[193]

Apart from a few loyal National Guard battalions and a handful of troops, the Revolutionary Army was the Jacobins' only defence against the dissident Guard battalions. But it was too small and too disorganized to be of much use. No effort was made to prepare it for action until 26 May, and it was formed into companies only on the 28th.[194]

Contrary to Herriot's view, it seems unlikely that fear of what the local Jacobins might do independently was the cause of the insurrection of 29 May.[195] They had too long a record of ineptitude, bungled theatrical plots, and failing support. The *Journal de Lyon*'s attacks on them tended more to mockery than fear-mongering. And if the bourgeoisie was in the grip of a *grande peur* it would be difficult to account for the tone of the *négociant* Fromageot's letter reporting the feast of the *sans-culotte* jurors on 9 May:

On est toujours ici dans une tranquillité parfaite; on craignait, hier, pour les

---

[190] *CM*, iv. 270 (25 May 1793); *Extrait des registres ... de la Convention*, p. 1.
[191] *CM*, iv. 270 (26 May 1793).
[192] *Département*, ii. 308–9 (28 May 1793); AD 42L33, Département and District (Lyon-Ville) to Municipalité, 28 May 1793.
[193] AC I²4, d. 74, address in the name of the section of Saint-Nizier (n.d.).
[194] *CM*, iv. 274 (28 May 1793).
[195] Herriot, *Lyon n'est plus*, i. 341.

suites d'un festin frugal et civique que les braves sans culottes se sont donnés en
Bellecour; ils devaient porter chacun leur plat et pas plus de deux bouteilles de
vin, ce qui paraissait beaucoup pour un seul plat ... ils en sont cependant sortis
assez tranquillement et n'ont fait d'autre bêtise que d'aller jeter bas un obélisque
antique et très curieux placé sur la place des Jacobins ...[196]

Like C. F. Dubost's estimate that there were at most a dozen committed
Jacobins in each *section*,[197] this suggests that their opponents were unim-
pressed by the strength of the Jacobins' local support.

By 28 May the anti-Jacobin movement had spread to two-thirds of the
sections, including all of those on the peninsula except for the l'Hôtel-Dieu
area.[198] It was by now broadly based both socially and geographically, but
the propertied classes and the *sections* of central Lyon played the dominant
role. Of seventeen clubs aligned with La Croisette up to 6 May, eleven
were in this area, including six of the seven which had provided the first
support for La Croisette's resistance to the Jacobins in February and
early March. The two main outbreaks of sectional opposition to the
Municipalité were just as firmly based in commercial peninsular Lyon:
seven of eleven *sections* active on 18 February, and twelve of eighteen
between 25 and 28 May.[199] All the known instigators of the sectional
assemblies on 18 February were prominent bourgeois—the surgeon Gilibert and his *négociant* brother, the solicitor Simon-Jean Adam and the
curé of Saint-Nizier, François-Marie-Thérèse Jolyclerc. Those arrested
for various acts of defiance towards the Municipalité in the fracas of the
same evening included both artisans and bourgeois.[200] More reliable
evidence is provided by the professions of the *commissaires de surveillance*
elected on 19 and 20 May in seventeen *sections* hostile to the Municipalité.
The presidents and secretaries of these 'permanent' *sections* were, like
the anti-Jacobin agitators of February, predominantly drawn from the
upper bourgeoisie. But amongst the sixty-four *commissaires surveillants*
whose occupations have been established,[201] the bourgeois majority

---

[196] Letter of 10 May cited Herriot, *Lyon n'est plus*, i. 326.

[197] AC I²4, d. 47, letter to the Convention, 25 May 1793.

[198] Rue Neuve, la Convention (le Griffon II), Port du Temple, la Pêcherie, Porte-Froc,
Rue Tupin, la Saône, la Croisette, Rue Buisson, la Grande-Côte II, Saint-Georges, Saint-
Nizier, Place Saint-Pierre, Rue Terraille, la Plâtre, le Change (see *Département*, ii. 296–7,
299, 303, 305–8 (25, 26, 28 May 1793); AD 42L72, d. 62, statement by Jacques Deaux,
section of Rue Terraille; 42L74, d. 63, denunciation of Desrieux, *section* of le Plâtre).

[199] See Appendix VI and Map 4.

[200] Merchants: 1 silk-merchant, 1 timber-merchant, 3 grocers, 1 butcher, 2 innkeepers,
1 merchant; professions: 2 lawyers, 1 teacher, 1 surgeon (Coste MSS 555, 565, 586, 597,
599, 610, 612).

[201] Out of 264 elected in these *sections* in May (there were 12 per *section*).

was smaller.[202] In this case there is less certainty that those elected were opposed to the Municipalité, though all continued to serve as *commissaires* under the regime which replaced it, and it seems likely that they supported the anti-Jacobins at least on the question of sectional permanence.

Socially, the anti-Jacobin movement in its early stages resembled the first *patriote* Municipalité of 1791. Merchants were more prominent in the sectional leadership than they had been amongst the early *patriotes*. But artisans were involved in significant numbers too, even in poor and previously radical areas like Saint-Georges and Port Saint-Paul (where the *commissaires* were mostly weavers), evidence that the political struggle of May 1793 was not being waged between distinct social groups. This is not to say that there was a massive anti-Jacobin following amongst the Lyonnais working classes. In particular, (in terms of their total numbers), there were few hatters or silk-weavers involved on either side. They held aloof from what was essentially a struggle between politicians whose preoccupations were mostly different from their own.

The propertied classes of Lyon finally found an organizational basis for political action in the new structures of sectional politics, centred on the *Comités de surveillance*, whose political potential was simultaneously being developed by the Parisian *sans-culottes*. With support from below and in most parts of the city, their spokesmen could claim much more convincingly than the Jacobins that they represented the community as a whole. Until now the sharpness of social conflict in Lyon and the alienation of the *patriotes* from the propertied classes had prevented the latter from establishing political dominance or from justifying their claim to rule in terms of revolutionary democratic ideology. The Rolandin–club alliance had succeeded in doing so for a time, and then the Jacobins. But by their élitism, by their rejection of the *sections* as the basic units of democratic politics, and by their alienation of the *menu peuple*, the Jacobins provided an opportunity for the propertied classes to rally popular support behind their leadership and to clothe it in the rhetoric of popular sovereignty.

With some justification, the Montagnards denounced this democratic posture as a façade. But it would be a mistake to reject as fraudulent the anti-Jacobins' protestations of *patriotisme* and respect for revolutionary principles. Only in a very restricted sense can the anti-Jacobin movement

[202] See Appendix VII.

be called counter-revolutionary. Because it was anti-Montagnard at a time when the Montagnards claimed to embody the principle of popular sovereignty, it was straight away classified as such and it has often been so classified by neo-Jacobin historians.[203] Some of its leaders were Fenillantists, like Gilibert and Jolyclerc who had both been members of the Société du Concert. Gilibert, a distinguished scientist, and physician, had been one of the authors of the *cahier* of the Third Estate. Jolyclerc had been the last vicar-general of Lyon under the old regime, but had strongly supported the Civil Constitution of the Clergy, earning himself the bitter condemnation of his former archbishop.[204] Such men might well have wanted to limit the effects of the democratic revolution. But this does not necessarily mean that they wished to revive the monarchy, and still less the *ancien régime*. The only certain construction which can be put on their behaviour in 1793 is that they regarded the Montagnard threat as sufficiently grave to require organized defence of the political gains of 1789 and the fundamental guarantees of property and individual liberty, representative parliamentary government, and the rule of law.

This is not to say that there were no covert royalists of a more reactionary kind amongst the *sectionnaires*. Two of the *commissaires surveillants* and one of the sectional leaders of late May can be identified as having signed the address drawn up in Lyon after the first invasion of the Tuileries (20 June 1792) expressing fervent devotion to the throne.[205] Another sectional activist, Edmé de Fréminville, later claimed to have been trying to exploit the situation in the interests of a restoration.[206] Covert royalists are naturally difficult to detect, and there were undoubtedly others amongst the anti-Jacobin activists. The sectional movement was a diverse anti-Jacobin coalition, and it included not only old régime *notables* (the *rentier* Jacques Bouvard, a former rector of the Charité, was president of Place Saint-Pierre's committee, and Charles-Joseph Jacob, a silk-merchant who had been a rector of the Hôtel-Dieu, was a member of le Plâtre's)[207] but also *patriotes* such as Denis Monnet and Denis Delorme, who was a member of the committee of le Change, a former

[203] e.g. A. Soboul, *The French Revolution 1787–1799*, trans. A. Forrest and C. Jones, 2 vols. (London, 1974), ii. 308.

[204] *Ordonnance de M. l'archévêque de Lyon primat des Gaules* (Lyon, 1791). On Gilibert, see Herriot, *Lyon n'est plus*, i. 139–40; on Jolyclerc, see M. Wahl, *Les Premières années de la Révolution à Lyon, 1788–1792* (Paris, n.d.), 298–323.

[205] François Privat, *huissier*; Gleyze, *cadet, rentier*; André Goiran, merchant broker (see AN F¹III, Rhône 6).

[206] See Riffaterre, *Le Mouvement anti-jacobin et anti-parisien à Lyon*, ii. 10 *et seq.*

[207] *Almanach* (1789).

notable, and apparently a Jacobin sympathizer as late as March 1793, when he signed with Chalier a denunciation of hoarders and 'le négociant égoïste et espéculant sans cesse'.[208] There is no evidence at all that the royalists were the real instigators of Lyonnais anti-Jacobinism, and the neo-Jacobin view of it as a royalist conspiracy cannot be sustained.

The Lyonnais anti-Jacobinism of spring 1793 does not belong to the history of the counter-revolution, but to that of the 'Republican Revolt of 1793' which, as M. J. Sydenham has pointed out, had its origins in a crisis of legitimacy which divided the republicans. Essentially, this was a movement of protest against the Convention's failure to erect new barriers against 'anarchy' in place of the discarded Constitution of 1791. It reflected widespread doubts, engendered by the Convention's own behaviour and that of its provincial agents, that the Convention was, or was capable of becoming, a suitable embodiment of national sovereignty: 'While there was no accepted Constitution, while the one embodiment of the sovereign authority of the whole nation, the National Convention, remained divided, discredited, and impotent, neither the general will nor the general interest had any final definition.'[209] This produced a degree of political uncertainty which the propertied classes found intolerable, and a real threat of chaos. The Convention seemed constantly to be giving ground to the popular democrats of Paris, whose threats of purges and intimidation and barracking of *députés* seemed to presage the anarchy which had haunted the propertied classes since the fall of the old regime. As the divisions amongst the *députés* increased, deepening the crisis of legitimacy and dimming hopes that the Revolution would realize the rule of law dreamed of in 1789, the departmental authorities in many parts of France began to express this disquiet openly, and to make more or less veiled threats of drastic action to protect the national legislature against the excesses of Parisian radicals.[210]

Lyonnais anti-Jacobinism shared some of the concerns of this movement. As early as December 1792 the club of La Pêcherie had repeated its main themes in a protest to the Convention:

Les Citoyens qui remplissent vos tribunes prennent depuis quelque temps à toutes vos délibérations une part qu'il ne leur appartient point de prendre

---

[208] *CM*, iv. 155 (25 Mar. 1793). See *CM*, iii. 673 (election of Delorme as a *notable*, 13 Dec. 1791); ibid. iv. 21 (14 Dec. 1792) (installation as president of the District Tribunal).

[209] M. J. Sydenham, 'The Republican Revolt of 1793: A Plea for Less Localized Local Studies', *French Historical Studies*, 12 (Spring 1981), 138.

[210] See B. Edmonds, ' "Federalism" and Urban Revolt in France in 1793', *Journal of Modern History*, 55 1 (Mar. 1983), 22–53.

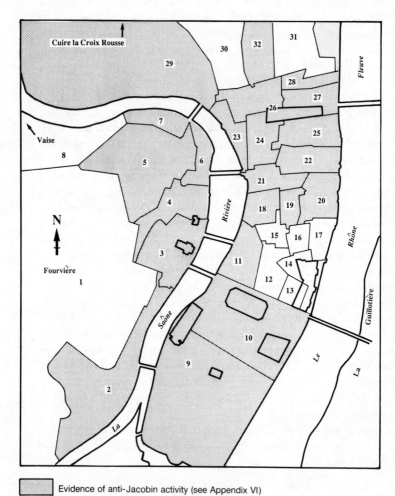

Evidence of anti-Jacobin activity (see Appendix VI)

5.   Anti-Jacobin activity in the *sections*, late May 1793

... Vos décrets rejetés, votre autorité méconnue, le nom français avili, voilà, Législateurs, voilà ce qui nous menace en ce moment ... que le même jour voie tomber la tête du tyran qui voulut assiéger Paris, et l'ambition des factieux qui chaque jour assiégent vos assemblées. Déjà dans nos Départemens on accuse les Parisiens d'oublier ce qu'ils nous doivent, de vouloir usurper une suprématie que la nature et la raison ne leur accordent pas.[211]

But genuine as these anxieties about the situation in Paris undoubtedly were, they would not by themselves have provoked insurrection in Lyon, any more than they did in those cities where they were expressed at least as vigorously and accompanied by more direct threats.[212] Generally speaking, bourgeois concern for parliamentary government and the rule of law did not go so far as to produce action to back up the declarations of protest. The legitimacy of the Convention was in doubt. So was the attitude it would take towards provincial enemies of the Montagne. But where the propertied classes were in control of local affairs they mostly preferred to ride out the crisis by a policy of *attentisme* which minimized the opportunities for Parisian intervention in their affairs.[213] Lyon, however, was incapable of presenting a united front to outsiders, and both factions in the local political struggle had already appealed directly to the Convention for deliverance from their enemies. It was clear that as things were the outcome was going to be decided by the national government. When it appeared on 28 May that the government's principal agents in the south-east were about to turn the tables decisively in favour of the Jacobins, their opponents sought to keep them out by seizing Lyon in the name of the people.

---

[211] *Adresse à la Convention nationale par la Société de Brutus, ci-devant la Pêcherie, à Lyon, département de Rhône-et-Loire* (Lyon, 30 Dec. 1792).

[212] 'Républicains, nous sonnons le tocsin, un feu violent dévore la République. Levez-vous, arrêtez les incendiaires ...' (*Les Nantais à tous les départements de la République* (7 June 1793), in *Secrétariat*, pp. 487–97).

[213] This point has been well made in M. Lyons, *Revolution in Toulouse: An Essay on Provincial Terrorism* (Berne, 1978).

6

From Anti-Jacobinism to 'Federalism'
29 May–24 June 1793

If the Jacobins are understood to constitute 'the part of the French bourgeoisie which was in 1789–94 most able to understand its historical function, the destruction of feudalism and, in 1793–4, the defence of the nation'[1], it is easy to assume, as they themselves did, that opposition to them represented a great conspiracy against the revolutionary nation. Seen from this point of view—as Mathiez, for example, saw it—the *journée* of 29 May in Lyon becomes the premeditated outcome of a royalist–Girondin plot supported by reactionary elements of the bourgeoisie.[2]

But if the insurrection which launched the biggest urban revolt against the Convention *cannot* be classified with the royalist counter-revolution, or even with Girondism, then a large cog is lost from the apparatus of neo-Jacobin historical justification of the Great Terror as a necessary response to internal as well as external threats. Without Lyon, the urban 'counter-revolution' amounts to little more than Marseille and Toulon, and to a lesser extent Bordeaux and Caen,[3] serious certainly, but hardly enough to justify the elaborate, nation-wide apparatus of repression that was assembled during the second half of 1793. What is worse for the neo-Jacobin position, is that it was the policies of the Montagnards and their local supporters which turned discontent into revolt in Lyon. The 'counter-revolutionary threat' here was produced by the very policies which have been justified as responses to it. Discarding the royalist–Rolandin–Girondin conspiracy theory reveals the fact that, however well the Jacobins may have understood their historic mission, they bungled it in Lyon. If any group can be blamed for the *journée* of 29 May, they

---

[1] P. Higonnet, *Class, Ideology, and the Rights of Nobles during the French Revolution* (Oxford, 1981), 175, paraphrasing C. Mazauric.

[2] See A. Mathiez, *The French Revolution*, trans. C. A. Phillips (New York, 1962), 334.

[3] See B. Edmonds, '"Federalism" and Urban Revolt in France in 1793', *Journal of Modern History*, 60 (1983), 22–53.

can—not the Girondins or the royalists, and least of all the Lyonnais Rolandins.

This is not to say that there were no Rolandins involved in the rebellion, though only two played a significant part,[4] or that there were no connections between the Girondins in the capital and the anti-Jacobin movement in Lyon. Whatever their political faults, the Girondins were astute enough to do what they could for their supporters in the big provincial towns. As we have seen, Chasset's decree banning the proposed Revolutionary Tribunal gave the Lyonnais anti-Jacobins a much needed victory. And Guadet cultivated the journalist J.-L. Fain, sending him both his own and Louvet's speeches against Robespierre.[5] But while the Girondins certainly encouraged Lyonnais anti-Jacobinism, they did not initiate it.

On 27 May news came that troops from Dubois-Crancé's headquarters at Grenoble were marching on Lyon.[6] Then the *députés* Nioche and Gauthier arrived, at the Municipalité's invitation, ostensibly to investigate the pillage of army stores.[7] Suspicions were aroused by the troop movements: 'nous ne savons quel est l'objet de leur mission, ni par qui ils ont été requis ... nous ne pouvons pénétrer le but de ces vues secrètes dans un moment où nos frontières ont besoin de tous nos défenseurs'.[8] But the Municipalité's supporters were jubilant, saying that 'les députés arrivent pour mettre à la raison tous les muscadins'.[9] On the 28th the *sections* reported 'des menaces faits pour cette nuit'.[10] They believed the troops' arrival to be imminent and demanded to know 's'ils doivent craindre et veiller, s'armer ou dormir en sûreté'.[11] At about noon a hostile

---

[4] Of Roland's correspondents of 1792, the joiner, Forret, was a provisional municipal officer from 30 May to October 1793, and Meynis was *procureur-général-sindic* of the Département during the rebellion. But the leading Rolandins, Vitet and Nivière-Chol, played no role (AD 42L101, d. B16; *CM*, iii. 674 (13 Dec. 1792)).

[5] AD 42L12, fos. 1–2, interrogation of J.-L. Fain, 4 brumaire, an II.

[6] *Copie de la lettre écrite par les administrateurs du Conseil général du département de Rhône-et-Loire ... à la Convention nationale sur les événements antérieurs à ceux du 29 mai dernier* (Lyon, 4 Kune 1793), 5.

[7] *CM*, iv. 269 (25 May). Except where otherwise indicated, dates given in the notes to Chaps. 6–8 refer to 1793.

[8] AN AFII43, plaq, 339, no. 23, Département to Minister of the Interior, 27 May. There were similar reactions in the *sections*: see *Les Commissaires des sections de la ville de Lyon réunies en comité les 29 et 30 mai 1793* (Lyon, 1793), 2.

[9] AD 42L71, denunciation by Clapier of Biolay, reported by Biolay, 17 brumaire, an II.

[10] *Département*, ii. 309 (29 May).

[11] Ibid.

delegation from 'un comité des sections réunies *ad hoc*'[12] asked Nioche
and Gauthier to send the troops back and to suspend the Municipalité.
When the *députés* refused, the *sectionnaires* demanded that the Département take measures to protect the city. The Département then took
the crucial step of calling out the National Guard.[13] The way was open
for military action against the Jacobins.

During the night a detachment of cavalry arrived and confirmed that
contingents of infantry were following. Delegates of the dissident *sections*
assembled in the library of the former Jacobin monastery in the *section*
of Rue Buisson. They proclaimed that the Municipalité had forfeited the
people's confidence, and at about 11.00 p.m. they repeated the demand
for its suspension.[14] Meanwhile, the Municipalité was reinforcing the
Arsenal with regular soldiers, placing cannon around the Town Hall, and
the battalion of Pierre-Scize at the powder-magazine. Officers from a
squadron of dragoons stationed at Serin on the city's outskirts and some
regular artillerymen declared their readiness to defend the Municipalité.[15]
But at about 7.00 a.m. on the 29th, probably with the connivance of its
commander, Gassendi, the Arsenal was occupied by the anti-Jacobin
battalion of Port du Temple. Soon after, the Comité des Sections moved
there, to be joined at about 1.30 p.m. by several members of the Département and the District. Then came the news that the battalion of
la Pêcherie, which had been ordered by the Municipalité to assemble on
the Place des Terreaux, had been fired on by snipers in the Town Hall.
This 'massacre' was seized on by the Departmental Directoire as a reason
for suspending all the members of the Municipalité from office. Claiming
now that their actions had legal sanction, the *sectionnaires* were in no
mood to heed the calls to disperse made by Nioche when he appeared at
the Arsenal later in the afternoon. When he refused to confirm the
Municipalité's suspension, the Comité des Sections ordered the National
Guard to march on the Hôtel de Ville.[16]

[12] 'Rapport fait par C. N. Nioche ... sur les malheureux événements arrivés à Lyon le
29 mai 1793' [Paris, 1793], in E.-L.-A. Dubois-Crancé, *Première partie de la réponse de
Dubois-Crancé aux inculpations de ses collègues Couthon et Maignet* (n.p., n.d.), 61–2.

[13] *Département*, ii. 309 (29 May).

[14] AD 31L20, fo. 86, minutes of Port Saint-Paul, 29 May; *Détail de ce qui s'est passé à
Lyon les 28 et 30 mai 1793 (extrait du Journal de Carrier)* (Lyon, [1793]), 4–5; Nioche,
'Rapport', p. 62.

[15] *CM*, iv. 273, 27–8 May; Fonds Coste MS 626, Ledoyen, adjutant-general, to Francière,
squadron commander of the 9th regiment of dragoons, 27 May.

[16] *Détail de ce qui s'est passé*, p. 5; *Les Commissaires des sections*, pp. 3, 6; *Procès-verbaux
des Conseils généraux du département de Rhône-et-Loire, des districts de Lyon et de la campagne
de Lyon relatifs à l'événement du 29 mai 1793* (Lyon, 1793), 5; Nioche, 'Rapport', p. 71.

After learning of the occupation of the Arsenal, the Municipalité hastily reinforced the Town Hall. Gauthier ordered Lyon's regular troops to come to its defence and the Committee of Public Safety requisitioned fourteen National Guard battalions which it considered reliable. But despite some snipers *en route* and cannon-fire from Jacobin guns on the Place des Terreaux and the Quai du Rhône, the two columns of *sectionnaires* who marched from the Arsenal late in the afternoon were able to crush the resistance from the Town Hall in something like two hours.[17]

The *députés* were under strong pressure to confirm the Département's suspension of the Municipalité, and by late on 29 May both of them were trapped in the Arsenal by hostile crowds.[18] They resisted until early on 30 May, when they issued a statement approving the Département's actions, commending the *sections*, disavowing their colleagues' approval of the revolutionary army, and admitting that the Lyonnais had been misunderstood. Soon afterwards they sent orders requiring the troops approaching Lyon to rejoin the Armée des Alpes. Later in the day they publicly endorsed the formation of a Provisional Municipalité of Lyon composed of two delegates from each of the thirty-four *sections* (including la Guillotière I and II).[19]

The cost in lives was high, but there was not the great slaughter which it suited both winners and losers to accuse each other of causing. At the time, anti-Jacobin estimates were as high as 400 dead, and soon after Thermidor they increased by 50 per cent. Similar figures have found their way into recent histories of the Revolution.[20] The only serious investigation soon after the event was done by Surgeon-General Tissot of the Lyon military hospital, who published a study of the deaths from gunshot wounds on 29 May with the aim of discrediting rumours that the Jacobins had used poisoned bullets and other fiendish methods. According to Tissot, there were twenty-six dead and thirty wounded,[21] and although he may have counted only casualties from gunfire, it seems

[17] *Les Commissaires des sections*, pp. 6–7; AN AFII43, no. 17, *Procès-verbal du Conseil du district de Lyon, en permanence à l'Hôtel Commun [29–30 mai]* (Lyon, 1793), 5–7.

[18] Nioche, 'Rapport', and A.-F. Gauthier, 'Observations', in *Première partie de la réponse de Dubois-Crancé*, pp. 65–8, 72–3, 85; *Les Commissaires des sections*, pp. 5–7; *Détail de ce qui s'est passé* pp. 11–12, 15.

[19] Nioche, 'Rapport', p. 74; *Procès-verbaux des Conseils généraux*, p. 8.

[20] AD 42L74, letter of Dubier, *cadet* (a participant in the fighting), 8 June; P.-E. Béraud, *Sur le siège de Lyon et sur les malheurs qui l'ont suivi. En Allemagne, 1794* (n.p., n.d.), 7; M. J. Sydenham, *The French Revolution* (London, 1965), 154.

[21] J. M. Tissot, *Observations sur les causes de la mort des blessés par des armes à feu dans la journée du 29 mai 1793 à Lyon* (Lyon, 1793), 1, 7.

unlikely that the total of dead and wounded was more than a few score. The only specific reference to the matter in the sectional records is consistent with this view. On 30 June 1793 la Croisette recorded that one of its inhabitants had been killed on 29 May and seven wounded.[22]

NATIONAL AND LOCAL CONTEXTS OF THE *JOURNÉE* OF 29 MAY

Riffaterre's careful study of the politics of the Lyonnais rebellion reaches the opposite conclusion to the neo-Jacobins' about the *journée* of 29 May. According to him, 'l'insurrection lyonnaise ne fut d'abord qu'une revolution municipale'.[23] Yet while it is true that historians like Mathiez and Thompson have jumped recklessly to their conclusions about long-prepared conspiracy and Girondin involvement from a few isolated fragments of evidence (notably, Chasset's correspondence with his cousin, C.-F. Dubost of la Croisette),[24] they were right to link 29 May with the national crisis of spring 1793.

Riffaterre's picture of a purely local conflict is misleading in several ways. We have seen that the activities of Montagnard *représentants en mission*, from Basire, Rovère, and Legendre to Dubois-Crancé, Nioche, and Gauthier, were among the principal causes of the rising. Just as the *sections* and the Département, aided by the Convention's decrees of 21 March (creating the *Comités de surveillance*) and 15 May (forbidding the Revolutionary Tribunal), were making some headway against a Jacobin Municipalité whose lack of local support was becoming obvious, the *représentants en mission*, having declared themselves for the Municipalité, generated fears that its dominance was to be secured by regular troops from Grenoble.[25] For anyone threatened by the Jacobin programme— that is, anyone likely to be categorized as a moderate, Feuillantist, *égoïste*, *riche insouciant*, lackey, hireling, or *vil suppôt* of the counter-revolution— it was no longer enough to rely on the spoiling tactics that had been used since March. The Jacobin Municipalité had to be removed before the

---

[22] AD 31L2, minutes of la Croisette, 30 June.

[23] C. Riffaterre, *Le Mouvement anti-jacobin et anti-parisien à Lyon et dans le Rhône-et-Loire en 1793* (Lyon, 1912–28), ii. 622–3.

[24] Mathiez, *The French Revolution*, p. 334; J. M. Thompson, *Robespierre*, 2 vols. (New York, 1968), ii. 35.

[25] Dubois-Crancé had in fact sent 1 regular battalion, 1 of volunteers from Mont-Blanc, 1 squadron of dragoons, and 15 guides (*Première partie de la réponse de Dubois-Crancé*, pp. 61–2).

représentants en mission gave it effective means of coercion.[26]

Though it is difficult to say how well-informed the Lyonnais *sectionnaires* were about developments in Paris—the arrests of militants by the Girondin Commission of Twelve, the street demonstrations of the 26th, the abolition of the Commission late on the 27th (which could hardly have been known in Lyon before the insurrection was under way)—or whether they sensed how close the showdown was between the Convention and the *sans-culottes*, the trend of events in the capital could only confirm the view that it was best to strike straight away. If the Girondins won out in the Convention, there was a good chance of having an anti-Jacobin municipal revolution legitimized. Amongst the denunciations of 'federalists' after the fall of Lyon was one against Martin, of Port du Temple, for spreading a rumour on the 28th that the Convention had already pronounced in favour of the *sections*, 'qu'il étoit arrivé dans la nuit un courrier de dépêche lequel lequel apportoit un décret qui supprimoit les clubs et autorisoit les assemblées permanentes'.[27] How much such hopes encouraged the rebels is uncertain. But even a less optimistic view could endorse the calculation that even if the Montagnards won control of the Convention, a successful insurrection would give the anti-Jacobins Lyon as well as Marseille, and the possibility of continued resistance would remain.

Coindre, the president of Port du Temple, was said to have read out a letter from Chasset on 26 May. The *section* of la Convention began its session on 27 May with a diatribe against those who threatened 'l'integrité de la représentation nationale' (a reference to *sans-culotte* threats against the Girondin *députés*), and referred to 'les projets qui se trament dans la capitale, et récemment dénonces à la Convention'. On 1 June Plat-d'Argent referred pointedly to the sacred indivisibility of the National Assembly.[28] So there is evidence to support Mathiez's belief in a connection between the national crisis of late May and the almost simultaneous rebellion of Lyon. But if anything prepared the *journée* of 29 May 'weeks in advance' (to use Thompson's phrase), it was not Girondin conspiracy but the Convention's loss of legitimacy over months

---

[26] '... les citoyens ... apprehendoient pour le jour l'arrivée des forces envoyées dans la ville de Lyon par les citoyens Dubois-Crancé et Albitte, et savoient d'ailleurs que ce jour étoit marqué pour l'exécution des complots ...' (Département to Minister of the Interior, 30 May, AN M669, d. 4, no. 9).

[27] AD 42L64, denunciation of Martin.

[28] Ibid. 42L79, denunciation of Coindre, 5 brumaire, an II; *Extrait des registres de la section de la Convention* (Lyon, 1793), 1; AD 31L49, minutes of Plat-d'Argent, 1 June.

of factional rivalry, mutual denunciation, and concessions to extra-parliamentary pressure.

The insurrection did succeed remarkably easily, and perhaps that has increased the appeal of the conspiracy theory. Jacobin fears of the counter-revolution, of its immanence, its subversive potential, and its power to strike suddenly without warning, might have seemed borne out perfectly by the events of the 29th, particularly given the venue. But an examination of the mechanics of the insurrection shows that there is no need to conclude that there was elaborate organization before the event with an uprising specifically in mind. The anti-Jacobins had had a lot of experience of co-ordinated opposition though the club movement and the campaign for sectional permanence. An established network of deliberative assemblies, authorized and encouraged by the Département, was well-prepared for the co-ordinated protest and mobilization of 27–9 May.

Again, the anti-Jacobins had the support of the majority of officers in most of the National Guard battalions. Denunciations made after the siege suggest that sections of battalions were sometimes drawn into the insurrection even if the battalion commanders refused to co-operate. This was said to have happened in le Change, where Delorme, who had succeeded Chalier as president of the Tribunal de Commerce, beat the call to arms himself. In Saint-Georges, two officers were said to have taken command on their own initiative and to have led the battalion to the Arsenal while others prevented the pro-Jacobin battalion commanders from approaching the men.[29] But the main factor in the rebels' victory was that there was a clear majority of battalions whose officers were united against the Municipalité. The Municipalité called fourteen battalions to its defence, but got significant support from only nine—all from the poorer, outlying *sections* or the Hôtel-Dieu area—while eighteen took some part in the attack on the Town Hall, including three of the fourteen on which the Municipalité was counting (Saint-Georges, Rue Thomassin, and la Grande-Côte II).[30] Even in the weaving areas the sectional move-

[29] AD 42L63, d. 55, denunciation of Delorme by Deléan, *notable*, 3 brumaire, an II; ibid. 42L75, d. B47, denunciation of Favel, *pâtissier*, and Jalliet by Pelletot *père*, 21 Oct.

[30] For the Municipalité: la Grande-Côte I, Belle-Cordière, la Gourguillon, l'Hôtel-Dieu, Plat-d'Argent, le Rhône, Bon-Rencontre, Port Saint-Paul, la Juiverie. Against (in addition to those mentioned above): la Guillotière I and II, la Croix-Rousse, Vaise, Port du Temple, Rue Tupin, Place Neuve, le Change, Rue Buisson, la Pêcherie, les Terreaux, Rue Terraille, Saint-Vincent, Place Confort, Porte-Froc (see *Département*, ii. 310 (29 May); *Les Commissaires des sections*, p. 9; *Détail de ce qui s'est passé*, pp. 7, 9; *Copie de l'adresses du bataillon de la Juiverie au Conseil général de la Commune Provisoire de Lyon* (Lyon, 1793); *Procès-verbaux des Conseils généraux*, p. 10; AD 42L80, d. 43, 42L64, d. 2, 42L75, d. Estournel, 43L3, fo. 198; AC I²3, ds. 28, 31, 67, I²7, d. 152; AN AFII, plaq. 339, no. 10).

ment had made sufficient inroads to create deep divisions in the National Guard units, notably in la Grande-Côte. Thus the insurrection completed the political realignment of the *sections* which had been going on since December 1792. Not all of them had displayed such a clear political tendency as Pierre-Scize or les Terreaux, but most had tended to respond consistently in moments of controversy. Broadly speaking, the poorer areas had been fairly consistently radical and the wealthier ones fairly consistently moderate or conservative.[31] The fighting on 29 May confirmed the earlier signs that some of the former were shifting their allegiances.[32]

Even if solid support had been forthcoming from traditionally radical areas on the slopes of la Croix-Rousse and across the Saône, the Municipalité would still have been in a difficult position militarily. To get to the key buildings in the central city—the Town Hall and the Arsenal— battalions from these areas faced a long march through hostile *sections*. In this sense the writing had been on the wall since 18 February, when Nivière-Chol's supporters had been able to swarm into the Town Hall unresisted. As the Jacobins had then lamented, 'la force armée requise dans les sections voisines de l'Hôtel-commun, étoient lentes [*sic*] à se rendre au poste qui lui étoit assigné, tandis que celle requise dans les sections des Sans-Culottes, étoit trop éloignée pour arriver aussi promptement que le besoin l'exigeoit.'[33] Lyon's social geography meant that military control would always be difficult to maintain against opposition from the propertied classes, even for a group with strong support amongst the *menu peuple*. Lacking that, the Jacobins were in a hopeless position unless they could obtain substantial outside help.

CLASS STRUGGLE?

But if 29 May was a victory for wealthy peninsular Lyon, restoring to it the dominance over the poorer outlying areas which had been under challenge since the rise of the clubs, it was not the straightforward class struggle it has often been taken for. According to one of several passages in *Lyon n'est plus* in which Edouard Herriot did his best to impose the

---

[31] See Appendix VI.

[32] AD 42L3, fo. 212, interrogation of Louis Lyon, silk-weaver, ex-commander of la Grande-Côte II, 8 brumaire, an II; 31L20, fo. 86, minutes of Port Saint-Paul (which sent *députés* to join the Committee of Sections at the Arsenal while the battalion marched half-heartedly to guard the Town Hall).

[33] *CM*, iv. 105 (18 Feb.)

maximum significance on the revolutionary struggles in his adopted city, Jaurès 'a vu que la sévère lutte engagée sur les bords du Rhône opposait non seulement des personnes mais des classes, la "classe ouvrière" et la "classe mercantile"'.[34] Yet when the conflicts of early 1793 culminated in armed struggle on the banks of the Rhône, the 'classe ouvrière' declined to play its part in this straightforward fashion. Despite the months of political tension, the years of social conflict, and the great inequalities which divided Lyon, the Jacobins' rhetoric against the counter-revolutionary *aristocratie bourgeoise* left the bulk of the population un-moved. Riding through Lyon at 8.00 a.m. on 29 May, Nioche made an observation which helps to explain both the *journée*'s outcome and the decision which he later made to abandon the Lyonnais Jacobins. As the *sections* tightened their grip on the Arsenal, he saw 'un peuple immense, tranquil et indifférent sur tout ce que se passoit'. His colleague Gauthier later noted how few heeded the Municipalité's call for defenders, and remarked on 'l'extrême minorité dans laquelle les patriotes restoient'[35] when night fell. One of the insurgents who set off from Bellecour towards the Town Hall, Jean-Salomon Fazy, son of the Swiss owner of the cotton-mill at Perrache, was also surprised by the great crowds of passive spectators: 'un peuple innombrable regardait défiler cette troupe dans le plus morne silence'.[36] this is in striking contrast to the great popular turbulence of the *journées* of June 1789, February 1790, and September 1792, sometimes in the face of regular troops as well as National Guards. It takes two collectivities to make a class struggle, but on this occasion the lower orders abstained overwhelmingly.

There was still violent hatred for the *muscadins* amongst the *menu peuple*. The insurgents were pelted with stones as they marched along the Quai du Rhône, and several of them were hacked to death in the darkness of the streets near the Hôtel-Dieu, where they sought refuge from Jacobin cannon-fire. *Sectionnaires* who were either wounded or got cut off from the main columns were attacked and beaten. *Mère* Jarrasson and her daughters, for example, were said to have dropped rubble out of their window on to wounded men trapped below, 'et toutes les trois crioient unaninement, il faut tuer les muscadins'. Seven similar incidents were reported, involving two day-labourers, a carter, a silk-weaver, and seven women, one the carter's wife, the other the wife of a turner. Fazy

---

[34] E. Herriot, *Lyon n'est plus* (Paris, 1938–40), i. 8.
[35] Nioche, 'Rapport', pp. 64–5; Gauthier, 'Observations', p. 85.
[36] J. Schatzmann, 'La Révolution de 1793 à Lyon vue par un témoin oculaire, Jean-Salomon Fazy', *AHRF*, 7 (1940), 97.

recorded attacks on wounded *sectionnaires* in the popular *quartiers* near the Hôtel-Dieu, and himself only just escaped with his life.[37] But these incidents fell a long way short of the organized popular support the Jacobins needed in their struggle to maintain control of the Town Hall.

It is true nevertheless that what support the Jacobins did still have was largely from below. Because the Municipalité's supporters generally did not come under suspicion during the Great Terror (the dossiers of which provide much of the evidence for political activists in 1793), they are harder to identify than their opponents. But some were arrested by the 'federalist' regime and others made depositions and petitions for compensation after the end of the siege. Of thirty-two defenders of the Town Hall who can be identified from these rather unreliable sources, including members of the Municipalité known to have taken part in the fighting, about a quarter were probably at least moderately well off—and some were very well off, like Mayor Bertrand and the confectioner and tobacco-merchant Doret[38]—while the rest were mostly skilled artisans in textiles or the luxury trades.[39]

But alongside the well-to-do supporters of permanence and their clientele—merchants, members of the professions, clerks, and servants[40]—there were also many artisans (more than a third of those identified by

---

[37] AC I²3, d. 67, denunciations of the Jarrassons by Marie Bruyan, hatter, and five others, 13 July; 42L56, d. 3, 42L39, fo. 73, Comité de Surveillance (Bon-Rencontre), 4 June; 31L57, interrogation of Monin, *affaneur*, 3 Aug.; 1L376, ds. 23–5, *affaire* Moulin, basket-maker, 27 June–13 July; *Détail de ce qui s'est passé*, p. 12; Schatzman, *La Révolution de 1793*, p. 98.

[38] The others were a schoolteacher, a grocer, a surgeon, the ex-noble Riard, and the *curé rouge* of Saint-Just, Bottin. For the Jacobins, the sources are warrants in *Procès-verbaux des séances de la Commission populaire, républicaine et de salut public de Rhône-et-Loire, 30 juin–8 octobre 1793*, ed. G. Guigue (Lyon, 1899) [henceforward *CP*], 433–45, 480–90; AD 42L148, d. Pitiot; 42L3, fos. 207–8 (both an II); 31L49, fo. 27, minutes of Plat-d'Argent, 18 July; 42L102, d. (B)62 (an II); 36L57, interrogation of Bourdillon, 31 July; 1L987, warrants, 27 June; 42L71, d. 3(48); 1L936, d. Villemure; 42L102, d. (B)62; 42L64, d. 2(64) (the last four all an II); AC I²6, d. 73, interrogation of Apiant (an II).

[39] 9 silk-weavers, 3 stocking-weavers, a printer, a comb-maker, a hatter, 2 turners (one of whom had been an *éligible* in 1790), a joiner, a ladies' hairdresser, a wallpaper-layer, 2 plasterers, a maker of playing-cards, a drink-vendor, and a *pâtissier*.

[40] Commerce: 6 *négociants*, a silk-merchant, a wine-merchant, a pharmacist, a stocking-merchant, 2 furniture-merchants, a merchant of *faïence*, a wax-chandler, a soap-merchant, a tile-merchant, a broker, 2 commission agents, 2 *rentiers*, the son of a silk-merchant. Employees: a bookkeeper, a *commis négociant*, 2 servants. Professions: a journalist, a surveyor-geometer, a musician, a lawyer, a schoolteacher. Army: the former *maréchal de camp*, Cortasse de Sablonnet. Justin Badger, son of an English weaver who had set up a substantial business in Lyon, can probably be classed with the *honnêtes gens*. An actor would probably be considered closer to the liberal professions than the *menu peuple*. For sources, see Appendix XII.

occupation) and petty retailers,[41] members of 'professions artisanales et boutiquières' who would not have been out of place socially with the Paris *sans-culottes* described by Soboul.[42] There were a few day-labourers as well. To judge by their professions, the insurgents were probably on average more prosperous than their opponents, and the presence among them of many members of the propertied classes differentiated them as a group from the Jacobins. But they were far too heterogeneous for us to speak of 29 May in terms of a conflict between *la secte mercantile* and the labouring classes.

Clearly, the vast majority of the *menu peuple* did not believe that their interests were at stake in this conflict. Just as clearly the propertied classes did, and in June they used the Jacobins' defeat to re-establish their political predominance. There remained a substantial popular element in the rebellion, but in terms of social composition, Lyon's leadership after 29 May had much more in common with the Municipalité of March 1790 than it did with those between then and 1793. By 'leadership' is meant (i) the presidents and secretaries of the *sections* who became provisional municipal officers on 30 May by virtue of Nioche and Gauthier's proclamation, and (ii) the presidents and secretaries who conducted the business of the *sections* (and provided a pool of replacements for the Municipalité) in June.

Of the forty *permanents* identified by profession in the first category[43] and sixty-two in the second, the majority were bourgeois of the more elevated sort—*négociants*, *rentiers*, lawyers—and only 20 per cent and 14.5 per cent respectively were artisans, *boutiquiers*, or wage-earners.[44] In terms of the social composition of political leadership, the *journée* of 29 May seems to have ended the democratic revolution which had begun in Lyon in 1790. But while it permitted the partial political demobilization of the *menu peuple* and a severe repression, these processes were to be limited by ideology and the city's political situation.

REPRESSION

The rule of the *sections* began with repression. There are only fragmentary records of it and there is no way of checking the Jacobin Gaillard's

---

[41] Textiles: 2 silk-weavers, a fabric-designer, a tailor, an embroiderer, a stocking-weaver, a dyer, a tapestry-weaver, a cloth-finisher. Other artisans: 2 wet-coopers, a shoemaker, a cutler, a hatter, a carpenter, a Launderer, a wig-maker, a clock-maker. Petty retailers: a baker, a tavern-keeper, a *charcutier*, a merchant of handkerchiefs, a wardrobe-dealer.

[42] A. Soboul, *Les Sans-Culottes parisiens en l'an II* (Paris, 1962), 445.

[43] Out of 68 listed in a placard dated 4 June (AN AFII43, plaq. 341, no. 4).

[44] See Appendix IX.

claim that more than 300 *patriotes* were held in chains by 6 June.[45] But information from disparate sources indicates that at least 100 people were arrested between 30 May and the end of June, forty-three of them on 29, 30, and 31 May. Many of these were treated arbitrarily. Only nine were tried before civil courts and nearly half were detained until the rebellion was crushed in October. Jean Mélizet, a silk-weaver, claimed that he was bashed with musket-butts while being taken to the Town Hall basement on 30 May and was then left without medical treatment for over four months, becoming permanently crippled as a result. Manlius Dodieu, the leading *sans-culotte* of la Juiverie, who was arrested in Bourgoin early in June, said that he was dragged to Lyon 'à grand trot au bout de ma chaîne'. Of those 'imprisoned patriots' listed after the rebellion whose occupations are known, the great majority (twenty-five in all) were artisans, and more than a third were silk-weavers.[46]

Arrest and physical violence were inflicted on a relatively[47] small number of suspected Jacobins, but it seems likely that the number of victims was limited not so much by lack of suspects or of enthusiasm for rounding them up, as by the need to avoid giving Dubois-Crancé any extra excuse for military intervention. Repression on a wide scale was restricted to the less provocative form of disarmament, still a severe punishment, 'le déshonneur le plus infamant'.[48] Six National Guard battalions—all in poor areas of Lyon—were disarmed.[49] Le Plâtre, which

---

[45] AD IL375, Gaillard to Pilot (the Jacobin postmaster at Lyon), [June].

[46] 9 Silk-weavers; 6 other artisans; 2 petty professions; 1 surgeon; 1 merchant/ manufacturer; 1 servant; 3 petty retailers; 2 priests (the *curé rouge* of Saint-Just, David Bottin, and his vicar, Carillion). During the whole rebellion the 'federalists' prisoners included an additional 21 silk-weavers; 7 other artisans; 2 petty retailers; 1 teacher; 1 priest; 1 servant; 3 day-labourers; 1 farmer. Of those identified by occupation, 10 were women: AC I²6, 49, Comité de Surveillance Républicaine; AD IL987, Certificats d'arrestation par la municipalité rebelle et de non résidence à Lyon pendant le siège (for those who obeyed the decree of 12 July to leave Lyon). Most of these documents date from Oct. 1793 to nivôse, an II: individual dossiers 1L376, nos. 23–5; 31L20, no. 63; 42L12, fo. 360; 42L39, no. 83; 42L75, no. B99. D. L. Longfellow, 'Silk Weavers and the Social Struggle in Lyon during the French Revolution, 1789–1794', *French Historical Studies*, 12 (1981), 22, gives a total of 460 arrests during the rebellion.

[47] Compared to the Terror of the year II when arrests ran into thousands. The highest estimate of the numbers of Jacobin sympathizers imprisoned between 29 May and the end of the rebellion in October is 469, contained in an unsigned, undated memorandum (AC I²6, 45) designed to rebut claims by Hébertists and others that Lyon was devoid of *patriotes*.

[48] AD 42L153, d. B(8), interrogation of Boze, *chapelier*, Montluel (an II).

[49] Saint-Georges, la Juiverie, Plat-d'Argent, Bon-Rencontre, le Rhône, Pierre-Scize (AD 31L20, fo. 90, minutes of Port Saint-Paul; 42L63, d. 78, Revolutionary Committee of le Rhône, 25 Oct.).

had strongly supported the insurrection, had disarmed thirty-four of its citizens by 1 June, and its minutes imply that similar operations were performed in most, if not all, *sections*.[50]

Still more thoroughgoing was the purification of institutions whose infiltration by the politically and socially suspect had been infuriating the *honnêtes gens* since 1790. Eighteen battalions of the National Guard were purged of suspect officers, in one case as many as twenty-six of them, but mostly between ten and twenty.[51] The État Major was also purged. At least four *Comités de surveillance* had to be renewed in the *sections*, and several days passed before politically acceptable presidents and secretaries could be extracted from Jacobin haunts such as Belle-Cordière, Bon-Rencontre, and Saint-Georges[52] to complete the Provisional Municipalité. Three weeks after the insurrection the new Municipalité gave the *sections* the means of controlling political participation systematically. All existing *cartes de section* were annulled. There were no precise instructions as to exactly what circumstances would justify refusal to renew the *cartes* (which identified 'tous les citoyens ayant droit de se présenter dans leur section'[53]) but there seems no reason to doubt that they were withheld from political undesirables in most, if not all, *sections*, as in the one complained of by Chollet in a denunciation of Duperret, a stationer, 'qui dit qu'il ne falloit point donner des cartes de section à ces clubistes et gens désarmés, on a appelé le concierge on lui défendit de ne [*sic*] laisser entrer aucun individu à l'assemblée sans carte de section. Duperret se levant demande la parole et dit qu'il falloit faire une seconde revue pour désarmer les gens suspects . . . ce qui fut arrêté . . .'.[54] According to Porte-Froc, 'les assemblées primaires sont les seuls juges de l'admission des membres de ces assemblées.' Other *sections* had anticipated the Provisional Municipalité's decision. L'Hôtel-Dieu had decided on 7 June to exclude from its assembly all those who had been disarmed. Plat-d'Argent had annulled all *cartes de section* issued before 12 June, and citizens considered unworthy of new ones were excluded from both the assembly and the National Guard. A member of Plat-d'Argent could be deprived of his *carte* on a denunciation signed by six citizens. Some *sections* were not so uncompromising. On 7 June Port Saint-Paul reversed its decision

[50] AD 31L35, Surveillance Committee of le Plâtre, 1 June.

[51] *CM*, iv. 289 (4 June 1789); AD 42L45, no. 2, nomination of officers, battalion of les Terreaux, 18 June.

[52] See Riffaterre, *Le Mouvement anti-jacobin et anti-parisien à Lyon*.

[53] *CM*, iv. 334–5 (20 June).

[54] AD 42L74, d. 2 (92), denunciation by Chollet, 31 Oct.

to exclude those disarmed after 29 May, and invited 'les citoyens désarmés à reconnaître leurs erreurs et à rentrer dans les bons principes' so that they could attend *section* assemblies again. But four days later, two citizens denounced by a member of the Comité de Surveillance 'pour l'avoir insulté et menacé de l'Armée des Alpes' were disarmed and barred from the assembly.[55]

All these measures were a direct reflection of the rebellion's anti-Jacobin origins and its primary aim of destroying the menace represented by the *anarchistes-massacreurs* in the Town Hall. There were strong forces in the *sections* for still sterner measures. The prisons containing Jacobins arrested after 29 May were handled like so many Pandora's boxes, and the more committed rebel *sections* became obsessed with the mechanics of preventing escapes. They elected *commissaires des prisons* to inspect cells and locks and check on the guards, and repeatedly exhorted the authorities to greater vigilance.[56] The courts were strongly criticized when they released suspects for lack of evidence. Legal quibbles, it was said, were being allowed to compromise the security of the city. There were calls for more arrests and for *visites domiciliaires* to locate suspects.[57]

Presented with a problem often faced by defenders of the rule of law—should its protection be extended to those against whom it is being defended?—the Provisional Municipalité held out against these pressures for most of June. It ordered the release of all those who had been detained illegally and emphasized the need to limit repressive activity to the proper authorities.[58] The Département, too, rejected demands from two *sections* for the summary judgement of the 'criminals of the 29th', warned that reprisals against Jacobin sympathizers would not be tolerated, and ordered strict adherence to the law in the treatment of prisoners.[59] For some, like the provisional *procureur* Didier Guillin, this was possibly an expression of sincere attachment to legality, but it would be unwise to assume, as Riffaterre does, that it reflects the new Municipalité's innate

[55] *Secrétariat*, p. 186, minutes of Porte-Froc, 24 June; AD 31L41, fo. 23, minutes of l'Hôtel-Dieu, 7 June; 31L49, fo. 10, minutes of Plat-d'Argent, 12 June; 31L20, fos. 90, 94, and 31L21, fo. 6, minutes of Port Saint-Paul, 3, 5, and 11 June.

[56] See e.g. AD IL375, extract from the minutes of Rue Terraille, 17 June; 31L2, fos. 13, 16, minutes of la Croisette, 30 June (recommending that the Jacobin prisoners be put in chains), 8 July; 31L21, fos. 19, 20, minutes of Port Saint-Paul, 5, 11 July; 31L41, fo. 30, minutes of l'Hôtel-Dieu, 21 July; *Secrétariat*, pp. 193, 205 (1, 7 July).

[57] AD 31L21, fo. 23, minutes of Port Saint-Paul, 18 July; 31L6, extract from the minutes of Saint-Nizier, 18 July; *Secrétariat*, pp. 188–9, minutes of Porte-Froc, 27 June.

[58] *CM*, iv. 282, 331 (1, 19 June).

[59] *Département*, ii. 318 (2 June).

moderation. Dramatic acts of retribution against the former Municipalité's sympathizers would clearly have increased the risk of an attack
by the Armée des Alpes, and large-scale arrests would have undermined
the claim that Lyon was united against a small minority of Jacobin
agitators.

But legal scruple and political prudence were soon overwhelmed by
the hatreds which pervaded the political struggle in Lyon. On the evening
of 26 June the Jacobin municipal officer Sautemouche was released from
prison into the midst of an angry crowd in the anti-Jacobin bastion of
Porte-Froc. He sought refuge in the sectional assembly, was thrown out,
cornered by the crowd, and hacked to death.[60] There were fears that this
would be followed by other murders and perhaps even prison massacres,
which would have discredited entirely the rebels' carefully constructed
image of moderation. It was partly this fear which, in July, prompted the
authorities to put some leading Jacobins on trial,[61] a decision which
greatly accelerated the drift towards civil war.

This account of 29 May has sought to qualify the neo-Jacobin view of it
as a straightforward counter-revolution generated by the social fears of
reactionary sections of the bourgeoisie. Instead, the focus has been on
firstly, the tightening nexus between local and national politics, and
secondly, the Jacobins' alienation of socially diverse sections of Lyon's
population. But this is not to deny that social fears played a part, or that
they contributed to the repressive zeal of the *sections*.

There was the old fear of what the working population might do or be
led to do by agitators or want, and undoubtedly the Jacobins were hated
for their attempts to stir up the masses, attempts which the insurgents
understood in terms of the basest criminality. The Jacobins were thought
to be threatening property, but not by means as sophisticated as the
agrarian law or anything like primitive socialism. In June the *section* of
Saint-Nizier described the deposed Municipalité's aims as having been
to disarm the rich in order to arm the poor, 'évidemment en vue du
pillage et du massacre'.[62] The Municipalité was believed literally to have
been 'un tha [*sic*] de va-nuds-pieds, de pillards' which 'avoit juré de

---

[60] Minutes of Porte-Froc, 27 June, in *Secrétariat*, pp. 188–9.

[61] See below, Ch. 7, pp. 227–8.

[62] *Lettre communiquée à la section II de Marseille, par le citoyen Pérouse et imprimée par ordre de la dite section* (Marseille, 1793), quoted in Riffaterre, *Le Mouvement anti-jacobin et anti-parisien à Lyon*, i. 206.

s'enricher de nos dépouilles';[63] and weeks after its overthrow the *sections* were still clamouring for confiscation of its members' property to make up for the public funds the Jacobins were thought to have stolen.[64] It was also believed that the Jacobins had bought their support amongst the *menu peuple*. Claude Bertholat, a silk-weaver arrested for fighting for the Jacobins on 29 May, was asked by a *juge de paix* first, whether he had not been a party to the September massacres, and secondly, whether he had not been paid to assist the plans of the Jacobin Municipalité.[65] Fears like these were widespread in 1793, of course, not only in Lyon but amongst the propertied classes generally. They were an important element in the Girondins' anti-Jacobin propaganda in the provinces, notably in Chasset's much-quoted warning to the Lyonnais to strike quickly against the Jacobin menace: 'Il s'agit de la vie et puis des biens'.[66] For the most part the provincial élites were not sufficiently alarmed to rise up in defence of life and property, but when they did so in Lyon, social fears increased the pressures for revenge which wore down the legalistic scruples of the rebel leadership.

IDEOLOGY AND POLITICS (1): LEGITIMIZING REBELLION IN JUNE 1793

The conflicting ideological patterns which emerged in the rebels' handling of repression are also apparent in their broader politics. To an extent, the tensions were those of the Revolution itself, tensions between the fundamental legitimizing concepts of popular sovereignty, the rule of law, and the right of resistance to oppression. 'Résister, avec la loi, à une oppression qui est la violation la plus audacieuse de toutes les Loix'[67] was the declared aim of the sectional movement. But how far should legitimate resistance go? With this question the problem of the rebels' aims emerges at the level of political theory.

In a letter to Garat, the Minister of the Interior, on 30 May, the Département defended the rebellion as a legitimate act of resistance while also paying its respects to the rule of law: it would await the decision of the government of France on the future of Lyon and the Provisional

---

[63] AD 42L68, d. 8, words attributed to Brest, *pâtissier*, in a denunciation (n.d.); *La Section Rousseau [Saint-Nizier] à ses concitoyens* (Lyon, [June] 1793), in *Secrétariat*, p. 496.

[64] AD 31L2, fo. 14, minutes of la Croisette, 1 July; 31L41, fo. 33, minutes of l'Hôtel-Dieu, approving le Plâtre's proposal, 3 July.

[65] Ibid. 1L987 (27 June).

[66] AN F1c III, Rhône 8, d. 3, no. 50, letter to Dubost, 15 May.

[67] *Extrait des registres de la section de la Convention*, p. 1.

Municipalité.[68] But its acceptance of the Convention's right to rule on the law was limited by the clear implication that Lyon would resist any attempt to re-establish the old Municipalité. Sectional statements on this issue reveal similar ambiguities. Rue Tupin declared an equivocal 'soumission aux loix émanées d'une représentation intègre et inviolable', and la Croisette 'le respect dû aux propriétés, aux personnes et à 'inviolabilité de la Convention'.[69] Some *sections* made more straightforward declarations of loyalty to the Convention, and delegates were elected on behalf of all of them to present Lyon's case to it. But in the seven *sections* for which there is evidence on this point, there appear to have been varying views of the delegates' objectives. Rue Neuve and la Croisette limited their delegates to justifying 29 May and rebutting Jacobin calumny. Porte-Froc and Port Saint-Paul wanted to ask the Convention to dismiss the Jacobin Municipalité and the Tribunal du District immediately, and to authorize the trial of the Jacobin prisoners in Lyon, with the Tribunal Criminel of Rhône-et-Loire as the court of last appeal. The Provisional Municipalité sent its own delegation to the Convention with instructions to request formal destitution of its predecessor, new elections, the recall of Nioche and Gauthier, and the extension to Lyon of the right of sectional permanence.[70] These demands implied recognition of the Convention's right to determine the legal status of the regime created by the *sections*. At least three *sections*, however, had so little confidence in the Convention's justice that they recommended detaining its two *représentants en mission* until the Lyonnais delegates had returned from Paris. And the decision to send other delegates to solicit support from Marseille and Bordeaux[71] suggests, at the very least, uncertainty as to whether resistance to oppression should, or could, be limited to the local context.

On 3 June, as news began to spread of the confrontation which had begun on 31 May between the Paris *sans-culottes* and the Convention, the appeal of continued resistance to oppression suddenly increased. By conceding the *sans-culotte* demand for the expulsion of twenty-nine *députés*, including many of those who had been taking the part of provincial moderates against their Jacobin opponents, the Convention ended

---

[68] AN M669, d. 4, no. 9, Département to Minister of the Interior, 30 May.

[69] AD 31L8, no. 1, declaration by Rue Tupin, 1 June; 31L2, fo. 2, minutes of la Croisette, 2 June.

[70] *CM*, iv. 281 (1 June); AD 31L2, fo. 2, minutes of la Croisette, 2 June; 31L20, fo. 88, minutes of Port Saint-Paul, 2 June.

[71] AD 31L33, extract from the minutes of Place Neuve, 2 June; 31L38, extract from the minutes of Porte-Froc (n.d.); 31L6, no. 1, extract from the minutes of Saint-Nizier; *CM*, iv. 281 (1 June).

the uncertainty which had allowed room for hope that it would legitimize Lyon's rebellion. Simultaneously, it provided both an act of oppression against which to offer continued resistance and grounds for denying the Convention any further right to embody the rule of law. On 3 June, for example, the *section* of la Saône circulated a denunciation of 'la faction des anarchistes à Paris et l'arrestation de 22 membres de la Convention par la minorité', and declared 'combien il est impossible et révoltant d'être gouverné par elle'.[72] The rule of law could continue under legislation passed before 31 May; but so too could resistance to oppression, defiance of the purged Convention, and measures against its agents and collaborators in the subversion of the law. The 'revolution' of 31 May–2 June thus gave the Lyonnais rebellion a new ideological coherence.

However, it is important not to over-emphasize the impact of the Parisian *journées* on the direction of the Lyonnais rebellion in June. While it is clear enough that they increased hostility to the Convention, it is also clear from the evidence we have seen that it had been regarded with hostility and suspicion by parts of the anti-Jacobin movement well before June. In the history of Lyon's rebellion, the main importance of the purge of the Convention was in loosening some of the constraints which had limited the direct expression of this hostility—constraints of ideology (repugnance to defying a legally constituted *représentation nationale*), prudence (fear of prejudicing a possibly favourable reception of Lyon's case at the bar of the Convention), and sectional politics (areas of opinion still favourable to the Convention). The extent of indignation at the treatment of the Girondins is hard to judge, but it does not seem to have been as powerful a force as in Bordeaux, for example, whose *députés* had been so prominent in the parliamentary opposition to the Montagne, and were so numerous amongst the victims of 31 May–2 June.[73] Reintegration of the expelled *députés* into a Convention free from the threat of force became a declared goal of the rebellion, but its leaders' main preoccupation was still the threat posed by the Montagnards' agents at Grenoble.

INCONSISTENCIES OF MONTAGNARD POLICY: DUBOIS–CRANCÉ AND LINDET

This threat had two contradictory effects on the politics of Lyon. On the one hand it encouraged military preparations and intransigent attitudes.

[72] AD 31L49, fo. 3, minutes of Plat-d'Argent, 3 June, summarizing la Saône's declaration.
[73] A. Forrest, *Society and Politics in Revolutionary Bordeaux* (Oxford, 1975), 104–7.

On the other, it imposed the necessity, at least in the short term, of avoiding giving Dubois-Crancé excuses to mount an attack on Lyon while it had virtually no means of defence. The Lyonnais were quite right to be worried about Dubois-Crancé, the dominant force amongst the *députés* with the Armée des Alpes. When he heard of the insurrection in Lyon, and deduced from the tone of their letters that Nioche and Gauthier were being held against their will, he wrote to warn the Committee of Public Safety of the military threat that would result if, as he feared, the counter-revolution had won control of Lyon.[74] Lyon's military importance was immense. With Auxonne, it was a principal supply centre for three armies (Alps, Italy, and Pyrénées-Orientales). It was second only to Paris as a centre of road and postal communications.[75] Its arsenal contained 83 artillery pieces, 782 muskets, over 10,000 sabres, and large quantities of powder, cartridges, cannon-balls, and shot. Its foundries were producing four cannon each day. Dubois-Crancé was saddled with 15,000 unarmed recruits, all of whom he thought could be provided with weapons if the suspects and *étrangers* in Lyon were to be disarmed (which says a good deal about his views of Lyon's politics). If the armies were deprived of these resources it would be bad enough. But he foresaw a worse possibility: a new Vendée centred on Lyon which would threaten his army's rear and cut off its supplies.[76]

On the morning of 2 June, in Chambéry, Dubois-Crancé ordered Kellermann to cancel the departure of 4,000 men for Toulon and to march on Lyon with ten infantry battalions, supported by cavalry and siege artillery. He expected that the city would be under attack in four or five days. But on reaching Grenoble on the evening of the same day, he found Nioche and Gauthier there. They thought that the insurrection was much less dangerous than he feared, and their safe return deprived him of his strangest justification for an immediate attack. Dubois-Crancé changed his decision, but not his belief that the Lyonnais insurrection should be crushed by force as soon as possible.[77]

By early June the Vendée and parts of the Lozère were in rebellion, Marseille and Lyon were on the edge of it, Bordeaux, Nîmes, Caen,

---

[74] *Actes*, iv. 421–6, Dubois-Crancé and Albitte to CSP, 2 June.

[75] Ibid.; *Première partie de la réponse de Dubois-Crancé*, p. 93; AN M669, d. 5, no. 3, *administrateur-général des Postes* to Minister of the Interior, 17 July.

[76] AG B^{3}103*, d. 1, inventory of the Lyon Arsenal, 19 May; *Actes*, iv. 459–61, Dubois-Crancé and Albitte to CSP, 5 June.

[77] AN AFII43, plaq. 340, no. 14, Dubois-Crancé and Albitte to Kellermann, 2 June (copy); *Actes*, iv. 459–61, Dubois-Crancé and Albitte to CSP, 5 June.

Grenoble, and Toulouse were showing signs of following suit, and the full extent of provincial reaction to the revolution of 31 May–2 June was still unclear.[78] In these circumstances, the moderate Committee of Public Safety was not inclined to encourage Dubois-Crancé's belligerence. Garat's *commissaires observateurs* were sending reassuring reports of Lyonnais patriotism.[79] Nioche and Gauthier's letter to the Committee of Public Safety on 3 June, while criticizing the use of force against the Municipalité, suggested that there was no reason to fear a counter-revolution in Lyon. Three days later, four moderate *députés* from *départements* near Lyon—Royer (Ain), Laurenceot (Jura), Serre (Hautes-Alpes), and Michet (Rhône-et-Loire)—sent a strongly worded note to the Committee urging it to restrain their colleagues in Grenoble. On 7 June the Convention passed a decree authorizing the *députés* in Grenoble 'à prendre toutes les mesures de sûreté générale propres à rétablir le calme et la tranquillité publique dans la ville de Lyon'.[80] But to make it clear that Dubois-Crancé and Albitte would bear responsibility for any precipitate action, the Committee wrote to them on the same day 'pour leur recommander de nouveau de ne user l'autorisation donnée par le décret qu'avec la plus extrême prudence'.[81] Temporarily, and with undisguised reluctance, Dubois-Crancé had to abandon thoughts of quick and drastic action against Lyon. This was a disastrous policy. By seeming to place Lyon at the mercy of Dubois-Crancé, the decree could only increase Lyonnais resentment. But the Committee prevented Dubois-Crancé from using his formally extensive powers, and so gave the rebel authorities time to consolidate themselves.

Lyon's fears were increased by a rumour that the 7 June decree had ordered the Armée des Alpes to attack. Feelings ran so high that ten *sections* demanded that no more artillery or munitions be released from the Arsenal:

Considérant que dans un moment où notre cité paroît menacée des plus grands malheurs, par la Perfidie des hommes qui se sont emparés exclusivement de la

---

[78] On the Lozère, see AN AFII43, extract from the minutes of the Département of Ardèche, 29 May; for other places, see Forrest, *Society and Politics*, pp. 99–100; W. Scott, *Terror and Repression in Revolutionary Marseilles* (London, 1973), 110–11; M. Lyons, *Revolution in Toulouse* (Berne, 1978), 42–3; Edmonds, '"Federalism" and Urban Revolt', pp. 22–6; Riffaterre, *Le Mouvement anti-jacobin et anti-parisien et Lyon*, i. 389 (on Grenoble).

[79] Pontheuil, a Lyonnais by birth, was sent to join Gonchon on 8 May. On their sympathy for the Lyonnais, see J. Garat, *Mémoires* (Paris, 1862), 248–9; AN AFII43, plaq, 339, no. 21, and 340, nos. 1, 3, Gonchon to Garat, 31 May, 2, 3 June.

[80] *Actes*, iv. 438–40, 476; *Moniteur*, xvii. 580.

[81] *Actes*, iv. 476.

représentation nationale lesquels ont osés [*sic*] des ordres pour faire porter sur notre ville touttes [*sic*] les forces qui avoient étés destinées à repousser nos ennemis et les ont mis à la disposition d'hommes qui nous avons droit de regarder comme nos plus grands ennemis, il est nécessaire de s'assurer de touttes l'artillerie et tous [*sic*] les munitions qui existent actuellement dans cette ville . . .[82]

The authorities did not act formally on this demand straight away, but they displayed complete intransigence in their response to an attempt at negotiation initiated by the Committee of Public Safety. On 3 June the Convention accepted its proposal to add Robert Lindet to the *représentants en mission* attached to the Armée des Alpes and to give him particular responsibility for Lyon. He left that day and arrived in Lyon on the 8th, unfortunately in the same coach as Chalier's ally, Gaillard, which compromised him in the eyes of the rebels from the start.[83]

Apart from this initial gaffe, Lindet seems to have behaved with great good sense, patience, and moderation, but he got nowhere. The Département refused to accept his credentials. His past political activities were questioned; he was told the *sections* had to be consulted; he was not told exactly when the Département would grant him an audience; he was denied copies of deliberations concerning his mission; and the Département even refused to give him details of the events of 29 May.[84] The Département was probably playing for time while exploring the prospects for a broad provincial coalition against the Convention, but it is not easy to see how a more accommodating response to Lindet could have been sold to the *sections*. Riffaterre blames the Département for inflaming opinion against the Convention by encouraging the rumours about the decree of 7 June when it knew from intercepted correspondence that they were false.[85] But a better outcome for Lindet's mission was hardly likely given the suspicions of *députés* which had been gaining strength in Lyon since March. Nioche and Gauthier's endeavours for the Jacobin Municipalité on 29 May provided excellent ammunition for the Département, which recalled 'le souvenir de la malheureuse journée du 29 mai [qui] a fait redouter aux citoyens de cette ville la présence de ce nouveau député, avec d'autant plus de raison qu'il a fait route avec un des premiers moteurs des troubles'.[86] Most telling of all was the belief that the Convention which had sent Lindet was now under the control of the

[82] AC I²4, no. 12, extract from the registers of Rue Buisson, 11 June.
[83] *Actes*, iv. 427; *CM*, iv. 298, 310 (8, 12 June); *Département*, ii. 339 (15 June).
[84] *Actes*, ii. 496–7, 508, 522, Lindet to CSP, 9, 10, 11 June.
[85] Riffaterre, *Le Mouvement anti-jacobin et anti-parisien à Lyon*, i. 383–4.
[86] *Départment*, ii. 339 (15 June).

factieux who had hatched Dubois-Crancé's mission (the decree of 7 June, even when properly represented, seemed further proof of this).[87]

On 9 June, at the request of the Provisional Municipalité, the *sections* considered whether they should recognize those of the Convention's decrees which had been passed after 31 May and whether they should accept Lindet's credentials. Both propositions were rejected, by a margin of twenty to two known resolutions in the case of the first, and twenty-eight to none in the case of the second. According to the Commune, a majority of *sections* called for Lindet's arrest.[88] Eight *sections* were openly intransigent, either calling for severance of all relations with the Convention or denouncing it violently.[89] Porte-Froc, as usual the most belligerent, declared Paris to be (amongst other things) in a state of revolt and the Convention to be dissolved. It appealed to the primary assemblies of all France to reject the Convention's decrees, and proposed that they should collaborate to save 'la chose publique'.[90]

There were signs of caution in some *sections*—Port Saint-Paul, la Croisette (which insisted that Lindet's 'caractère de représentant' be respected), and la Grande-Côte I (which stressed that withdrawal of recognition from the Convention should only be temporary). But even these *sections* took a hard line on some of the main issues dividing Lyon from the Convention. La Croisette favoured establishing links with other *départements*, and Port Saint-Paul wanted the convocation of the primary assemblies of Rhône-et-Loire, measures regarded in Paris as 'federalist' and therefore counter-revolutionary. La Grande-Côte would only consider recognizing the Convention if the Commission of Twelve was re-established.[91] Overall, it seems clear that by the end of the second week of June, opinion in the *sections* was heavily in favour of removing Lyon, at least temporarily, from the jurisdiction of the Convention, though there was uncertainty as to how much further the revolt should go, and on what terms it might end.

There were divisions of opinion within this consensus, but they are difficult to link with particular individuals, and more difficult still to link with groups. In support of his thesis that the Lyonnais were tricked into

[87] AD 1L375, Fréminville, Mollet, and Genet-Bronze (*députés* of the *sections*) to Coindre in Paris, 9 June; 31L41, fo. 23, minutes of l'Hôtel-Dieu, 11 June.

[88] AD 1L375; *CM*, iv. 304 (11 June).

[89] AD 1L375, extract from the minutes of Saint-Georges, 9 June.

[90] Ibid., Projet d'adresse aux français, proposed by Porte-Froc, 9 June.

[91] Ibid.; AD 31L21, fo. 6, minutes of Port Saint-Paul, 11 June.

war with the Convention by a small faction of intriguers,[92] Riffaterre
suggests that there were two factions in the rebel Municipalité, one
relatively moderate, represented by the *procureur* Didier Guillin, the other
intent on war with the Convention, represented by Francois Bémani, the
rather mysterious president of the *section* of la Convention.[93] Just as he
reads much into nuances between *sections* which were, as we have just
seen, by no means clear or consistent in their recommendations and which
were confused about the political situation, so also Riffaterre finds parties
and fixed positions in debates where there is insufficient evidence to
attribute a consistent policy to any of the participants, much less to
definable groups of them. Bémani's demand 'que l'on emploie la plus
grande surveillance pour ôter an citoyen Robert Lindet tous les moyens
de nous nuire' is given as evidence that he belonged to 'le parti de la
rupture', and Guillin's reasoning that Dubois-Crancé's military position
was not strong enough to threaten Lyon places him in 'celui de la paix'.[94]
Yet Guillin had urged that Lindet's credentials should be not recognized
when the matter was first considered by the Municipalité, and after
Bémani had read an inflammatory address by Lanjuinais, had successfully
advocated its publication.[95] All that can be said about his position is that,
like the majority of the provisional municipal officers, departmental and
district councillors, and *sectionnaires* who took part in these discussions
in the second week of June, he appears to have denied the Convention's
authority over Lyon while hoping for the moment to avoid open hostilities.

As well as verbal assaults on the Convention, there were, it is true, a
number of statements urging caution. But since both could come (as in the
case of Guillin) from the same mouth, the most plausible interpretation of
them seems to be that after the first wave of indignation died away, even
some outspoken critics of the Convention realized that Lyon's position
was too weak to risk such provocative acts as the arrest of Lindet. Lindet
thought he saw growing reluctance to break with the Convention, and
there was no open opposition to his departure on the 16th.[96]

Essentially, the rebels seem to have been playing the same game as the

---

[92] Riffaterre, *Le Mouvement anti-jacobin et anti-parisien à Lyon*, ii. 615.

[93] Bémani, a *négociant*, resigned as president of the Provisional Municipalité after being
denounced as foreign-born and not long resident in Lyon (AD 31L9, no. 1, extract from
the minutes of la Convention, 31 May).

[94] Riffaterre, *Le Mouvement anti-jacobin et anti-parisien à Lyon*, i. 367–71, 397–80.

[95] *Actes*, iv. 496, Lindet to CSP, 9 June; *CM*, iv. 305 (11 June).

[96] *Actes*, iv. 583, Lindet to CSP, 16 June.

Committee of Public Safety, keeping open the possibility of negotiation with the other side and waiting until the political situation in the rest of France became clearer. Despite a report by Fain that to pursue negotiations with the Convention would be useless, as it was dominated totally by the anarchists, he was sent back to Paris, and suggestions that the delegation be recalled were rejected.[97] But to recognize that the rebels were not willing to destroy all possibility of reconciliation with the Convention is not to accept Riffaterre's speculation (largely based on Lindet's letter just cited) that the Municipalité was ready to accept the Parisian revolution in return for acceptance of its own. Distrust of the Convention had been developing for too long to be dissipated, as Riffaterre suggests, by the news that a decree of 8 June had forbidden Dubois-Crancé to weaken the forces guarding the alpine frontiers.[98] After all, this additional restraint on him might last only as long as the Piedmontese threat. It is not this decree, or 'l'indécision habituel aux modérés',[99] but the caution dictated by Lyon's precarious situation which explains the Municipalité's failure to break all links with the purged Convention in the first half of June.

THE CALLING OF THE PRIMARY ASSEMBLIES

Two days after Lindet's departure, the Département and members of the six *districts* under its jurisdiction convoked the primary assemblies of Rhône-et-Loire to elect delegates who were to meet in Lyon on 30 June, 'considérant ... que c'est au peuple, en exerçant sa souveraineté, à juger la violation de ses droits, à les rétablir et à sauver la patrie'.[100] It may seem surprising that, having trodden so carefully while other rebel areas had broken openly from the Convention within a few days of learning of the purge,[101] the Département now set about creating a local substitute for the Convention. The explanation appears to be that by mid-June the

---

[97] *CM*, iv. 298, 8 June; AD 42L12, fo. 5, interrogation of Fain, 4 brumaire, an II; 42L75, d. B(13), passport issued to Fain by the Municipalité, 8 June.

[98] Riffaterre, *Le Mouvement anti-jacobin et anti-parisien à Lyon*, i. 393, 395. The decree was proposed by the CSP on 8 June and voted the same day, after representations by *députés* from *départements* exposed to Piedmontese attack (*Actes*, iv. 483, CSP, 8 June).

[99] Riffaterre, *Le Mouvement anti-jacobin et anti-parisien à Lyon*, i. 255.

[100] *Département*, ii. 347–8 (18 June).

[101] Bordeaux set up a *Commission populaire* in the first week of June, and by the 9th had withdrawn recognition from the Convention (Forrest, *Society and Politics*, pp. 109–10). On 6 June the Marseille *sections* re-established the Tribunal Populaire in direct defiance of the Convention, and then set about organizing a Departmental Army on the 10th (Scott, *Terror and Repression*, pp. 112, 115).

provincial anti-Jacobin movement seemed strong, and victory over the Convention possible. As well as Marseille and Bordeaux, there was evidence that the anti-Jacobin movement had substantial support in Nîmes, Montpellier, Tarascon, Lons-le-Saunier,[102] and within a number of departmental administrations. By 1 June, three *départements* (Ain, Jura, and Saône-et-Loire) had agreed to send representatives to a new national assembly in Bourges, and by the 10th, representatives of these and three more *départements* (Côte-d'Or, Ardèche, and Mont-Blanc) were conferring with the authorities in Lyon.[103] In Bordeaux, the Provisional Municipalité's deputation met with an enthusiastic welcome, and the arrest of two Montagnard *députés* in the Gironde became known in Lyon on the 12th. Lyon's delegates to Bouches-du-Rhône reported the rout of the anarchists from Aix and Marseille to the smallest village.[104] Closer at hand, the Isère seemed to be on the point of breaking with the Convention. It was known in Lyon on 10 June that the Département of the Isère had convoked the primary assemblies to meet on the 20th to discuss the events in Paris, and two of its administrators deputed to Lyon on the 15th made no secret of their sympathy for the rebels.[105]

These developments, the apparent hesitancy and timidity of the Convention, the weakness of Dubois-Crancé's position, and the enthusiasm expressed by some *sections* for the idea, make the Département's decision to convoke the primary assemblies quite comprehensible.[106] It had been toying with the possibility since the 12th at the latest, when it had called for two representatives of each *district* to be sent to Lyon to discuss it.[107] It had also been assessing the likely strength of an anti-Parisian confederation. On 10 June, *administrateur* Jean-Jacques Tardy was secretly dispatched with Gauthier, one of the delegates of the Jura, to consult with the Gironde and other *départements*, 'leur communiquer les instructions verbales dont ils ont été chargés'. They and the delegates sent to Marseille carried accounts of 29 May, proclamations of their

[102] Anti-Jacobin addresses from Nîmes and Lons-le-Saunier were read in la Juiverie on 16 and 17 June (AD 31L16, fos. 6, 7). The Comité Général des Sections de Tarascon promised aid to Lyon on 7 June (Coste MS 631). On 17 June a delegation from the *sections* of Montpellier denounced the violation of the Convention (*CM*, iv. 321).

[103] Riffaterre, *Le Mouvement anti-jacobin et anti-parisien à Lyon*, i. 388–9.

[104] AD 31L16, fo. 2, minutes of la Juiverie, 12 June; Fonds Coste MS 632, Pelzin and Jacquet to the Provisional Municipalité.

[105] *CM*, iv. 301 (10 June); *Département*, ii. 346 (18 June).

[106] *CM*, iv. 309 (12 June), mentions the Convention's decree of the 8th.

[107] The minutes of Port Saint-Paul mention a delegation from nine *sections* to the Département with this request (AD 31L21, fo. 7 (13 June)).

respective *départements*, and a list of thirty-eight *départements* which were seen as potential allies. Others in the north were expected to send delegates to Strasbourg and Rennes, and all were to be invited to help form an assembly at Bourges.[108] This was a tentative, exploratory mission which came to nothing, but it indicates the optimistic estimates conceived in Lyon of the potential strength of the departmental movement in the Midi, stimulated by a flow of exhortations and promises which required a special committee to handle them.[109]

Riffaterre rightly stresses that the stated objectives of the departmental movement were hardly counter-revolutionary. The assembly at Bourges was to be composed of substitutes (*suppléants*) for the existing *députés*, or, failing that, provisional *députés*. It was itself to be provisional, dissolving when the purged *députés* were readmitted to the Convention.[110] No doubt this was a cloak for men with more drastic measures in mind—Lindet heard remarks (presumably during his meetings with the Département) to the effect that 'il fallait une autre Convention'.[111] But while some of them may have been bitterly opposed to the purged Convention, it is hard to believe that the twenty-one members of the Département and *districts* of Rhône-et-Loire who signed the order of 18 June were out to destroy the Republic. They had all either survived the purge of the Département after 10 August or been elected or re-elected since then. Not much else is known about their politics. Some had served the old regime or the constitutional monarchy. But the ex-noble Servan was not amongst the signatories, and the only member of the Département known to have had royalist associations, Tardy,[112] was on his way to Bordeaux. Those about whose politics anything positive is known were all former *patriotes*. Dubost had been president of the Club Central in 1791 and a *notable* under Vitet, while Richard, Pipon, and Maillan had been regarded as extremists before 29 May. The last two had served on the Jacobin Committee of Public Safety of Rhône-et-Loire.[113]

For the *sectionnaires*, as for the Département, calling the primary assemblies was in a sense a defensive measure as well as a challenge to

---

[108] This information derives from a report of a search of Tardy's papers carried out in Limoges on 16 June (AD 1L375, extract from the minutes of the CSP of Haute-Vienne).

[109] *Département*, ii. 339 (15 June).

[110] Riffaterre, *Le Mouvement anti-jacobin et anti-parisien à Lyon*, i. 391–2.

[111] *Actes*, iv. 538, Lindet to CSP, 12 June.

[112] His son made a royalist declaration before his execution during the Terror (Riffaterre, *Le Mouvement anti-jacobin et anti-parisien à Lyon*, i. 240).

[113] AD 42L12, fo. 23, interrogation of J.-F. Dubost, 8 brumaire, an II; [J. Chalier?], 'Tableau de réforme', Fonds Coste MS 609, [March, 1793]; *CM*, iv. 253 (14 May).

the Convention. It sought to lift responsibility for future action from the *sections* of Lyon and the authorities assembled there, and to place it on the people of Rhône-et-Loire. It also reduced Lyon's isolation, in appearance at least. As the *section* of la Convention had argued on 9 June (taking some liberties with recent history), 'les sections de cette cité ... ne peuvent et ne doivent s'isoler des autres districts du Département qui dans la journée du 29 mai ont fait cause commune avec elles ...'.[114]

In the second half of June, Lyon's anti-Jacobin insurrection, its quarrel with the *députés en mission*, and its defiance of the Convention looked like merging into a general movement against the purged Convention. The city's leaders were content henceforth to follow in the wake of this movement. Like most of the 'federalist' cities, Lyon began an odd and self-deceptive game of bluff, emitting terrible threats against the Montagnards ('vils scélérats, factieux impudents, vous osez menacer des hommes libres ... nous aussi savons marcher contre les rebelles à la volonté nationale') while taking at face value similar bellowing from elsewhere ('tous les citoyens étoient prêts à partir ... que tous périroient ou extermineroient les traîtres: oui tous, tous ...') and the promises of phantom or, at most skeleton, bodies like the Assemblée Centrale de Résistance à l'Oppression des Députés des Communes et Assemblées Primaires des Départements Réunis, Séante à Caen.[115] Lyon, like the others, was waiting for someone to go over the top.

But Lyon was even more reticent than most. Marseille and Bordeaux did at least establish and dispatch departmental armies intended to subdue Paris. Lyon made only gestures. On 19 June the Municipalité drew up a plan for a departmental army, inspired by the examples of the Eure, Calvados, and Bouches-du-Rhône. Its organization was haphazard in the extreme, and the Département, while aware of the project, does not appear to have taken steps to begin recruitment outside Lyon.[116] Neither the army's size nor its objectives were specified. The *sections* were simply asked to enrol volunteers, who would be formed into battalions when there were sufficient numbers and paid 30 *sous* a day. The money was to be raised by voluntary subscription or, failing that, by a progressive tax on the rich. Only fifteen *sections* sent delegates to a meeting on 21 June

---

[114] AD 1L375, extract from the minutes of la Convention, 9 June.

[115] *Adresse du peuple de Lyon à la République française* (Lyon, [14 June] 1793), in *Secrétariat*, p. 528; report of a session of the Commission Populaire, Bordeaux, in *CP*, p. 347; *Lettre* [from the ACRODCAPDRSC] ... *aux Assemblées populaires de Rhône-et-Loire* (n.p., [early July]) (Fonds Coste 4480).

[116] *CM*, iv. 328–9 (18–19 June); *Département*, ii. 350 (19 June).

to discuss details of recruitment, and there are records of enrolments in only two. Some *sections* were said to have greatly exceeded their quotas; others, like Port Saint-Paul, were still being exhorted to fill theirs on the 27th.[117] But by 28 June confidence in Lyon's ability to raise a substantial force had apparently waned, for the idea of an independent attack on Paris was dropped in favour of waiting until the Marseillais force could link up with Lyon's.[118]

It is easy to see why Riffaterre concluded that Lyon's 'adhérence au mouvement fédéraliste fut hésitante, inactive, superficielle',[119] assuming federalism to mean a campaign of co-ordinated action by the *départements* to bring Paris into line. But in the sense in which the Montagnards understood federalism—rejecting the purged Convention's authority and acting independently of it—many of the *sections* were decidedly federalist. They strongly supported the Département's decision to appeal to the primary assemblies and thus to seek a new repository for the popular sovereignty which the Convention could not embody while 'un-free'. Only a minority of sectional statements on this issue have survived. Nine of them unequivocally demanded convocation of the assemblies, and three of the nine (Rue Buisson, Porte-Froc, and le Gourguillon) wanted their delegates to be given 'des pouvoirs les plus amples'.[120] Plat-d'Argent was undecided, and l'Hôtel-Dieu opposed holding elections 'motivé sur la crainte qu'elle a de voir le fédéralisme s'établir'.[121]

Assuming that the 'federalist' implications of what was proposed were not lost on the other *sections*, and considering that federalism had been a capital crime since 16 December 1792,[122] the numbers of voters in the assemblies on 24 June were (if we can trust the figures) surprisingly high. Riffaterre gives the totals in two *sections*—la Juiverie, 154, and Port Saint-

---

[117] AC I²4, fo. 14, meeting of Rue Buisson, 22 June; AD 31L18, no. 2, list of volunteers, la Juiverie (there was one recruit by 24 July, and no more for more than a month thereafter); 31L2, fo. 21, minutes of la Croisette (which claimed 21 volunteers); 31L21, fo. 14, minutes of Port Saint-Paul, 27 July.

[118] *CM*, iv. 356 (28 June).

[119] Riffaterre, *Le Mouvement anti-jacobin et anti-parisien à Lyon*, ii. 615.

[120] AD 31L30, fo. 15, 31L21, fos. 6, 8, 31L2, fo. 5, 31L21, fos. 7, 8, minutes of le Gourguillon, 17 June (approving Porte-Froc's proposal), Port Saint-Paul, 12, 15 June (recording Place Saint-Pierre's and la Convention's opinions), la Croisette, 9 June (recording le Rhône's opinion), Port Saint-Paul, 17 June (approving Rue Tupin's opinion), and 13 June (mentioning that 9 *sections* approved the plan); AC I²4, fo. 14, minutes of Rue Buisson, 24 June.

[121] AD, 31L49, fo. 12, minutes of Plat-d'Argent, 14 June; minutes of l'Hôtel-Dieu, 16 June.

[122] M. J. Sydenham, *The Girondins* (London, 1961), 137.

Paul, 83—to back his contention that the département's policy did not have much support.[123] Yet the figures are not low compared with the votes in most *sections* during the municipal elections of 1792, especially since voting now could be seen as an act of rebellion and would not go unnoticed in these once radical *sections*. Riffaterre did not have access to some of the sectional records that are now available, according to which two other previously radical *sections* attracted about as many voters as the two he was aware of.[124] True to its tradition, Pierre-Scize produced only 54 votes, and le Rhône 25. But there were high votes in le Change (235) and in two commercial *quartiers* of the peninsula, Rue Buisson (249) and Rue Neuve (302).[125] Support for this challenge to the Convention seems to have been greater than Riffaterre thought, particularly considering that of the eight *sections* whose votes are known, only three had been involved in the rebellion from its beginnings. If votes comparable to those in le Change, Rue Neuve, and Rue Buisson were recorded in other firmly anti-Jacobin areas, the total would have been high by the standards of local government elections during the Revolution.[126] So we can speak of relatively strong, though far from unanimous, support in the *sections* for establishing a temporary alternative to the purged Convention.

The Municipalité's views are hard to judge at this point. Delegates were sent to Roanne, Villefranche, Montbrison, and the *département* of the Isère, possibly to justify what was being done in Lyon. But there was a decline in attendance at meetings after 18 June which may have been due to unhappiness with the Département's decision. Nevertheless, the Municipalité acquiesced in it by formally convoking the primary assemblies.[127]

IDEOLOGY AND POLITICS (2): DIRECT DEMOCRACY

Lyon was now openly defying the Convention, but it could not risk denying the fundamental revolutionary idea, 'the ideology of pure democracy, that is ... the idea that the people are power, or that power is the

---

[123] Riffaterre, *Le Mouvement anti-jacobin et anti-parisien à Lyon*, i. 445.

[124] Belle-Cordière: 103; Plat-d'Argent: 98.

[125] The figures in this paragraph come from extracts from minutes dated 24 June: AD 31L45, 31L48, 31L19, 31L26, and 31L13, except for Rue Buisson: AC I²4, fo. 13.

[126] If an average of 250 voted in the more prosperous peninsular *sections* (15), and 100 in the other 19, the total could have been more than 5,600. (For comparison, see above, Chaps. 4, 5.) All *sections* seem to have elected representatives (*CP*, p. 5 (1 July)).

[127] Riffaterre, *Le Mouvement anti-jacobin et anti-parisien à Lyon*, i. 445; *CM*, iv. 337 (20 June).

people'.[128] Furet has demonstrated brilliantly the relationship of the concept of plot to this idea, plot as the hidden counter-power, always redoubtable, constantly threatening the fragile reign of democracy.[129] The relationship was understood by those who, in many cases reluctantly, tried to translate Lyon's case into the language of democracy. However much they might privately have wished to turn back the political clock to 1791, to limited suffrage and representative government untainted by direct democracy, they could not risk providing fuel for the propaganda campaign which would inevitably come from the Montagne, designed to assimilate Lyon's rebellion with the counter-revolution. A Lyonnais address of 2 June had accurately predicted the charges: 'Ils vous diront que c'est l'ouvrage de l'aristocratie triomphante; ils vous diront que les sans-culottes ont ete égorgés par les riches ... que les riches de Lyon sont des Brissotins, Rolandins, des modérantistes, des aristocrates, des contre-révolutionnaires, que la cocarde blanche est arborée; ils vous diront qu'ils veulent le retour de la tyrannie, de la féodalité et du despotisme....'.[130]

The immediate danger was that a version of the rebellion along these lines would be conveyed to the peasantry around Lyon, and this address was composed with them very much in mind. From the start the rebels had been nervous about peasant reactions to the rising of 29 May. On that day, both sides had appealed for support from the countryside, and according to Gonchon,[131] 11,000 peasant guardsmen responded by marching to Lyon. To whose appeal they were responding is not clear. According to an anonymous letter to *député* Basire, they came to crush counter-revolution, which is quite plausible given Lyon's reputation: 'on rassembloit toutes les campagnes des environs qui sont arrivées dans le lendemain en nombre de 15 à 20 mille hommes soit de ce département, de celui de l'Ain et de Cher [*sic*], qui trouvant la besogne faite, à sens contraire, ont éte obligés de changer d'idées, en convenant qu'on les avoit trompés.'[132] The Département publicly claimed to have strong rural support, but its minutes reported that 'dans toutes les campagnes et villes

---

[128] F. Furet, *Interpreting the French Revolution*, trans. E. Forster (Cambridge, 1981), 54.

[129] Ibid., 54–7.

[130] *Les sections de la ville de Lyon aux habitants du département et de toutes les municipalités voisines* (Lyon, [2 June] 1793).

[131] C. Gonchon, *Conchon aux citoyens de la section des Quinze-Vingts, Fauxbourg Saint-Antoine* (Lyon, [14 June] 1793), in *Secrétariat*, p. 523.

[132] AN F⁷4590, d. Basire, letter of 2 June.

des environs, jusqu' à Grènoble, [on disait] que la ville de Lyon étoit en pleine contre-révolution'.[133]

Knowing that Montagnard propaganda would seize on any hint of counter-revolution to mobilize the peasantry against Lyon provided a powerful reason for proclaiming revolutionary democratic orthodoxy. Even Porte-Froc felt the need to end its particularly violent diatribe against the Convention with advice to the authorities to persuade Lindet 'que le peuple de Lyon ne veut que la liberté, l'egalité, l'unité et l'indivisibilité de la République'.[134] The rebellion's social and political heterogeneity pushed its leaders further towards ideological conformity. Their popular support derived to a great extent from *clubiste* anti-Jacobinism which had been largely a response to the Jacobins' abandonment of the forms of direct democracy practised in Lyon since 1790. To maintain this support it was necessary to respect the *sections'* autonomy and role as interpreters of the popular will.

At the very moment when they regained political supremacy in Lyon, the propertied classes were thus obliged to behave consistently with the 'ideology of pure democracy', a striking illustration of Furet's point about revolutionary politics becoming 'a matter of establishing just *who* represented the people, or equality, or the nation; victory was in the hands of those who were capable of occupying that symbolic position'.[135] But throughout the rebellion there had been evident tension between this necessity and aspirations to a rule of law policed by conservative representative forms of political authority.

In theory, the idea that the popular will emanated from the *Assemblée primaire* of the *section*, meeting *en permanence*, was as fundamental to the Lyonnais rebellion as to the Parisian *sans-culotterie*: 'la volonté générale du peuple s'exprime dans les assemblées primaires, dans les sections ...'.[136] This doctrine was used to legitimize the insurrection of 29 May and the Provisional Municipalité which emerged from it, an assembly of delegates of the *sections* embodying their collective authority. Nevertheless, sectional supremacy lay mainly in the realm of symbol and theory. The *sections* sent delegations to the Town Hall almost daily, and frequently voted on matters submitted to them by the Municipalité. But they were careful to avoid seeming to issue the Municipalité with

---

[133] AD 1L375, Département and Districts of Lyon to the Convention, 4 June; *Département*, ii. 310 (30 May).

[134] AD 1L375, Projet d'adresse aux français, 9 June.

[135] Furet, *Interpreting the French Revolution*, p. 48.

[136] *Adresse du peuple de Lyon à la République française*, p. 13.

directives, except for ordering their representatives to remain at their posts (with four *sections* preferring the word 'invitation' to 'ordre'). La Croisette and la Convention formally resolved to call their resolutions 'émissions du vœu de la section' rather than 'arrêtés', and la Convention, which had proclaimed the *sections*' rights so uncompromisingly on 27 May, took a quite different view of them after the Jacobin Municipalité was no more: 'Il est d'une nécessité indispensable que les sections agissent constamment comme sections, autrement il en résulteroit ... qu'après avoir délégué ses pouvoirs, le peuple continueroit à les exercer dans ses sections et c'est cet abus qui a produit les maux que nous souffrons.'[137] What it was 'to act as *sections*' was not made clear, but it obviously did not mean to exercise direct sovereignty.

Ironically, it was the more anti-Jacobin *sections* which, when it suited them, were to seek the widest scope for sectional authority, notably Porte-Froc in the legal quarter of the city, which took it upon itself late in June to threaten an attack on Grenoble unless two Lyonnais being held there were released. La Croisette strongly criticized this, observing 'que c'est une déclaration formelle de guerre civile et que c'est aux autorités supérieures à prendre des pareilles mesures'.[138] Porte-Froc also tried to mobilize the *sections*' collective authority to force the Département and the Municipalité to take stronger action against Jacobinism, but for a long time it was frustrated by its opponents' adroit appeals both to the hierarchy of powers and to sectional autonomy. At the beginning of June Porte-Froc proposed that an organization should be set up to gather and transmit the *sections*' opinions to the authorities, but none of the other *sections* would endorse it and it took until 12 July to win majority support. La Croisette was particularly opposed to the proposal: it would destroy sectional independence, just as the *clubs de quartier* had been destroyed by the Club Central. Further, a *Secrétariat* such as Porte-Froc proposed would rival the constituted authorities and fall into the hands of factions. It was not until war with the Convention had become inevitable that the proposal was finally adopted, and even then more than a quarter of the *sections* do not seem to have supported it.[139]

---

[137] AD 31L20, fo. 21, reproduced in the minutes of Port Saint-Paul, 12 July.

[138] AC I²4, fo. 13, Rue Buisson's minutes reporting Porte-Froc's proposal, 27 June; AD 31L2, fo. 13, minutes of la Croisette attacking it, 28 June.

[139] Minutes of Porte-Froc, 3 June, in *Secrétariat*, p. 157; AD 31L41, fo. 38, minutes of l'Hôtel-Dieu, 12 July; 31L2, fos. 3, 25, minutes of la Croisette, 3 June, 1 Aug. The last document records a letter from organizers of the Secrétariat claiming that 23 *sections* had accepted it. It began its deliberations on 2 August (*Secrétariat*, p. 2).

While the debate over the Secrétariat was partly about how far to take the conflict with the Convention, it is also interesting as a guide to the continuing strength of autonomist sentiment in the *sections*. Until the Secrétariat was finally established, an extraordinarily clumsy system had to be used so that they could consult together without compromising their autonomy. This cost the *sections* a good deal in effort, talk, and delay. Before they felt able to express their collective view, a proposal for a conference had to be communicated to all thirty-four of them, which, with Lyon's topography, meant much hard walking. After each *section* had elected a delegate, a meeting would take place in one of their assembly rooms, proposals would be debated, and a scheme or recommendation agreed upon. This would then be submitted to each assembly for its approval at which stage modifications might be generated, requiring further consideration by all thirty-four. Other evidence of this extreme delicacy in matters concerning sectional independence is to be found in the records of la Croisette, the inter-class *quartier par excellence* and the bastion of anti-Jacobin *clubisme* in April and May. Proposals from other *sections* were not considered by its assembly until they had been vetted by a committee. Visiting delegates were not allowed to remain while their proposals were discussed.[140] And la Croisette's opposition to any form of centralization of sectional activity helped to ensure that the Secrétariat had mimimal powers, making it nothing more in practice than a clearing-house for determining the balance of opinion in the *sections*, mostly on uncontentious issues of day-to-day administration.[141] In the matters of sectional autonomy and permanence, and in the frequent (fortnightly) renewal of sectional delegates to the Provisional Municipalité, the rebellion maintained some genuine continuity with the traditions of popular democracy in Lyon, which may explain the persisting support for it in these areas where Lyonnais popular democracy had been strong.

Exploitation of the Jacobins' ideological weapons went beyond these limited exercises in direct democracy. With sectional permanence established, the unanimist rhetoric borrowed from them was used to justify rooting out the remnants of Jacobinism and popular radicalism in Lyon, an early demonstration of the adaptability of modern democratic thought.

---

[140] AD 31L2, fo. 8 (10 June). It took 4 days for a resolution by Rue Terraille to win approval from half the *sections* (31L12, p. 1).

[141] The regulations are in *Secrétariat*, pp. 1–2. Article 5 reads: 'The General Secrétariat cannot deliberate under any circumstances. In creating this institution the *sections* do not in any way intend [to renounce] their direct and fraternal relations, nor the right to present their positions directly to the administrative bodies...'.

Early in the campaign for permanence Jean Gilibert had found unanimist grounds for dissolving the clubs:

La souveraineté des peuples réside dans les assemblées primaires parce que c'est là où il nomme ses délégués et mandataires, c'est là seulement où il peut exprimer sa volonté générale, les clubs, les Sociétés partielles, n'expriment que des volontés individuelles. Leurs séances doivent cesser au moment de la convocation des assemblées primaires, le peuple doit alors se montre grand par une masse de citoyens réunis et n'en plus souffrir d'izole [*sic*].[142]

In June this principle was integrated with the imperative of defending the people against its enemies to make the destruction of the clubs a patriotic duty: 'tout individu, toute association quelconque qui tenteroit de faire prévaloir sa volonté sur celle des assemblées primaires, doit être considéré comme rebelle à la souveraineté nationale, et traité comme ennemi du people.'[143]

Most of the clubs seem to have been closed down early in June, like those of Le Gourguillon and La Juiverie.[144] On 8 June l'Hôtel-Dieu expressed alarm at reports of meetings of 'le cercle dit bellecour' (the Cercle Delglas was suspected of aristocratic tendencies), 'motivé sur ce que les Sociétés populaires étant suspendu [*sic*] ce seroit donner prétexte aux malveillants de dire: les Riches seuls ont le droit de s'assembler'.[145]

In practice, however, permanence tended to restrict the *droit de s'assembler* along just these lines. Deprived of their *clubs de quartier*, artisans were in most cases unlikely to be able to find time for the permanent sectional politics which superseded them. Some *sections* tried to overcome this problem: '[P]our ne pas arracher les ouvriers à leurs travaux journaliers', l'Hôtel Dieu held only one meeting daily, between 6.00 p.m. and 9.00 p.m. Rue Buisson and Plat-d'Argent followed a similar practice. But la Juiverie met generally at 3.00 p.m., and Port Saint-Paul met twice daily from 10.00 a.m. to midday and from 6.00 p.m. to 9.00 p.m. Despite its solicitude for labouring men, l'Hôtel-Dieu decided that either its Bureau (the president and secretaries) or its Comité de Surveillance would be in continuous session between 10.00 a.m. and 6.00 p.m. daily, which would have made it virtually impossible for manual workers to hold these offices. And the Bureau had the power to convoke the *sections* whenever it

---

[142] Coste MS 612, evidence against Jean Gilibert *l'aîné*, speech of 18 Feb.

[143] *Adresse du peuple de Lyon à la République française*, p. 13. See also AD 31L20, fo. 3, minutes of Port Saint-Paul, 9 June.

[144] AD 31L30, fo. 6, minutes of le Gourguillon, 3 June; 31L16, minutes of la Juiverie, 11 June.

[145] Ibid. 31L41, fo. 24, minutes, 8 June.

wished.[146] Such arrangements made serious participation in sectional politics a heavy burden for anyone whose livelihood depended on long hours of exhausting work. Even for the well-to-do, 'permanent' politics must have been trying, which meant that those able and determined enough to attend regularly were given the chance to manipulate or dominate sectional proceedings.

The propertied classes did a good job of dressing up their rebellion in democratic clothes. But the fact that it was primarily *their* rebellion remains unmistakable in the social composition of its institutions and in the belief that by ejecting the *sans-culotte* Municipalité the natural order in Lyon's affairs had been restored, or at least an unnatural one removed: 'La municipalité de Lyon dans ce temps-là n'étoit que des navets et autres ouvriers et qui se faisoit vivre les uns aux autres aux dépens de la ville.'[147] The Provisional Municipalité's policy on *subsistances* points to the same conclusion. The 'pain de l'égalité', which had been the *patriotes*' ideal since the early days of the Vitet Municipalité, was replaced by two types of bread—white bread and an inferior 'pain national'—with an indemnity paid to the poor instead of to the bakers. The rationale was to prevent price rises by allowing bakers to make a good profit on the better bread. This was supported by twenty-eight *sections* and opposed by only two, but it was unpopular with the poor because a greater outlay had to be made at the baker's shop than under the subsidized price system, and there was no certainty of receiving the indemnity.[148] Prices rose anyway, from $4\frac{1}{2}$ *sous* per pound on 29 March (with a 1 *sou* subsidy) to $5\frac{1}{2}$ *sous* for *pain national* on June 17 (with a 1 *sou* indemnity).[149]

The *sections* were divided over the *maximum*, which the Département reluctantly introduced to Rhône-et-Loire on 19 June—reluctantly, because Lyon's already daunting supply problems would be worsened by limiting the price that could be paid for grain. In early July, at least nine *sections* were demanding the suspension of the *maximum*, though there was support for it in the working-class areas of Port Saint-Paul and Pierre-Scize. On 6 July it was abolished within Rhône-et-Loire.[150]

---

[146] Ibid., minutes of l'Hôtel-Dieu, 9 June; 31L49, fo. 1, Plat-d'Argent, 1 June; 31L16, 31L21, minutes of Port Saint-Paul and la Juiverie, *passim*; AC I²3, fos. 1–13, minutes of Rue Buisson, 1–27 June.

[147] AD 42L80, d. 68, statement alleged in a denunciation of Litandon, [an II].

[148] *CM*, iv. 322–3 (17 June); AC I²4, d. 15, submission by Rue Buisson on food supplies, [June 1793].

[149] *CM*, iv. 174–5, 322–3.

[150] *CP*, p. 38. At least 9 *sections* opposed the *maximum* in early July; Port Saint-Paul and Pierre-Scize supported it. On this issue, see Riffaterre, *Le Mouvement anti-jacobin et anti-parisien à Lyon*, i. 425 n. 1.

These policies all threatened the interests of poorer consumers, and it is interesting that there was very little popular opposition to them, or indeed to the rebel regime itself as its regressive social character (viewed from the standpoint of the popular democrats) became more apparent. On 17 June Port Saint-Paul reported that 'le peuple crie beaucoup' because of the non-execution of the *maximum*, but there is no evidence of public protest about this time. The first substantial popular uprising after 29 May was not until 2 July, when a crowd of women—200, according to one report—and some silk-weavers, including former *club-istes*, chased the *permanents* of Saint-Georges from their assembly. There followed arrests and disarmaments, and the disorders in Saint-Georges seem to have ceased.[151] But the rarity of resistance to the rebellion should not surprise us. The reasons for it are clear enough, though they are not quite as simple as the Jacobin explanations in terms of the repressive economic power of the merchant class would suggest. They lie in continuing popular anti-Jacobinism, straightforward political repression of militants, and the elimination of political organization in the *quartiers* apart from the *assemblées permanentes*.

It has sometimes been suggested that the Lyonnais rebellion—and the 'federalist' movement more generally—represented an effort to prop up the liberal values of 1789 against the rising tide of terror and dictatorship,[152] which is what the rebels said they were about. That many of them aspired to establish the rule of law and a stable, conservative hierarchy of powers based on the broad representation of property is not in question. But, just as in 1789 the propertied classes had not dared to act out a liberal revolution in Lyon, preferring to offer verbal support and encouragement to the *patriotes* at Versailles, so they dared not attempt an experiment in political liberalism in mid-1793. Instead they used protective colouring from the Jacobin palette, with the result that both sides in this civil war bombarded each other with the same rather lurid political rhetoric and explored the same themes of plot and counter-revolution. (For example, the Lyonnais produced 'evidence' that Chalier was in the pay of the princes at Coblenz.[153]) The rebels used Jacobin methods, too, and not just, as Riffaterre suggests, under the pressure of

---

[151] AD 31L23, d. 2, Denis Monnet, president of the Comité de Surveillance of Port Saint-Paul, to the president of the *section*, 17 June; *CM*, iv. 368–9 (3 July).

[152] This is the main thesis of H. Wallon, *La Révolution du 31 mai et le fédéralisme en 1793 ou la France vaincue par la Commune de Paris*, 2 vols. (Paris, 1886).

[153] 'Histoire de la Révolution de Lyon', in *Secrétariat*, p. 459, *pièce justificative*, no. cxxxiv (this was published in June 1793).

the increasing military threat in July.[154] From the first, the *sections* repressed dissent by Jacobin means—purges, Surveillance Committees of trustworthy militants with wide powers to eliminate (politically if not physically) arbitrarily defined suspects, detention without due process of law, all fuelled by the oxygen of the Terror, denunciation: 'Il faut ... bien vous persuader qu'un dénonciateur est l'homme le plus honorable lorsque la patrie est en danger.'[155]

To make these points is not to accuse the rebels of political apostasy or failure in some historical mission. If they were to sustain their struggle against the Montagne they had to use such methods. And they had to borrow from the repertoire of popular democracy if they were to maintain the support from below which was a major strength of the rebellion. But, ironically, the further they took the logic of popular sovereignty and resistance to oppression, the stronger the position of the royalists became.

---

[154] Riffaterre, *Le Mouvement anti-jacobin et anti-parisien à Lyon*, ii. 616.
[155] AD 42L39, d. 167, address by Gérin, 6 June.

7

From Federalism to Civil War

The convocation of the primary assemblies opened a direct route to civil war, but that was by no means an inescapable destination. Far from rallying to Lyon's call, Rhône-et-Loire was very cool about the Département's initiative. Even Montbrison, a town of over 4,000 inhabitants with a volubly anti-Jacobin Municipalité, could produce only eighty voters on 24 June, and in several *cantons* the vote was either quite derisory, like Belleville (thirteen out of 1,600 registered voters) and Charlieu, or non-existent (in the *cantons* around Roanne, in Beaujeu, and in some parts of the *district* of Lyon-Campagne). In Saint-Étienne, one of the three *sections* formally refused to nominate a delegate. Altogether, twenty of the *département*'s eighty-three *cantons* did not vote on 24 June, including half of those in the *district* of Roanne.[1]

As a result, more than half of the 200 *députés* from the six *districts* who met in Lyon on 30 June were from Lyon-Ville and Lyon-Campagne.[2] Nevertheless, the assembly felt able to announce on 1 July that it constituted the Commission Populaire, Républicaine et de Salut Public de Rhône-et-Loire, and on 4 July that 'la représentation nationale actuelle n'est ni entière ni libre ... qu'il [le peuple de Rhône-et-Loire] demande la réunion, dans le plus bref delai, d'une représentation nationale libre et entière ... que, jusqu' au rétablissement de son intégralité et de sa liberté, les décrets rendus depuis le 31 mai sont regardés comme non-avenus, et qu'il va prendre des mesures pour la sûreté générale ...'.[3] In effect, the Popular Commission had declared itself the only legitimate instrument of popular sovereignty in the *département* until such time as there existed a national assembly to its liking. It was attempting to turn the rebellion of Lyon into the rebellion of Rhône-et-Loire, and declaring the

---

[1] Riffaterre, *Le Mouvement anti-jacobin et anti-parisien à Lyon et dans le Rhône-et-Loire en 1793* (Lyon 1912–28), ii. 98–100; AD 42L36, extract from the minutes of l'Union (Place Neuve), 24 June.
[2] 101 out of 197 (Riffaterre, *Le Mouvement anti-jacobin et anti-parisien à Lyon*, ii. 98).
[3] *CP*, pp. 4, 26.

département's temporary secession from the Republic.

But the *Journal de Lyon*, which was totally committed to the rebellion, conceded that at one point the assembly had seemed likely to reject this measure.[4] Contemporary accounts suggest that most of the Lyonnais members were determined on the break, while some from elsewhere were alarmed by the idea.[5] Probably, many rural *députés* followed the example of Béthenod of L'Arbresle, who left the Commission immediately after the decision of 4 July and resigned his functions.[6] Forty-eight names on the lists of *députés* from rural *districts* do not appear at all in the proceedings of the Commission or amongst the papers signed by its members, and it seems likely that most of these withdrew in protest at the decision of 4 July.

Various accounts, including Béthenod's,[7] attribute the decision to the intervention of the fugitive Girondin, Birotteau.[8] When he rose to speak, the outcome of the discussion was still uncertain. But Birotteau put on a bravura performance: the Convention, he announced, was dominated by a handful of depraved royalist stooges, and Paris had been reduced to anarchy. The overthrow of the Montagne was just around the corner: only eleven *départements* were in favour of the 'counter-revolution' of 31 May, and the northern *départements* were already marching on the capital, where most of the population was awaiting them as liberators. According to Béthenod, the assembly was then seized by 'un entousiasme [*sic*] général, excité en grande partie par la présence et le discours de Birotteau'. By 9.00 p.m. the break with the Convention had been voted.[9]

But if Birotteau's lurid view of Paris was necessary to change some minds, to the Lyonnais delegates at least it was not new. For nearly three weeks Lyon had been flooded with versions of the situation in the capital that were just as highly coloured as Birotteau's and contained extra details calculated to touch Lyonnais susceptibilities—Lyon systematically calumnied by the propagation of Tallien's report and by Legendre's tirades, seductive parallels between Paris in late June and Lyon in late

---

[4] *Journal de Lyon*, 5 July, p. 394.

[5] Riffaterre, *Le Mouvement anti-jacobin et anti-parisien à Lyon*, ii. 120–3, 140.

[6] AD 1L36, minutes of L'Arbresle, 5 July.

[7] Ibid.; *Journal de Lyon*, 5 July, p. 394; 42L3, fo. 80, *Commission Militaire*, interrogation of Verdun; Fonds Coste MS 647, 'Opinion de L. Guyot, lue le 17 août 1793 à la Commune'.

[8] A *député* from Pyrénées-Orientales, Birotteau was a persistent critic of the Montagne and was placed under guard on 3 June. He escaped, was proscribed on 12 July, and stayed in Lyon intermittently between 4 and 25 July. (See M. J. Sydenham, *The Girondins* (London, 1961), 202, 216–17; Riffaterre, *Le Mouvement anti-jacobin et anti-parisien à Lyon*, ii. 392.)

[9] *CP*, pp. 22–3 (4 July); AD 1L376; *Journal de Lyon*, 5 July, p. 394.

May—plus accounts of success after success for the departmental movement in the north and in the Midi, armies marching on Paris, and a
Parisian majority (twenty-eight *sections*, said Fain) against the Jacobin
clique.[10] All sorts of rumours had been floating in to be duly consecrated
in the sectional records. The *sectionnaires* who had violated the Convention had repented and now realized that the hand of 'la faction
[Jacobine] désorganisatrice' lay behind the Vendée rebellion; bread had
been dumped into the Seine as part of a plot to incite further popular
atrocities; the Jacobins aimed to divide France in two, one to be delivered
to the royalists, the other to foreign powers. These rumours seem to have
been widely believed; Lindet was certainly convinced that they were
doing great harm.[11] The Popular Commission's decision needs to be
understood not just as an oratorical triumph for Birotteau, but as the
product of confusion, anxiety, and misplaced optimism in a context of
deeply rooted suspicion of the Convention.

The reports from Paris were bolstered by the news from the main
centres of departmental resistance, Caen,[12] Bordeaux, and particularly
Marseille. A pamphlet entitled *Manifeste: Marseille aux républicains français* and dated 12 June promised that an army of 1,200 men would reach
Tarascon by 28 June *en route* to Paris. By 4 July the force from Marseille
was known to have reached the Durance south of Avignon, and to be preparing for a crossing against Avignonnais opposition. For over two weeks
the *sections* at Lyon had been discussing a plan to send a force to Valence
to accompany the Marseillais on the rest of their journey. On 21 June
they were already asking the well-to-do to provide billets for 'nos
frères Marseillais qui nous attendons de jour à autre [*sic*]'.[13] The Lyonnais
rebels could thus believe that, by joining the war against the Convention,

[10] See AD 1L375, letters from Durand and Fain (Lyonnais delegates in Paris), 13 and
14 June; 31L21, fo. 12, minutes of Port Saint-Paul, 23 June; 31L2, fo. 8, minutes of la
Croisette, 17, 28 June; 31L49, fo. 16, minutes of Plat-d'Argent, 23 June; 42L86, d. 89,
denunciation of Saint-Genis, delegate of Rue Buisson in Paris in June, [an II]; *Rapport fait
au Conseil-général de la Commune provisoire de Lyon* ... (Lyon, [June 1793], 15–16.
[11] AD 31L21, fo. 12, minutes of Port Saint-Paul, 23 June; 31L2, fo. 8, minutes of la
Croisette, 17 June; Lindet to CSP, 9 June (*Actes*, iv. 497).
[12] *Journal de Lyon*, 3 July, p. 387; *Lettre des commissaires de la ville de Lyon près la ville
de Bordeaux à leurs concitoyens. Bordeaux, le 26 juin 1793* (Lyon, 1793), 1.
[13] AD 31L21, fo. 10, minutes of Port Saint-Paul, 21 June. See also *Manifeste: Marseille
aux républicains français. 12 juin 1793* ... (Marseille, 1793); AD 42L39, letter from agents
of the Provisional Municipalité in Condrieu (reporting news from Tarascon), 28 June; AC
I²4, fo. 14, minutes of Rue Buisson, 20 June; AD 31L2, fo. 12 minutes of la Croisette,
22 June. In fact, the Marseillais force was closer to 500 men (W. Scott, *Terror and Repression
in Revolutionary Marseilles* (London, 1973), 115).

they were not only defending France against the Parisian anarchists, but also aligning themselves with a powerful movement of resistance.

LE COBLENZ DU MIDI

Bad timing dogged Lyon throughout the Revolution. Its municipal revolution came noticeably late and its popular democratic movement early. The Jacobins won office prematurely, in circumstances which made political instability inevitable, and the anti-Jacobins mounted their insurrection four days before the national government fell into the hands of the Montagne. Now Lyon threw in its lot with a departmental movement which, unknown to most Lyonnais, was already rapdily disintegrating. In the last ten days of June it was crumbling in the Isère, Ain, and Drôme. Dubois-Crancé had overcome the 'federalists' of Grenoble with the help of the popular societies and was turning his attention to the Marseillais army, which he rightly judged to be easily containable. But thanks to confusion and some suppression of information by the Département, the Lyonnais were not aware until late in July that their city was becoming isolated.[14]

At the beginning of July the Lyonnais administrations finally took the step of arresting a Montagnard *député*, Noël Pointe, who was on his way to take over the supervision of the arms factory in Saint-Étienne, his home town. On 6 July the rebels passed another milestone when the Popular Commission abolished the *maximum* ('cette loi spoliatrice') in Rhône-et-Loire. This measure, the first to contradict a law passed before 31 May, was meant to please the rural *districts* and to attract grain to Lyon, and it was supported by the majority of the *sections*.[15] Then, on 9 July, a battalion of National Guards was sent to Saint-Étienne to deal with discontent provoked by the arrest of Pointe and by the pro-Lyonnais policy of the mayor, Praire-Royet.[16] Securing Saint-Étienne gave Lyon access not only to weaponry, but to the Forez, with its ripening crops.

On 8 July the Commission announced the appointment of Louis-François Perrin, formerly Comte de Précy, as commander of the Depart-

---

[14] See AC I²4 13 (27 June; notes of proceedings of Rue Buisson, 29 June); AD 31L2, fo. 12 (27 June). fo. 13 (28 June). See Riffaterre, *Le Mouvement anti-jacobin et anti-parisien à Lyon*, i. 456–61; Journal de Lyon, 17 July, p. 425 (claiming that 66 Départements supported the departmental movement).

[15] *CP*, pp. 9, 28–9, 38 (2, 4, 6 July); *Journal de Lyon*, 5 July, p. 394; *Actes*, iv. 163.

[16] *Département*, ii. 382 (5 July); *Journal de Lyon*, 5 July, p. 394, 12 July, p. 412; *CP*, p. 57 (9 July). On the situation in Saint-Etienne, see C. Lucas, *The Structure of the Terror: The Example of Javogues and the Loire* (Oxford, 1973), 41–2.

mental Army, thus creating another large obstacle to reconciliation with the Convention. The *Journal de Lyon* referred to him as 'Perrin *dit* Précy', elaborate arrangements were made to dispense him from taking the republican oath, and he was kept as far as possible out of the public eye.[17] But those responsible for appointing him can hardly have been unaware of his service as a lieutenant-colonel in Louis XVI's constitutional guard or his connection with the *émigré* royalist Comte de Virieu. Those who were in the dark found out when Birotteau strongly criticized his appointment during a debate in the Popular Commission.[18] A small group of committed royalists may well have been responsible for manœuvring him into the post, but there seems to have been no serious opposition from more moderate opinion in the *sections* or the authorities.

More dangerous still was the Commission's direction that the Criminal Tribunal of Rhône-et-Loire should try the Jacobins arrested on and after 29 May, despite the Convention's decree of 21 June suspending all legal proceedings against them. Sectional opinion was so strong against the 'criminals of the 29th'[19] that the Commission had little choice here. Failure to proceed with the trials would have alienated its strongest supporters. The Provisional Municipalité was as set on punishing the Jacobins as the *sections* were, and it forced the Tribunal's hand by publishing a list of charges against the prisoners and setting up the required *jury d'accusation*.[20]

Chalier was brought for trial on 15 July, condemned to death, and executed the next day as an instigator of murder and civil war. On 22 July Riard also was executed.[21] As Riffaterre has shown, Chalier was condemned on thin, circumstantial evidence of incitement to murder by judges who would have feared for their lives if they had acquitted him. The real reason for his execution was the strength of feeling against him in Lyon. Riffaterre further argues, persuasively, that Chalier was regarded as a kind of class traitor, who abandoned an honourable position amongst the merchant class in order to manufacture popular disorder and hatred of the rich in a city which feared these more than almost anything.

[17] *CP*, p. 51 (8 July). See Riffaterre, *Le Mouvement anti-jacobin et anti-parisien à Lyon*, ii. 33, 35–7, 38; *Journal de Lyon*, 11, 18 July, pp. 408, 432.

[18] Ibid. pp. 429–32.

[19] See e.g. AC I²4, fos. 13, 15, notes of meeting of Rue Buisson, 27 June, address by Droits de l'Homme (Rue Tupin), 26 June; AD 31L2, fo. 12, minutes of la Croisette, 27 June; 31L16, fo. 14. minutes of la Juiverie, 28 June; 31L41, fo. 32, minutes of l'Hôtel-Dieu, 26 June.

[20] *CM*, iv. 362, 370–4.

[21] *CP*, pp. 404–5, 441.

Just as he had for Vitet, Chalier satisfied the anti-Jacobins' need for anthropomorphic explanations of the political disasters which had deprived the *honnêtes gens* of their natural right to rule: it was Chalier who had brought the city to its present pass, 'le premier auteur de tous les troubles de Lyon', 'l'auteur de tous nos maux'.[22]

Great crowds celebrated the execution of the *patron des pauvres*, and there is no evidence of popular protest against it. If six weeks of 'federalist' rule had caused the working classes of Lyon to regret the overthrow of the Jacobins, they did not choose this moment to express their feelings. The only sour note was due to a maladjustment of the guillotine, apparently caused by crowds clambering over the platform before the execution. After four drops of the blade it still took the executioner's knife to decapitate Chalier entirely: 'Quelques claquements de main furent étouffés par l'indignation que fit éprouver le mauvais succès de *l'instrument. On le plaignit*.'[23] Possibly this dreadful fiasco discouraged the authorities from staging any more public executions after Riard's, who was an easy target as an ex-noble and an *étranger*. But their reluctance to provide Jacobin martyrs was probably also related to the weakness in Lyon's position which became increasingly obvious in the second half of July.

It was another disaster of timing to execute Chalier, whom Robespierre admired as the first unmasker of Roland, a week after the reconstitution of the Committee of Public Safety with a terrorist majority (10 July) and in the same week as the murder of Marat (13 July), who 'had served the Montagnards as a kind of safety valve'.[24] Now his popular following demanded violent action in place of his violent words. Negotiations acceptable to the new committee would anyway have required the Lyonnais to back down on the main fronts: recognizing the Convention and disbanding the Popular Commission. But disavowing Chalier's execution meant acknowledging the guilt of the Commission which had authorized it, the Municipalité which had engineered it, and the *sections* which had been baying for it. It should be stressed, though, that even without the death of Chalier, a settlement would have been difficult, for many Jacobins had quickly identified Lyon's rebellion with the counter-revolution.[25] On

---

[22] *Journal de Lyon*, 17 July, p. 430. Riffaterre, *Le Mouvement anti-jacobin et anti-parisien à Lyon*, i. 301–3.

[23] *Journal de Lyon*, 17 July, p. 430.

[24] N. Hampson, *A Social History of the French Revolution* (London, 1963), 190. Robespierre himself did not join the Committee until 27 July. See J. M. Thompson, *Robespierre* (New York, 1968), ii. 73.

[25] See *Jacobins*, v. 268 (21 June).

4 June the Committee of Public Safety had received their Lyonnais counterparts' version of the events which had led to their downfall, denouncing as usual the Département which had sponsored the revolt ('ou Riches Egoistes au Royalistes outrés') and the counter-revolutionary 'classe mercantile'. Not only Dubois-Crancé and Albitte, but other observers in Lyon supported this view, and Legendre told the Paris Jacobins that of the Lyonnais authorities the Municipalité alone was *patriote*.[26]

Meanwhile, demands for action against 'federalism' were coming both from the Paris Commune and from leading Montagnards like Barère and Jeanbon Saint-André (who proposed the decree of 7 June empowering Dubois-Crancé and his colleagues to deal with the situation in Lyon).[27] After discussing Lyon on 15 and 16 June, the Committee obtained a decree from the Convention suspending the presidents and *procureurs* of the administrations there and summoning them to Paris.[28]

In the first half of July there were grounds for the belief that indulgence was only encouraging the spread of insurrection. Couriers of the Ministry of Justice were arrested in Calvados and Eure. The illegal Tribunal Populaire of Marseille was in session. There were new troubles in Seine-et-Marne and Nîmes. Baudot claimed that Toulouse was about to send 15,000 men against Paris.[29] While royalism in the Midi seemed to be beaten with the rout of Charrier's forces in the Lozère,[30] the 'federalist' threat increasingly worried the Committee of Public Safety. Encouraged by rumours that Roland was leading the revolt in Lyon (he was actually in hiding at Rouen), Saint-Just's report of 8 July linked the Lyonnais revolt with Roland and the 'Girondin conspiracy'.[31]

Lindet offered the rebels a last way out through a proposal which the Convention adopted on 26 June. All who had signed 'des arrêtés tendant à faire méconnaître l'existence de la Convention Nationale'[32] were given three days to recant. But this came at the wrong time, when euphoria in the rebel camp was reaching its peak. And in any case the *procureur-général-syndic* of Rhône-et-Loire, Meynis, seems to have done his best to

[26] AN AFII43, plaq. 339, CSP of Rhône-et-Loire to CSP of the Convention, 27 May; *Jacobins*, v. 245 (10 June).
[27] *Actes*, iv. 402, 452, n. 1, 478.
[28] Ibid. 571, 573, 577, 590.
[29] Ibid. 571–2, 609–11; M. Lyons, *Revolution in Toulouse* (Berne, 1978), 48.
[30] *Actes*, iv. 609, Chateauneuf-Randon and Malhes to the Convention, Mende, 18 June.
[31] AN F⁷4394¹, d. 7, no. 4, CSG to Minister of the Interior, 4 July; E. Herriot, *Lyon n'est plus* (Paris, 1938–40), ii. 84, 174.
[32] Cited ibid. ii. 86.

suppress news of the decree.[33] Certainly, there were no responses to the offer in Lyon,[34] and on 3 July, on Couthon's motion, another decree arraigned the *procureurs* of the authorities at Lyon, and held all members of these authorities responsible with their lives for the safety of their prisoners.[35]

Although it did appear in June that the Committee was seeking a peaceful resolution of the crisis in the provinces, its negotiating position was based on the unrealistic expectation that the leaders of Lyon's rebellion could be persuaded to throw themselves on the Convention's mercy. The decree of 3 July hardened its position, making the sacrifice of the *procureurs* a pre-condition for any accommodation with Lyon. Such was the depth of Lyonnais suspicion of the Convention and hostility to the local Jacobins that it is difficult to conceive of a settlement being reached on this basis as long as there were any hopes for the success of the departmental coalition. Either the *procureurs* had to submit to arrest or the *sections* had to overthrow them. There was no sign of these things happening. And to suspend proceedings against the imprisoned *anarchistes-massacreurs* would have produced furious dissent from the *sections*, and possibly a prison massacre, as well as casting doubt on the legitimacy of the resistance to oppression on 29 May. In the unlikely event of the Convention allowing the indecision of the Committee to continue while the military crisis deepened, the eventual outcome would probably still have been the use of force as proposed by Dubois-Crancé.

That is speculation. What is certain is that civil war was made nearly inevitable by the election of a Committee of Public Safety with a majority which shared Robespierre's commitment to unremitting war against the aristocratic conspiracy. Early in June Robespierre himself had diagnosed the troubles in Lyon, Marseille, and Bordeaux as counter-revolution. He was defending the *sans-culottes* and the leaders of the Paris National Guard who had made the 'revolution' of 2 June, and he justified what they had done as a necessary response to the conspiracy which had manifested itself in the revolts of Lyon and other provincial cities. This speech was greeted coldly by the Convention at first, but when Robespierre sat down he was applauded.[36] He had put forward the idea

[33] AD 42L12, Commission de Justice Populaire (henceforth the CJP), interrogation of J.-F. Bonamour and J.-B. Buiron-Gaillard, members of the Département of Rhône-et-Loire, 23 brumaire, an II; 42L33, retraction of Bonamour, 22 July.

[34] See below, p. 237.

[35] See Herriot, *Lyon n'est plus*, ii. 150.

[36] See A. Mathiez, *The French Revolution*, trans. C. A. Phillips (New York, 1962), 334.

that 29 May represented a counter-revolutionary threat as part of a rationale for the Convention's capitulation to the *sans-culottes*.[37] To quote Furet, Robespierre's 'sermons' had both 'the tremendous power of deciding who was included in the people'[38] in its war with counter-revolution, and the capacity to focus suspicion on individuals and groups. All the same, rigour against Lyon should not be seen simply as a policy forced on the Committee by Robespierre and his close allies, Saint-Just and Couthon. Now that terror against the enemies of the people was becoming the mainspring of government policy, it was natural for strong measures to be taken against a city that had long been regarded as an epicentre of conspiracy. The likelihood, the imminence, of a Lyonnais counter-revolution had been commonplace in *patriote* thinking since 1790. Even moderates like Vitet, Alquier, and Boissy had proclaimed its destiny as the home of counter-revolution in the Midi.[39] After 29 May, with Lyon displaying classic symptoms of counter-revolution—'une municipalité patriote détruite', 'des centaines de patriotes ensevelis dans les cachots', and 'la Représentation nationale méconnue'—it was automatic for Jacobins to assume that what had happened there was what had been feared for so long. The principal remaining question was how much repression to use on which categories of the population of 'le Coblenz du Midi'.

Within forty-eight hours of its formation, the renewed committee was busy manufacturing decrees against Lyon for ratification by the Convention. Acting on a report by Couthon which emphasized the dangerous military situation, the Convention decreed on 12 July that Lyon was in a state of rebellion, denounced as traitors those administrators who had convoked or co-operated with the Popular Commission of Rhône-et-Loire, confiscated rebel property, and ordered loyal citizens to leave Lyon within three days. No further public or private funds were to be remitted there. On the same day another member of the Committee, Hérault-Séchelles, had a motion adopted which made the withholding of military supplies a capital offence. Two days later Dubois-Crancé got the decree he had been waiting for: he and his colleagues were authorized to send a force sufficient to subdue Lyon.[40]

---

[37] Robespierre's implacable hostility to 'federalist' Lyon was demonstrated again a month late, when he treated talk of conciliation with the murderers of Chalier as an outrage (see below, n. 83).

[38] F. Furet, *Interpreting the French Revolution*, trans. E. Forster (Cambridge, 1981), 70.

[39] AN F¹ᶜIII, Rhône 8 (10 Nov. 1792), cited in P. Mansfield, 'The Missions of Collot d'Herbois: A Study in his Political Career', Ph.D. thesis (Macquarie University, 1985), 274.

[40] Herriot, *Lyon n'est plus*, ii. 188–92, 195; *Actes*, v. 256.

At Grenoble, he and Albitte had been chafing under the restraints imposed on them: 'ce n'est point ici affaires d'opinions, c'est révolte, c'est une conspiration bien évidente . . . Mais la Convention nous paralise, elle ne nous ordonne rien, elle défend même de dégarnir les frontières. Les généraux flottent et sont plus incertains que nous, et sans nôtre activité tous les départements où nous sommes seroient aujourd' hui coalisés avec Lyon . . .'.[41] The *députés* had made little more than gestures towards negotiating a peace. Their *Proposition* of 1 July required Lyon to accept both Lindet's credentials and the Convention's authority, to agree to the trial of the Jacobins by courts nominated by the Convention, and to provide 10,000 muskets for the Armée des Alpes.[42] A few days later they deputed General Sériziat, who belonged to a wealthy Lyonnais merchant family, to advocate submission, and on 11 July two Lyonnais district administrators detained in Chambéry were sent home with an address from Dubois-Crancé and Gauthier disclaiming any desire to use force against the Lyonnais and expressing the hope that they would submit voluntarily.[43] Neither the Municipalité nor the Popular Commission considered these proposals seriously, and the address of the 11th misfired completely because the Commission had already seen the *députés*' letter of 27 June which revealed their commitment to a military solution.[44] Even in the address, which was relatively mild, the threat of force was only thinly disguised, and the Commission published it, with a critique, as evidence of the *commissaires*' perfidy.[45]

The continued intransigence of Lyon gave the *députés* ample justification for an attack, and all that stood in the way of one was Kellermann's refusal to lead it: 'Je ne puis disposer d'une seule troupe de plus sans compromettre toute la frontière depuis Genève jusqu' au Val de Barcelonnette', he said.[46] He would march on Lyon only if Dubois-Crancé

---

[41] AG B³103*, Dubois-Crancé and Albitte to the Jacobin Club of Paris, 27 June. (Copy sent to Kellermann by the Département of Rhône-et-Loire, dated 6 July. This might have been altered or even concocted to influence the general, but it is consistent with the *députés*' behaviour about this time.)

[42] AD 1L375, Proposition des représentants du peuple à l'armée des Alpes, undated, signed Albitte.

[43] *CP*, pp. 32–3 (5 July); Finds Coste MS 645, 'Observations pour Charles Sériziat', undated; AD 42L33, no. 39, Matheron and Pecollet to the Département of Rhône-et-Loire.

[44] *CP*, pp. 377–84.

[45] *CM*, iv. 366 (2 July). *CP*, pp. 25–6 (4 July) and 383–4 (text of the *députés*' 11 July address, reprinted by the Commission).

[46] The accusations included: 'vous avez pillé l'Arsenal, détruit les ressources de nos armées, vouz avez puisé dans les caisses nationales les fonds destinés à leurs besoins . . . vous avez détruit à main armé une autorité constituée dont vous pouviez réclamer la cassation . . . vous avez incarcéré sans distinction tous les citoyens qui n'étoient pas de votre

took responsibility for the frontiers. But continued delay was made more difficult by the Convention's decree of 14 July, which gave Dubois-Crancé a trump card to play as soon as he could claim to have explored all possibilities of negotiation. However, developments in Lyon seemed briefly to increase these possibilities.

ONE STEP BACK: THE ACCEPTANCE OF THE MONTAGNARD CONSTITUTION

In the second week of July it was rumoured that troops were already marching on Lyon,[47] and more authority was concentrated in the hands of those responsible for defence. The Popular Commission's Committee of General Security, formed on 1 July, became the principal policy-making body, maintaining (in theory at least) general supervision over a military committee of twenty men which was formed on 13 July (half from Précy's staff, the rest from the civil administrations). The formation of a 9,600 strong Departmental Army was ordered by the Commission on the same day.[48] On 14 July the Commission gave the Committee of General Security vague powers 'à prendre, contre les détracteurs de la chose publique, les mesures de sûreté générale qu'il jugera convenables'.[49] The Commission then assumed a virtually dictatorial role, destituting two *district* administrators suspected of Jacobinism, and issuing orders directly to the Département and the Municipalité.[50] Lyon was responding to military threat much as the Convention was, by giving wide and arbitrary powers to men who seemed capable of organizing defence, and turning a blind eye to their politics.

Recruitment, barrack-building, and fund-raising went slowly, but Précy quickly put together an experienced general staff: Agniel de Chene-lette, formerly *gros-major* of the Toul regiment and chief artillery instruc-tor at Metz and La Fère; Ferrus de Plantigny, formerly a sub-lieutenant

opinion ... et tandis que depuis trois ans votre ville est l'asygle [*sic*] des malveillants, de tous les conspirateurs du Midi contre la Liberté, vous avez fait arbitrairement incarcérer des voyageurs, des fonctionnaires publics, des militaires qui se rendoient à leur poste, sur la plus absurde dénonciation' (*CP*, pp. 378–9).

[47] AD 1L376, no. 23, Blanchard to Gras, member of the Popular Commission, 11 July; 1L378, no. 2, minute of the CSG of Rhône-et-Loire requesting surveillance of the movements of Dubois-Crancé's forces.

[48] *CP*, pp. 6–7, 88–9 (1, 13 July).

[49] Ibid. 92.

[50] AD 2L10, minutes of the District of Lyon-Ville, 13 July (destitution of Bourbon and Berthelot); 1L378, pp. 4, 6, minutes of the CSG of Rhône-et-Loire, 12, 16 July; 42L32, d. B8, pp. 1–14, requisitions of CSG, 10–11 July.

in the Guyenne regiment; Vallès, another ex-officer, who had served in the force sent to Lyon after the 1786 riots; Griffet de la Beaume, an ex-officer of engineers, who appeared in Lyon on 13 July; Cudel de Montcolon, Précy's nephew and also an ex-officer. All were nobles. Cudel de Montcolon was an *émigré* who used the *nom de guerre* of Gardel.[51] These men brought more than a whiff of Coblenz to the rebellion. They were certainly not in Lyon to help restore the integrity of the national representation.

But Précy's plans to build a Lyonnais army were hampered by a series of blows to morale as the Convention's measures against 'federalism' began to take effect. On 14 July, near Nîmes, the vital Rhône bridgehead at Pont-Saint-Esprit was taken by Carteaux from the Nîmois 'federalists'. The Département of Saône-et-Loire was co-operating fully with the *députés* at Grenoble and helped them to establish a direct link with Paris via Mâcon.[52] Always alert for an opportunity to disadvantage Lyon, the Mâconnais blocked the grain bought for the city. The Provisional Municipalité toyed with the idea of sending a force 'pour faciliter la libre circulation des bleds', but had to drop it for lack of troops to send.[53] Reverchon and Delaporte, on mission to Rhône-et-Loire, Saône-et-Loire, and the Ain under a decree of 12 July, made Mâcon their headquarters and took steps to stop all communications and commerce with Lyon.[54] The Ain and the Isère were advocating acceptance of the Constitition; Clermont-Ferrant (Puy-de-Dôme) and Privas (Ardèche) had rallied to the Convention. Promises of aid made in early June came to nothing, and all Lyon heard from its allies now were requests for men (Saint-Chamond), muskets (Jura and Orne), and cannon (Roanne).[55] There was little comfort in Rhône-et-Loire. A great departmental federation had been planned for 14 July, but only two detachments of National Guards presented themselves from outside Lyon. And against the Département's

[51] AD 42L3, Commission Militaire, 14 Oct. and 2 Nov., interrogations of Louis Griffet Labaume (*sic*) and Cudel de Montcolon; entries on Ferrus de Plantigny, Valles, and Agniel de Chenelette, in A. Portallier, *Tableau général des victimes et martyrs de la Révolution en Lyonnais, Forez et Beaujolais* (Saint-Etienne, 1911).

[52] *Actes*, v. 276–8 (16 July); E.-L.-A. Dubois-Crancé, *Deuxième partie de la réponse de Dubois Crancé aux inculpations de ses collegues Couthon et Maignet* (?, n.d.), 148–50; AG B³6, d. 7, Albitte to the Minister of War, 17 July.

[53] *CM*, iv. 401 (15 July).

[54] *Actes*, v. 243; AN F¹ᶜIII, d. 3, nos. 43 and 45, Minister of the Interior to CSP, 23 July, *directeur des Postes* to Postal Administrators at Châlons-sur-Marne, 17 July.

[55] *CM*, iv. 400 (15 July), p. 114 (18 July); *Département*, ii. 421–2 (17 July); AD 1L376, extract from an unsigned letter from Annonay, 13 July; 1L378, notes of proceedings of CSG of Rhône-et-Loire, 13, 17 July; 31L21, minutes of Port Saint-Paul, 14 July.

instructions, the District of Villefranche was busy distributing copies of the Jacobin Constitution.[56] From Bordeaux the usually euphoric Lyonnais delegation reported that 'les mouvements de la Gironde sont très lents et ne répondent pas à cette enthousiasme qui a éclaté dans le commencement', while the optimism generated by news received on 12 July that the Marseillais rebels had taken Avignon was dampened on the 22nd when a Marseillais delegation announced that their troops were still there.[57]

Lyon had still to learn the full extent of the disaster. On 24 July the Bordelais army, only 400 strong, turned back after marching only fifty kilometres, and the next day, after a light bombardment by Carteaux's artillery, the Marseillais retreated from Avignon.[58] It is not clear when news of these events reached Lyon. Nothing was said officially. Even as late as 15 August a Lyonnais wrote confidently to a friend that 'aujourd' hui arrive une avant-garde des Marseillais au nombre de sept cents, l'on nous assure que leur armée est de quinze mille hommes, sous peu de jours ils seront à Lyon ...'.[59] This might well have been deliberate misinformation, for it was written during the siege when letters from Rhône-et-Loire were being routinely intercepted by the authorities elsewhere. But there can be little doubt that the Popular Commission kept quiet about the worst news, or that in late July it began to moderate its own policy in response to the first intimations of the collapse of the departmental movement.

On 19 July, the day after it received the news that the Ain had accepted the Constitution, the Commission decided to submit it to the *sections* after all, explaining that this did not represent a departure from its principled refusal to recognize decrees passed since 31 May, because 'le plan de constitution' was not a law 'mais un simple projet qu'il [le peuple Français] a le droit d'examiner'.[60] Exploring again the theoretical possibilities of the concept of popular sovereignty, the Commission

---

[56] Riffaterre, *Le Mouvement anti-jacobin et anti-parisien à Lyon*, ii. 240; *CP*, p. 109 (18 July).

[57] AD 42L34, B21, the Lyonnais delegates at Bordeaux to the Commune of Lyon, 7 July; *CP*, pp. 79, 133.

[58] A. Forrest, *Society and Politics in Revolutionary Bordeaux* (Oxford, 1975), 157; *Actes*, v. 456–7, Rovère to the Convention, 2 Aug.; A. Doppet, *Mémoires politiques et militaires de Général Doppet* (Carouge, 1797), 132.

[59] AD 42L74, no. 4, copy of an unsigned letter to Duchamp, merchant at La Tour du Pin, dated Lyon, 15 Aug. Similar hopes of assistance from the Midi were expressed in another unsigned letter of 12 August (42L81, no. 33).

[60] *CP*, p. 118 (19 July).

argued that 'l'examen d'une constitution quelconque est un acte de souveraineté et que nul n'a le pouvoir d'en restreindre l'exercice'.[61] No answer was given to a questioner who enquired whether constitutions from other sources would be given equal treatment.[62] No one asked whether the Commission had grounds for reassessing the information from Paris which it had previously published, namely that the Constitution was a grotesque fraud concocted in four days and the keystone of a plot to found an eternal dictatorship.[63] Nor, it seems, did anyone ask the president of the Commission, J.-E. Gilibert, to reconcile this change of policy with his published criticisms of the Jura Département for presenting the Constitution to the primary assemblies. Gilibert had maintained that to present the document to the people, even accompanied by such desirable amendments as the Jura had provided, implied recognition of the Montagnard minority's right to act as a constituent body, and that, given its origins, the Constitution could only be vicious and inadequate. More pragmatically, he had argued that acceptance of the Constitution by a majority would greatly increase the Convention's authority and would enable it to time new elections to suit itself.[64] What had happened by 19 July to drive these considerations into the background was that Gilibert's basic assumption—that the purged Convention was not recognized by most of France—had become untenable, and the Commission now risked the ideological disaster of being found marching in the opposite direction to the *volonté générale*, which for all practical purposes could not be distinguished from the *volonté majoritaire*.[65] If the Lyonnais authorities could not afford to go all the way towards full recognition of the Convention which had outlawed them, neither could they afford to stand virtually alone in their refusal to submit the new constitution to popular judgement. But in burying Gilibert's scruples they gave away all pretence that their rebellion was a crusade for constitutionalist rectitude.

It is impossible to say whether the decision of 19 July was engineered by a peace faction within the Commission. In terms of expediency it had

[61] *CP*, p. 118 (19 July).

[62] *Journal de Lyon*, 21 July, p. 442.

[63] *CP*, pp. 8, 34, 46 (1, 5, 8 July); *Lettre des commissaires de la ville de Lyon [à] ... Bordeaux*, p. 4.

[64] *Observations sur le rapport fait par deux commissaires du département du Jura, à l'Assemblée générale de la Commission populaire, républicaine et de salut public de Rhône-et-Loire* (Lyon, [12 July] 1793), 1–6.

[65] See M.J. Sydenham, 'The Republican Revolt of 1793: A Plea for Less Localized Local Studies', *French Historical Studies*, 12 (1981), 137.

something to offer both compromisers—an olive branch for Paris—and intransigents—buying time by giving the *députés* reason to hope that Lyon was preparing for peaceful submission. But it did not alter the fundamental situation. The Popular Commission still claimed sovereignty over Rhône-et-Loire, and it went on with its military preparations.

Elsewhere, attempts were being made to find a way out of the rebellion, if not for Lyon at least for some of its administrators. Members of the Département could regard themselves as less compromised than the députés to the Popular Commission. They had not taken part directly in the decision to withdraw Rhône-et-Loire from the Convention's jurisdiction, and since then they had confined themselves mostly to administrative functions, executing the orders of the Commission, taking no initiatives of their own, and avoiding responsibility for political decisions. On 8 July, for instance, the Département refused the Commission's request to destitute the pro-Jacobin *directeur des Postes*, Pilot, on the ground that only the Commission had authority to do so without permission from the Directoire des Postes in Paris.[66] Between 22 and 24 July six administrators, one councillor, the president, and the *procureur-général syndic* tried to exculpate themselves by way of the decree of 26 June, of which they claimed to have been previously ignorant. They declared that they recognized the Convention and all its decrees and retracted all their statements to the contrary. Several of them continued nevertheless to take part in the rebellion.[67]

In the last ten days of July the Provisional Municipalité also tried to reach an accommodation with the Convention. On 20 July, at Guillin's suggestion, the Municipalité voted to send a delegation to *députés* Reverchon and Delaporte at Mâcon, seeking the withdrawal of their 'arrêtés désastreux qui supposement un état d'affaires qui n'existe pas'—presumably the prohibitions against trade with Lyon—and inviting them to see the situation in Lyon for themselves.[68] The presence of Reverchon at Mâcon may have seemed a spark of hope: he came from Saint-Cyr-au-Mont-d'Or near Lyon,[69] and at least he was not Dubois-Crancé. On 24 July, after receiving an encouraging response from Reverchon and Delaporte, who agreed to let Lyon have two boat-loads of wheat and to consider making a visit, and presumably knowing that delegates from three nearby *départements* had come to Lyon to recommend recognition

---

[66] *Département*, ii. 393.

[67] AD 42L33, 22 July, 1L376, 24 July.

[68] *CM*, iv. 411–12 (20 July).

[69] *Actes*, v. 243 n. 3; A. Kuscinski, *Dictionnaire des conventionnels* (Paris, 1917), 422.

of the Convention, twenty-six provisional municipal officers, including Guillin and Bémani, joined ten members of the Département and five of the District in recognizing the Convention 'comme le seul point central et de ralliement de tous les citoyens français et républicains'.[70]

This was less a retreat than a shifting of ground. Only 'les décrets ... concernant l'intérêt générale de la République' were recognized, and so those directed specifically at Lyon were not. It was further stated that the signatories 'résisteront de toutes leurs forces à l'oppression, quelque forme qu'elle prenne'. The declaration was contradictory: it seemed to recognize the revolution of 2 June, yet it refused to accept the Convention's sovereignty over Lyon. Its real meaning was that Lyon abjured the departmental movement of protest and rebellion against the purging of the Convention, the movement which nearly eight weeks before had seemed a means of merging what had been done on 29 May into the will of the people, and reverted to the original justification of resistance to specific local acts of oppression. Abandonment of the departmental movement and of 2 June as grounds for defying the Convention did not mean that Lyon was ready to capitulate. It simply put the rebellion back on its original footing of resistance to Montagnard control, without removing the major obstacles to settlement: in Lyon, hostility towards the deposed Jacobins and the *représentants en mission*; in the Committee of Public Safety, the desire to eliminate all possibility of further provincial dissent and to avenge the *patriotes égorgés*. When he argues that, but for bad luck and misunderstandings, a negotiated peace might have been achieved at the end of July, Riffaterre[71] fails to appreciate that the ending of the 'federalist' phase of the rebellion left its fundamental, intractable causes unaltered.

Of the obstacles to negotiation, the most easily removable, in appearance at least, was the Commission. But it refused to go away. One reason for this was that its members did not have even the straw of the 26 June decree to clutch at: as one of them said, speaking of the Département's recantation: 'sa soumission lui garantit son pardon; mais vous, pouvez-vous l'espérer ...?'[72] The Commission's role in any settlement would most likely be sacrificial, and, believing that the conciliators were deliberately isolating it, it bitterly criticized the other authorities for acting independently.[73] It considered dissolving itself or asking the primary assem-

---

[70] *Département*, ii. 436 (24 July).
[71] Riffaterre, *Le Mouvement anti-jacobin et anti-parisien à Lyon*, ii. 450–76.
[72] *Journal de Lyon*, 30 July, p. 469.
[73] Ibid. 26 July, p. 458, 27 July, p. 461.

blies to pronounce on its future, but instead accepted its Committee of General Security's proposal to carry on regardless, basing the decision, once again, on the wonderfully adaptable principle of popular sovereignty: 'c'est au peuple souverain à rappeler ses mandataires'. Then the Commission neatly outmanœuvred the conciliators and brought itself into line with the other authorities by recognizing the Convention: 'la liberté ainsi que l'intégralité de la Convention paraissant rétablie, d'après l'arrêté des Corps administratifs'. But, 'conformément à la loi', it would remain 'en état de résistance à l'oppression, jusqu' au rapport des décrets rendus contre le Département de Rhône-et-Loire et la ville de Lyon', decrees which had been 'surpris à la Convention sur des faux rapports'.[74] This was a rationale for continued resistance whatever the results of the referendum on the Constitution of 1793.

Those who now wanted a quick negotiated end to the revolt were obviously numerous, or they would not have been able to isolate and embarrass the Commission in this way. But not all partisans of negotiation were prepared for total surrender. Sixteen of the provisional municipal officers who signed the declaration of 24 July remained in office long after the outbreak of civil war.[75] Eleven ceased to attend the Commune, but only three of these formally resigned.[76] Other members of the Commune resigned or retracted at one time or another, but some of them continued in office or, like Guillin, served as soldiers during the siege.[77]

[74] Ibid. 26 July, p. 458; *CP*, pp. 143–4 (25 July); *La Commission populaire ... de Rhône-et-Loire à ses commettants* [27 July], in *CP*, pp. 460–1.

[75] Péricaud (despite having retracted in accordance with the decree of 26 June) and Privat signed as members of the Works Committee of the joint authorities of Lyon on 20 Sept. (AD 42L32, no. B38); Girin as provisional municipal officer and member of the same committee on 4 Oct. (ibid., no. B51); Bémani for the Committee of Five on 16 Sept. (ibid., no. B38); Royer as president of the Military Committee on 13 Sept. (42L34, no. 80); Pieron as provisional municipal officer on 1 Sept. (42L34, no. 65); Grognier was named for official business on 2 Sept. (42L32, no. 53); Desmartin signed a list of prisoners on 7 Sept. (ibid., no. 54); David Figuet and Louis Buisson admitted continuing their functions despite having retracted (42L12, interrogations by the CJP, 22 brumaire, an II); Ray, one of the delegates sent to Paris with Lyon's acceptance of the Constitution, served in the Lyonnais army from 20 Aug. to the end of the siege; Coindre and Mazard attended the last two meetings of the Provisional Municipalité on 17 Aug. and 5 Oct.; Condentia and Martel attended the last meeting (*CM*, iv. 442, 444).

[76] Guillon and Mongin (AD 42L34, nos. 32, 36 (20 July, 3 Aug.), Derion-Duplan (31L4, no. 13 (26 July)).

[77] J.-B.-M. Roches admitted continuing to serve as president of the Municipalité's Comité de Police et de Surveillance from 29 Aug. to 9 Oct., despite having given his retraction to the Committee of Public Safety in Paris and to Javogues on 25 or 26 July (AD 42L12, fo. 9, interrogation by CJP, 8 brumaire); Barthélemy Forest also continued in office after his resignation was rejected (42 L101, B16, prisoners of *arrondissement* Rousseau (Saint-Nizier)).

There is no evidence to explain why these men persisted, but their decision can be understood in terms of the long-standing Lyonnais distrust of the Convention and the persistence of the sectional support for the rebellion which had been its motor all along. On 26 July a delegation representing fourteen *sections* promised the Commission full support, and during the last few days of July nineteen requested it to continue its functions.[78] Numerically this was not a great majority, but the nineteen included nearly all of the *sections* of the peninsula, the area in which the sectional movement had its roots. Twelve of the *sections* in this area which had supported permanence late in May still supported the Commission in late July. But most of those poorer, outlying areas which had been anti-Jacobin in May now abstained from the declarations of loyalty. Four of the *sections* which signed them were in the traditionally radical l'Hôtel-Dieu area, which had been heavily purged of Jacobin militants. Probably there had been some waning of the popular anti-Jacobinism which had swelled the ranks of the *permanents* in May, but the recalcitrants remained in control of commercial Lyon. The changing pattern of support for the rebellion is also apparent in the analysis of sectional personnel (see Appendix X). Those who seem to have embraced rebel politics publicly only in July—and stayed involved for at least a month—included fewer artisans and *boutiquiers* than the earlier activists. The proportion of artisans was markedly smaller than among the *commissaires surveillants* of May–June, and also than among those sectional officials of June–July who seem to have dropped out before August. The proportion of upper bourgeois and ex-noble activists exceeded 60 per cent.

None of the sectional assemblies was openly hostile to the Commission. Most seem to have continued to execute its orders and to have adapted to, rather than dictating, the authorities' more conciliatory policy. There was some opposition early on to the negotiations with Reverchon and Delaporte: la Convention sought the other *sections'* support for a declaration that the *députés'* duty called them to Rhône-et-Loire, and expressed deep suspicion of them for stopping at Mâcon, 'où ils ourdissoient des projets dangereux au préjudice des Lyonnais' instead of coming to Lyon to discover for themselves 'les sentiments et la profession de foi' of its citizens.[79] But after the Commission recognized the Convention, even

---

[78] *CP*, pp. 145, 150, 158 (26, 27, 31 July).

[79] AD 31L21, fo. 23, minutes of Port Saint-Paul, 20 July. Port Saint-Paul supported the declaration.

Porte-Froc was sufficiently chastened to propose sending a sectional delegation to Mâcon.[80] On 31 July a majority (according to the *Journal de Lyon*) accepted an address which conceded, in effect, the impossibility of restoring the purged *députés* to the Convention, but demanded the withdrawal of all the decrees against Lyon. Some *sections* issued separate manifestos requesting new elections to replace the Jacobin Municipalité definitively. L'Hôtel-Dieu, despite having decided on unconditional recognition of the Convention, authorized the Commission to continue 'ses fonctions relatives aux mésures de sûreté générale jusqu'au moment où l'assemblée nationale aura statué sur l'état de la ville de Lyon'.[81]

So there remained substantial support within the city for continued resistance, presumably based on the hope that the Convention might undergo a change of heart or be forced by defeat on the frontiers to concede an amnesty to the rebels and accept the destitution of the Jacobin Municipalité. For the irreconcilable royalists, on the other hand, now more influential than ever, the reasons for pressing the rebellion against the Convention to the point of war remained the same as they had always been.

Even if Reverchon and Delaporte had been prepared to support the lifting of the decrees against Lyon, it is hard to imagine the Committee of Public Safety agreeing to this, particularly after Robespierre joined it on 27 July. He seems to have been firmly committed not just to a military solution of the 'federalist' crisis, but to 'making a terrible example of all the criminals who [in Lyon, Marseille, Toulon, the Vendée, the Jura, etc.] have outraged liberty, and split the blood of patriots'.[82] According to one account, he angrily rejected a proposal for the destitution of the overthrown *Commune patriote* when it was suggested by Garat, Minister of the Interior, to encourage the submission of Lyon.[83]

Attempts to negotiate with the *députés* at Mâcon seem to have been made by a delegation of Lyonnais, though they had no credentials and it

---

[80] Minutes of Porte-Froc, 25 July, in *Secrétariat*, p. 238.

[81] *Journal de Lyon*, 2 and 3 Aug., p. 481; minutes of Porte-Froc, 25 July, in *Secrétariat*, pp. 238–9; AD 31L21, fo. 25, minutes of Port Saint-Paul, 24 July; 31L2, fo. 24, minutes of la Croisette, 27 July; 31L41, fo. 44, minutes of l'Hôtel-Dieu, 27 July.

[82] Thompson, *Robespierre*, ii. 67. See also G. Walter, *Robespierre* (Paris, 1961), i. 407–8. Both these authors date the 'catechism' in which Robespierre wrote these words to July 1793, which seems probable.

[83] J. Garat, *Mémoires* (Paris, 1862), 252–3; ' "*J'entends*", dit-il: "*vous nous proposez de détruire une commune patriote; c'est contre les principes, et le gouvernement révolutionnaire est fait pour les maintenir, et non pour les anéantir.*" Tout se tut devant ces paroles ...'. Garat claimed to have made the proposal to the Committee of Public Safety, and that Couthon seemed inclined to accept it.

is unclear whom they were representing. They promised to obtain a declaration from the *sections* recognizing the Convention and agreeing to end the trials and executions in Lyon.[84] But on 31 July a jury indicted twelve Jacobin municipal officers, and all the *députés* got from the *sections* was *Le peuple de Lyon à tous les François*, proclaiming support for the Popular Commission and demanding (not requesting as the *députés* had hoped) the annulment of the decrees against Lyon as an indispensable condition for any settlement. Reverchon and Delaporte were not prepared to negotiate on this basis: 'le Département de Rhône-et-Loire doit s'abandonner absolument à la clémence nationale'. Earlier they had hoped that only the administrations were committed to the demands for withdrawal of the decrees. Now they were convinced that 'les Lyonnais ... ont suivi les errements de la Commission', and they were unwilling to negotiate with the *sections* unless they withdrew recognition from the rebel authorities. So long as most of the *sections* were controlled by supporters of the rebel administrations, the negotiations started by Guillin on 20 July could achieve nothing. The *représentants* advised the Committee of Public Safety to make no concessions.[85]

Their attitude was hardened further by restrictions that various *sections* placed on the acceptance of the Constitution. Riffaterre regards the heavy vote in favour of the Constitution on 28 July as an indication of the rebellion's failing support.[86] But it cannot be seen simply as a vote for the Convention and against rebellion. On 24 July the Popular Commission received a letter from Kellermann announcing his intention to march on Lyon, and communicated its contents to the *sections*.[87] All the subsequent attempts by the Lyonnais authorities and *sections* to placate their opponents, including the acceptance of the Constitution, must be interpreted in the light of their knowledge that an attack was imminent.

The Commission's first reactions to the letter were conciliatory. It permitted the departure of a squadron of dragoons and an artillery company which had been kept in Lyon against Kellermann's wishes since early July, and released three *conventionnels* who had also been detained in Lyon.[88] With all of the authorities agreed that the decrees of the

[84] *Actes*, v. 358 (24 July).

[85] *CP*, pp. 476–7, 480–90; *Actes*, v. 399, 454–6 (27 July, 2 Aug.); AC I²3, no. 187 (copy), Reverchon to Davallon (an acquaintance in Lyon).

[86] Riffaterre, *Le Mouvement anti-jacobin et anti-parisien à Lyon*, ii. 622.

[87] *CP*, p. 137 (24 July); *Journal de Lyon*, 25 July, p. 457; AD 31L2, fo. 22, minutes of la Croisette, 22 July.

[88] *Journal de Lyon*, 26 July, p. 457; *CP*, p. 144 (25 July); AN F¹ᵃIII, Rhône 8, d. 2, no. 2, Buonarroti (to the Convention?), Vienne, 27 July. The *conventionnels* were Dherbez-Latour, Sauteyra, and Buonarroti (AG B³103*, d. 24, CP to Kellerman, 24 July).

Convention concerning France's general interests should be accepted, and the only apparent means of preventing an attack being to convince Kellermann of Lyon's republicanism, it is hardly surprising that most of those whose voted are recorded in the archives accepted the Constitution unreservedly. No doubt the 'yes' vote was further increased by the widespread (and, for Lyon, comforting) illusion that the referendum heralded the end of the Convention and new elections.[89]

More surprising is the degree of reluctance to accept the proposed constitution as it stood.[90] At a time when unanimous and unqualified acceptance would clearly have improved the prospects for generous treatment by the Convention, it was a sign that the intransigents' strength that so many votes for acceptance contained restrictions or reservations.[91] In several cases, it is true, procedural devices were probably used to attach various qualifications to resolutions of acceptance. But the fact remains that ten of the twenty-four *sections* whose proceedings have survived were controlled by men unwilling to take this opportunity for a *rapprochement* with the Convention.

With no show of enthusiasm, acceptance of the constitutional proposal was proclaimed in Lyon on 30 July,[92] and sectional delegates taking the voting results to Paris passed through Mâcon on 2 August. Reverchon, Javogues, and Delaporte received them, but having already been informed that 'la majeure partie des sections n'ont émis qu'un vote conditionnel et restrictif', they were sceptical of the delegates' claim that 'ce n'etoit qu'un vœu de la part des sections, et que l'acceptation n'en restoit moins pure et simple'. They left the Lyonnais with an impression of inflexibility: 'notre Commission populaire les indigne beaucoup; ils disent que c'est un ramas d'aristocrates et qu'il n'en faut pas l'état major composé de cy-devants en un mot notre ville a besoin d'être mise à neuf ...'.[93] After the meeting the *députés* informed the Committee of Public Safety that the Lyonnais wanted a general amnesty and the quashing of the decree of 12 July, but recommended that no concessions should be made before Lyon had accepted all of the decrees and a garrison. It seems unlikely

---

[89] See M. J. Sydenham, *The French Revolution* (London, 1969), 172.

[90] See Riffaterre, *Le Mouvement anti-jacobin et anti-parisien à Lyon*, ii. 416–31.

[91] 5,152 votes were recorded for unqualified acceptance, 2,049 for acceptance with restrictions, and 45 for rejection of the Constitution.

[92] *CP*, p. 154 (30 July). Two of Garat's agents were in Lyon that day and reported that the proclamation was done 'avec fort peu de pompe et d'éclat, on n'y a fait que ce qu'on ne pouvoit pas absolument empêcher' (P. Caron (ed.), *Rapports des agents du Ministre de l'Intérieur dans les départements, 1793–an II*, 2 vols. (Paris, 1951), ii. 60).

[93] AD 42L39, no. 51, Hugues Perrin to the *section* of la Croisette, 3 Aug.

that they would have taken a different view even had they known the full voting figures on the Constitution, and less likely still that a letter more sympathetic to the Lyonnais would have persuaded the Committee of Public Safety to relent.

After receiving the letter from Mâcon and the manifesto *Le peuple de Lyon à tous les François*, the Committee, which had already ruled out any relaxation of the decrees against Lyon, reiterated the order to attack with all available forces:[94] 'Il est aisé de voir, par les termes de leur adresse aux Français, que les dominateurs de cette ville rebelle ne veulent point de paix et qu'ils cachent, sous les mots sacrés de liberté et d'égalité, de République une et indivisible, des intentions contre-révolutionnaires.'[95] Billaud-Varenne and Saint-André had already decided that acceptance of the Constitution by rebel cities was an obvious deceit, and the Jacobin Club of Paris was informed on 9 August that 'les intrigants de Lyon ont remplacé les patriotes qui avaient été désignés pour assister à la fête du 10 août [à Paris] par des contre-révolutionnaires'.[96] The Lyonnais delegates to Paris would find, as they expected, that the Convention had decided against them.[97]

At Bourg, Dubois-Crancé had decided on his plan of attack. He was just as certain that Lyon would have to be reduced by force as he had been in early June,[98] although now there was little chance of a combined Lyonnais–Marseillais army being formed he was not so worried by the rebellion and believed that Lyon could be occupied quickly and painlessly. Kellermann could delay his attack no longer. Marching from Bourg on 6 August, he reached the environs of Lyon on the 7th and captured the hamlet of Caluire, but he was unable to seize his next target, La Croix-Rousse, which had been hastily fortified. There was a skirmish that day, and on 9 August, after three demands for unconditional surrender had been rejected by the Commission the siege began.[99]

A peaceful end to the rebellion could only have been achieved if the

(30 July, 2, 4 Aug.). The presence of the truculent Javogues is unlikely to have softened the atmosphere during this encounter. (On 20 July Claude Javogues of Montbrison was sent on mission to the *départements* of Ain, Allier, Isère, Ardèche, Haute-Loire, Puy-de-Dôme, and Drôme (ibid. 320). See Lucas, *The Structure of the Terror*.)

[95] *Actes*, v. 467 (4 Aug.).

[96] *Jacobins*, v. 339.

[97] AD 42L39, no. 55, letter of Hugues Perrin to Terra, Paris, 11 Aug.: 'Nous sommes Lyonnois: c'est un crime.'

[98] *Deuxième partie de la réponse de Dubois-Crancé*, pp. 203, 224, 249, letters of 17, 21, and 28 July.

[99] *CP*, pp. 241–2, 245; *Deuxième partie de la réponse de Dubois-Crancé*, p. 266, proclamation of 8 Aug.; AG B³103*, d. 30, *députés en mission* to the president of the Convention, Bourg, 6 Aug., Kellermann to CSP, 10 Aug., Kellermann's ultimatums of 8 and 9 Aug.

A peaceful end to the rebellion could only have been achieved if the Popular Commission had dissolved itself after the authorities' statement of 24 July. The intransigents in the *sections* might then have been dislodged, or at least sufficiently demoralized for full submission to be made to the decrees of 26 June and 12 July. Without the Commission and its committees, there could not have seemed much hope of organizing the defence of Lyon. The demoralized administrations and the *sections* with their clumsy methods of consultation were hardly capable of it. The fall of the Commission might also have convinced the *députés* that they should wait for the rebellion to collapse of its own accord. Instead, between 24 July and 2 August they became more convinced that the partisans of rebellion still controlled Lyon, though they continued to regard them as a small Machiavellian minority who dominated the city by force, intrigue, and misinformation.

Riffaterre argues that the attack on Lyon only went ahead because Reverchon and Delaporte were unaware of the strong vote in favour of the Constitution.[100] But the two *députés* were swayed less by their impressions of public opinion in Lyon in general than by their unquestionably correct belief that 'l'influence des meneurs n'est pas encore neutralisée'.[101] Neither they nor the Committee believed that the *meneurs* (ringleaders) should be negotiated with: 'nous ne pensons pas que la Convention Nationale puisse honorablement transiger avec une poignée de factieux'.[102] 'La Convention ne peut et ne doit rien écouter que la loi et la justice sont satisfaites.'[103] Both, again rightly, believed that the *meneurs* would have to be removed by force. There was no fundamental misunderstanding between the opposing sides about the crucial matters that divided them. The Committee of Public Safety correctly understood that Lyon was under the control of men whose suspicion of the Convention prevented their acceptance of its authority over Rhône-et-Loire. Lyon correctly understood that the Committee of Public Safety insisted on nothing less than unconditional recognition of the Convention's absolute sovereignty.

The Committee of Public Safety's identification of anti-Jacobinism with counter-revolution removed any possibility of a settlement along the lines suggested by Lindet in June and by Garat's agent, François Melletier, in July: to suspend hostile measures against the Lyonnais and patiently

---

[100] Riffaterre, *Le Mouvement anti-jacobin et anti-parisien à Lyon*, ii. 476.
[101] *Actes*, v. 454, letter of 2 Aug.
[102] Ibid. 399 (27 July).
[103] Ibid. 473 (4 Aug.).

to dispel their mistrust of the Convention. The Committee translated into policy a Jacobin hostility to Lyon that was based on deep and long-standing suspicions of 'the home of counter-revolution in the Midi', suspicions which were distilled into certainty by the anti-Jacobin insurrection of 29 May and Lyon's adhesion to the 'federalist' movement. The assumption that anti-Jacobinism must be rooted in royalism converged with Lyon's sinister reputation and understandable fears that its rebellion posed a grave strategic threat. Belief in the need for a harsh and uncompromising stand against the anti-Jacobins of Lyon was not limited to the terrorists of the Committee; it had been responsible for the attempts by various *députés en mission* to prop up the Jacobin Municipalité in the spring. The same assumption lay behind the decree of 12 July, which, as Melletier observed, inflamed opinion in Lyon and stood as a large barrier to conciliation.[104] Even Dubois-Crancé decided that there should be 'quelque adoucissement au décret du 12'[105] when, to his surprise, the *sections* refused to negotiate after a week's fighting. But the Convention only amended the decree in the direction of greater severity.[106] Provocations like the appointment of Précy, the execution of Chalier, and the publication of *Le peuple de Lyon à tous les François*—in all of which royalists probably had a hand—removed what chance there had been of Paris relenting. But after the renewal of the Committee of Public Safety on 10 July that was a very small chance.

As well as making civil war virtually inevitable, the Montagnards' difficulty in understanding the rebellion as anything other than outright counter-revolution led them to underestimate the Lyonnais willingness to resist. By definition, the people and the counter-revolution were mutually exclusive. The people could not willingly submit to the aristocratic yoke. Hence Lyon's persistence in revolt must be the work of 'a handful of seditionaries' (*une poignée de factieux*) tyrannizing—or duping—a population which was—or would be if correctly informed—thirsting for liberation. But as we have seen, there was still a good deal of sectional support for the rebellion in late July, and this was to continue well into the siege.

[104] AN F¹ᶜIII, Rhône 8, d. 3, no. 30, letter to Garat, 20 July.

[105] *Actes*, vi. 7, letter to CSP, 16 Aug.

[106] On 23 July the Convention ordered the sequestration of property of those who failed to leave Lyon in accordance with the decree of 12 July (Herriot, *Lyon n'est plus*, ii. 271).

8

The Siege

The uniqueness of Lyon's revolutionary experience is demonstrated most clearly in the nine-week siege of summer and autumn 1793. Several other cities came under attack by the forces of the Convention, but none resisted nearly so hard or so long, except for Toulon, which had the assistance of the British fleet. Clearly, Lyon's resistance was only made possible by the active involvement of large numbers of its citizens. The documents of the Terror refute the Jacobin myth that the revolt was engineered and sustained by the thousands of nobles, foreigners, and priests who had flocked to Lyon since 1789. Pelat and Cayrol's study[1] of those executed for counter-revolution after the siege shows an almost exact correlation between the birthplaces of 1,901 victims of the Terror in Lyon and the geographical recruitment of Lyon's population in the eighteenth century. Four-fifths of them were described as residents of Lyon, and on the socially selective evidence of the lists of the *contribution patriotique* (1789)[2] and of *éligibles* (1790), 65 per cent can be shown to have lived in Lyon in 1789. Ex-nobles represented 6.3 per cent of the condemned, and more than half of this group (67 out of 120) were Lyonnais. While it is true that less than half of the 130 clergy executed were Lyon-born (53), the great majority of the rest came from Rhône-et-Loire or the neighbouring *départements* of the Ain and the Isère. So, Lyon's resistance was overwhelmingly resistance by Lyonnais.

It is very difficult to estimate how many were directly involved in the defence of Lyon. Maintaining an army for more than two months, and manning such ancillary services as working parties to build and repair

---

[1] See H. Pelat and M. Cayrol, 'Tableau de la Contre-Révolution à Lyon d'après 1 901 condemnations à mort prononcées à la suite du siège de la ville', DES thesis (Université de Lyon, n.d.), 19–30, 49–53.

[2] The *contribution* of 1789 was not obligatory for day-labourers and poorer manual workers, and the published list of taxpayers was far from being a comprehensive directory of the male population. These figures do not take account of the reinforcements obtained from the Forez in September, some at least of whom were tried by the Commission Révolutionnaire at Feurs.

fortifications and fire-fighting units to cope with the incendiary bombardments of September, must have required full- or part-time participation by many hundreds of people. But it is hard to count even the participants in the more obvious activities of civil and military rebellion, the ones which most interested the terrorist authorities. And it is even more difficult to say how their involvement was secured. Those arraigned for having served in the ranks of the Lyonnais army were likely to plead in mitigation ignorance, confusion, hunger, coercion, or all four. In many cases this is likely to have been true. But it would be a mistake to accept too easily that the population was tricked or coerced into participation by a small core of committed (royalist) rebels—*une poignée de factieux* again, the first line of defence against the truth that this was a civil war. There are good reasons for believing that committed support for Lyon's resistance was greater than has usually been thought.

Riffaterre suggests that participation in sectional permanence was derisory even before the rebellion reached the point of open hostilities.[3] Unfortunately, nearly all the detailed sectional records stop well before the siege, very few give voting figures, and it is impossible to say how many regular attenders there were, apart from presidents and secretaries. Plat-d'Argent (a socially mixed *section* of the peninsula) and la Juiverie (poor and pro-Jacobin before 29 May) had average attendances of 65 and 66 at those meetings (four and three respectively) for which figures were recorded in the period after the creation of the Popular Commission. In each case the lowest figure recorded was 56.[4] If something like 65 men attended each of the *sections* fairly regularly, the total of committed *sectionnaires* in the month or so before the siege would have been about 2,080. It could have been rather higher, since the more prosperous *sections* of the peninsula were likely to have contained more supporters of permanence. Possibly, then, there were well over 2,000 committed *sectionnaires* from whom civilian and military personnel could be drawn during the siege. This was no great number, but it can hardly be described as a handful and is not much less in proportion to the city's population

---

[3] C. Riffaterre, *Le Mouvement anti-jacobin et anti-parisien à Lyon et dans le Rhône-et-Loire en 1793* (Lyon, 1912–28), i. 229–31, 445–6. Riffaterre's perspective on these figures was affected by his questionable decision to compare them to the extraordinarily high voting-figures recorded by l'Hôtel-Dieu before 29 May (see above, Ch. 5).

[4] AD 31L49, minutes of Plat-d'Argent, 19, 20 July, 2, 12 Aug; 31L16, minutes of la Juiverie, 7, 22, 31 July. La Grande-Côte I, a very poor weaving *quartier*, recorded 72 votes in the election of its president on 27 July (42L39, no. 156), the polls having been open from 9.00 a.m. to 7.15 p.m.

than the *sans-culottes* were to that of Paris in the year II.[5]

As we will see, the size of the Lyonnais army is also hard to establish, and estimating its committed component, as distinct from those who served under threat or to get bread, is harder still. But some rough calculations are possible. Not every *section* proved capable of contributing a reliable battalion to the force, and Précy was obliged to reduce the number of fighting battalions from twenty-eight to twenty. A plausible figure for the number of committed soldiers can be reached on the basis of there being two élite companies (the grenadiers and *chasseurs* who did most of the fighting) for each of these twenty battalions, and fifty-eight men per company. To these should be added the companies of gunners, made up of twenty-eight men per *section* and at a guess half as many dragoons.[6] This would make 3,160 full-time soldiers quartered in barracks or manning front-line posts, which is consistent with other evidence. The rest of the Lyonnais army was made up of fusiliers, many of whom were probably forced to serve, and many of whom deserted.[7] Their officers and NCOs, though, are likely to have been committed rebels, 400 of them on the basis of two fusilier companies for each of the twenty battalions.[8] Taking into account *section* officials and *commissaires de surveillance*— there were fewer in both these categories after the fighting broke out, but in all perhaps ten per *section*—together with members of the Provisional Municipalité and other authorities, it would be reasonable to think in terms of 4,000 men committed to the defence of Lyon in August and September.

These militants' ability to maintain control of Lyon and elicit co-operation from the rest of the population was based on more than coercion and misinformation. One factor was their effective use of the *sections*

---

[5] The proportions are: 'federalist' activists in Lyon, 1.39%; *sans-culotte* activists in Paris, 1.57%. This is based on a figure 'somewhat exceeding 10,000 as the number of active popular democrats' in Paris in the year II (calculated by R. R. Palmer from Soboul's *Les Sans-culottes parieiens en l'an II*, in 'Popular Democracy in the French Revolution: Review Article', *French Historical Studies*, 1 (1960), reprinted in F. A. Kafker and J. J. Laux, *The French Revolution: Conflicting Interpretations* (New York, 1968), 290). Lyon's total population is taken as 150,000 and Paris's as 636,000 (see G. Rudé, *The Crowd in the French Revolution* (Oxford, 1959), 243).

[6] On the organization of the Lyonnais army, see P[asseron], 'Mémoires d'un pauvre diable', *Revue du Lyonnais*, 3 (1838), 361; *CP*, pp. 76–7 (13 July); AC I²3, 112, authorization by Précy for the Bordeaux (l'Hôtel-Dieu) battalion to form 1 grenadier and 1 *chasseur* company of 50 men and 10 officers each (n.d.).

[7] See below, *The Armies*.

[8] The regulations for the Departmental Army provided for 10 officers per company (*CP*, p. 87 (13 July)).

and particularly the sectional *Comités de surveillance*. Being in effect a committee of sectional representatives, the Provisional Municipalité had the advantage of more direct lines of communication with the *sections* than any of its predecessors. And both it and the Popular Commission continued to rely heavily on the *sections' Comités de surveillance* for administration and repression. As they had done since the third week of June, the committees collected denunciations, designated suspects, and had them disarmed or arrested. The Municipalité's own Committee of General Security confined itself to deciding whether those arrested should be held for trial, and that task also went to the committees later.[9] Levels of zeal varied. The minutes of the committee of Vaise seldom record more than 'la lecture du procès verbal de la dernière après quoi n'étant rien survenu de nouveau la séance à été levée'.[10] So inoffensive was this rebel committee that it continued to meet, apparently unnoticed, for more than a fortnight after the Convention had recaptured Lyon. But other committees had interpreted their powers more broadly from the outset and had used them rigorously, assuming, for instance, that they had the right to annul the *cartes de section* without waiting for the Municipalité's permission, conducting disarmaments on their own initiative, and adjudicating complaints of unjustified disarmament themselves.[11]

The siege widened the committees' powers further. In June they had been charged with surveillance of the bakeries, and later the distribution of indemnities to the poor and food rationing became part of their functions, obviously increasing their ability to exert political control. It is likely that many *sections*, like la Croisette, also made their committees responsible for recruitment, and they were confirmed in this function in August. During the siege the committees requisitioned labourers to work on the fortifications and conducted domiciliary visits.[12]

As well as being the administrative backbone of the rebellion, the *Comités de surveillance* provided an element of continuity in sectional personnel which would otherwise have been lacking. Most of the *sections*

[9] AD 42L32, d. C41.

[10] AD 31L36 (1 June–27 Oct.).

[11] e.g. AD 31L49, no. 5, minutes of Plat-d'Argent, 5 June, conferring a range of powers on its committee; 31L16, fo. 2, minutes of la Juiverie, 12 June; ibid., fo. 21 (12 July); 42L12, fo. 308, interrogation of Hugues Bergeon, *commissaire de surveillance* of la Juiverie.

[12] AD 42L39, committee of Port Saint-Paul to Committee of Police (Municipalité), 1 June; 31L47, extract from the minutes of the committee of Place Confort, 4 June; 31L2, fos. 11–15, minutes of la Croisette, 5 July–17 Aug.; 42L93, d. 70, Comité Particulier de Sûreté Générale to the *Comités de surveillance* ([late Aug?]); 42L71, d. Clergier, denunciation by Serlin; 31L24 committee of Saint-Pierre to the *Corps administratifs réunis*, 23 Sept.

held fortnightly or monthly elections of their presidents and secretaries, but the committees were not renewed *in toto* during the period of the rebellion. Only those who resigned were replaced. Despite the fragmentary records, it can be established that forty-eight of those who were *commissaires surveillants* in June still held the office in September. In three *sections* about half the *commissaires* served continuously during this period; in one *section* the figure was as high as three-quarters; and in four others it was a quarter.[13]

It is not possible to determine how many *commissaires* were intransigents, or how many, like the scrivener Hivert, a veteran *clubiste* of les Terreaux, used their positions to assist persecuted *patriotes*.[14] Nor is it possible to judge with certainty which committees were particularly active. Nevertheless, those which continued to function and to co-operate with the authorities in the last three weeks of the siege, after Lyon had been completely surrounded, can be regarded as strongly committed to the defence of the city. There are records of fourteen *sections* which had both committees and sectional *Bureaux* functioning after 22 September. At least fourteen more had one or the other.[15] So, in the last desperate stage of the rebellion, one or both of the forms of sectional organization adopted at its beginning survived in at least twenty-eight of the *sections*. Only at the last did it cease to be a rebellion of the *sections*, and this helps to explain its resilience.

Just as it had before the siege, the rebels' network of *sections* and committees helped to retain cross-class support and prevented wealthy peninsular Lyon, the heartland of the rebellion, from becoming isolated. Much confusion has surrounded this enduring support from below, partly

---

[13] See Appendix XI.

[14] 'Hivert écrivain membre du Comité de surveillance section de la Liberté [les Terreaux] siège et avant [*sic*] de manière qu'il semble qu'il y a resté pour servir les patriotes, il étoit de la nomination du 20 mai et auparavant il étoit un des fondateurs de la société populaire, et il n'a jamais abandonné la société . . .'. (He was said to have spoken in favour of *patriotes* and warned them when they were denounced.) (AC I²7, d. 17, Arrests, *section* de la Liberté, 29 ventôse, an II.)

[15] Surveillance Committees still co-operating with the administrations late in the siege were: Porte-Froc (*CP*, p. 298 (1 Oct.); Place Saint-Pierre (*Secrétariat*, p. 125 (3 Oct.)); Place Confort (ibid., p. 128 (4 Oct.)); Place Neuve (AD 42L39, no. 263 (1 Oct.)); la Pêcherie (ibid., nos. 80–2 (30 Sept., 5–6 Oct.)); Port Saint-Paul (ibid., no. 98 (3 Oct.)); la Grande-Côte I (ibid., no. 166 (8 Oct.)); Port du Temple (ibid., no. 200 (5 Oct.)); Saint-Georges (ibid., no. 240 (5 Oct.)); Rue Neuve (ibid., no. 231 (29 Sept.)); Bon-Rencontre (ibid., no. 68 (4 Oct.)); le Gourguillon (ibid., no. 72 (23 Sept.)); Rue Tupin (ibid., no. 122 (29 Sept.)); le Rhône (ibid., 29 Sept.); le Change (ibid., 30 Sept.). The *sections* not mentioned in the Secrétariat's minutes between 25 Sept. and the end of the siege were: Port Saint-Paul, Plat-d'Argent, Saint-Vincent II, and Bon-Rencontre (*Secrétariat*, pp. 113–30).

because neo-Jacobin historians have usually ignored it, while anti-neo-Jacobin historians who have noticed it have tended to exaggerate it. From Collot d'Herbois to Richard Cobb, those who have actually looked at the dossiers of the Terror have been obliged to abandon the Montagnards' early characterization of the rebel militants as 'a handful of seditionaries' drawn from 'the aristocratic and mercantile sect' and its lackeys. Soon after their arrival to supervise the repression, Collot and Fouché became 'convaincus qu'il n'y a d'innocent dans cette infâme cité que celui qui fut opprimé ou chargé de fers par les assassins du peuple'.[16] In the 1950s, while working on the Revolutionary Armies of the year II, Cobb formed the impression that 'à Lyon tout le peuple sectionnaire prend part aux combats du siège'.[17] Alfred Cobban seized on this to suggest that Soboul's version of the Montagnard–sans-culottes alliance ignored contrary provincial evidence.[18] But in fact the menu peuple's support for the defence of Lyon was not as great as Cobb thought. Some popular anti-Jacobinism certainly carried over into August and September, but the evidence on rebel militants during the siege shows only one category (grenadiers below the rank of captain) in which the participation by artisans and boutiquiers was greater than their approximate proportional representation in the general population. The involvement of silk-weavers was low, and this is a good indication of the poorer artisans' attitude to the rebellion in its final stages. Amongst sectional personnel identifiable by occupation, the proportion of artisans, boutiquiers, and weavers is lower for the siege period than for any other category except those in office for over a month after 1 July.[19] In general, the upper social categories were much more prominent amongst rebel militants after July than before. Nevertheless, the cross-class character of the rebellion held, and its ability to recruit committed soldiers from the menu peuple helped not only militarily, but by continuing to validate the democratic rhetoric of a people's resistance to oppression.

LE PREJUGÉ EST CONTRE NOUS

It was important, too, that the rebels could continue to see themselves as targets of the same great conspiracy between Lyonnais Jacobins and

[16] Quoted in P. Mansfield, 'The Missions of Collot d'Herbois: A Study in his Political Career', Ph.D. thesis (Macquarie University, 1985), 298.

[17] R. Cobb, Les Armées révolutionnaires: Instrument de la Terreur dans les départements, avril 1793–floréal, an II, 2 vols. (Paris, 1961–3), i. 49.

[18] A. Cobban, The Social Interpretation of the French Revolution (Cambridge, 1971), 126.

[19] See Appendix X.

Montagnards which had justified the insurrection of 29 May. This meant that the rationale for holding out in the siege had the same communal, anti-Jacobin basis as the sectional movement of May. The threat was against Lyon as a community as well as against property and order. As long ago as September 1792, it was said, Dubois-Crancé had marked Lyon as 'une ville à exterminer': 'Depuis quinze jours notre ville est assiégée par les ordres du brigand Dubois-Crancé, parce que nous n'avons pas voulu rétablir une Municipalité qui avoit eu la barbarie d'arrêter le massacre de vingt mille citoyens'; 'la Convention avoit donné ordre de faire marcher des troupes sur Lyon ... les troupes s'avancent sur nous pour remettre les clubs et l'ancienne municipalité et nous forcer imposition de 30 millions [sic]'; 'si l'on appercevoit qu'on ne put pas repousser la horde de Dubois de Crancé on se porteroit aux prisons pour y égorger les scélerats pour lesquels il venoit'.[20] Dubois-Crancé unwittingly encouraged this mentality with threats which might have been copied out of the Brunswick Manifesto ('craignez ... que votre entière destruction ne serve d'exemple à quinconque serait tenté de vous imiter ...'), and the authorities deliberately fostered it with material like the letter supposedly addressed to him by Danton: 'Dussions-nous même abandonner le Montblanc au Tyran Sarde, peu nous importe... il faut la [la ville de Lyon] réduire en cendres. Distribuer à force les assignats, ne les compte pas...'[21]

Dubois-Crancé was regarded as 'le chef de la conspiration'[22] against Lyon. In the wake of his consistent support for the Jacobin Municipalité and his dispatch of troops to Lyon on 28 May, there had come his attempts to mount an attack in June and July and his denunciations of Lyon's 'révolution prétendue républicaine' as 'faite en faveur du *royalisme* ou du *fédéralisme*'.[23] He had elaborated a wild plot-thesis involving foreign powers and the royalists of the Lozère and Vendée, but centring on

---

[20] *Les Lyonnois à l'armée dirigée contre eux par Dubois-Crancé* (Lyon, n.d.) (Fonds Coste MS 4555), 1; AD 42L75, d. 18, letter signed Dussurgey, 21 Aug., intercepted at Marcigny; AB BB3, 77 liasse 2, letter signed Dutel, 17 Aug.; AD 42L70, d. 97(2), denunciation of Cholet, stocking-merchant, by Billet, 24 Oct.

[21] E.-L.-A. Dubois-Crancé, *Deuxième partie de la réponse de Dubois-Crancé aux inculpations des ses collègues Couthon et Maignet* n.p., n.d.), 70, 'Les représentants du peuple envoyés près l'Armée des Alpes aux Lyonnais', 25 Aug., signed Dubois-Crancé and Gauthier; AN AA531487, no. 41, printed copy of a letter attributed to Danton, *Actes*, vi. 98–9; Dubois-Crancé to the Convention, 30 Aug., denying the letter's authenticity.

[22] AD 31L21, fo. 16, minutes of Port Saint-Paul, 29 June.

[23] Dubois-Crancé, Albitte, and Gauthier, *Proclamation des représentants du peuple envoyés près l'Armée de Alpes* (Grenoble, 3 July 1793), 7.

Lyon's determination to create a separate state in the Midi by exploiting
the linguistic differences between the 'langue d'oc' and the 'langue d'oïl',
and the provincial cities' envy of Paris.[24] No one had done more to equate
the Lyonnais rebellion with counter-revolution, and the intense hostility
to him in Lyon is understandable.

Of course, as he observed himself, it suited the rebel leaders to focus
animosity on him. Denouncing an individual *député* with a personal
grudge against Lyon was less compromising and less likely to alienate the
hesitant than denouncing the national government.[25] But he had made
himself an easy target for attacks representing him as a fanatical enemy
of Lyon. His presence with Kellermann's army was a major argument
for continued resistance.

There was more than this working against submission. Paralleling and
feeding on Jacobin denigration of their city as an epicentre of counter-
revolutionary conspiracy, something like collective paranoia emerged
amongst the Lyonnais, a belief that 'le préjugé est contre nous'.[26] The
theme was developed in la Convention's declaration on 27 May: '[C]ette
Cité, trop constamment calomniée', had been singled out for attack and
denied rights freely enjoyed by others (specifically, the right of sectional
permanence). Soon after, another pamphlet began with 'Les Lyonnais,
longtemps avilis dans l'opinion publique ...'.[27] Variations on the theme
recur in letters, addresses, and sectional minutes. A participant in the
journée of 29 May wrote, admittedly with hindsight, that 'depuis longtemps, Lyon était proscrit'.[28] Belief in the existence of a campaign of
calumny was reinforced during June and July. At Condrieu, the Provisional Municipalité was told, the inhabitants believed that 'nous sommes
des assassins qui lapidons et guillotinons tous les patriotes ...'. Despite
Lyon's demonstrated love of liberty and obedience to the law since 1789,
'la calomnie nous a jusqu'à présent poursuivis, nos véritables sentiments
ont été étouffés par des factieux'.[29] On 3 July, after an interview with the

---

[24] See *Deuxième partie de la réponse de Dubois-Crancé*, pp. 112–27 ('Proclamation des
représentants ... aux citoyens du département de l'Isère' (Grenoble, 22 June 1793)).

[25] E.-L.-A. Dubois-Crancé, *Discours sur le siège de Lyon prononcé au Club des jacobins à
Paris* ... (n.p., n.d. [an II]), p. 3.

[26] *Journal de Lyon*, 5 Mar. 1793, p. 394.

[27] *Lettre d'un citoyen de Lyon à son ami sur les événements de la journée du 29 mai 1793*
(Lyon, 1793), 1.

[28] Cited in J. Schatzmann, 'La Révolution de 1793 à Lyon vue par un témoin oculaire,
Jean-Salomon Fazy', *AHRF*, (1940), 101.

[29] AD 42L39, letter to the Provisional Municipalité from its *commissaires* in Condrieu,
29 June; *Les citoyens de la ville de Lyon à leurs frères des districts ... de Rhône-et-Loire* (Lyon,

député Gauthier, a Lyonnais described the former's views as follows:

Les Lyonnois sont des aristocrates, des contre-révolutionnaires, la journée du 29 n'est due qu'à un parti depuis longtemps préparé; ... déjà cinq sections ont manifesté leur désir pour le Gouvernement monarchique ... un esprit de parti bien décidé et bien connu dirige les sections et la cœur blanche bientôt aborée sera le signal de la contre-révolution ... nous sommes Lyonnois, par conséquent entachés du prétendu vin locale, et comment d'ailleurs faire entendre raison à des hommes qui se croyent demi-dieux ...?[30]

The feelings of persecution went deeper than this belief in the Montagnards' bias against Lyon. They fed on Lyon's uneasy relationship with the countryside and on its sense of isolation in a sea of peasant hostility which the revolution had made more threatening. This was connected with old tensions rooted in problems of food supply, and attributed, for example, to greedy peasants extorting excessive prices while taking advantage when they could of subsidized bread intended for city-dwellers.[31] It was believed—and not only by political moderates—that it was the peasants who had benefited most from the Revolution and were favoured by the taxation system. Yet what use had they made of the liberty conferred on them? 'Les gens de la campagne en abusant de cette liberté se coalisent pour nous vendre les denrées à des prix excessifs.'[32] Or, as it was stated in the *section* of Port Saint-Paul on 30 July:

les habitants de la campagne jouissant jusqu'à présent eux seuls des faveurs de la révolution, sont assez riches pout n'être pas pressés de vendre leurs denrées, au point qu'ils disent qu'ils ne soucient pas de les vendre, qu'ils ont assez d'assignats, on a observé de plus que depuis trois ans ils ne payent aucune imposition et qu'eux-mêmes sont étonnés qu'avec des guerres telles que nous avons on ne leur en demande point.

Earlier, the same *section*'s president had called on the Département to put Lyon's case more forcibly to the peasantry: 'comme les citoyens de la campagne sont presque les seuls qui [ont] commencé a recueillir les fruits de la Révolution et ... [doivent] considérer par cette raison la convention comme la source d'où découle leurs richesses, et [peuvent]

June 1793), in *CP*, p. 329.
[30] Coste MS 642, anonymous letter, 3 July (possibly by one of the district administrators detained by Dubois-Crancé in Grenoble late in June).
[31] See e.g. the address by the club of la Croisette on this subject; AC I²4, d. 45, fo. 40, 6 Mar.; *CM*, iv. 136 (8 Mar.).
[32] AN F⁷3686⁶, d. 7, no. 19, Charles George *l'aîné* to Roland ([late 1792]). See also AD 1L646, letter of Mayor Bertrand, 27 Mar.

par là être facilement trompés'. These fears that *nos frères de la campagne* ('enfants de la nature' with 'la crédule confiance des simples agriculteurs') would make easy targets for 'Maratization' produced an earnest but fruitless campaign to explain Lyon's case to the countryside.[33]

Not only was the revolution seen as favouring the peasantry; it was seen by some as actively working against the interests, and perhaps even the survival, of the cities. Jacobinism blended Roman republican austerity with a Rousseauist idealization of rural life and contempt for wealth and sophistication. Besides harming Lyon's interests as a producer of luxury goods, this led easily to the assumption that the big cities were the sewers of old regime corruption—unless repeated acts of revolutionary heroism proved the contrary. By mid-1793, Marseille having ruined its record, the category of hero-city consisted of Paris alone. It was not easy to see where, or even whether, the great centres of commerce and industry fitted into the Jacobin Utopia of small producers, artisans, and peasants content with economic independence, the dignity of their toil, and a modest living. Some Lyonnais concluded that Jacobinism had become a war against the cities. 'Je crois que nos ennemis ont juré la destruction des villes parce qu'ils ont soutenus la Révolution', wrote one of Roland's correspondents in December 1792, 'et ils n'ont que ce seul moyen qui est de faire crier contre le luxe, parce que les villes ne peuvent vivre sans la luxe.' (This reasoning was based on the standard assumption in revolutionary discourse that one's enemies are counter-revolutionaries behind the mask of patriotism.) A pamphlet dated 30 May declared that under the Jacobin Municipalité, 'tout le commerce était proscrit ainsi que les jeunes gens attachés aux maisons de commerce'. Two days into the siege a private letter sent to Thiers put the matter more bluntly: 'On vous tend le piège d'écraser les grandes villes, les scélérats veulent nous réduire tous a traîner la charrue afin de nous rendre serfs.'[34]

Many sympathizers of the rebellion, it seems, felt profoundly threatened by what the Revolution looked like becoming under Montagnard management. With the siege, all these fears seemed on the brink of

---

[33] AD 31L21, fo. 27, minutes of Port Saint-Paul, 30 July, 30 June; *Les Sections de la ville de Lyon aux habitants du département et de toutes les municipalités voisines* (Lyon, [2 June] 1793); *Adresse des 32 sections ... aux habitants de la campagne* (Lyon, [17 June] 1793); *Les citoyens de la ville de Lyon à leurs frères des districts et communes du département de Rhône-et-Loire et à tous leurs frères de la République* (Lyon, [c. 11 June] 1793).

[34] AN F¹ᵃIII, Rhône, d. 1, no. 92, Billiotet to Roland, 6 Dec. 1792; *Lettre communiqué à la section II [de Marseille] par le citoyen Pérouse ...* (dated Lyon, 30 May 1793), cited in Riffaterre, *Le Mouvement anti-jacobin et anti-parisien à Lyon*, i. 206; AD 42L63, d. 10, Demarest *fils* to Baillard, 11 Aug.

realization. Besieged Lyon become a hothouse of rumour and mis-information, and it was easy to turn the Montagnards' rhetoric against themselves: Dubois-Crancé was making counter-revolution behind the mask of patriotism. After the siege, many Lyonnais claimed to have been told they were fighting royalists: 'on a été dans le doute pendant presque tout le siège'.[35] Jean-Baptiste Sarrazin, a stocking-weaver, said that he thought Dubois-Crancé was a royalist, and General Doppet, who was with the government troops when they entered Lyon on 9 October, found evidence of similar ideas amongst the defeated soldiers.[36] Many Lyonnais believed simply that the attackers were brigands with nothing more in mind than pillage. This belief, born of the fear that democracy might endanger property, fed by memories of the previous year's looting, and linked with the Jacobins and Dubois-Crancé by the revolutionary taxes planned in May, was one of the main themes in both personal and official justifications for resistance.[37]

In the year II, captured Lyonnais soldiers had everything to gain by persuading the terrorist authorities that they had been misled. But against the background of confusion created by the siege and deliberately fostered by the rebel authorities, their claims should be taken seriously. Decisions to support the rebellion were influenced by the consensus of the street, the barracks, the café, and the food queue, where rumour ruled. As the city was steadily cut off from outside information there was little else to go on, and little else to hope for than that the siege was indeed part of a conspiracy which might fall apart in time to save Lyon.

[35] AD 31L57, no. 171, fo. 13, interrogation of J.-B. Berruyer, dealer in gold leaf, by the Municipalité of Sens (Yonne), 22 brumaire, an II; 42L3, Military Commission, fo. 158, interrogation of J.-B.-C. Sarrazin *fils*, stocking-weaver, 27 brumaire. See also 42L3, fos. 53, 101, interrogations of C. Bied-Charreton, lawyer, 25 Oct., J.-B. Guérin, ex-regular soldier, 16 brumaire; 42L153, d. B7, interrogation of Claude Boze, hatter, by Vacher, *juge de paix* at Montluel, n.d.

[36] A. Doppet, *Mémoires politiques et militaires du Général Doppet* (Carouge, 1797), 141.

[37] Some characteristic examples: AD 42L86, no. 102, denunciation of Prudhon, postal employee, who was said to have described the Republic's armies as 'des brigands [qui] ne venoient que pour égorger les hônnetes gens et piller la ville'; ibid., B29, Gaspard Semenol, of Montbrison, who came to Lyon because 'l'on disoit que c'étoit l'armée des brigands que tout étoit au pillage'; 42L33, B60, anonymous denunciation of a plot for Dubois-Crancé's army to bombard various *quartiers* of Lyon, 'principalement contre les quartiers riches ... les clubistes des quartiers *battus* et ceux de *l'autre côté de l'eau* doivent dans la bagarre se réunir, en armes de différentes espèces, entrer dans les maisons sous prétexte de secourir, y voler et assassiner et augmenter le feu, ils assassineront aussi dans les rues. Plusieurs seront déguisés en femmes et des femmes aussi armées se réuniront à eux. Tout cela est arrêté pour le restant de cette semaine ...'. The threat of pillage is stressed in *Le Peuple de Lyon à tous les François* (Lyon, [31 July] 1793), in *CP*, pp. 476–7; *Liberté, Egalité: République une et indivisible—proclamation du général* (Lyon, [3 Sept.] 1793), in *CP*. pp. 539–40.

ROYALISTS AND PITT'S GOLD

For some, there was a much more positive rationale for resistance. To royalists the siege offered a chance to weaken the Republic's grip on the Midi, and perhaps even to open the way for a Piedmontese invasion by forcing the diversion of French troops from the Alpine frontier. The royalists' role has been closely studied by Riffaterre, who, having concluded that there was little support for the rebellion from other sectors of opinion, relies heavily on their presence to explain why Lyon held out for so long. Amongst the probable royalists in the civil administrations were P.-E. Béraud, the provisional *procureur* of the *commune* from 4 August to 5 October; Jean-François Fauré-Montaland, formerly *lieutenant-général criminel* at Lyon, a member of the Popular Commission's Committee of General Security; and an ex-*avocat du Roi*, Fleury-Marie Courbon-Montviol, president of the Commission from 10 September to the end.[38] Other crypto-royalists were undoubtedly working beside them, and it is quite likely that they came to dominate policy-making as military issues began to push all others into the background.

Royalists certainly did dominate the army. At least fifty-nine ex-nobles fought for Lyon, thirty-one as officers. Seven of them are known to have been *émigrés*: the three Allier brothers, Cudel de Montcolon, Gabriel-François de la Roche-Négly, Charles-Gaspard de Clermont-Tonnerre, and Henri-Isidore de Mélon, a veteran of the Camp de Jalès.[39] But most of them were moderate constitutionalists rather than reactionary diehards. Even the denouncers of the year II could come up with only a few cries of 'vive le roi', and flourishings of *fleurs de lis*. Précy himself was regarded as a constitutional monarchist, and Vallès's memoirs and those of other royalists who took part in the rebellion stress that outright counter-revolutionaries had little influence. The contempt for the Lyon-

---

[38] See Riffaterre, *Le Mouvement anti-jacobin et anti-parisien à Lyon*, ii. 10–94. Courbon-Montviol and Fauré-Montaland signed the royalist address to the King of 30 June 1792 (AN F^{1c}III, Rhône 7, d. 3). Fauré-Montaland declared his royalism before his death (AD 42L12, Commission de Justice Polulaire, fo. 104). Béraud was probably the author of *Relation du siège de Lyon contenant le détail de ce qui s'y est passé* (Neuchâtel, 1794), a work with a marked royalist bias. On its authorship see Riffaterre, *Le Mouvement anti-jacobin et anti-parisien à Lyon*, i. 140–1.

[39] Riffaterre, *Le Mouvement anti-jacobin et anti-parisien à Lyon*, ii. 68; AD 42L3, Commission Militaire, interrogations of de Melon and Cudel de Montcolon, 9 and 12 brumaire; entry on Rimberg (La Roche-Négly's *nom de guerre*) in A. Portallier, *Tableau général des victimes et martyrs de la Révolution en Lyonnais, Forez et Beaujolais* (Saint-Étienne, 1911), 391.

nais rebels ('boutiquiers republicains') expressed by *émigré* purists gives weight to this view.[40]

There were rumours at the time that not only royalists but British gold—4 million *livres* of it—propped up the Lyonnais resistance. This is possible but there is no firm proof. Riffaterre argued that there must have been outside help because the Lyonnais could not possibly have raised enough from their own resources to fight for sixty days.[41] It is true that voluntary contributions were hard to come by. By 19 July the *section* of Port Saint-Paul had collected only 2,666 *livres*, though 1,636 *livres* came in during the next week. La Croisette had collected 5,345 *livres* by 20 July. On 16 August, however, the General Committee adopted a sectional plan for forced payments, backed by threats (and not empty ones) of billeting and confiscation. This seems to have worked, and between 13 August and 8 September la Croisette paid 51,955 *livres* into the military treasury.[42] Since la Croisette was not a rich *quartier*, it is not inconceivable that two *contributions civiques* levied during the siege brought in at least half of the 6 million *livres* expected. After the siege, rich Lyonnais frequently admitted to paying taxes of 2,000, 6,000, and even 15,000 or 16,000 *livres*.[43] As well as this, the rebel authorities confiscated large sums from the *receveur* of the *district* of Lyon-Ville (369,507 *livres*), the departmental *payeur général* (422,830 *livres*), the *directeur des subsistances militaires* (100,000 *livres*), and the Mint (276,488 *livres*). More funds were obtained from the confiscation of church orna-

---

[40] [A. Guillon de Montléon], *Histoire du siège de Lyon, des événements qui l'ont précédé et des désastres qui l'ont suivi . . .* (Paris and Lyon, 1797), 139. On Précy's politics, see Riffaterre, *Le Mouvement anti-jacobin et anti-parisien à Lyon*, ii. 50. See also R. Fuoc, *La Réaction thermidorienne à Lyon (1795)* (Lyon, 1957), 58; J. Vallès, *Réflexions historiques sur quelques chapitres d'un ouvrage de M. l'Abbé Guillon, de Lyon, ayant pour titre: Mémoires pour servir à l'histoire de Lyon pendant la Révolution* (Paris, 1825), 68, 73; Béraud, *Relation du siège de Lyon*, pp. 108, 113.

[41] Riffaterre, *Le Mouvement anti-jacobin et anti-parisien à Lyon*, ii. 93–4.

[42] AD 31L21, fo. 22, minutes of Port Saint-Paul, 19, 27 July; 42L33A, p. 1, Finance Committee, 20 July, 13, 14, 17, 22 Aug., 1, 8 Sept.; *CP*, pp. 185–8 (16 Aug.); 42L32, no. 30, General Committee of Public Safety, 16 Aug., 27 Sept. (ordering the billeting of 4 soldiers on Pierre Michel, Rue Sainte-Catherine, for refusing to pay 15,000 *livres* for the second *contribution civique*).

[43] After the siege, J.-C. Perrochia, *marchand-fabricant*, was executed for paying 15,000 *livres*, and Antoine Moirié, grocer, for paying 16,000. These sums were given in the lists of rebels executed and may have been exaggerated (Portallier, *Tableau général*, pp. 311, 347). But it was not unusual for an admission to be made of having paid 4,000 *livres* (e.g. Boulard de Gatelier, a former *échevin*, aged 81, who also had troops billeted on him. He escaped lightly, being fined 8,000 *livres* (AD 42L12, p. 130, interrogation, 19 brumaire; Portallier, *Tableau général*, p. 55)).

ments, and the possessions of those who had fled the city.[44]

The expenses of the siege are hard to determine. Until mid-September Lyon could requisition much of the food and other supplies needed for the army, so the main outlay was paying the troops. This was estimated in July to cost about $6\frac{1}{2}$ million *livres* for 9,600 men over a year. Even though the rates of pay proposed then—$1\frac{1}{2}$ *livres* per day for an ordinary soldier—appear to have increased during the siege to 2 *livres* and eventually to 5 *livres* a day for a *caserné* (front-line soldier),[45] Riffaterre's generous estimate of 4,200 troops over sixty days at roughly three times the rate originally envisaged can hardly have cost more than $1\frac{1}{2}$ million *livres*. There were non-military wages and other costs as well—for example, one man employed in the fire brigades was paid 8 *livres* a day for three weeks.[46] But it seems at least possible that the rebels were able to meet the necessary outlays from their own resources.

It is thus unnecessary to invoke foreign involvement to explain the stubborn resistance of Lyon. But in some respects it merited the Jacobin accusations of *lèse-nation*. Even before the siege, not only the leadership but most of the *sections* seem to have adopted a policy of no enemies to the right. In July several *sections* (including the usually moderate la Juiverie and la Croisette) sprang to the defence of the brothers Julien de Vinézac, *émigrés* from an ancient Ardèchois noble family. They were on Précy's staff and had been denounced (presumably as royalists) by an unnamed provisional municipal officer. They resigned, but served later during the siege. Précy himself threatened to resign over this issue, protesting that 'par des dénonciations on cherchoit a désorganiser l'armée départementale'.[47] Eleven days later the *section* of Saint-Nizier circulated a proposal that Précy be given all the necessary powers to organize Lyon's

[44] AD 42L32, no. 49, Comité Particulier de Salut Public, 1 Sept.; ibid., no. B26, statement by Verset, *receveur du district* (Lyon-Ville), 3 Sept.; 42L106, no. 25, statement of losses to the Mint, n.d. [after the siege]; AC I²17, d. Blachette, *payeur-général* of Rhône-et-Loire; Coste MSS 647, 649, record of confiscation of funds from the *directeur des subsistances militaires*, 31 Aug., Commission des Cinq, authorization to requisition church property, n.d.; *CP*, p. 188 (16 Aug.).

[45] *CP*, p. 428, Tarif, appointemens et solde de la force départementale de Rhône-et-Loire (17 July); AD 31L61, p. 5, interrogation of Jacques Pey, clerk, Comité de Surveillance Générale de Lyon, 20 Oct.; 31L57, fo. 78, interrogation of Simon Stirlet, *garçon* brewer, Temporary Commission, 9 brumaire.

[46] AD 31L61, no. 32, interrogation of J.-B. Barcy, locksmith, Comité de Surveillance Générale de Lyon, 20 Oct.

[47] AD 31L2, fo. 22, minutes of la Croisette, 22 July. The 'citoyens Jullien' were supported by Rue Neuve (ibid.), la Juiverie (31L16, fo. 24 (20 July), Porte-Froc, and Place Neuve (minutes of Porte-Froc, 22 July, in *Secrétariat*, p. 233).

defence 'sans l'avis des autorités constituées, dans un moment pressant où l'on n'a pas le temps à délibérer'. La Croisette and Porte-Froc endorsed this, but the other *sections*' reactions are not known.[48] In its *Observations sur un arrêté de Dubois-Crancé et Gauthier*, the Popular Commission indignantly denied that either *émigrés* or the Comte de Virieu (who was not an *émigré*) held posts of responsibility in Lyon.[49] It is barely conceivable that it was unaware of the *émigrés* already on Précy's staff, but the denial was disingenuous anyway, for by appointing him and allowing him to choose his principal subordinates, the Commission had opened the door wide to aristocratic infiltration.

Committed rebels tolerated the royalists because they could envisage no greater political evil than the triumph of the Jacobins. Similar thinking affected their attitudes to the war effort during months of deep military crisis for France. In June and July their refusal to release desperately needed military supplies had been in marked contrast to the policy of 'federalist' Toulouse, whose leaders were extremely anxious to avoid compromising France's defences against Spain, and Bordeaux, which refused to recall its battalions from the war in the Vendée.[50] By September, news of French defeats was being greeted enthusiastically: 'Aucune autre idée hors celle d'une délivrance n'avoit place chez nous. Les patriotes les plus zélés écoutoient avec plaisir et répétoient à l'envi que les Autrichiens approchoient de Paris.'[51] Some of this talk clearly came from royalists like the scrivener Chapuis, who said that the French had lost 18,000 men at Toulon, and that the English would soon be at Lyon and would harm no one but *patriotes*. Some of it was wishful thinking: Dubois-Crancé would be caught between two armies when Piedmont invaded Savoy. The Commission's claim that the siege had been mounted at the cost of exposing the frontiers encouraged the hope that the Piedmontese could advance without meeting serious resistance.[52]

[48] AD 31L2, fo. 25, minutes of la Croisette, 1 Aug., endorsing Saint-Nizier's proposal; minutes of Porte-Froc, 2 Aug., in *Secrétariat*, p. 245.

[49] *CP*, p. 469.

[50] Ibid. 47–8, 113 (8, 18 July); M. Lyons, *Revolution in Toulouse* (Berne, 1978), 50; A. Forrest, *Society and Politics in Revolutionary Bordeaux* (Oxford, 1975), 273.

[51] Schatzmann, 'La Révolution de 1793 à Lyon', p. 107.

[52] AD 42L70, no. 93, denunciation of Chapuis, 29 brumaire; 42L75, pp. 23–4, d. Desgranges, extract from an unsigned, undated letter, according to which the Austrians and Piedmontese had almost reached Dauphiné; 42L81, B18, no. 33, letter addressed to Mme Miège at the Croix-Rousse, 12 Aug., according to which the Piedmontese were in the Valais and poised to seize Savoy; Fonds Coste MS 4524–111026, *Proclamation de la Commission populaire ... la section du peuple françois dans le département de Rhône-et-Loire* (Lyon, [19 July] 1793).

On the civil war in the west there were mixed feelings. While welcoming the Republic's 'avantages à la Vendée', Lyon's delegates in Bordeaux wrote pointedly of the considerable resources being diverted there.[53] There was talk of outside help for most of the siege, but not much concern about whether it came from Bordeaux, Marseille, Piedmont, or Switzerland: 'On nous parle des Suisses et des Piémontois. Donnez-nous en des nouvelles sûres ... Les autorités de cette ville n'ont jamais eu je vous le jure aucune intelligence avec l'étranger, mais dans notre situation ils sont préférables aux brigands.' But as the besieging forces grew and no help came, such hopes began to wear thin: 'Je crois que l'on amuse les Lyonnois en leur fesant entandre [sic] que les suisses doivent venir à leurs secours, ce sera comme les Marseilllois et je crois bien que Lyon est perdu.'[54]

'FEDERALIST' TERROR

A variety of fears, hopes, and confusions combined with intense anti-Jacobinism and, for a minority, royalism to prolong the resistance of Lyon. But there were limits to the voluntary support that could be obtained for the war effort, and repression was increasingly used to supplement it. On 7 July the Popular Commission had opened the way for the indiscriminate harassment of dissidents throughout the *département* by ordering the arrest of 'tout individu qui ne seroit pas muni d'un passeport ou qui tenteroit de diviser les citoyens, en provoquant la désobéissance auxdits lois et décrets [antérieurs au 31 mai], ou à l'exécution des mesures arrêtées par l'assemblée [the Popular Commission] pour le maintien de la sûreté publique'. The District of Lyon-Ville interpreted the commission's order as requiring the arrest of 'tous ceux qui propageroient d'autres principes que les siens'.[55] With the approach of open hostilities, the General Committee of Public Safety ordered the arrest of all those suspected of complicity with the Jacobin Municipalité, 'même ceux qui auroient été mis en liberté',[56] and naturally enough the repression intensified during the siege. Lack of a *carte de section* or consorting with suspects were both grounds for arrest, and on 26 August came an order

---

[53] AD 42L34, d. B31, letter to the Provisional Commune, 7 July.

[54] Letter of Blanc, leather-merchant, quoted in H. Pelat and M. Cayrol, 'Tableau de la Contre-Révolution à Lyon', p. 17; AD 4273, no. 41, letter (n.d.) among papers seized from V.-A. Déplasse, a member of the Saint-Étienne expedition.

[55] *CP*, p. 38 (8 July). AD 2L10, fo. 41, minutes of the District Council (Lyon-Ville).

[56] AD 42L32, no. 19, Comité Général de Salut Public, 1 Aug.

for those 'reputés suspects' to be expelled from the city. It was alleged after the siege that between 150 and 200 people were forced to cross the lines the next day, 'dans le dessein prémédité de les faire périr et tuer par les patriotes de l'armée du siège et par les muscadins'. Intentionally or not, several of those driven from Lyon on this and other occasions seem to have been killed or wounded in cross-fire.[57] The *députés* in charge of the siege claimed that 20,000 Lyonnais left the city in accordance with the decree of 12 July,[58] but many of them may in fact have been forced departures. To deal with those actively subverting Lyon's defence, a *Comité militaire* was created late in August with the power to impose death sentences, and at least three people were condemned to be shot.[59]

DEFENDING LYON (2): ISOLATION AND ENCIRCLEMENT

On 9 July 1,500 men had ridden out of Lyon to secure Saint-Étienne. It is unnecessary to follow their expedition in detail[60]—or Lyonnais military operations as a whole—but some episodes from the *sortie en Forez* are worth recounting for the insight they offer into Lyon's fatal lack of rural support.

It was rather like the *volontaires'* descent on Dauphiné during the Great Fear of 1789, a troop of sons and servants of the notability and the merchant élite, fed and equipped at their own expense, doing the social rounds of the Forez between skirmishes with the peasantry, and, on this occasion, bouts of club-wrecking. They were resisted from the beginning. As the column approached Rive-de-Gier the tocsin was rung in several villages. Near Saint-Chamond it was fired on by snipers hidden in the wheat-fields.[61] After killing some of their attackers and purging Saint-

---

[57] Ibid., nos. 37, 41, Comité Particulier de Salut Public, 26 Aug.; AD 42L75, d. B99, deposition in favour of Anne Firmin, sewing-maid, by Lambert, *commissaire de police*, 4 nivôse; 1L987, Ambroise Chapilliot, silk-weaver, to the Temporary Commission, n.d., claiming to have been expelled from Lyon under fire at 11.00 p.m. on 11 Sept.

[58] *Moniteur*, xvii. 756 (26 Sept.).

[59] *CP*, pp. 541, 552 (3, 17 Sept.), sentences on Antoinette Raymond, the wife of a metal-founder (for spying), Joseph Basson, district administrator, and C.-J. Marque, watchmaker (both for sedition). Étienne Dumas, surgeon, claimed to have seen 3 people shot by the rebels (AC I²6, no. 49, Temporary Committee, list of imprisoned *patriotes*).

[60] There is a good brief account in C. Lucas, *The Structure of the Terror: The Example of Javogues and the Loire* (Oxford, 1973), 38–60. On the size and composition of the detachment, see *Actes*, v. 286, Noël Pointe to the Convention; AD 42L160, fo. 154, Commission de Justice Populaire at Feurs, interrogation of Lattard *fils*, 4 frimaire; Riffaterre, *Le Mouvement anti-jacobin et anti-parisien à Lyon*, ii. 217, 225.

[61] *Journal de Lyon*, 17 July 1793, p. 425.

Chamond of *anarchistes*, the Lyonnais enjoyed the hospitality of the local élite: 'le meilleur ton y régna ... l'on n'aurait pas cru que les convives étaient des soldats marchant le sac sur le dos'.[62]

After 'l'exécution du Club', and having removed the church bells which had sounded the alarm against the Lyonnais, the main force departed, leaving behind a small garrison. On 12 July they arrived at Saint-Étienne, 'ville ... d'ouvriers féroces' and much less agreeable. Its 'Jacobin' *sections* proved uncooperative and the local business men were dull company. But there was the satisfaction of comprehensively wrecking the club, including the floor-boards, and the Municipalité collaborated enthusiastically. *Clubistes* were arrested and arms were despatched to Lyon.[63]

From Saint-Étienne a detachment of Lyonnais was sent to Montbrison at the invitation of the Municipalité of that aristocratic little town. Since the *clubistes* there were few, disturbances caused by the Municipalité's supporters were used as a pretext for the usual arrests and demolition work, which were well under way when the Lyonnais arrived on 22 July.[64] But the warm welcome of the Montbrisonnais was overshadowed by the hostility of peasants encountered *en route*, with whom there were several skirmishes, and still more by the attack on Montbrison by peasant National Guards from *cantons* near Boën (3 August).[65]

The attack was repelled without much difficulty and disarmaments were carried out in the vicinity of Boën and Moingt, but the episode underlined (and no doubt increased) the lack of enthusiasm for the cause of Lyon which the rural population had already demonstrated by ignoring the elections for the Popular Commission and voting overwhelmingly in favour of the Jacobin Constitution. Towards the end of July there were manifestations of hostility to Lyon in every *district* of Rhône-et-Loire, particularly Villefranche, where the *cantons* of Anse and Beaujeu quashed the powers of their *députés* to the Commission. Villié-Morgon and Beaujeu took the opportunity to reiterate Beaujolais separatist demands. In the *district* of Lyon-Campagne itself, Saint-Genis-Laval and Brignais resisted

---

[62] C.-J. Puy, *Expédition des Lyonnais dans le Forez, juillet à septembre 1793* (Saint-Étienne and Lyon, 1889), 24, cited in Riffaterre, *Le Mouvement anti-jacobin et anti-parisien à Lyon*, ii. 226. Puy was an officer in the Saint-Étienne expeditionary force.

[63] *Lettre écrite par les commissaires envoyés par la ville de Lyon à Saint-Etienne* (Lyon, 1793) (Fonds Coste MS 4502); Lucas, *The Structure of the Terror*, pp. 39 n. 2, 42; Riffaterre, *Le Mouvement anti-jacobin et anti-parisien à Lyon*, ii. 226–7.

[64] Coste MS 630, Valette and Mondon, *commissaires* of the Département of Rhône-et-Loire, to the Département, 2 June; Lucas, *The Structure of the Terror*, pp. 39, 42–3, 51–2.

[65] Lucas, *The Structure of the Terror*, p. 53; *CP*, pp. 172–3 (5 Aug.).

the Commission with impunity, while at Chaponost and Francheville in early August, National Guards requisitioned for the defence of Lyon refused to march and were sent home by their commander. Still closer to Lyon, the Guardsmen of Saint-Genis-Laval, also mobilized in August, marched not to defend Lyon but to join Kellermann's army.[66] These places were only a few kilometres from Lyon, and their blatant defiance is a measure of its failure to control its hinterland.

After evacuating Saint-Étienne on 26 August in the face of growing popular agitation, the Lyonnais expedition withdrew to Montbrison. Less than a fortnight later, with troops under Javogues approaching from the south-west and Couthon's forces from the west, Montbrison too was evacuated (8 September). The *muscadins* took a week to return over the hills to Lyon, confiscating what grain and other food they could as they passed through the fertile country near Feurs.[67]

Peasant resistance to 'federalism' was naturally intensified by these activities, but its roots lay in the fear that victory for Lyon would bring in its wake a revived seigneurial system. Lyonnais of all estates had after all been 'feudal' landowners only four and a half years before, and Lyonnais had attempted to defend 'feudal' property against the peasant revolution in 1789. Rumours abounded that Lyon was now controlled by *ci-devants* ('J'ai vu monter la garde rigoureusement par les seigneurs, prince et marquis, baron et riche négociant qui ne la montoit [*sic*] pas cy-devant et depuis le 29 mai il l'a monté'[68]), and the Popular Commission did not help to dispel by rejecting a proposal to ratify the decree of 17 July which abolished all remaining manorial dues without compensation.[69]

Dubois-Crancé and his colleagues played adroitly on Forezian separatism by creating the *département* of the Loire from the *districts* of

---

[66] See Riffaterre, *Le Mouvement anti-jacobin et anti-parisien à Lyon*, ii. 431–7; AD 1L378, CSG of Rhône-et-Loire, 11 July; 42L69, fos. 16–17, denunciation of the Pellissard brothers and their servant Estienne, 6 July; 42L79, nos. 22–3, report on Laroche, former mayor of Chaponost; 32L42, d. C15, Comité Particulier de Salut Public, order to disarm Saint-Genis-Laval, 16 Aug.

[67] AN M669, d. 5, no. 17, district administrators to the Minister of the Interior, 30 Aug.; *Actes,* vi. 407, 410–11, 413, 549, CSP, 10 Sept., Couthon to the CSP, 10 Sept., Dubois-Crancé, Gauthier, and Delaporte to the CSP, 10 Sept., Javogues to the CSP, 17 Sept.; AD 42L3, fo. 32, Commission Militaire, interrogation of Pierre Chappuis Maubourg, noble, of Montbrison, 24 Oct.; 42L160, no. 143, denunciation of Coindre and Vachon by P.-E. Parias *père*; Lucas, *The Structure of the Terror,* p. 40.

[68] AD 42L53, no. 25, d. Claude Stize, declaration by Claude Machique to the Comité de Surveillance of Saint-Galmier, 25 brumaire. See Lucas, *The Structure of the Terror,* p. 55.

[69] *Journal de Lyon,* 25 July 1793, p. 454.

Roanne, Montbrison, and Saint-Étienne (12 August), and won over la
Guillotière by attaching it to the Isère, so ending its detested administrative subjection to Lyon (14 August).[70] But even without these measures, Lyon is unlikely to have received significant support in August and
September from areas which had given none in June and July, when
the prospects of the departmental movement had been much brighter.
Rejected by the countryside, and with little worthwhile support in nearby
towns, Lyon had to rely on its own resources, scant in food but more
substantial in arms and men.

THE ARMIES

On 31 July the *Journal de Lyon* claimed that a force of about 3,000 men
had been assembled in the barracks.[71] Even assuming this figure to be
correct, which is doubtful, it fell far short of the 9,600 men planned for
in July. Volunteers were few. Many fled to the countryside to avoid
conscription, and there were moves by the *sections* to sequester their
properties.[72] At least one battalion, la Juiverie, decided by majority vote
not to take part in the Departmental Army, and there was an attempt to
have the neighbouring battalion of Port Saint-Paul follow suit. Only
twelve men had been recruited in la Juiverie by 4 August.[73] Part of the
trouble seems to have been that the soldiers were not being paid regularly.
On 9 August the battalion of le Gourguillon, composed largely of 'citoyens
vivans [*sic*] de leur travail', complained that it had received no pay at all,
despite having served for several days.[74] Appeals to patriotism and selection by lot produced some men from la Croisette, but not enough, so the
final fifty required had to be requisitioned. Nevertheless, forty-six had
been found for the first of la Croisette's companies by 6 August. Several
sections used selection by lot. One case has been found of a purchased
replacement.[75]

[70] *Deuxième partie de la réponse de Dubois-Crancé*, pp. 4–6, 8.

[71] *Journal de Lyon*, 31 July 1793, p. 473.

[72] AD 31L21, fo. 25, minutes of Port Saint-Paul, 22 July; 31L2, fo. 26, minutes of la
Croisette, 3 Aug.

[73] *Journal de Lyon*, 27 July 1793, p. 464; AD 42L64, nos. 27, 36, denunciation of Paillasson
fils aîné to committee of Port Saint-Paul, n.d., denunciation of Bertrand, commander of la
Juiverie's battalion; 31L38, miscellaneous papers of la Juiverie, no. 2, register of volunteers,
24 June–4 Aug.

[74] AD 42L44, no. 304, letter to Précy.

[75] AD 31L2, fos. 22, 28, minutes of la Croisette, 23–5 July, 6 Aug.; 42L93, no. 5,
declaration by J.-L,-G. Rivoyron; 42L85, d. B32, agreement signed by Thimonier, hatter
and ex-soldier, to replace Rivoyron. The price was 200 *livres* and 2 pairs of shoes.

But in wealthy Saint-Nizier there were signs of enthusiasm. The whole sectional assembly enrolled itself 'par un mouvement spontané' on 19 July, and twenty-four men from the artillery company alone were in barracks by 5 August. Even Pierre-Scize had fifty-five men in barracks on 9 August.[76] But if the *sections* provided an average of fifty men each by 9 August, the total at the beginning of the siege could not have been much more than 2,000, including contingents said to have come from outside Lyon.[77]

Fortunately for the rebels, Kellermann's force was also inadequate. On 6 August the Convention was told that 20,000 men had been sent against Lyon, but Dubois-Crancé later gave the figures as 13,000 infantry (many of them peasant levies), 100 gunners, and five squadrons of cavalry. Kellermann felt unable to press the attack in August. He had only twelve cannon, he was short of horses, and he did not have enough boats to co-ordinate the sections of his army divided by the Rhône. Even with the 4,000 extra troops he was sent about 19 August, he was short of the 25,000–30,000 men he considered necessary to take Lyon quickly. To make matters worse, these forces had to be stretched between the Rhône and the Saône to secure his communications. Further difficulties arose in mid-August, when he was sent to counter a Piedmontese incursion into the *département* of Mont-Blanc.[78] So, unable to take Lyon by storm, the *députés* decided to reduce it by bombardment, with frequent barrages of incendiary cannon-balls and mortar-shells, interrupted occasionally by calls for submission. Failing that, they hoped to surround the city completely with the help of the peasant levies being raised by Couthon, Maignet, and Châteauneuf-Randon in the Puy-de-Dôme, Allier, Lozère, Haute-Loire, and Ardèche.[79] The planned three-pronged attack pre-supposed sufficient troops to cut off Lyon from the surrounding country-side, and depended on Couthon's force occupying the area on the right bank of the Rhône to the south-west of the city which controlled access

[76] AD 31L21, fo. 23, minutes of Port Saint-Paul, 19 July; 31L6, no. 4, list of artillerymen, Saint-Nizier company, 5 Aug.; 42L45, dossier de l'Armée lyonnaise, report by Graff, captain of Pierre-Scize.

[77] The *Bulletin du département de Rhône-et-Loire*, 2 (9 Aug.) (in *CP*, p. 244), claimed that 330 men from rural *districts* were already in the barracks.

[78] AG B³103*, ds. 23, 30, Kellermann to the Minister of War, 23 July, 25, 28 Aug., *députés en mission* with the Armée des Alpes to the Convention, 6 Aug., Minister of War to the *députés en mission*, 19 Aug.; E. Herriot, *Lyon n'est plus* (Paris, 1938–40), ii. 320; *Actes*, vi. 95, the *députés en mission* to the CSP, 24 Aug.

[79] AG B³103*, d. 2, Council of War, 14 Aug.; *Actes*. vi. 81, 95, 155–6, 412, letters of the *députées en mission* with the Armée des Alpes, 23, 24, 28 Aug., 10 Sept.

to the peninsula by way of the Mulatière bridge.[80] Lyon had to be completely encircled, not only to weaken its resistance by starvation, but 'pour éviter que le débordement de ces coquins ne fît dans ces montagnes [du Forez] une nouvelle Vendée'.[81]

Several contingencies slowed the build-up of the besieging army. Kellermann was unable to force the Piedmontese back through the mountain passes until 9 September; Carteaux's force, having taken Marseille on 25 August, was unable to join the siege because it was needed to meet the threat posed by the English landing at Toulon; the *muscadins* in the Forez captured a small detachment under General Nicolas, thereby severing communications between the *représentants* outside Lyon and Couthon and his colleagues; the Lyonnais foothold in the Forez had to be destroyed to secure the *département* of the Loire.[82] The escape of the *muscadins* from Montbrison was another set-back, for besides providing Lyon with additional food and about 500 more men, including a number of Montbrisonnais refugees, their depredations in the Forez plain made it difficult to provision the Convention's armies.[83] And finally, despite the strength of feeling against Lyon, the recruiting efforts of Couthon and his colleagues did not meet with great enthusiasm initially, partly because of the harvest, and the number of troops at their disposal grew very slowly. It was not until 17 September that forces from the west were able to complete the stranglehold on Lyon.[84] Nevertheless, Dubois-Crancé was gradually adding to the regular troops encamped near Lyon, until by 28 September more than 21,000 of them were involved in the siege, quite apart from the peasant levies. An important consignment of siege-artillery was received about 10 September.[85]

Lyon was able to hold out as long as it did only because it managed to build up its full-time forces considerably from the small beginnings of

[80] *Deuxième partie de la réponse de Dubois-Crancé*, pp. 102, 249; Herriot, *Lyon n'est plus*, ii. 288, 321.

[81] *Députés* with the Armée des Alpes to the CSP, 9 Sept., in *Deuxième partie de la réponse de Dubois-Crancé*, p. 107.

[82] Ibid. 107; *Actes*, vi. 112, 281, Dubois-Crancé and Gauthier to the Convention, 4 Sept., Albitte, Escudier, Gasparin, and Nioche to the Convention, 25 Aug.

[83] *Actes*, vi. 154, 246–7, 407, 410, 499–500, Couthon, Chateauneuf-Randon, and Maignet to the CSP, 28 Aug., 2 Sept., Couthon to the CSP, 10 Sept., Javogues to the CSP, 10 Sept., Chateauneuf-Randon to the CSP, 15 Sept.; AD 42L3, p. 32, Commission Militaire, interrogations of Chappuis Maubourg, 24 Oct.

[84] *Actes*, vi. 407, 411, 551, Couthon to the CSP, 10 Sept., Javogues to the CSP, 10 Sept., Dubois-Crancé and Gauthier to the CSP, 17 Sept.

[85] Ibid. 411, Dubois-Crancé, Gauthier, and Delaporte to the CSP, 10 Sept; Riffaterre, *Le Mouvement anti-jacobin et anti-parisien à Lyon*, ii. 611.

August. As we have seen, only sparse evidence is available on the numbers of full-time rebel troops (*casernés*). Riffaterre's estimate of an average of about 4,200 between 11 August and 7 September[86] is based unsatisfactorily on reports from different officers and posts at various times between these dates, and although it is lower than the figure of about 5,000 given by several of those who served under Précy, it is a generous estimate on the available evidence. Even if we add the 330 men recruited from elsewhere in Rhône-et-Loire and the 226 gendarmes requisitioned by the Département to the figure of 3,160 arrived at earlier, the total is well short of 4,000.[87] The return of the force from Saint-Étienne in mid-September bolstered the Lyonnais army considerably, but by then there were losses from the fighting as well as from desertion. Figures for five out of eight barracks on 6 September gave a total of 237 men absent without leave. Late in the siege, reinforcements for the front-line troops were frequently drawn from the fusiliers of *bataillons du centre*, but they often proved unreliable and wholesale desertion of posts became common towards the end.[88]

For some weeks, holding out was made easier by the way the siege was conducted. So many *députés en mission* (eight of them) were involved in its organization that co-ordinating the attack was difficult: Dubois-Crancé quarrelled with Couthon and Maignet, Javogues with Gauthier.[89] Besides, Kellermann resisted orders to bombard Lyon for more than a week, and other soldiers were half-hearted about the siege. There is evidence, too, of fraternization between the Convention's soldiers and the rebels.[90]

On the other side of the fortifications, the military leadership of the rebellion proved competent and made the best of Lyon's defensive advantages. Opinion was divided about these and some thought them inconsiderable. But the rivers and hills to the north and west gave some protection, and old fortifications in the Croix-Rousse were skilfully incorporated into a system of redoubts and fortified houses by Agniel de

---

[86] Riffaterre, *Le Mouvement anti-jacobih et anti-parisien* à Lyon, ii. 540–1.

[87] Schatzmann, 'La Révolution de 1793 à Lyon', p. 104; P[asseron], 'Mémoires', p. 361; Vallès, *Réflexions historiques*, p. 64; AD 42L45, dossier de l'Armée lyonnaise, d. Guignard.

[88] AC I²3, nos. 144–7, reports on troop numbers, 6 Sept.; Schatzmann, 'La Révolution de 1793 à Lyon', p. 107.

[89] See *Première et deuxième parties de la réponse de Dubois-Crancé, passim*, and *Discours sur le siège de Lyon*, pp. 6–7; *Actes*, vi. 549, Javogues to the CSP, 17 Sept.

[90] Riffaterre, *Le Mouvement anti-jacobin et anti-parisien à Lyon*, ii. 48; Vallès, *Réflexions historiques*, p. 39; *Actes*, vi. 412, Dubois-Crancé, Gauthier, and Delaporte to the CSP, 10 Sept.; AD 42L3, no. 139, Commission Militaire, interrogation of Antoine Bernard, surveyor, lieutenant-colonel in the Lyonnais army, 23 brumaire.

Chenelette. According to Kellermann, the walls, copses, and ravines of the Croix-Rousse were good natural defences, and effectively concealed the Lyonnais artillery. The fortified houses would have to be destroyed one by one before the Croix-Rousse itself could be captured. On Agniel de Chenelettes's military ability and Précy's, contemporaries were agreed. They and their experienced staff officers appear to have made the best of things, including a good supply of small arms and some light cannon from the Arsenal and Saint-Étienne. There was also a foundry in Lyon which produced larger cannon under the direction of an English engineer.[91] General Sériziat had said that 3,000 men and a reserve of 6,000 could successfully defend Lyon. If access to the Forez and food supplies had not been cut off in mid-September, Précy might have proved him right. Fortified by hopes of Piedmontese intervention, he wanted to fight to the death.[92]

By the end of September the shortage of food in Lyon was critical. It was no longer possible to draw supplies from nearby *cantons*, as had been done in August. Only soldiers received bread now. For the rest, the authorities could only provide a few almonds and small amounts of oatmeal. Meat from horses killed in battle was sold for 2 *livres* a pound.[93] After the capture of the heights of Sainte-Foy to the south-west on 29 September, the last small agricultural area fell into enemy hands and it was now possible for the besiegers to bombard the entire city at will. By the end there were said to be no habitable houses left in the *section* of Bon-Rencontre. Despite these set-backs, the Lyonnais were still able to mount counter-attacks on 2 October.[94]

But with no outside help materializing, defeat by starvation became the most likely prospect, and calls for surrender began to be heard in the

---

[91] Guillon de Montléon, *Histoire du siège de Lyon*, ii. 2, 4; [P]asseron, 'Mémoires', p. 361; AG B³103*, Kellermann to the CSP, 10 Aug.; Dubois-Crancé, *Discours sur le siège de Lyon*, p. 4; *Actes*, vi. 7, Dubois-Crancé to the CSP, 16 Aug.; Hampshire Record Office, Wickham Papers 1/125/1, Relation de la sortie de Monsieur de Précy de Lyon en 1793. (Précy was in regular correspondence with Wickham during the latter's period as a British agent at Berne.)

[92] P. Ballaguy, *Un général de l'an II: Charles Sériziat (1756–1805)* (Lyon, 1913), 76; Hampshire Record Office, Wickham Papers 1/125/1.

[93] AD 42L3, fo. 168, Commission Militaire, interrogation of François Rivière, ex-regular army *adjutant sous-officier*, who led troops to get wheat from Duerne; 42L34, 49, receipt for wheat and rye, 12 Aug.; *Deuxième partie de la réponse Dubois-Crancé*, p. 229, 'Rapport d'un citoyen de Lyon' (4 Oct.); pp. 243–4, 'Déclaration d'un Lyonnais sur la situation des rebelles'.

[94] Doppet, *Mémoires*, p. 159; AD 42L39, no. 67, request for wine by the Comité de Surveillance of Bon-Rencontre; AG B³103*, report by Colonel Sandoz, 1–2 Oct., Doppet to the Minister of War, 9 Oct.

sections. On 8 October they were allowed to meet to discuss the situation, and next day twenty-three of them sent representatives to sue for peace. Précy had been making plans for escape in such circumstances, but he feared that if they became known the city's defences would be totally abandoned before anyone could get out. He secretly told the most reliable soldiers and administrators to meet at Vaise during the night of 8/9 October, and early that morning about 700 men fought their way along the bank of the Saône through Saint-Rambert and Saint-Cyr and then into the Beaujolais hills. But losses from enemy fire and persistent peasant harassment had reduced their number to 80 by early on 10 October, and only a handful, including Précy, made it to Switzerland.[95] Meanwhile, on 9 October Lyon was occupied without further resistance.

[95] AC I²4, nos. 9, 9 *bis*, Réunion des commissaires des sections, 8 et 9 octobre 1793; Hampshire Record Office, Wickham Papers 1/125/1.

9

Conclusion

Survival in revolutions is a matter of keeping in step or keeping out of sight. Lyon was too big and too important strategically and economically to keep out of sight, and simply being a major centre of luxury production made it an object of suspicion for advanced *patriotes*. Its politics were shaped by deep social conflicts which put it out of step with Paris at crucial stages of the Revolution and invited political intervention from the capital. Its social élites were too terrified of popular disorder to initiate a local revolution in 1789, and too alienated from the *menu peuple* to impose their leadership even under the very limited democracy of 1790. During the constitutional monarchy, when bourgeois *patriotes* hostile to the élites ran Lyon with the support of the clubs, the city won a deserved but short-lived renown for pioneering popular democracy. But the *patriote* Municipalité's constant conflicts with the Département and with the general staff of the National Guard, which the *patriotes* appealed to Paris to resolve in their favour, enhanced another and more enduring reputation: that of a city harbouring a secret army of aristocrats, in league with the Lyonnais élites, against whom the Vitet Municipalité was waging a desperate struggle. That was the picture Chalier painted when he took his personal vendetta against the Département to Paris in 1792.

Late in 1792, while the Montagne was forging its own alliance with the popular democrats of Paris, Vitet's alliance with the clubs was falling apart. His Municipalité was undermined by the September crisis which the Paris Jacobins, being out of power, were able to turn to their advantage, and it soon lost its patriotic credentials when its patron, Roland, was reclassified by the Jacobins as an enemy of the people. Chalier and his allies exploited this situation and their influence in the Club Central to establish a Municipalité committed to the Montagne. Its plebeian character, its vague but threatening rhetoric of social equality, its half-baked terrorist initiatives, and clumsy Montagnard intervention in support of it, finally provoked the political mobilization of the propertied classes in a movement of protest that had its origins in some of the clubs and soon swept to a majority of *sections*. At the same time the Jacobins became isolated. Their authoritarian, centralist methods threatened the traditional autonomy of the clubs, and their inability to meet the social and economic demands of the *menu peuple* not only cost them much of their popular following, but generated popular support for the anti-Jacobin *sectionnaires*.

From this point on, for reasons which were primarily ideological, Montagnard policy towards Lyon became increasingly counter-productive. Certainly, there were good military reasons for vigilance against sedition in the second city. But when their policy of unswerving support for an unpopular Jacobin minority only increased anti-Jacobin activity, the Montagnards did not reconsider their policy but felt confirmed in their belief that the tentacles of aristocratic conspiracy had strangled *patriotisme* in Lyon, perverting the civic morals of its population. Their refusal to see anything but incipient counter-revolution in the sectional movement became self-fulfilling. The *sectionnaires* interpreted the dispatch of troops to Lyon on 28 May as another, perhaps decisive, instalment of Montagnard support for the Jacobin Municipalité, and this was a prime factor in the insurrection of 29 May. In June, mistrust engendered by the partisan approach of successive teams of Montagnard *députés* spoiled what little chance there was of a conciliatory Lyonnais response to Lindet's mission in a climate of opinion inflamed by the purge of the Convention.

Resentment of the Convention's factionalism and its apparent submissiveness to the *sans-culottes* undoubtedly helped to produce a legitimacy crisis which prepared the way for rebellion, but more important in precipitating the civil war was this direct experience of Montagnard revolutionary government through the *députés en mission*. A sectional address of 14 June described the latter as part of a deep-laid plot to subjugate France and compared them with the great tyrants of history, 'les Néron, les Tibère, les ducs d'Albe, les Inquisiteurs d'Espagne et de Portugal, enfin les Daïre du Japon'.[1] They were travelling dictators sent with illicit powers to oppress the *départements* at will, and their activities were a condemnation of the Convention, which had arrogated 'la faculté de se dissoudre elle-même par l'envoi de ses membres dans les départements': 'Quels sont ces lâches despotes qui osent ainsi venir établir dans les départements cette atroce dictature, désorganiser les pouvoirs, violer toutes les loix de la justice et de l'humanité, soudoyer d'infâmes agitateurs?

---

[1] *Adresse du peuple de Lyon à la République française* (Lyon, 14 June 1793), in *Secrétariat*, p. 527.

et ils se disent les représentants du peuple!'[2] The behaviour of the *députés en mission* provided the most powerful rationale for the resistance to oppression which, with the forming of the Popular Commission, became the secession of 4 July. It was a convenient rationale, but none the less a genuine part of the motivation of the rebellion.

As has been noted elsewhere, there were other towns, including Bordeaux and Toulouse, where the activities of inept fire-breathing *députés* such as Chabot helped to push provincial communities into the 'federalist' revolt, and to this extent I reject the view of the Montagnard repression and the Great Terror as necessary responses to internal as well as external threats. In several places, and in the most notable single instance of urban rebellion during the French Revolution, Montagnard repression helped to create internal threats. This is not to say that the deployment of *députés en mission* for recruiting, food-procurement, and political stabilization did not, overall, contribute significantly to the survival of the Convention and the Republic. Even quite committed terrorists like Collot d'Herbois could do a competent job, astutely assessing local situations and leaving départements more stable and submissive than they had been when he arrived.[3] But in Lyon the reverse happened, because the men who went there were mostly heavy-handed, ill-informed, and deeply prejudiced by years of *patriote* tirades against Lyon.

When the long-predicted rebellion occurred, the Montagnards felt fully confirmed in their diagnosis of Lyonnais anti-*patriotisme*. It was a Rolando-Girondin federalist conspiracy, feeding on Lyon's particularism and envy of Paris, and with royalism lurking, according to taste, either in the wings or behind the *patriote* masks of Rolandin hypocrites. Elements of this remarkably durable myth have persisted into recent neo-Jacobin history, but most of them are quite baseless.[4] For one thing, feeling against the Convention itself was too pronounced for the Girondins to have a following in Lyon. For another, the connections between the Lyonnais revolt and those *députés* who could even loosely be termed Girondins were as tenuous from June to September as they had been in May. Three *députés* of Rhône-et-Loire might be considered Girondins,

[2] AC I²4, d. 10, minutes of Rue Tupin, 12 June; *Adresse aux armées, aux citoyens et à tous les départements de la République françoise par les autorités constituées réunies à Lyon* (Lyon, [June] 1793), 4.

[3] See P. Mansfield, 'The Missions of Collot d'Herbois: A Study in his Political Career', Ph.D thesis (Macquarie University, 1895), 102–261.

[4] See B. Edmonds, ' "Federalism" and Urban Revolt in France in 1793', *Journal of Modern History*, 55 (1983), 22–53.

but only one of them, Charles Chasset, had anything to do with the revolt, and he does not appear to have played any role in the rebellion between mid-May and his arrival in Lyon on 8 July, a few days after Birotteau. Like Birotteau, he left before the end of the month, and spent much of his time proselytizing for the anti-Jacobin cause in the countryside. Birotteau's speech of 4 July was important, but there is no evidence that he made any other contribution to the rebellion and he quickly became alarmed by the infiltration of *aristocrates* into its ranks. The fact that the rebels used pamphlets written by some of the purged *députés* indicates eagerness to be seen as part of a broad movement of resistance rather than particular enthusiasm for the Girondins.[5]

The notion that the rebellion was 'Rolandin'[6] is equally baseless. After 29 May, as before it, Roland's closest political associates were either absent or took no part in it. Vitet, who left the Convention pleading illness in late February, stayed at his country house near Lyon, but he did not enter the city until forced to do so during the siege and he gave no indication that he approved of the rebellion.[7] Even Billemaz, who had been so violently opposed to the Jacobin Municipalité, played no discernible part in the revolt. If Roland was in some sense the guiding light of the rebels, it is strange that there is no reference to him or his virtues in the dozens of pamphlets they put out, except for the *Adresse des Nantais*.

'Federalist' was another label the Montagnards applied to the revolt, and the one that stuck most firmly. The only justification for it lies in the Département's flirtation with the departmental movement and the doctrine of the right to resist oppression. At a theoretical level, there were certainly federalist implications in the assertion that the primary assemblies were the organs through which resistance should be conducted. With the Convention acting under duress, the rebels were saying, sovereignty reverted to the *Assemblées primaires*. When they chose to do so, these could delegate their sovereignty to a body such as the Popular

---

[5] See A. Patrick, *The Men of the First French Republic: Political Alignments in the National Convention of 1792* (Baltimore, 1972), 327–8 (the other *députés* with Girondin connections were Lanthénas and Marcellin-Béraud); C. Riffaterre, *Le Mouvement anti-jacobin et anti-parisien à Lyon et dans le Rhône-et-Loire en 1793* (Lyon, 1912–28), i. 392; *Journal de Lyon*, 14 July 1793, p. 340.

[6] The term is used in Riffaterre, *Le Mouvement anti-jacobin et anti-parisien à Lyon*, i. 311, and in L. Trénard, 'La Crise sociale lyonnaise à la veille de la Révolution', *Revue d'histoire moderne et contemporaine*, 2 (1955), 45.

[7] AN AFII, plaq. 343, correspondence of Vitet, 3 Apr. 1793–24 nivôse, year II, nos. 71, 76, 78, 82–3, 87.

Commission, which could then speak as 'les délégués de la section du peuple François dans le département de Rhône-et-Loire'.[8] The implications of this could be regarded as 'federalist' in the most extreme sense, implying the division of the French people into a conglomerate of tiny republics which could create coalitions if they wished, but which were fundamentally sovereign and autonomous.

But there is no evidence that this or any other kind of federalism was seriously intended to be permanent. After the 'Conspiration de Lyon' was discovered in 1790, it was frequently rumoured that the royalists were plotting to divide France so that the old regime could be more easily restored. Such plots were said to involve the creation of a new capital and the separation of the Midi from the north, and royalist agents were certainly thinking in such terms as late as March 1792.[9] Buzot's proposals for a Departmental Guard to protect the Convention were cleverly represented by his Montagnard opponents as smacking of similarly divisive tendencies. These accusations led to the resolution of 25 September which declared the Republic to be one and indivisible. Within three months, federalism—which had not long before been canvassed by Chabot at the Jacobin Club of Paris as a possible basis for a new constitution—was a pejorative term, ranking second only to royalism in the vocabulary of political abuse, a heresy furiously denounced by politicians of all colours. The notion of a federalist plot was given further credence when the Austrian offensive of spring 1793 coincided with unrest in the provinces. Since Cloots alleged that Mme Roland's salon had seriously discussed the division of France into a federation of states, it was inevitable that Lyon would be considered the seed-bed of this new and insidious form of counter-revolution.[10] But there is no evidence for any of these accusations, or for Dubois-Crancé's claim that Lyon was the linchpin of a federalist plot to separate the Midi from the north. Lyon was certainly influenced by the so-called 'federalist movement', but only in the sense that the hope of linking up with a great departmental coalition encouraged the intransigence of June and early July. It was in Marseille, not in Lyon, that there was talk of unifying the Midi against the Montagnards in the north. It was Marseille and Bordeaux which conceived grandiose schemes of departmental federation. And while the Bordeaux moderates proselytized vigorously and systematically in the first fortnight

    [8] *CP*, p. 493 (2 Aug.).

    [9] Riffaterre, *Le Mouvement anti-jacobin et anti-parisien à Lyon*, ii. 59; E. Herriot, *Lyon n'est plus* (Paris, 1938–40), i. 42.

    [10] See M. J. Sydenham, *The Girondins* (London, 1961), 125–7, 193–4.

of June, sending out a total of nine delegations, in several instances with briefs to visit nine or ten *départements*, the three long-distance delegations from Lyon went straight to Bordeaux or Marseille and stayed there.[11]

There is no evidence to show that Lyon favoured the secession of the Midi, or that ill-feeling towards the north of France played a direct part in the rebellion. In a pamphlet printed in Lyon, Barbaroux wrote of 'cette barrière que les dictateurs élèvent entre le Nord et le Midi' and of the 'Maratized' northern cities, but this theme is not prominent in Lyonnais propaganda. On the contrary, Lyon's delegates in Paris praised the spirit of the northern *départements* and exhorted the Lyonnais to emulate their presumed energy.[12] There was seldom pronounced feeling against Paris *per se*. The Paris Jacobins and the Commune were strongly criticized, but they were generally distinguished from the Parisian population, which, it was said, had been 'deceived' or 'oppressed' and was now awaiting the moment to throw off its chains.[13] There were general references to usurpation of the nation's rights by Paris, particularly during the sectional meetings which discussed Lindet's credentials, but when the capital was discussed in detail it was emphasized that the majority of its population could be counted on to join the struggle against Jacobinism. As elsewhere in the Midi, the relatively low price of bread in Paris was a cause of dissatisfaction, but the blame was placed on Jacobin conspirators who ransacked the public treasury to keep themselves in power through bread subsidies.[14] For the Lyonnais rebels, as for those of Bordeaux and Caen, the conspiracies of 'la faction', not the perversity of Paris, had caused the political crisis. In material published in Lyon, only Rabaut Saint-Étienne's pamphlet and the *Adresse des Nantais* came close

---

[11] See W. Scott, *Terror and Repression in Revolutionary Marseille* (London, 1972), 115–16; A. Forrest, *Society and Politics in Revolutionary Bordeaux* (Oxford, 1975), 212. AD 42L12, fo. 9, Commission of Popular Justice, interrogation of J.-J. Tardy, 6 brumaire, an II; 1L375, letter of Pelzin and Jacquet, *commissaires* of the Provisional Municipalité in Marseille, 6 June; 42L87, d. 10, interrogation of Subrin by the Temporary Commission, 11 frimaire, an II.

[12] *Barbaroux à ses commettants* (Lyon, 1793); *Rapport au Conseil-général de la commune de Lyon par l'un des commissaires de section ... à Paris* (Lyon, [June, 1793]), 7; AD 1L375, J.-L. Fain to the Provisional Municipalité, 14 June.

[13] e.g. AD 31L21, fo. 9, minutes of Port Saint-Paul, 18 June; 31L2, fo. 16, minutes of la Croisette, 7 July; *Lettre des commissaires de Lyon à Bordeaux* (Lyon, [15 June] 1793), 6. Exceptional in this respect is an *Adresse à la Convention nationale par la Société de Brutus, ci-devant la Pêcherie, à Lyon, département de Rhône-et-Loire* (Lyon, 1792), which indirectly accused 'les Parisiens ... de vouloir usurper une suprématie que la nature et la raison ne leur accordent', and raised fears of economic exploitation (p. 5).

[14] See Scott, *Terror and Repression*, p. 95; *Rapport au Conseil-général de la commune*, p. 11.

to anathematizing Paris as comprehensively as the Montagnards were anathematizing Lyon.[15]

Nor is there any evidence of Lyonnais aspirations for their city to become the capital of either France or the Midi. This is unsurprising, given the city's economic difficulties and lack of regional dominance. And it was for these reasons, as well as because it needed a powerful central government to protect its trading interests and its food supplies, that Lyon did not want a federal system for France. Some of the rebels' ideas were compatible with federalism. Some of the rebels were mildly sympathetic to proposals which the Montagne had branded federalist, such as finding a more placid location than Paris for the National Assembly. But the rebellion as a whole was federalist only in the broad sense in which the Jacobins of Lyon and elsewhere were federalist: its leaders were prepared to use the local authorities to push through those illegal and extraordinary measures which they considered to be justified by the political crisis. Regionalism and particularism have been prominent themes in recent writing about the French Revolution. But important as these seem to have been in the politics of many communities, and reasonable as it may seem to be to suspect their influence in Lyonnais 'federalism', this rebellion cannot be traced back to old rivalries, traditions, and aspirations, and still less to Lyonnais 'nationalism' or hostility to centralization. Rather, it was a direct product of the revolutionary crisis.

Both the city and its élites were too divided for politicization to proceed in a way that was consistent with the integrative, populist rhetoric of *patriotisme*. Social disorder and the precocity of popular democratic organization confirmed the political reticence of the possessing classes— which the *patriotes* interpreted as secret sympathy for the counter-revolution. By trying to defend themselves with such weapons as the *volontaires*, the rural conservatives of the Departmental Directoire, and the general staff and élite companies of the National Guard, they gave credence to the accusations of aristocracy levelled at them by the early *patriotes*. When at last they began to mobilize politically to meet the threat posed by the Jacobin Municipalité, they found themselves in an ideological trap. Every act of anti-Jacobinism confirmed Montagnard suspicions of counter-revolutionary conspiracy in Lyon. Similarly, each

[15] See Forrest, *Society and Politics*, p. 247; A. Goodwin, 'The Federalist Movement in Caen in the Summer of 1793', *Bulletin of the John Rylands Library*, 42 (1959–60), 216; *Secrétariat*, pp. 493, 537.

Montagnard intervention in support of the *anarchistes-massacreurs* fed Lyonnais fears of a conspiracy organized by the Commune and the Jacobin Club of Paris. With each side understanding the other's policy in this light, there was little hope of settling the conflict by negotiation. Revolutionary ideology, the interpretation of politics as an unending struggle between the people and the aristocratic plot, contributed powerfully to the making of the Lyonnais civil war.

Revolutionary ideology also prepared the way for the massive repression which followed the fall of Lyon. By then it had become impossible for the most optimistic Jacobin to dismiss the rebels as 'une poignée de factieux', and it was clear that many more Lyonnais supported or acquiesced in the rebellion than actively opposed it. In August the *député* Javogues, on mission in Saint-Étienne, encouraged the Committee of Public Safety to believe that the people of Lyon would strike against the *muscadins*.[16] But no such rising occurred. Since the people and *patriotisme* were one, the conquerors of Lyon found it easy to believe that the mass of its population were not of the people but victims of a vicious local disease which disqualified them collectively from the French nation's mystic revolutionary union. The ground was well prepared for this. In July Saint-André had told the Convention that 'A Lyon, il n'est pas étonnant qu'il y ait un si grand nombre d'aristocrates, car cette ville est corrompue par la richesse et le luxe, mais bientôt ils baisseront la tête, car ils sont lâches, et les Sybarites ne peuvent devenir des Spartiates.'[17] After three months of stubborn resistance, Lyon's problem came to seem more intractable, a case of profound civic degeneracy. The signs of widespread complicity in the revolt—drawing on all sections in society—and the failure of the mass of the population to oppose it, perplexed Jacobin ideologists, for whom the social base of counter-revolution was axiomatically aristocratic, *haut bourgeois*, and clerical, and in whose eyes the identification of people and revolution was complete. Where the people rose up against the Convention, the unanimist, integrative, and populist arguments of Jacobinism became nonsense. Fouché was later to put the problem succinctly: 'C'est calomnier la nature et la Révolution que de croire que la masse du peuple puisse être corrompue.'[18] A community which produced such an aberration, defying the fundamental principles of the Jacobin revolution, was a pathological case which called

---

[16] *Actes*, v. 804 (7 Aug.).

[17] *Journal de la Montagne*, 3 (7 July), cited in Riffaterre, *Le Mouvement anti-jacobin et anti-parisien à Lyon*, ii. 189–90.

[18] *Actes*, x. 653, Fouché to the Convention, 21 ventôse, year II.

for the most drastic remedies. These were provided in the famous, ferocious decree of 12 October (18 vendémiaire, an II):

Art. 3. La ville de Lyon sera détruite. Tout ce qui fut habité par le riche sera démoli; il ne restera que la maison du pauvre, les habitations des patriotes égarés ou proscrits, les édifices specialement employés à l'industrie et les monuments consacrés à l'humanité et à l'instruction publique.

Art. 4. Le nom de Lyon sera effacé du tableau des villes de la République. La réunion des maisons conservées portera, désormais, le nom de *Ville-Affranchie*.

Art. 5. Il sera élevé sur les ruines de Lyon une colonne que attestera à la posterité les crimes et la punition des royalistes de cette ville, avec cette inscription: Lyon fit la guerre à la liberté; Lyon n'est plus.[19]

This drastic solution to the problem of Lyon was not just a blunt instrument of war policy. Nor was it just an expression of frustration and outrage at the length and cost of the siege. It evolved naturally from Jacobin ways of thinking about counter-revolution in general and Lyon in particular, ways of thinking which were developed still further by Collot d'Herbois and Fouché, the chief agents of the Terror at Commune-Affranchie, when they told the Convention 'qu'il n'y a d'innocent dams cette infâme cité que celui qui fut opprimé ou chargé de fers par les assassins du peuple'.[20] Collot later declared that the majority of *ci-devant* Lyonnais could only be regenerated if they were scattered throughout the Republic: 'En les disséminant parmi les hommes libres ils en prendront les sentiments. Ils ne les auront jamais, s'ils restent réunis.'[21] The hyperbole is evident; the depopulation of Ville-Affranchie was never seriously contemplated. But it remains the case that Lyon as a community found itself, like returned *émigrés*, non-juring priests, and nobles of unproven patriotism, officially categorized amongst the enemies of the people.

The history of Lyon from 1789 to 1793 is a striking example of the influence of what Hunt calls 'the rhetoric of conspiracy' on the course of the Revolution in France. But it also illustrates the relationship between social conflict and revolutionary politics. Few communities suffered as much as Lyon did from the French revolutionaries' obsession with conspiracy. I have tried to show, however, that it became a target largely because social conflicts prevented it from conforming to the model of revolutionary solidarity which the Jacobins held up to France, from

---

[19] *Moniteur*, xviii. 104.
[20] *Actes*, viii. 653, 26 brumaire, year II.
[21] *Actes*, viii. 668, Collot to Robespierre, 3 frimaire, year II.

blending into their 'Garden of Eden' (to quote Hunt again) in 'the mythic present of the regenerated national community'.[22] Other places, quieter, less divided, with less politicized plebeians and more dominant élites, could play their parts more or less convincingly in the revolutionary-democratic fantasy. But deep social divisions prevented Lyon from showing a united front to outsiders or taking the line of *attentisme*: timely adjustment to changes of direction in Paris. And they played a major role in shaping the pattern of local politics which led to Lyon's refusal of Jacobin leadership in May 1793, and then left it stranded at centre-stage, cast as the enemy of liberty.

[22] L. Hunt, *Politics, Culture and Class in the French Revolution* (London, 1986), 38–9.

10

Postscript: The Terror

Wherever it was applied with severity under the direct control of Paris, the Terror distorted local politics and gave central roles to new sets of individuals. Nowhere was the latter more evident than in Ville- (soon Commune-) Affranchie. Exhaustive examination of the new conditions, institutions, and actors in Lyonnais affairs must be left for another book. The aim here is simply to complete my account of the revolt with a survey of its immediate aftermath, making extensive use of existing research.

Two factors dominated the Committee of Public Safety's policy towards the defeated city during the ten months from early October 1793 to mid-Thermidor, year II (late July 1794). One was a determination to make a genuinely horrific example of Lyon. Mansfield has persuasively argued, contrary to many earlier historians, that this was a collective determination, and not the decision of the chief terrorists on the spot, Collot d'Herbois and Fouché.[1] The aim was to deter further revolt at a time of continuing military crisis. Toulon was still in British hands, Bordeaux not yet occupied by the Convention's troops, and the Vendée far from subdued. The battle of Wattignies, one of the early signs that the war was beginning to go France's way, was not fought until 16 October. Spanish and Piedmontese armies were still a threat. It counted for little that the danger of widespread urban revolt had passed with the collapse of the 'federalist' movement. The advocates of remorseless repression had only been in full control for two months, and they had not changed their view that the conciliatory and indecisive tactics of the previous majority in the Committee of Public Safety had allowed counter-revolution to run wild. Furthermore, they were under intense pressure from below to take action on a variety of fronts. Only a month earlier, on 5 September, the Convention had been surrounded by great crowds and invaded by *sans-culotte sectionnaires* demanding action against aristo-

---

[1] P. Mansfield, 'The Repression of Lyon, 1793–4: Origins, Responsibility and Significance', *French History*, 2 (1988), 74–101.

crats and hoarders. It had responded with the draconian Law of Suspects, ordering their detention until the peace. Repression of the *aristocratie marchande* at Lyon was a convenient way of appeasing the *sans-culottes* and deflecting the criticisms of the 'Hébertiste' left.

A second major element in the Montagnards' policy towards Lyon derived from their perception of its population as almost totally corrupted. Not only did this produce the ideological problems already discussed—and the terminological difficulties which led one *Comité révolutionnaire* in Lyon to describe Antoine Roullet, who had been a lieutenant in the rebel army, as 'aristocrate, quoique sans-culotte'[2]—it raised an immediate practical difficulty as well. Elsewhere in the provinces the Terror normally proceeded under the overall direction of *représentants en mission*, who acted as *agents de liaison* between the Committee of Public Safety and repressive organs staffed mainly by reliable local elements. But this was not thought possible at Commune-Affranchie. 'Les hommes sûrs étant très rares',[3] *patriotes* had to be implanted there with sufficient powers to root out the counter-revolutionaries and regenerate the rest. This was revolutionary colonization.[4]

The originator of the policy of colonization was Georges Couthon, although it was left to others to carry it out. After the Committee of Public Safety's destitution of Dubois-Crancé and Gauthier on 1 October for their failure to win a quick victory, Couthon found himself in charge of[5] punishing Lyon more drastically than he thought justifiable. Not that he had a higher opinion of the Lyonnais than his colleagues—in fact he made one of the more striking comments on their collective *incivisme*: 'Je crois que l'on est stupide ici par tempérament et que les brouillards du Rhône et de la Saône portent dans l'atmosphère une vapeur qui épaissit également les idées.'[6] But he was humane enough to conclude that this somewhat diminished the responsibility of most of them for their political errors, and that the way to proceed was by executing the ringleaders and re-educating the misled. For both purposes he recommended sending a

[2] AD 42L100, d. B39, no. 42, 23 frimaire.
[3] Collot to the CSP, 17 brumaire, year II: *Actes,* viii. 287.
[4] R. Cobb, *Les Armées révolutionnaires: Instrument de la Terreur dans les départements, avril 1793–floréal an II,* 2 vols. (Paris, 1961–3), ii. 788, 790.
[5] His colleagues were Laporte and Maignet. On Couthon's policy, see Mansfield, 'The Repression of Lyon', and M. Morineau, 'Mort d'un terroriste ... Prolégomènes à l'étude d'un juste: "Aristide" (ci-devant Georges) Couthon, précédé d'un coup d'œil sur ses bibliothèques', *AHRF* 55 (1983), 328–30.
[6] Letter to Saint-Just, 20 Oct., cited in E. Herriot, *Lyon n'est plus* (Paris, 1938–40), iii. 40.

colony of energetic *patriotes*, who were desperately needed to reinforce the few worthy of trust in 'cette terre étrangère'.[7]

To supplement the Commission Militaire, created during the siege with the relatively straightforward task of identifying and condemning rebels captured bearing arms, Couthon created the Commission de Justice Populaire for those taken unarmed and for non-combatants. The latter began its operations on 21 October, and specified a policy similar to Couthon's: 'it would only strike "les grands coupables" and separate "le séducteur de l'homme séduit"'.[8] But by this time it had already been made clear to Couthon that such a policy fell far short of the great acts of national vengeance against traitors in the Midi for which Robespierre and other leading Jacobins, including Hérault de Séchelles, Barère, and Saint-André, had been calling.[9] Not only had Couthon and his colleagues let Précy and other leading counter-revolutionaries get away, they had indulgently described scenes of reconciliation between republican troops and Lyonnais on 9 October. On 21 vendémaire (12 October) Hérault and Robespierre sent Couthon a copy of the decrees that had been passed against Lyon that day, accompanied by a long, frosty letter: 'Vous avez paru vous abandonner à un peuple qui flatte les vainqueurs ... il faut démasquer les traîtres et les frapper sans pitié ... faites exécuter, avec une sévérité inexorable, les décrets salutaires que nous vous adressons.'[10] Although he had begun to organize the demolitions and executions, Couthon was not prepared to apply the decree in the harsh manner expected by Robespierre. He asked to be replaced.[11]

By appointing Collot d'Herbois and Fouché to succeed Couthon on 9 brumaire (30 October), the Committee of Public Safety gave further proof of its intention to increase the level of repression. Both had harshly applied the Terror *en province*. Collot in particular had a long record of loyal Jacobinism and a shorter but impressive one as an administrator in the Committee itself.[12] Mansfield has shown that he was not, as has long been claimed, engaged in a personal vendetta against Lyon. On the

---

[7] *Jacobins*, v. 465 (17 Oct.).   [8] Cited in Mansfield, 'The Repression of Lyon', p. 85.

[9] Ibid. 77–9.   [10] Letter of 12 Oct., cited in Herriot, *Lyon n'est plus*, iii. 28–9.

[11] Mansfield, 'The Repression of Lyon', p. 85.

[12] See P. Mansfield, 'The Missions of Collet d'Herbois: A Study in his Political Career', Ph.D. thesis (Macquarie University, 1985), 1–205, for Collot's early career and his missions to Nice, Orléans, the Nièvre, and the Oise; L. madelin, *Fouché (1759–1820)* (Paris, 1901), vol. i, chaps. 3, 4. Montaut was originally to accompany these two to Commune-Affranchie, but because of illness he was replaced by Chateauneuf-Randon on 2 frimaire (22 November) (see Herriot, *Lyon n'est plus*, iii. 33).

contrary, he was less rabidly anti-Lyonnais than many of his colleagues, and initially opposed the plan to send a colony of *patriotes* there on the ground that there was enough local talent.[13] But he was prepared to carry out the Convention's orders, as he had conscientiously carried out orders before, and to apply the Committee's policy as he (correctly) understood it.

Despite Collot's early reservations, his and Fouché's mission was from the beginning an exercise in revolutionary colonization. The Lyonnais Gaillard, a *patriote opprimé* who won rapturous applause from the Paris Jacobins on 19 October, persuaded the latter ten days later to nominate a batch of nine *patriotes* (including himself) to accompany Collot to Commune-Affranchie the next day.[14] They were the first of many. On 20 brumaire (10 November) Collot, Fouché, and Laporte constituted the Commission Temporaire de Surveillance Républicaine. They were unanimous that the local authorities, though reconstituted as far as possible with their former *patriote* membership, were unreliable and incapable of acting with the necessary vigour. The Commission Temporaire was formed to supervise and energize them, but it had a wide range of other functions and powers. First, it was to be the *députés'* principal executive arm, with one section (*permanente*) for Lyon and the other (*ambulante*) for the *départements* of the Rhône and the Loire (and in practice the surrounding *départements* as well). It was to be an agent of de-Christianization, using measures such as the arrest of priests, the prohibition of masses, and the replacement of the Sunday holiday by the *décadi*. It was to administer the redistribution of wealth from the Church and the suspect rich to the politically virtuous poor. It was to apply a heavy revolutionary tax. It was to ensure, by armed force if necessary, the application of the *maximum* and the provisioning of Lyon, which brought it into conflict with the peasant communities in *départements* as far apart as Mont-Blanc, the Loire, Ain, and Ardèche. (In this respect at least, Commune-Affranchie benefited from the presence of the Commission, for the surrounding *départements* needed forceful persuasion to send food to federalists.) This was not the anarchical Terror that Thermidorian writers later attributed to the 'Commission infernale' but a generally disciplined experiment in the application of ultra-Jacobinism and *sans-culotte* principles.[15]

[13] Mansfield, 'The Repression of Lyon', pp. 84–9.

[14] *Jacobins*, v. 470, 486, 493 (19 Oct., 8, 11 brumaire).

[15] R. Cobb, 'La Commission temporaire de Commune-Affranchie (brumaire–germinal an II): Étude sur le personnel d'une institution révolutionnaire', in *Terreur et Subsistances 1793–1795* (Paris, 1965), 55–80. C. Lucas, *The Structure of the Terror: The Examples of Javogues and the Loire* (Oxford, 1973), 200.

But the Commission Temporaire was not just ultra-Jacobin, it was anti-Lyonnais. This feeling, Cobb argues, was reinforced by provincial and social antagonisms. Mainly Parisians, Moulinais, and Nivernais, the *commissaires* took great satisfaction in the humbling of 'l'orgueilleuse ville de Lyon', 'la citadelle même de "l'aristocratie bourgeoise"'.[16] And they made no effort to hide their feelings. They informed the reconstituted authorities of Commune-Affranchie, the cream of Lyonnais Jacobinism: 'Vous avez tous de grands torts à expier, les crimes des rebelles lyonnois sont les vôtres.'[17]

Anti-Lyonnais feeling was also strong in the detachment of the Parisian *Armée révolutionnaire* which arrived, nearly 2,000 strong, on 5 frimaire. Its commander, Ronsin, informed Paris 'que, dans cette commune, forte de 120 000 habitants, on trouverait à peine je ne dirai pas 1 500 patriotes, mais 1 500 hommes qui n'avaient pas été complices de la rébellion'.[18] Cobb has analysed—in all their varieties of emphasis—the motives behind the formation of Revolutionary Armies in the year II: 'volonté punitive, un certain chantage aux massacres', war on counter-revolution and 'fanatisme', protection of food convoys, requisitioning, application of the *maximum*, repression of brigandage, encouragement of popular societies and *sans-culotte* minorities, especially in rural areas.[19] Most of these aims were pursued by the army in Lyon and the surrounding countryside between Frimaire and Germinal. But while some provincial armies followed policies dictated by local conditions or the interests of particular *députés en mission*, the ones in Commune-Affranchie acted primarily as agents of the central government.[20] They were directly involved in many aspects of physical repression, making arrests, carrying out *visites domiciliaires* (perhaps the most effective method of generalizing political terror in the city[21]), guarding the tribunals and the guillotine during executions, and carrying out or assisting in executions themselves.

Assistance to the local *patriotes* was given liberally, though received with little enthusiasm. Three members of the Parisian army (Parein, Corchand, and Armé) and one from the Nièvre contingent (Brunière) served on the Commission Révolutionnaire or Commission des Sept (in

[16] Lucas, *The Structure of the Terror*, p. 60.
[17] Ibid. 59.
[18] Cited in Herriot, *Lyon n'est plus*, iii. 142.
[19] Cobb, *Les Armées révolutionnaires*, ii. 264–5.
[20] Ibid. 536–7. Small detachments from the Nièvre and Allier were there as well.
[21] Ibid. 540.

practice, des Cinq) formed by the *députés* on 7 frimaire to accelerate the rate of executions. Only one member of this body, the *dessinateur* Fernex, was Lyonnais. Antoine Lafaye, a former legal official, came from near Saint-Étienne but had long been a member of the Paris Jacobin Club. Of the *étrangers* chosen to invigorate the *Comités révolutionnaires* (much to the latters' indignation), forty-nine were drawn from the Parisian army and seven from those of the Allier and the Nièvre. Revolutionary soldiers formed a large part of the Jacobin Club of Commune-Affranchie and played a prominent part in its tumultuous affairs.[22]

With the arrival of the Revolutionary Army from Paris, Collot was in a position to do what he was there for, 'faire de grandes choses'. So far Collot and Fouché had been relying mainly on the tribunals created by Couthon, their only important innovation being the Commission Militaire of Feurs (20 brumaire), which complemented and soon entirely replaced the Commission de Justice Populaire there.[23] But Collot became frustrated at the slow pace of the repression, complained at the enormous administrative load with which he was burdened, fretted at the inefficiency of the local *Comités révolutionnaires* (one of them, he informed Robespierre, had let Chalier's executioner go free), and denounced the legacy of 'indulgence' left by Couthon's inadequate measures.

To signal the end of half measures, Collot, Albitte, and Fouché declared on 3 frimaire that Ville-Affranchie was 'en état de guerre révolutionnaire', and resolved to increase drastically the rate of executions: 'Cela est encore lent pour la justice du peuple entier, qui doit foudroyer tous ses ennemis à la fois, et nous nous occuperons à forger la foudre.'[24] On the same day, the Commission Temporaire decided to achieve this by executing the rebels *en masse*, by cannon-fire, thus translating into practice the favourite revolutionary image of the thunderbolt launched by an outraged people. There is perhaps no plainer evidence of how closely habitual rhetoric came to represent reality in the minds of committed Jacobins.

The thunderbolt in fact produced a bloody shambles, and the excuse could not be made for the Commission and the *députés* that they were too lost in their abstractions to comprehend what the reality would be like: the Commission's minutes state that troops were to be present to

[22] Ibid. 335 n. 119, 542; Herriot, *Lyon n'est plus*, iii. 147. Armé was the secretary of the Commission des Sept; the others mentioned were judges.
[23] Lucas, *The Structure of the Terror*, pp. 242–7.
[24] Herriot, *Lyon n'est plus*, iii. 134–5.

finish off those not killed outright by the cannon.[25] Sixty men were chained together on the Brotteaux plain and killed by these methods on 14 frimaire, and 211 more the next day. The many still alive after the cannonades were shot or sabred to death. There is evidence that the soldiers who carried this out were sickened by it, and after the 15th even the Commission Temporaire had no stomach for more. It resolved 'que l'on écrive aux Représentants du peuple que ce mode n'a pas eu l'exécution que l'on auroit désiré, de prendre a'autres moyens plus sûrs'.[26] There were no more *mitraillades,* but executions by firing-squad and guillotine continued at a rapid rate.

No qualms were expressed about any of this by the Lyonnais Jacobins. On the contrary, there was open exultation. 'Encore des têtes, et chaque jour des têtes tombent!', wrote Achard to Gravier; 'Quelles délices tu aurais goûtées [*sic*], si tu eusses vu, avant hier, cette justice nationale de deux cent neuf scélérats! Quelle majesté! Quel ton imposant! Tout édifiait!'[27] This unnervingly intense elation was expressed frequently in the public and private correspondence about the executions. Writings to the Convention, on 14 frimaire, Dorfeuille described the coming mass destruction of counter-revolutionaries by 'le feu de la foudre' as 'la fête de la vertu'; Pilot assured Gravier that his health was improving 'par l'effet de la destruction des ennemis de notre commune patrie'.[28] Expressing such enthusiasm was of course prescribed by Jacobin orthodoxy: 'la *soif de la sang* est devenue un trait de l'orthodoxie révolutionnaire et le programme même de la politique gouvernementale'.[29] But it was more than mere conformism. These men had all committed their lives to the Jacobin war against aristocratic conspiracy. For Jacobins, the revolt of Lyon had both confirmed the reality of the conspiracy and offered a chance to eliminate conspirators in sufficient numbers to hope that the way might at last be clear to the Utopia Achard had promised the Club Central in August 1792: 'la France et la terre entière seront rendus à la liberté primitive qu'accorda la nature'.[30] Or as Collot put it more pro-

---

[25] Herriot, *Lyon n'est plus,* iii. 136–7.

[26] Ibid. 178.

[27] Achard to Gravier, 17 frimaire, in E. B. Courtois, *Rapport fait au nom de la commission chargée de l'examen des papiers trouvés chez Robespierre et ses complices ...* (Paris, year III), 306.

[28] Herriot, *Lyon n'est plus,* iii. 175–6; letter of 13 frimaire, in Courtois, *Rapport ... de la commission,* p. 296.

[29] Cobb, *Les Armées révolutionnaires,* ii. 537.

[30] J. Achard, 'Discours prononcé au Comité central le 27 août l'an 1ᵉʳ de la République française par-devant MM les commissaires de la Convention nationale envoyés à Lyon pour y établir le calme et la paix' (Coste MS 534).

saically: '[e]n faisant périr les scélérats, on assure la vie de toutes les générations des hommes libres'.[31] There was a chiliastic element in the terrorist mentality which exulted in the mass killings of the winter of the year II.

It also had a social element. It was now axiomatic that the city's political degradation was caused by its rich: 'Les riches Lyonnois ont tué l'énergie qui devoit animer soixante-mille individus indigens [sic], ils ont comprimé sans cesse par la misère, l'élan qui les portoit vers la liberté.'[32] Eliminating the counter-revolutionary rich served two purposes here: punishment for treason, and removal of the power to degrade exercised *ci-devant* by 'cette classe d'êtres monstrueux, vampires de la société, sangsues de tous les peuples, êtres vils et méprisables, qu'on nomme négocians [sic]'.[33] Laws of 12 July and 12 October provided for the distribution of sequestered rebel property to indigent oppressed *patriotes*,[34] and so Commune-Affranchie appeared to represent an opportunity for social levelling *sans-culotte* style, without fundamentally threatening the principles of 1789. Taken out of context, some rhetoric associated with this has been interpreted as socialism,[35] and Babeuf read the *Instruction* of the Commission Temporaire as '[l']expression de la sainte et sublime doctrine communiste'.[36] It certainly envisaged heavy taxation of the rich, 'proportionnée à leur fortune et à leur incivisme', and the nationalization of agricultural production, excepting 'une indemnité' for the producer.[37] But it was in essence war taxation, combined with an unusually explicit statement of *sans-culotte* (and Robespierrist) doctrine on *subsistances*.[38] As with Jacobin social policy generally, attacks on the rich were justified by the exceptional circumstances created by war and rebellion, as well as by the presumption that *incivisme* or, at the

---

[31] Letter to Duplay, 15 frimaire, cited in Herriot, *Lyon n'est plus*, iii. 172.

[32] *Rapport fait au nom du Comité de salut public sur la situation de Commune-Affranchie par J. M. Collot d'Herbois. Le 1 nivôse* (Paris, year II), 4.

[33] 'Discours d'Achard à la Société populaire de Commune-Affranchie, le 18 pluviôse an II', in Courtois, *Rapport ... de la commission*, p. 308.

[34] *Moniteur*, xvii. 121; xviii. 104.

[35] For examples, see Herriot, *Lyon n'est plus*, iii. 112.

[36] Quoted in Cobb, 'La Commission temporaire', p. 55.

[37] See Herriot, *Lyon n'est plus*, iii. 109–12. The use of revolutionary taxes was by no means exceptional in the year II, and does not constitute evidence that the Terror at Commune-Affranchie had a special social character.

[38] See Mansfield, 'The Missions of Collot d'Herbois', pp. 404–14, for the necessary evidence on the point of war taxation. There is an excellent discussion of the limitations of Jacobin social policy in Lefebvre's *Compte rendu* of Herriot's *Lyon n'est plus*, (*AHRF*, 18 (1946), 78).

least, *égoïsme* were endemic amongst the rich, particularly in this region.

Nevertheless, these aspects of the Terror in Lyon exemplify the social preoccupations of Jacobinism, with its consciousness of the Republic's mission to protect the poor,[39] to abolish mendicancy as an affront to human dignity (without, however, providing much more than statements of intention in this regard, such as the *arrêté* of 24 brumaire[40]), and to limit the rights of property in order to guarantee the necessities of life. And while the *Instruction* contains no critique of private property in general, it approaches it with a degree of revolutionary abandon which is far from the spirit of reverence for its inviolability expressed in the Declaration of the Rights of Man and the Citizen in 1789: 'Il ne s'agit pas ici d'exactitude mathématique ni de ce scrupule timoré avec lequel on doit travailler dans la répartition des contributions publiques; c'est ici une mesure extraordinaire qui doit porter la caractère des circonstances qui la commandent. Agissez donc en grand; prenez tout de qu'un citoyen a d'inutile.'[41] The terrorists at Commune-Affranchie did not go as far as Saint-Just, whose Ventôse decrees provided for the permanent redistribution to *patriotes* of the property of suspects, but they expressed a crusading zeal to exploit the opportunity that the counter-revolutionaries of Lyon had given them. Informing the Convention on 21 ventôse (11 March 1794) that the population of Lyon was desperately short of necessities, Fouché went on: 'Vous pouvez ... les satisfaire aisément ... l'opulence qui fut si longtemps et si exclusivement le patrimoine du vice et du crime, est resitutée au peuple; vous en êtes les dispensateurs; les propriétés du riche conspirateur lyonnais, acquises à la République, sont immenses, et elles peuvent porter le bien-être et l'aisance parmi des milliers de républicains.'[42] Very little of this social policy was actually put into practice. Mansfield maintains that the *députés* showed no interest in applying the measures of 24 brumaire,[43] and the Convention decreed on 19 October that, contrary to its earlier legislation, the property of

---

[39] See Lucas, *The Structure of the Terror*, pp. 290–3, 323–4, for comments on this aspect of terrorism in the Loire.

[40] 'Là où il y a des hommes qui souffrent', announced Collot, Fouché, and Albitte, 'il y a des ennemis de l'humanité ... Tous les citoyens infirmes, vieillards, orphelins, indigens seront logés, nourris et vêtus aux dèpens des riches de leurs cantons respectifs, les signes de la misère seront anéantis' (cited in Herriot, *Lyon n'est plus*, iii. 104–5).

[41] Cited ibid. 111.

[42] Letter of 21 ventôse: *Actes*, x. 654.

[43] See Mansfield, 'The Missions of Collot d'Herbois', pp. 413–14, and Lucas, *The Structure of the Terror*, pp. 282–93, where it is concluded that Javogues's more ambitious essay in reshaping society through revolutionary taxation in the Loire also had little practical effect.

rebels was not to be redistributed amongst *patriotes* but sold off like that of *émigrés*.[44] Though the matter has not been studied systematically, not much property seems actually to have been reallocated, and when it was it was probably done mostly by Lyonnais *sans-culottes*[45] operating outside the letter (though perhaps in their view within the spirit) of revolutionary law.

Nothing at all came of schemes to republicanize commerce 'pour soustraire les pauvres au despotisme alimentaire des millionnaires', or of the plan by the *deputés* Reverchon and Dupuy to create 'un noyau républicain de commerce et d'industrie' by establishing 300 workshops for 'patriotes peu fortunés', and prohibiting businesses with a turnover of more than 10,000 or 12,000 *livres* per year.[46] But it remains important that for nine months Lyon was ruled by Jacobins who spoke as though they intended to implement *sans-culotte* social doctrine. And if they did not do a great deal in practice to show that the poor had much to hope for from the Jacobin Republic, they did show that the rich had much to fear from it.

But despite its reputation as a centre of *ultracisme*, Commune-Affranchie saw only sporadic episodes of de-Christianization, even with the presence of two specialists in the field, Couthon and Fouché. The festival of Chalier on 20 brumaire (10 November) is notorious for its donkey 'habillé en Monseigneur' and the smashing of church ornaments. Possibly Fouché would have done more in this direction, but the arrival of Collot gave political repression absolute priority. It was only after Collot's departure that Fouché secularized the cemeteries of the Rhône (17 nivôse (6 January 1794)) as he had earlier those of the Allier and Nièvre. But by this time the Convention had decreed the *liberté des cultes*, and the de-Christianizers were under attack. In this respect, as in most others, the Terror at Commune-Affranchie was focused on the specific targets that the revolutionary government set for it.[47]

---

[44] *Archives parlementaires de 1787 à 1860*, lxxxvii (Paris, 1910), 28.

[45] Property held under seal (except Précy's) was restored to its owners by a decree of 14 pluviôse (2 February 1795), and that of executed rebels to their heirs by decrees of 14 floréal (31 May) and 21 prairial (9 June) (see R. Fuoc, *La Réaction thermidorienne à Lyon (1795)* (Lyon, 1957), 39).

[46] See C. Riffaterre, *Le Mouvement anti-jacobin et anti-parisien à Lyon et dans le Rhône-et-Loire en 1793* (Lyon, 1912–28), i. 346–8.

[47] See P. Mansfield, 'Collot d'Herbois and the Dechristianizers', *Journal of Religious History*, 14 (1986–7), 409–12; Herriot, *Lyon n'est plus*, iii. 90–1, 160–1. The proportion of clergy amongst those executed in the Rhône was 7.2%, compared with 6.5% nationally (D. Greer, *The Incidence of the Terror during the French Revolution: A Statistical Interpretation* (Gloucester, Mass., 1935), 161, 163).

LES AMIS DE CHALIER ET DE GAILLARD

Having besieged Lyon in order to liberate the Municipalité of December 1792, the *députés en mission* had little choice but to reinstate it, and to commence the round-up of counter-revolutionaries they revived the thirty-two sectional *Comités révolutionnaires* which had been appointed by the Municipalité in May 1793. But they had increasing difficulty with the local *patriotes*. As well as shaping the domestic history of Commune-Affranchie in the year II, the resulting conflicts indirectly but profoundly affected the fate of the revolutionary government itself.

It was only three days after the fall of Lyon that Couthon and his colleagues created the Comité Central de Surveillance because they had become convinced that the sectional committees were too undisciplined and preoccupied with personal vendettas. On 2 brumaire (23 October) they created a commission, the majority of whose members were to be chosen by the *députés*, to collaborate with the Comité Central in investigating abuses and ensuring the security of confiscated valuables.[48] Collot later placed the committees under the still stricter surveillance of the Commission Temporaire. The frictions this produced were a familiar feature of the Terror in many places as the revolutionary government tightened its grip on organizations controlled by local militants, but in the case of Lyon they were exacerbated by contempt for the Lyonnais from one side and indignation on the other at the *députés*' failure to implement the redistributive provisions of 12 July and 12 October. The committees were intermittently purged and disciplined, but the *députés*' dissatisfaction with them remained. On 5 pluviôse (24 January 1794) Fouché, Laporte, and Méaulle finally abolished the sectional committees altogether for abusing their powers and persecuting the innocent, replacing them with nine *Comités de canton*.[49] The final blow to the *sections*, the mainstays of popular democracy in Lyon, was thus delivered by the agents of Jacobin centralism.

It was not so easy to get rid of the Municipalité and the Société Populaire des Jacobins de Commune-Affranchie, despite their constant encouragement of the clamours for redistribution of confiscated property. On 12 brumaire (2 November) the Municipalité presented a list of 918 'contre-révolutionnaires, agioteurs et accapareurs' whose property should be divided according to the decree of 12 July. Instead the Lyonnais

---

[48] *Arrêté* by Collot, Laporte, Châteauneuf-Randon, and Maignet; AC, I²1.

[49] *Rapport de Fouché ... sur la situation de commune-Affranchie* (Paris, year II), 3–4; see also Herriot, *Lyon n'est plus*, iii. 322.

patriotes received indemnities from public funds, amounts between 100 and 240 *livres* distributed to 242 individuals between 19 brumaire (9 November) and 18 nivôse (7 January 1794).[50] Indignation over such paltry compensation for their sufferings further soured relations between the Lyonnais Jacobins and the *députés*. There were also repeated outbursts about offices in the revolutionary administration, particularly in the *Comités révolutionnaires*, whose members were paid 2,000 *livres* per year. On 12 brumaire (2 November), for example, a member denounced 'la perfidie des gens à écritoire pour accaparer toutes les fonctions administratives et en écarter les pauvres sans-culottes'. The meeting then adjourned to continue a *scrutin épuratoire* of the committees.[51] But after the arrival of the Revolutionary Army, the Jacobin Club itself was extensively colonized by *sans-culotte* soldiers, *frères Parisiens*, and other *étrangers*, who did their best to deflect the meetings from these issues.

The Lyonnais fought back by exploiting differences between officers and men of the Revolutionary Army.[52] Discontent mounted to such an extent that on 16 nivôse (5 January) the *députés* were openly criticized at a meeting of the Lyonnais Jacobins. There was talk of denouncing them to the Committee of Public Safety, and even of the guillotine.[53] After weeks of disorder in the club (and, it was hinted, sexual debauchery in its public galleries), this was too much for Fouché, who appeared at the next day's meeting and threatened to dissolve the Société. To ensure its good behaviour he also delegated two members of the Commission Temporaire to attend its sessions. This elicited somewhat more prudent behaviour from the club, and when the Lyonnais dared to rehearse their grievances they were now answered by the voice of revolutionary orthodoxy. Late in Nivôse an attempt was made to squeeze out discussions of contentious issues by introducing regular and lengthy orations on the Declaration of the Rights of Man. Mention of relief for the indigent (in effect, the redistribution issue) brought censure for wasting 'un temps précieux destiné à l'instruction dont la société doit s'occuper sans interruption puisque les représentants ont pris toutes les mesures les plus efficaces pour anéantir la mendicité'. When the veteran Lyonnais Jacobin Perez returned to the charge in Ventôse with a report on the case for indemnities, he was told that the word 'indemnité' could not be used, as

---

[50] Riffaterre, *Le Mouvement anti-jacobin et anti-parisien à Lyon*, i. 343 n. 3.

[51] AD 34L9, minutes of the Société Populaire des Jacobins de Commune-Affranchie.

[52] Ibid., minutes of 10, 12, 13–17 nivôse; see Cobb, *Les Armées révolutionnaires*, ii. 791.

[53] AD 34L9, minutes of the Société Populaire des Jacobins de Commune Affranchie, 16 nivôse. See also Herriot, *Lyon n'est plus*, iii. 278.

the *représentants* had spoken only of 'un secours provisoire'.[54]

But for all their complaints about the invasion of committees by 'les gens à écritoire', the local *sans-culottes* had some satisfaction *vis-à-vis* their claim to places in the revolutionary bureaucracy. Of 176 members of *Comités de surveillance* identified by Longfellow from his estimated total of 500, nearly all were artisans or *boutiquiers*; 33.5 per cent were weavers and 10.2 per cent were cobblers. Weavers were still more prominent amongst the *gardiateurs des scellés*, who were paid 40 *sous* a day to protect property placed under seal after the arrest of suspects or awaiting sale on behalf of the nation following the execution of 'counter-revolutionaries'. There were perhaps 2,000 of these officials, and of 333 identified by trade, Longfellow found 20 to be hatters, 43 stocking-weavers, and more than half (175), silk-weavers. Work on the demo-litions—desultory and, fortunately, inefficient—employed thousands more at 40 *sous* a day.[55]

This reflects mainly the belief that such *civisme* as was to be found in *la ville maudite* would be amongst the poor. It also reflects the fact that artisans, particularly weavers, were less involved in the rebellion, both in terms of absolute numbers and proportionately. Furthermore, the 37-member *noyau* of the Jacobin Society also had a majority of silk-weavers (14) and artisans in related trades (6),[56] men who were in a position to allocate jobs which were particularly desirable at a time when the local economy was in chaos. For a short time, large numbers of the *menu peuple* of Lyon were able to exploit the apparatus of state for their own material benefit, and to exercise power over their social superiors. Together with the *mitraillades*, this aspect of the Terror at Commune-Affranchie symbolized for the properties classes the Revolution's essential crimin-ality.

This evidence qualifies the claim that '[t]he correlation between humble social position and militancy breaks down for the provinces'.[57] Unlike the

[54] AC I²6, 119, minutes of the Société populaire des Jacobins de Commune-Affranchie, 26 nivôse, 8 ventôse. (These minutes are divided between the communal and departmental archives. Those for 28 ventôse–18 prairial are in the former, and the rest (9 brumaire–14 thermidor) in the latter.)

[55] D. L. Longfellow, 'Silk Weavers and the Social Struggle in Lyon during the French Revolution, 1789–1794', *French Historical Studies*, 12 (1981), 31, 36–7.

[56] AC I²6, 106 (14 floréal). The rest of the *noyau* consisted of 10 artisans in various trades outside the textile sector, 1 stocking-weaver, 1 hatter, 2 *négociants*, a merchant, a teacher, and a government official.

[57] D. M. G. Sutherland, *France 1789–1815: Revolution and Counterrevolution* (London, 1985), 456. The evidence for this statement appears to depend rather heavily on the example of Toulouse.

imported terrorists of the Commission Temporaire, the local militants were predominantly of the lower orders. The picture is complicated by the fact that most of the leading Lyonnais Jacobins, and particularly those who had the ear of Robespierre, were far from humble: Gravier and Bussat had modest means, but Emery was the son of a merchant hatter, Pilot was the *directeur de la Poste*, and Achard was a surgeon, though from an artisan family. Their position was ambiguous. They defended their socially *sans-culotte* compatriots against the *représents en mission* and they conspired for the removal of Fouché, but they did not challenge the authority of the revolutionary government, and their dependence on one of its principal architects would have made that impossible in any case. Pending a minute re-examination of terrorist personnel such as Richard Andrews is pursuing in Paris, it can be suggested that Commune-Affranchie saw something like Soboul's much-criticized version of the conflict between bourgeois revolutionary government (the *députés*) and the remnants of a popular movement (the *amis*), with the special relationship between Robespierre and people like Gravier hiding the true nature of the conflict from the former.[58]

There was also something resembling the nightmares of pillage which had haunted the well-to-do since 1789. The sequestrations themselves were not pillage, for they were prescribed by law, just as forfeiture of property (in cases of lese-majesty and suicide, for example) had been under the old regime. But the *députés* at Lyon repeatedly claimed that property that had been sequestrated or was under seal was being stolen on a large scale by *gardiateurs* and members of the *Comités revolutionnaires*: 'les gardiens dilapident tout, d'accord avec les administrateurs qui soutiennent cette anarchie'.[59] There is no doubt that many thefts occurred, though it would be nearly impossible to estimate their extent, given that the only authorities whose records might have thrown light on it are plausibly alleged to have been implicated, and that the accusations came principally from *députés en mission* who were engaged in a bitter political struggle with the local authorities. In so far as weavers and hatters were

---

[58] See R. M. Andrews, 'Réflexions sur la conjuration des égaux', *Annales Économies Sociétés Civilisations*, 24 (1974), 73–106; id., 'Social Structures, Political Elites and Ideology in Revolutionary Paris, 1792–94: A Critical Evaluation of Albert Soboul's *Les Sans-culottes parisiens en l'An II*', *Journal of Social History*, 19 (1985), 71–112; R. Cobb, *The Police and the People* (Oxford, 1970), part 2.

[59] Reverchon to Couthon, 28 germinal, in Courtois, *Rapport ... de la commission*, pp. 312–14; for an example of similar charges, see Laporte to Couthon, 24 germinal, ibid. 320–2. (Reverchon had been ordered to replace Fouché on 7 germinal: Herriot, *Lyon n'est plus*, iii. 503.)

involved, they may well have felt justified in appropriating property from those when they saw as their exploiters. Other Lyonnais *patriotes* could have regarded helping themselves as executing the Convention's proclaimed policy of recompensing them for their sufferings from the property of the people's enemies.

This question was important in the battle between *étrangers* and Lyonnais, but more than revolutionary careerism and the spoils of victory were involved. Many of the local Jacobins had long been taking the risks of revolutionary politics in what was now generally agreed to have been the capital of counter-revolution. They had repeatedly warned Paris of the dangers of revolt, but the help they sought had not been forthcoming. (They did not consider that they might not have needed it had they acted more adroitly.) Yet now outsiders were treating them with suspicion and at times with open contempt. Dodieu, who had paid dearly for his precocious *sans-culottisme*, used terms reminiscent of the 'federalists' in a speech demanding adequate provisioning of 'cette cité envers laquelle on n'a garde [*sic*] de vouloir faire revivre la tâche du péché original'. Bussat complained, not unjustifiably, that 'déjà on a répandu à Paris qu'il n'y a pas de patriotes dans cette cité'.[60] On 9 pluviôse (28 January) the Jacobins resolved 'qu'une commission soit nommée pour recueillir tous les traits de patriotisme qu'ont donné les habitants de cette commune depuis le 29', and a brochure was published summarizing their struggle against 'l'aristocratie la plus nerveuse, la plus puissante' from 1789 to the summer of 1793, when those who had escaped imprisonment marched against 'leurs propres foyers pour les incendier'.[61]

The Lyonnais tried to prop up their reputation by emphasizing their links with Chalier, whose remains were carried through Paris on 30 frimaire in an elaborate ceremony which elevated him to the status of a republican martyr alongside Marat and Le Peletier. The next day the Convention approved Couthon's proposal that his bust be placed in the Panthéon and an official life be written for purposes of public instruction.[62] The Lyonnais Jacobins called themselves 'les amis de Chalier' and swore 'honneur aux mânes de Chalier par l'imitation de ses vertus'.[63] When Gaillard, the hero of 10 August, committed suicide at the end of Frimaire—for reasons which remain obscure but which they found it con-

[60] AC I²6, 108, 113 (8 brumaire, 22 pluviôse).

[61] Ibid. 121; *Adresse de la Société populaire de Commune-Affranchie. A tous les Jacobins Montagnards de la République* (Commune-Affranchie, year II), 1, 3.

[62] Herriot, *Lyon n'est plus*, iii. 239–40, 245–6.

[63] AC I²6, 108 (8 brumaire).

venient to describe as 'désespoir patriotique'—he was adopted as a second patron saint and they became 'les amis de Chalier et de Gaillard'.[64] But these tactics cut no ice with the *frères étrangers*. Duvicquet, secretary of the Commission Temporaire, attacked the *amis de Chalier* at their meeting of 28 nivôse for proposing to send copies of their proceedings to the countryside ('vous voulez leur apprendre ce qu'ils scavent [*sic*] mieux que vous'). He then advised them to enrol in the army (c'est par là que vous effacerez le crime que pèse sur vos têtes'), and twisted the knife with: 'Lyonnais, si vous aviez été républicains vous auriez prévenu la mort du vertueux Chalier'. Fouché made the same point in a published attack on the *amis*.[65]

While the *amis de Chalier et de Gaillard* could not hope for much sympathy from the chiefs of the revolutionary colony, they had a valuable political resource in Paris: the sympathy of Robespierre. As we have seen, he had several *protégés* amongst the Lyonnais Jacobins, notably Achard, who on 16 nivôse (5 January 1794) was given the important post of *agent-national* at Commune-Affranchie. Achard supported the *amis* in their struggle with the *étrangers*, and after resigning his post on 9 germinal (21 March), he left to press their case with Robespierre.[66] Claude Gravier, one of the founders of the original popular societies of Lyon, was a *juré* of the Tribunal Révolutionnaire de Paris and, it seems, an intimate of Robespierre. The Lyonnais Emery, Fillion, and Musson were also *jurés*. Pilot, one of the Jacobin *noyau*, bought goods for Robespierre's landlord, and in Nivôse promised to buy stockings for Robespierre.[67] Whether or not he got his stockings, Robespierre gave unqualified public support to the Lyonnais Jacobins, extravagantly praising '[les] services rendus par les amis de Chalier; il les connaît tous; il connaît aussi ses persécuteurs'.[68]

The politics of Commune-Affranchie became intimately involved with

[64] *Règlements de la Société populaire de Commune-Affranchie* (Commune-Affranchie [24 floréal], year II).

[65] AC I²6, 111; *Rapport de Fouché*. A resolution critical of Gaillard seems to have been passed by the Lyonnais Jacobins on 28 frimaire, but was rescinded the next day. The nature of the criticism is not clear. (See *Journal de Ville-Affranchie et des départements de Rhône et Loire. Rédigé par D'Aumale*, 37 (8 nivôse), 221.)

[66] J. Rousset, 'Un chirurgien jacobin: L'Infernal Achard', *Albums du Crocodile*, 32 (1964), 19–20. In the year III Courtois described Achard as 'le fournisseur de la famille Duplay et de Robespierre, auxquels il envoie bas, huile et savon' (Courtois, *Rapport ... de la commission*, p. 19 n. 86). Duplay was Robespierre's landlord.

[67] Letters to Gravier, 13 frimaire and 25 nivôse, in Courtois, *Rapport ... de la commission*, pp. 296–7.

[68] *Jacobins*, vi. 216–17 (23 messidor). See also his speeches of 1 and 11 germinal, ibid. 7–8, 37.

the struggle between the revolutionary government and its critics. During the Indulgents' campaign to relax the Terror, a Lyonnais petition for mercy was sent to the Convention, where it was read on 30 frimaire (20 December), the day before Collot arrived in Paris to defend himself and the policy he had been sent to Lyon to implement.[69] He received the support of the Committee of Public Safety, the Convention, and the Paris Jacobins,[70] but the horrors of the *mitraillades* were beginning to turn even Jacobin opinion against his implementation of *terrorisme à l'outrance* and against the extraordinary institutions which had been created to carry it out. Concurrently, a programme of normalization and centralization was under way, impelled both by the determination of the Committee of Public Safety to remove the possibility of further opposition and the need for central regulation of the war economy. This process found its main legislative expression in the decree of 14 frimaire (4 December 1793) establishing revolutionary government for the duration.[71] In Commune-Affranchie, 'la capitale de l'administration d'exception', the Commission Temporaire and the Parisian Revolutionary Army (the only one to escape abolition by the decree) were now clearly under threat. Their critics were given plenty of ammunition by quarrels amongst senior officers and some individual excesses.[72]

Accusations of 'Hébertisme' had also made the Revolutionary Army vulnerable as the Committee of Public Safety extended its offensive from the moderates to the ultra-revolutionary left. Ronsin, the army's commander-in-chief, had set out for Paris a week before Collot, having written to the Cordeliers extolling the virtues of the *mitraillades*. The publication of this early in the third *décade* of Frimaire led to attacks on Ronsin in the Indulgent press, and he was arrested by order of the Convention (27 frimaire (17 December)) soon after he arrived in Paris.[73] Collot had little choice but to defend Ronsin, for if a campaign were mounted against the authors of the *mitraillades*, Collot would be an obvious target. He persuaded the Jacobins to support Ronsin and the latter's ally, Vincent, *sécretaire-général des bureaux* at the Ministry of War. This made further concessions towards the Indulgents impossible:

---

[69] See N. Hampson, *The Life and Opinions of Maximilien Robespierre* (London, 1974), 218, 242.

[70] *Jacobins*, v. 570 (1 nivôse); *Moniteur*, xix. 29.

[71] See A. Soboul, *The French Revolution 1787–1799*, trans. A. Forrest and C. Jones, 2 vols. (London, 1974), ii. 355–7.

[72] See Cobb, *Les Armées révolutionnaires*, ii. 792–3.

[73] Ibid. 537, 791; Hampson, *Maximilien Robespierre*, p. 217.

'Collot's intervention was decisive because it forced the Committee of Public Safety to abandon its benevolent neutrality towards the Indulgents, which would henceforth have split the Committee itself.'[74] Collot, and the policies he had carried out at Commune-Affranchie, were major obstacles to any gradual winding down of the Terror by the steady elimination of secondary figures accused of 'excesses'.

After their release from gaol on 13 pluviôse (1 February), Vincent and particularly Ronsin provoked the government with talk of a rising and a new purge of the Convention. On the night of 23/4 ventôse (13/14 March) the Hébertists were arrested, and they were executed ten days later. It was this blow against *ultracisme* which gave Fouché, Delaporte, and Méaulle the excuse they needed to dissolve the Lyonnais Jacobin Club on 6 germinal. But while the *amis de Chalier* certainly had views on repression and *subsistances* that were similar to Hébert's, their politics remained Robespierrist. They had continued to use their influence with Robespierre against Fouché, who, vulnerable because of his de–Christianizing past, was now firmly out of favour with the revolutionary government and particularly with Robespierre. Perhaps already informed that the Jacobin Club's papers had been seized (5 germinal), Robespierre seems to have anticipated its dissolution. Two orders of the Committee written in his hand and dated 7 germinal (27 March) recalled Fouché and prohibited further persecution of the Lyonnais *patriotes*.[75]

This victory against their most determined enemy did the *amis* little good. The remaining *députés* were hardly less critical of them than Fouché, attacked them for constantly complaining to their allies in Paris behind the *députés'* backs, and intimated that the *amis* were making the situation in Lyon unmanageable.[76] In the longer term, the departure of Fouché contributed substantially to the downfall of the *amis'* chief protector. It restored to the Convention an able politician strongly antagonistic to Robespierre, who in turn attacked Fouché's conduct in the provinces and particularly his persecution of the Lyonnais *patriotes*.[77]

[74] Hampson, *Maximilien Robespierre*, p. 218.

[75] Herriot, *Lyon n'est plus*, iii. 503–4.

[76] Letters of Laporte to Couthon, 24 germinal, and Reverchon to Couthon, 21, 27, 29 germinal, 7 floréal, in Courtois, *Rapport ... de la commission*, pp. 310, 311–13, 320.

[77] Robespierre did not actually name Fouché in his speeches on Lyon (see above, n. 82), but the attacks on the persecutors of the *amis* and on the Commission Temporaire were clearly directed against the former. ('A Commune-Affranchie, les aristocrates ont calomnié les amis de Chalier, en les traitant d'Hébertistes ... [Robespierre] regardait comme conspirateurs ceux qui poursuivraient les amis de Chalier' (*Jacobins*, vi. 37).)

Fouché's leading role in the intrigues which brought down the Robespierrists needs no elaboration here.

The last meeting of the Jacobin Club of Lyon was on 14 thermidor
(1 August 1794) and its main business was to draft a letter, signed by
Achard, praising the Convention's recent victory over the conspirators
and their allies in the Committee of Public Safety: 'la République est
encore une fois sauvée'.[78] Revolutionary orthodoxy triumphed over
loyalty to Robespierre, but the new order had no place for the *exaltés* of
Commune-Affranchie. On 6 fructidor Reverchon and Laporte, having
dissolved the Société Populaire des Jacobins de Commune-Affranchie,
created a new *noyau* to establish another. Amongst the twenty-six names
were three of the early Rolandin *patriotes*, the surgeon Michel Carret,
Perret, formerly director of the Mint and acting mayor in 1792, and
another surgeon, Grandchamp, who had served a term as president of
the Club Central during the constitutional monarchy. The others included
a teacher, an artist, a third surgeon, a *fabricant voyageur*, formerly *commis
aux domaines royales*, three military officers, two officials, two linen-
drapers, an apothecary, two gilders, and two *dessinateurs*, who belonged
to the élite of the old Fabrique. Only one was an ordinary silk-weaver.
These men were to determine the composition of the new club and to
assist in a purge of the administrations.[79] As elsewhere, Thermidor began
the process of restoring full political control to the *honnêtes gens* and the
hommes à talent.

SOME OUTCOMES

The Jacobins made Lyon pay a heavy price for the revolt which their
own policies had done so much to provoke. Estimates of the number of
people executed there during the Terror vary from 1,876 to 1,907, 11 per
cent of the victims in the whole of France.[80] At least twice as many people

---

[78] AC I²6, 139.

[79] *Au nom du peuple français: Les Représentants du peuple envoyés à Commune-Affranchie
pour y faire cesser l'oppression ... Reverchon et Laporte* (Commune-Affranchie, year II), 6–
7. For the occupational identification, see also AD 1L203, list of the Comité Révolutionnaire
of the *canton* of la Convention, 3 vendémiaire, year III.

[80] Based on Greer's figure (16,954) in *The Incidence of the Terror*, p. 26. On the various
estimates of the numbers executed in Lyon, see D. L. Longfellow, 'The Silk Weavers of
Lyon', Ph.D. thesis (Johns Hopkins University, 1979), p. 330, and H. Pelat and M. Cayrol,
'Tableau de la Contre-Révolution à Lyon d'après 1901 condamnations à mort prononcées
à la suite du siège de la ville', DES thesis (Université de Lyon, n.d.). The discrepancies
appear to arise from doubts about how many of those sentenced to death managed to escape
execution.

were held as suspects for varying periods and underwent the ordeal of judgement by the Revolutionary Tribunal.[81] Together with the *noyades* at Nantes and the trials of the 'factions' in Paris, this death-toll—and the *mitraillades*—did much to attach the stigma of brutality to the Revolution and the Jacobins, to turn European opinion against both, and to isolate those outside France who could be linked with Jacobinism.

It was not mass murder, however, for it was carried out according to laws enacted by the National Convention, and could even be justified by laws passed before the expulsion of the Girondins, such as those of 16 December 1792, which made threatening the unity of the Republic a capital offence.[82] Nor was it indiscriminate slaughter, though the lack of defence lawyers or appeal procedures, together with pressure to lift the rate of executions, obviously increased the risk of innocent people being convicted. Judgements by the Commission Révolutionnaire produced 1,673 executions in the twenty weeks between its formation on 7 frimaire (27 November) and the suspension of its activities on 24 germinal (13 April), whereas the two tribunals it replaced had taken eight weeks to produce 213 executions.[83] But even this rapid-fire tribunal took some care to discriminate between guilt and innocence. As Lefebvre pointed out, the Commission acquitted 29 per cent of defendants in Frimaire, 48 per cent in Nivôse, and 60 per cent in Pluviôse, 1,252 as against 1,322 convictions.[84] There was preliminary interrogation of prisoners, and there was a great deal of documentary evidence to identify those involved in the revolt, evidence which, according to the best study of this question, the Commission Révolutionnaire consulted regularly.[85] It was not prepared to act blindly on the evidence provided by the *Comités révolutionnaires*, which was just as well if we accept the denunciations of the latter by Fouché, Laporte, and Reverchon. But there are some indications that the committees, too, were not as wilfully vindictive as has been maintained. Like the Commission Révolutionnaire, their job was to apply extremely harsh laws which defined indictable behaviour very loosely. On some occasions they made arrests reluctantly, and tried to minimize the significance of an offence. The committees provided lengthy moral portraits

---

[81] See Longfellow, 'The Silk Weavers of Lyon', p. 331.

[82] See Greer, *The Incidence of the Terror*, pp. 13–14.

[83] Based on the figures in Glover, *Collection complète des jugements rendus par la Commission révolutionnaire etablié à Lyon par les représentants du peuple en 1793–1794* (Lyon, 1869), 1–45.

[84] Lefebvre, *Compte rendu* of *Lyon n'est plus*, p. 74.

[85] Mansfield, 'The Missions of Collot d'Herbois', pp. 370–81. See also Herriot, *Lyon n'est plus*, iii. 136.

of their prisoners. Bataillon-Affranchie (Port du Temple) agonized over Lafont *aîné*, 'd'abord zélé patriote', who erred only on the eve of 29 May, when 'l'on le vit avec étonnement dévier et parler un langage *modéré*'. Finally it decided 'qu'il n'est point assez habile à intriguer'. Mitigating circumstances were frequently reported. Georges Rémi, painter, 'très pauvre, ayant le défaut de boire et inconséquent dans ses actions et ses propos'; Perronneau *père*, 'un peu dévot, mais d'une conscience pure, peu éclairé sur la révolution, a tombé facilement dans l'erreur'; Louis-Gaspard Rivoiron, officer in the 'federalist' army, 'n'est pas riche, et trop bête pour être un contre-révolutionaire'.[86] Personal relationships and money may often have had a part in these appeals for clemency, just as they may have influenced arrests and denunciations. The only certain conclusion is that the committees provided information in favour of many defendants, as well as describing their alleged crimes against the Revolution.

All that said, it remains that this was an ideological crusade and that the terrorist authorities were prone to equate anti-Jacobinism with counter-revolution. The repressive laws offered plenty of scope for condemning people merely for verbal attacks on the Convention. Billemaz, the founder of the clubs, seems to have taken no part in the rebellion, but he was still executed as 'un contre-révolutionnaire enragé', presumably for his pronounced anti-Jacobinism in 1792–3 and for his associations with Roland.[87] The circumstances of the year II certainly provided opportunities to pursue vendettas by political denunciation.

Some final general points can be made about the repression of Lyon. It was above all an exercise in what might be called high Jacobinism, the Jacobinism of the great committees which aimed single-mindedly to consolidate the Republic by force. It was not allowed to become an assault on the propertied classes *per se*, despite all the socio-political rhetoric against the rich. On 10 nivôse the Jacobin Ozet complained 'qu'on a délivré ce jour d'hui des millionnaires, des nobles contre-révolutionnaires', and proposed that to prevent such abuses the Commission Révolutionnaire should post lists of those acquitted each week. The motion was rejected out of hand, and the proposer was attacked for impugning revolutionary justice.[88] The rich were under particular suspicion of economic as well as political crimes, and so they were more

---

[86] AD 42L101, ds. 4, 7, 8, 11, 12; 42L100, d. B39.

[87] A. Portallier, *Tableau général des victimes et martyrs de la Révolution en Lyonnais, Forez et Beaujolais* (Saint-Étienne, 1911), 41.

[88] AD 34L9, Société Populaire des Jacobins de Commune-Affranchie, minutes.

likely to be arrested. They may also have been less likely to be acquitted,[89] but then they had been more involved in the revolt. Evidence from two recent studies is consistent with Greer's general conclusion that the Terror had little to do with class war,[90] even though some Lyonnais Jacobins would have welcomed one.

So the exercise in repression at Lyon achieved its main aim, the extermination of large numbers of people involved in the revolt. But this book has argued that Jacobin policies were the main cause of revolt, and that it is misleading to mount a defence of the siege and its aftermath as having been necessary to save the Republic from its enemies. Intimidation was probably called for to discourage disruption of the war effort, to limit the extent of protest against Jacobin policy, and to extract taxes, labour, and other resources on the unprecedented scale of the year II. Undoubtedly, there was hostility to the revolutionary government in many provincial towns. But many severe measures of intimidation had already been taken by October 1793, both by legislation and by popular punitive action. The 'federalist' movement had collapsed ignominiously; the Jacobin Constitution had been accepted overwhelmingly. It is difficult to see how the level of violence used in Lyon could have been needed as a deterrent. Rather, it appears as a product of the paranoia which pervaded the leading Jacobins' thinking, their routine mistrust of the *aristocratie mercantile*, and their contempt for Lyon. This led them first to multiply the internal enemies of the Republic and then to kill them in a repression which cannot be seen in the terms sometimes used to characterize the Terror as a rational response to real threats.[91]

There is no disputing the general effectiveness of the Committee of Public Safety as a wartime government, but its policy towards Lyon must be regarded as a costly blunder. Estimating the costs would require extensive study of the drastic economic decline caused by the loss of population—both through emigration and an increased death-rate, particularly in the appalling winter of 1795—the disorganization of industry, and endemic violence, criminal and political. This last reached a peak in the White Terror of 1795 and contributed greatly to the Directoire's

[89] See Longfellow, 'The Silk Weavers of Lyon', pp. 334–6.

[90] Ibid.; Mansfield, 'The Missions of Collot d'Herbois', pp. 420–2. Mansfield points out that the proportion of victims of the Terror in Lyon who came from Greer's 'upper middle class' was lower than in several other départements, including the Seine (p. 421).

[91] See R. R. Palmer, *The World of the French Revolution* (London, 1971), 115. It should be emphasized that Professor Palmer was discussing the Terror in general here, and that he believed the excesses at Lyon to have been a perversion of the government's policy.

failure to stabilize the Republic. For most of the 1790s, local government in Lyon and its region was virtually paralysed. Another consequence, ironically, was 'une opposition politique à la centralisation française et à Paris, coupable d'avoir voulu faire un exemple aux dépens du Lyonnais'.[92]

In one respect, however, the Terror and its aftermath helped to achieve an important objective of 1789, that of equating power and property. In Lyon this link had been threatened by the emergence of popular politics in a particularly spirited form, and by the political education of large numbers of the *menu peuple*. The 'federalist' repression struck one blow at the Lyonnais popular movement by destroying the clubs, and the *représentants en mission* a still more damaging one by their abolition of the *sections* as units of political action.

White Terror continued the process of destruction, this time by eliminating many of those who had used the popular democratic movement as a springboard to municipal office. Murder gangs decimated the *sans-culottes* who had been in public office in 1792 and 1793. Some left Lyon for the relative safety of the *faubourgs*, the countryside, or towns further afield, but a decree of 5 ventôse, year III (23 February 1795) confined Jacobins who had been public officials in 1793–4 to the *communes* in which they had held office. This allowed them to be dealt with at their enemies' leisure, particularly after the anti-terrorist Comité Révolutionnaire of Lyon ordered that lists of residents, written in 'caractères très lisibles', should be posted near the entrance of every building 'à une hauteur commode'. Those taken to prison to await trial for abuses of power could be killed either on the way there, while their National Guard escorts turned a blind eye, or in the prisons themselves, where the murder gangs operated with impunity in the spring of 1795. Louis Dubois, Claude Vital, Jean Roullot, Roullot's wife, and J.-B. Carteron were killed in the great prison massacres of 14–17 floréal, year III; Roux (a *notable* in 1792–3), Joseph Fernex, and Charles Turin were victims of separate murders during the year III.[93] In various ways, then, the 'federalists', the Montagnards, and the White Terrorists all helped to diminish the threats from below which had deprived the propertied classes of full political supremacy during the early years of the Revolution at Lyon.

[92] M. Garden, 'La Révolution et l'Empire', in A. Latreille (ed.), *Histoire de Lyon et du Lyonnais* (Toulouse, 1975), 302. On the problems of the later 1790s, see Fuoc, *La Réaction thermidorienne*; R. Cobb, *Reactions to the French Revolution* (Oxford, 1972).

[93] On 7 brumaire, year II, the *Comités de canton* had been replaced by a single Comité Révolutionnaire de Surveillance du District de Lyon (see Fuoc, *La Réaction thermidorienne*, pp. 69–70, and on the massacres, pp. 63, 76, 122–96).

APPENDIX I

The Distribution of Poverty in Lyon, 1790–1793

Section	Population in 1794[a]	No. aided by the Société Philanthropique in 1790[b]
Saint-Georges	3,578	2,190
Le Gourgillon	5,175	743
Porte-Froc	4,084	1,360
Place Neuve	3,284	976
Le Change	2,966	994
La Juiverie	3,605	1,300
Port Saint-Paul	3,412	1,172
Pierre-Scize	3,171	1,050
Saint-Vincent I	2,971 ⎫	
Saint-Vincent II	2,503 ⎭	1,440
La Grande-Côte I	2,676 ⎫	
La Grande-Côte II	3,239 ⎭	1,500
Le Griffon I and II	4,069	745
Les Terreaux	3,253	220
La Pêcherie	3,339	390
Place Saint-Pierre	2,888	265
Le Plâtre	4,096	477
Rue Neuve	3,496	545
Saint-Nizier	3,616	170
Rue Tupin	2,800	175
La Croisette	2,637	562
Rue Buisson	2,523	400
Bon-Rencontre	2,192	484
Plat-d'Argent	2,675	650
Rue Thomassin	2,448	424
Port du Temple	3,201	299
Place Confort	3,579	500
L'Hôtel-Dieu	3,503	750
Belle-Cordière	3,032	500
Bellecour I	3,728 ⎫	
Bellecour II	3,551 ⎭	1,600

Appendix I—*contd.*

By *Canton*	Average estimated rental value of houses (1791)[c]	No. granted tax relief in 1793 because of indigence[d]
Nord-Ouest	1,580	78
Nord-Est	3,780	83
Hôtel-Commun	3,500	12
Halle-aux-Blés	2,740	79
Hôtel-Dieu	2,630	85
Fédération	4,310	35
Métropole	1,300	359
Ancienne-Ville	—	144
Montagne	—	184

[a] Figures based on the census completed in January 1794. (See C. Riffaterre, *Le Mouvement anti-jacobin et anti-parisien à Lyon et dans le Rhône-et-Loire en 1793* (Lyon, 1912–28), i. 104–5.)

[b] J.-P. Gutton, *La Société et les pauvres: L'exemple de la généralité de Lyon* (Paris, 1970), 55.

[c] From M. Garden, *Lyon et les Lyonnais au XVIIIe siècle* (Paris, 1970), 23.

[d] *CM*, iv. 426 (26 July 1793).

APPENDIX II

The Silk-Weaving, Hat-Making, and Stocking-Weaving *quartiers*, 1788–1789

Quartier	Population in 1794	No. of Workshop masters 1788–9	Compagnons	Average rental value of workshops (*livres*)
Silk-weaving				
Saint-Georges	3,578	472	—	105.5
Porte-Froc	4,084	314	—	—
Port Saint-Paul	3,412	492	—	—
Pierre-Scize	3,171	462	—	81.4
La Juiverie	3,605	297	—	—
Le Change	2,966	204	—	—
La Grande-Côte	5,915	705	—	159.5
Saint-Vincent	5,474	549	—	159.6
Bon-Rencontre	2,192	235	—	—
Bellecour	7,279	200	—	—
Rue Buisson	2,523	102	—	—
Plat-d'Argent	2,675	152	—	—
Hat-making [a]				
Place Confort	3,579	9	247	—
Rue Thomassin	2,448	9	244	—
Belle-Cordière	3,032	11	351	—
Bon-Rencontre	2,192	17	420	—
Bellecour	7,279	13	358	—
Place Confort	3,579	94	46	—
Belle-Cordière	3,032	38	66	—
Bon-Recontre	2,192	77	59	—
L'Hôtel-Dieu	3,503	75	68	—

Source: AC I², 46 *bis*.

[a] *Quartiers* with over 250 master and *compagnon* hatters.
[b] *Quartiers* with over 100 master and *compagnon* weavers.

Relative Affluence of the *sections* of Lyon[a]

A		B	
(1)	(2)	(1)	(2)
Less than 5%	More than 20%	5–10%	15–20%
Saint-Georges	*Saint-Georges*	Le Gourguillon	*Rue Belle-Cordière*
Port Saint-Paul	*Port Saint-Paul*	Porte-Froc	Rue Buisson
La Juiverie	*La Juiverie*	Place Neuve	Rue Neuve
Pierre-Scize	*Pierre-Scize*	Le Change	Le Griffon
Saint-Vincent	*Saint-Vincent*	La Pêcherie	*La Pêcherie*
La Grande-Côte	*La Grande-Côte*	La Croisette	
L'Hôtel-Dieu	*L'Hôtel-Dieu*	Bon-Rencontre	
Rue Belle-Cordière	*Le Change*	Plat d'-Argent	
	Place Neuve	*Rue Thomassin*	*Rue Thomassin*
	La Croisette	Port du Temple	
	Bon-Recontre	Place Confort	
	Plat-d' Argent	Bellecour	
	Porte-Froc		

C		D	
(1)	(2)	(1)	(2)
10–15%	10–15%	More than 15%	Under 10%
Les Terreaux	Le Gourguillon	*Place Saint-Pierre*	*Place Saint-Pierre*
Le Plâtre	*Le Plâtre*		*Les Terreaux*
Rue Neuve			*Saint-Nizier*
Saint-Nizier	Place Confort		Bellecour
Rue Tupin	*Rue Tupin*		Port du Temple
Rue Buisson			
Le Griffon			

[a] Two criteria have been used to determine the relative affluence of the *sections* of Lyon at the time of the Revolution: (1) the percentage of *éligibles* according to the table in AD 1L332–5, Élections 1790–1; (2) the percentage of the population given assistance by the Société Philanthropique in 1789 (from J.-P. Gutton, *La Société et les pauvres: L'exemple de la généralité de Lyon 1534–1789* (Paris, 1970), 55). The only census giving population figures per *section* was completed in January 1794 (see C. Riffaterre, *Le Mouvement anti-jacobin et anti-parisien à Lyon et dans le Rhone-et-Loire en 1793* (Lyon, 1912–28), i. 105). In view of

the lapse of time between the various sets of figures used, this ranking should be regarded as a rough guide only.

The *sections* have been grouped in ascending order of affluence. Those in italics appear twice under A and/or B or C and/or D, and so can be classified as 'poor' or 'wealthy' with some confidence.

Changes in the *sections* of Origin of Municipal Councillors (including the Mayor and *procureur*), 1790–1792

	1790	1791	1792
Poorest sections *(classified under both A(1) and A(2))*			
Saint-Georges (1)		1	1
Port Saint-Paul (7)			1
La Juiverie (6)	1		1
Pierre-Scize (8)		1	2
Saint-Vincent I, II (9, 10)	1	1	1
La Grand-Côte (11, 12)			3
L'Hôtel-Dieu (29)		1	1
TOTAL	2	4	10
Sections *classified under A and/or B*			
Rue Thomassin (26)	1		1
Rue Belle-Cordière (30)			3
La Pêcherie (16)		1	
Le Change (5)			
Place Neuve (4)	1	1	
La Croisette (22)			
Bon-Rencontre (24)			1
Plat-d'Argent (25)			
Porte-Froc (3)	3		
TOTAL	5	2	5
Sections *classified under B and under C or D*			
Port du Temple (27)		3	
Place Confort (28)			1
Le Gourguillon (2)			
Bellecour I, II (31, 32)	7	3	
Rue Buisson (23)	2		
Rue Neuve (19)	2	1	
Le Griffon I, II (14, 13)		1	4
TOTAL	11	8	5

	1790	1791	1792
Sections *classified under C and D*			
Les Terreaux (15)		1	
Le Plâtre (15)	1	2	1
Saint-Nizier (20)	1	2	
Rue Tupin (21)	2	1	1
Place Saint-Pierre (17)	4	6	2
TOTAL	4	6	2

[a] Two councillors were from the *faubourg* of la Guillotière which was attached to Lyon in 1791.

APPENDIX V

Municipalité of Lyon, March 1790[a]

	Occupation	Rent Assessment (livres)	Section[b]
Mayor			
Fleury-Zacharie-Simon Palerne de Savy	ex-*conseiller* in the Cour des Monnaies	600	31
Procureur			
Jean François Dupuis	lawyer	400	3
Municipal Officers			
Jérôme Maisonneuve*	merchant hatter	600	31
Mathieu-Marc-Antoine Nolhac	ex-*échevin*	750	3
Jean-Baptiste Dupont	*négociant*	450	19
André Lagier	bourgeois		9
Louis Felissent *l'aîné*	*négociant*	850	18
Jos. Fulchiron	banker	1,000	19
Luc Candy	mercer	400	21
Jacques-Fr. Vauberet-Jacquier	ex-*échevin*	1,000	31
Jos. Vachon	baker	200	21
Jos. Vidalin	*négociant*	410	23
Jean-Marie Bruyset *fils aîné*	*imprimeur du Roi*	1,400	31
Jos.-Marie Goudard *le jeune*	*négociant*	335	32
Jos. Courbon	*custode-curé* of Ste-Croix		
Claude-Jn-Marie Dervieu de Varey	bourgeois	1,600	31
Jn-Pre Granier *l'aîné*	*négociant*		31
Claude Charmetton *l'aîné*	*négociant*		26
Jn-Marie Servan *l'aîné*	draper	100	20
Louis Berthelet*	bourgeois	300	6
P.-A. Faure	*négociant*	1,200	23
Jn-Fois Vitet	*avocat*	800	3

Note: * denotes *patriotes*

[a] The material for these tables has been compiled from *Procès-verbaut des séances des corps municipaux de la ville de Lyon, 1787–an VIII*, 4 vols. (Lyon, 1900–1904), and AC G, *Contribution mobilière*, 1791.

[b] See Appendix IV for the corresponding names of the *sections*.

Municipalité of Lyon, December 1791

	Occupation	Rent Assessment (livres)	*Section*
Mayor			
Louis Vitet*	physician	900	29
Procureur			
Luc-Antoine de Rozière de Champagneux*	*avocat*	500	4
Municipal officers			
Claude Arnaud-Tizon *cadet**	linen-draper	900	20
Claude Bonnard	master stocking-weaver		8
Denis Breton			34
Claude Carron	silk-weaver		9
Joseph Chalier*	*négociant*	320	19
Jean-François Chalon	silk-weaver		21
Antoine Chapuy*	shoemaker		18
Gilbert Combe-Pachot	*négociant*	800	18
Joseph-Honoré Curet			33
Toussaint Gleyze			27
Antoine Henri	master stocking-weaver		1
François-Joseph Lange*	'artiste'		31
Eusèbe Morénas*	mercer	150	27
Antoine Nivière Chol	*négociant*	800	13
Jean-François Perret	controller of the Mint	400	27
Nicholas-Simon Picard	mercer		15
Joseph Rivaux	commission agent		20
Jean-Marie Roland*	inspector of manu-factures		31
Jean-Antoine Sicard*	mercantile broker	300	16
Antoine Vingtrinier*	furrier	1,000	32

Note: * denotes Rolandins.

Appendix V—*contd*.

Municipalité of Lyon, December 1792

	Occupation	Rent Assessment (livres)	*Section*
Mayor			
Antoine Nivière-Chol*	*négociant*	800	13
Procureur			
François-Auguste Laussel	ex-priest, journalist		
Municipal officers			
Louis Bédor	silk-weaver	10	11
Antoine-Marie Bertrand	*négociant*	100	18
Dominique Bicon	silk-weaver	20	8
Jean-Marie Biolet		600	9
Etienne Boyet	gauze-weaver	50	29
Pierre Chazot	stocking-weaver	50	7
Jean-Jos. Destéphanis	printer's clerk	70	26
Louis Dubois	silk-weaver	70	1
François Francalet		100	24
Toussaint Gleyze*	*négociant*	360	6
Claude Gravier	vinegar-maker	80	30
Jean-François Milou	taxation clerk	240	21
Vincent Noel	actor	200	11
Jean Richard	bookkeeper	150	10
Gilbert Roch	second-hand furniture-dealer	30	11
Jean Sallier	*rentier*	216	14
Odo Sautemouche	ink-retailer	120	28
Charles Turin	stocking-weaver	45	30
Thomas Villard	hatter	60	30
Julien Vanrisamburgh*	*négociant*	1,080	13

Note: * denotes Rolandins.

APPENDIX VI

Sectional Politics, 1791–1793

	The National Guard controversy, June 1791[a]	Payment of municipal officers, Oct. 1792[b]	The Anti-Appelant campaign, Mar. 1793 (Clubs)[c]	Permanent before May 1793[d]	Large-scale disarmament and/or collective repentance after 29 May 1793[e]
Poorest sections					
Saint Georges			Xc	*	X
Port Saint-Paul	Xc (& *section*)	X	Xc	*	X
La Juiverie	Xc			*	X
Pierre-Scize	Xc				X
Saint-Vincent I	Xc ⎱	X	Xc	*[?]	
Saint-Vincent II		X	Xc		
La Grande-Côte I	Xc ⎱	X			
La Grande-Côte II		X		*	
L'Hôtel Dieu	Xc	X	Xc		
Sections *classified under A and/or B*					
Rue Thomassin		X	Xc		
Rue Belle-Cordiere	Xc	X		*	X
La Pêcherie	Xc	X		*	
Le Change		X		*	
Place Neuve	Xc	X		*	
La Croisette					
Bon-Rencontre		X	(Xc)		X
Plat-d'Argent	Xc	X	Xc		X
Porte-Froc		X	(Xc)	*	

Sections classified under B and C or D

Port du Temple	*		*	
Place Confort	X			X
Le Gourguillon	Xc			
Bellecour I	*		*	
Bellecour II	*		*[?]	
Rue Buisson			*	
Rue Neuve	*		*	
Le Griffon I	*		*	
Le Griffon II	*		*	

Sections classified under C and D

Les Terreaux	Xc	*
La Plâtre	*	*
Saint-Nizier	*Xc	*
Rue Tupin	*	*
Place Saint-Pierre	*	(Xc)

Key: X = *patriote*, pro-Jacobin; * = pro-Département, anti-Jacobin; ( ) = club split; c = club.

a AC 1L818, Organisation de la Garde nationale, délibérations des sections, 17 June 1791; AD 31L20, fo. 36, minutes of Port Saint-Paul, 17 June 1791.

b AN DIII216, d. 4, extract from the minutes of the Municipalité of Lyon, 29 Oct. 1792.

c C. Riffaterre, *Le Mouvement anti-jacobin et anti-parisien à Lyon et dans le Rhône-et-Loire en 1793* (Lyon, 1912–28), i. 44–5.

d *CM*, iv. 100 (18 Feb. 1793) (for Saint-Nizier, Place Neuve, Rue Neuve, la Pêcherie, Place Saint-Pierre, les Terreaux, le Griffon I, Porte-Froc); ibid. 104 (18 Feb.) (for la Juiverie); *Extrait des registres de la section de la Convention* (Lyon, 1793) (for Port du Temple, Griffon II); AD 31L20, minutes of Port Saint-Paul, 27 May 1793 (also for le Plâtre, la Croisette, Rue Buisson, la Grande-Côte II, Rue Tupin, Saint-Vincent (which division is not specified); AN AFII43, plaq. 339, no. 26, extract from the minutes of the Département of Rhône-et-Loire, 26 May 1793 (for Saint-Georges and Bellecour I); Cost MS 610, interrogation of J.-J. Pascal, *avoué*, 5 Mar. 1793 (for le Change).

e AD 31L34, report by the Comité de Surveillance of le Plâtre, 10 June 1793 (for Saint-Georges); 31L20, fos. 88, 91, minutes of Port Saint-Paul, 2, 3 June 1793 (for Bon-Rencontre, la Juiverie, Plat-d'Argent); 31L21, fo. 2, minutes of Port Saint-Paul, 8 June 1793 (for Pierre-Scize); 31L2, fo. 1, minutes of la Croisette, 1 June 1793 (for la Fédération II); 31L49, fos. 3, 10, minutes of Plat-d'Argent, 3, 11 June 1793 (for Belle-Cordière, le Gourguillon); 31L41, fo. 21, minutes of l'Hôtel-Dieu, 31 May

APPENDIX VII

Commissaires de surveillance, May–June 1793
(elected 19 May in 17 dissident *sections*)

Name	Occupation	*Section*
Albert *père*, J.-A. (RE)	ironmonger	Port du Temple
Allegret, P.-N. (E)	silk-weaver	Port Saint-Paul
Assada, L.-B.	silk-weaver	Port Saint-Paul
Bavet, J.-A.	factor	Port Saint-Paul
Benoit, Pierre[a](E)	silk-weaver	Port Saint-Paul
Boullet, Pierre	silk-weaver	Saint-Georges
Bourdon	silk-weaver	Le Change
Bouvard, Jacques[b](E)	*rentier*	Place Saint-Pierre
Brachet, Jean	handkerchief-merchant	La Croisette
Bret, François[c]	bookseller	Rue Neuve
Bonand	grocer	Rue Buisson
Bruno (E)	commission agent	Le Change
Buis	joiner	Le Plâtre
Caby, Jean[d]	stocking-weaver	Port Saint-Paul
Chantre, Claude (E)	stocking-weaver	La Croisette
Chazat, Jacques	notary	Rue Neuve
Choulet, Ignace[c] (E)	*pâtissier*	La Juiverie
Clapisson, Georges	stocking-weaver	La Croisette
Corderier, François (E)	gilt-merchant	Le Plâtre
Creppu, Claude (E)	lace-merchant	La Croisette
Delamorte, Antoine[e]	leather-merchant	Le Change
Delorme, Denis[f] (E)	factor	Le Change
Dervieu	jeweller	Saint-Nizier
Deschaux[g]	commission agent	Rue Neuve
Duter	millwright	La Croisette
Favel *aîné*, M.[h] (E)	locksmith	Rue Neuve
Floret *cadet*, J.-B.[i] (E)	*négociant*	Saint-Vincent (I)
Fourcherau, J.-B.	jeweller	Saint-Nizier
Gaillard, Antoine	silk-weaver	Port Saint-Paul
Gardiveau, Etienne	builder	Port Saint-Paul
Gerin, Camille	surveyor	Rue Neuve
Gleyze *cadet*, Joseph (E)	*rentier*	Port du Temple
Gonnet, Dominique[j] (E)	ex-*procureur*	La Juiverie

Appendix VII—*contd.*

Name	Occupation	*Section*
Goiran, André[k] (RE)	merchant commission agent	Rue Neuve
Grangier (E)	*marchand-fabricant*	Saint-Vincent II
Greppo, Jacques (E)	farrier	La Croisette
Guillon	*négociant*	Saint-Vincent II
Gutton, Philibert (E)	*marchand-fabricant*	La Grande-Côte II
Hivert	scrivener	Les Terreaux
Jacob, Charles-Joseph[l] (E)	*négociant*	Le Plâtre
Jarnieux, Alexis	*ouvrier*	Saint-Vincent I
Jouty, Joseph (E)	*rentier*	Saint-Vincent II
Lacour, J.-C.	turner	Port Saint-Paul
Lecuyer *père*	linen-draper	Rue Neuve
Martin, Pierre	merchant tailor	Le Change
Martinon *aîné*[m]	*négociant*	La Croisette
Michaud *aîné*, Jacques	mason	Saint-Vincent II
Mignard, A.-M. (E)	fan-merchant	Place Saint-Pierre
Mignot	mercer	La Croisette
Monnet, Denis	silk-weaver	Port Saint-Paul
Pariat, Louis (E)	grocer	Port du Temple
Pascal, J.-J. (E)	*avoué*	Place Neuve
Patreday	tailor	Port Saint-Paul
Labry *dit* Petit (E)	carpenter	Saint-Nizier
Poncet, Antoine	silk-weaver	Port Saint-Paul
Ricard, G.-A.[n] (E)	*négociant*	Les Terreaux
Roland, Claude	*grammairien*	La Juiverie
Romany, J.-A.	silk-weaver	Le Plâtre
Rossignol	silk-weaver	Saint-Vincent II
Rousset, Claude	silk-weaver	Port Saint-Paul
Thierry, Jean (E)	mercer	Rue Tupin
Vasseras, Joseph	silk-weaver	Saint-Vincent II
Vincent, François	*rentier*	Place Saint-Pierre
Willermoz, Antoine	*négociant* mercer	Rue Buisson

Note: R = signed royalist petition, June 1792 (AN F[lc] III, Rhône 6). E = éligible in 1790.

[a] Lieutenant in the National Guard, 1790 (AD 31L20, fo. 3, minutes of Port Saint-Paul, 19 Jan. 1790); chosen as elector, 25 May 1791 (ibid. fo. 13).

[b] Rector of the *Charité*, 1789 (*Almanach*, 1792).

[c] Captains in the National Guard, 1790 (*CM*, i. 229 (30 Jan. 1790)).

[d] Often elected secretary or president in sectional assemblies from 1791 to 1793 (AD 31L20, fos. 37–73, July 1791–Feb. 1793).

[e] Société Philanthropique, 1792 (*Almanach*, 1792).

ᶠ *Notable* 1791–2 (*Almanach*, 1792), president of the Tribunal de Commerce, Nov. 1792 (*CM*, iv. 20 (14 Dec. 1792).

ᵍ *Commissaire* of the Société Philanthropique, 1792 (*Almanach*, 1792).

ʰ *Notable*, 1791–2 (*Almanach*, 1792); *maître-garde* of the locksmiths' guild, 1789 (*Almanach*, 1789).

ⁱ Captain in the National Guard, 1790 (*CM*, i. 221 (26 Jan. 1790)).

ʲ *Syndic des procureurs aux cours de Lyon* in 1789 (*Almanach*, 1789).

ᵏ President of the Société Philanthropique of Rue Neuve, 1792 (*Almanach*, 1792); Captain in the National Guard, 1790 (*CM*, i. 221 (26 Jan. 1790).

ˡ Rector of the Hôtel-Dieu, 1781–3 (*Almanach*, 1789).

ᵐ Captain in the *National Guard*, 1790 (*CM*, i. 20 (11 Feb. 1790)).

ⁿ *Conseiller*, Département de Rhône-et-Loire (*Almanach*, 1792).

APPENDIX VIII

Organized Anti-Jacobinism in Early 1793

Anti-Jacobin Clubs, March–May 1793 (those in italics were in Central Lyon)

March

Le Plâtre, La Croisette, Rue Tupin, Saint-Nizier, Place Saint-Pierre, La Pêcherie (AC I²4, d. 45, fo. 42, 10 Mar. 1793), Le Griffon I, Saint-Georges (ibid., fo. 44, minutes of La Croisette, 26 Mar. 1 Apr. 1793).

May

(In addition to the above) Place Neuve, Le Gourguillon, Le Change, *Rue Buisson, Rue Thomassin, Port du Temple, La Fédération, Les Terreaux*, La Grande-Côte, Port Saint-Paul (ibid., fos. 51–2 (5–7 May 1793)).

Anti-Jacobin sections, *February–May 1793*

February

Le Plâtre, Saint Nizier, La Pêcherie, Rue Neuve, le Griffon (I and *II, Place Saint-Pierre*, les Terreaux, Saint-Vincent, la Juiverie, Place Neuve (*CM*, iv. 100, 104 (18 Feb. 1793)).

May

Le Plâtre, Saint-Nizier, la Pêcherie, Rue Neuve, le Griffon I and *II, Port du Temple*, Porte-Froc, *Rue Tupin, Bellecour I, la Croisette, Rue Buisson*, la Grande-Côte II, Saint-Georges, *Place Saint-Pierre*, le Change (*Département*, ii. 296–7, 299, 303, 305–8 (25, 26, 28 May)), Port Saint-Paul, Saint-Vincent (AD 31L20, minutes of Port Saint-Paul, 27 May 1793)). (The documentation on this point is very patchy and the number of *sections* involved was almost certainly higher.)

Anti-Jacobin sectional personnel in Lyon, May–June 1793

	Population of cantons (%)	*Commissaires surveillants*, May–June	Provisional Municipalité, list of 4 June	Sectional personnel, June
Nobles	4.6	—	—	4 (6.5)
Clergy		—	—	3 (4.8)
Upper bourgeoisie	22.1	18 (28.1)	20 (50.0)	34 (54.8)
Merchants		16 (25.0)	4 (10.0)	5 (8.1)
Lesser professions, clerks	5.7	3 (4.7)	8 (20.0)	7 (11.3)
Artisans and *boutiquiers*	22.3	14 (21.9)	7 (17.5)	5 (8.1)
Silk-weavers	27.0	12 (18.7)	—	3 (4.8)
Journaliers, servants	18.2	1 (1.6)	1 (2.5)	1 (1.6)
TOTAL	99.9	64 (100.0)	40 (100.0)	62 (100.0)

Note: In view of the well-known difficulties of deducing social and economic status from occupational descriptions, this and the other tables should be interpreted with caution.

APPENDIX X

Support for the Rebellion after June

Anti-Jacobin sectional personnel in Lyon, 1793 (% in brackets)

	Population of cantons (%)	June–July only	In office for over a month after July 1	In office during siege (8 Aug.–9 Oct.)	In office June–Mid Sept.	All holders of sectional office
Nobles	4.6	0	5 (10.4)	1 (1.6)	2 (2.3)	8 (2.3)
Clergy		1 (1.3)	0	5 (7.9)	3 (3.4)	12 (3.4)
Upper bourgeoisie	22.1	35 (46.0)	26 (54.2)	32 (50.8)	29 (33.3)	148 (42.4)
Merchants		11 (14.5)	9 (18.8)	12 (19.0)	22 (25.3)	66 (18.9)
Lesser professions, clerks	5.7	3 (3.9)	3 (6.2)	4 (6.3)	4 (4.6)	23 (6.6)
Artisans and *boutiquiers*	22.3	12 (15.8)	3 (6.2)	6 (9.5)	17 (19.5)	55 (15.8)
Silk-weavers	27.0	12 (15.8)	2 (4.2)	3 (4.8)	8 (9.2)	28 (8.0)
Journaliers	18.2	2 (2.6)	0	0	2 (2.3)	9 (2.6)
TOTAL	99.9	76 (99.9)	48 (100.0)	63 (99.9)	87 (99.9)	349 (100.0)

The 'Federalist' Army

	Rank unknown	Fusiliers below the rank of captain	Grenadiers below the rank of captain	Fusiliers above the rank of captain	Grenadiers above the rank of captain
Nobles	10 (5.4)	12 (2.5)	6 (1.2)	4 (3.7)	27 (26.2)
Clergy	1 (0.5)	9 (1.9)	1 (0.2)	0	0
Upper bourgeoisie	22 (11.8)	61 (12.9)	50 (9.9)	35 (32.1)	22 (21.4)
Merchants	15 (8.0)	50 (10.6)	45 (8.9)	21 (19.3)	13 (12.6)
Lesser professions, clerks	19 (10.2)	75 (15.9)	79 (15.6)	3 (2.7)	3 (2.9)
Artisans, *boutiquiers*	74 (39.6)	172 (36.5)	203 (40.2)	32 (29.4)	20 (19.4)
Silk-weavers	22 (11.8)	38 (8.1)	31 (6.1)	12 (11.0)	7 (6.8)
Journaliers	18 (9.6)	32 (6.8)	56 (11.1)	2 (1.8)	4 (3.9)
Domestiques	4 (2.1)	16 (3.4)	20 (4.0)	0	0
Miscellaneous	2 (1.1)	6 (1.3)	14 (2.8)	0	7 (6.8)
TOTAL	187 (99.9)	471 (99.9)	505 (100.0)	109 (100.0)	103 (100.0)

Long-Serving *commissaires de surveillance*

Place Saint-Pierre

This is the only committee for which there is a full set of signatures dated late in the siege (on a complaint against an attempt by the presidents of Place Saint-Pierre to expel the committee from its rooms). Nine names correspond to those on a list of early June: Jacques Bouvard (*rentier*, ex-rector of the *Charité*), A.-M. Mignard (fan-merchant), Francois Vincent (*rentier*), Gagnieur *l'aîné*, Raymond, Prodon, Sionet, Lanvin, and Jean-Baptiste Faure (AD 31L24, Comité de Surveillance of Guillaume-Tell (Place Saint-Pierre) to the constituted authorities, 23 Sept., 42L39, Commission Populaire Républicaine (henceforth CPR) documents, no. 142, list of members of the committee elected on 19, 20, and 21 May).

La Croisette

Bertrand, Jacques Greppo (farrier), Georges Clapisson, Creppu (lace-merchant), Miallet ('rich', according to the terrorist Comité de Surveillance), Mignot (haberdasher) (AD 31L2, d. 4, minutes of la Croisette, 2 June–22 Sept.; supplementary papers, 2 June, 22 Sept., *Secrétariat*, pp. 117–33).

Place Confort

Étienne Bonnet (merchant hatter), Bossant (spirit-merchant), Benoît Girard (ironmonger, *éligible* in 1790), Aimé Lafage (faience-merchant), François Poix (éligible in 1790) (AD 31L47, extracts from the minutes and supplementary papers of Place Confort, 30 May–22 Sept. 42L39, CPR documents in evidence against members of the *sections*, nos. 132–3, 136–7, 139, Comité de Surveillance of Place Confort, 1–2, 6–12, 24 Sept.).

Rue Neuve

F.-L. Boydelatour (Bois de la Tour) (*négociant*), François Brette (bookseller), Jacques Chazat (notary), Favel (locksmith), André Goiran (merchant and commission agent) (CPR documents, nos. 1221–3, 225–6, 228, 230–1, 238; AD 42L66, d. Boydelatour, nos. 19, 20; 42L75, d. Favel; 42L99, no. 3, interrogations (n.d. [vendémiaire–germinal], an II); 42L116, no. 31, detainees of Rue Neuve, 23 frimaire, an II; 1L986, requisition signed Chazat, 31 May).

le Change

Delamorte (leather-merchant), Denis Delorme (commission agent) (AD 42L39), CPR documents, nos. 83–6 (31 Aug. 2, 7, 30 Sept., *Secrétariat*, p. 94; 42L72, ds. Delamorte, Delorme).

La Juiverie

Hugues Bergeon (*rentier*), Dominique Gounet (*avoué*), Claude Rolland (school-master) (AD 42L12, fo. 308, CJP, interrogation of Bergeon and Gounet, 4 frimaire, an II; 31L26, supplementary documents, Comité de Surveillance, Rue Neuve, petition of 11 June, signed Bergeon, Rolland for la Paix (la Juiverie); 42L39, CPR documents, no. 191 (Sept.), *Secrétariat*, p. 94).

L'Hôtel-Dieu

J.-F. Commoy, H. Delorme, Denis Pinet, T.-A. Laboré (*Secrétariat*, pp. 102, 112; AD 31L42, Comité de Surveillance of Bordeaux (l'Hôtel-Dieu), supplementary papers; AC I²3, no. 84, statement signed by committee members, 3 Sept.).

Rue Thomassin

Simon *aîné* (*rentier*), Jean-Baptiste Venet (metal-founder, *éligible* 1790), Claude Faucheux (printer-bookseller), Henri Ferlat (merchant mirror-manufacturer) (AD 42L39, CPR documents, nos. 232–3 (signed documents, 4 June, 8 Oct.)).

Bon-Rencontre

Brochet (weaver of crêpe de Chine) (AD 42L39, CPR documents, nos. 73, 67–8 (4 June, 3–4 Oct.); 42L68, d. Brochet, denunciations Oct./brumaire, an II).

Le Plâtre

Jacques Devilars, Buis (AD 42L67, d. Boudet, papers signed by Devilars, 23 Aug., 14 Sept., 5 Oct.; 42L68, d. Buis, interrogation, 9 frimaire; 31L34, Egalité (le Plâtre), supplementary documents, 10, 15 June).

Pierre-Scize

Gaspard Revol (merchant and manufacturer of faience) (AD 31L19, Pierre-Scize, supplementary papers, nos. 2, 7 (3 June, 1 Sept.)).

Port du Temple

Joseph Gleyze, *cadet* (*rentier*) (AD 31L43, Port du Temple, supplementary papers, signatures of the Comité de Surveillance, 3 June; 42L39, CPR documents, no. 20, signed document, 5 Oct.; 42L101, no. 13, prisoners of Bataillon-Affranchi, vendémiaire–germinal, an II).

Le Gourguillon

J.-M. Flechet (*rentier*) (AD 31L20, minutes of le Gourguillon, 1 June; CPR documents, no. 72 (23 Sept.); AD 42L95, d. Flechet, inventory of his effects, n.d. [an II].

La Pêcherie

J.-A. Sicard (broker) (AD 42L39, CPR documents, no. 81 (5 Oct.); 42L86, no. B57, d. Sicard, denunciation by the Comité Révolutionnaire of la Pêcherie, 18 nivôse, an II).

La Grande-Côte II

Benoît Bédor (silk-weaver) (AD 31L26, Rue Neuve, correspondence, address to the Provisional Municipalité, 11 June, supported by la Côte II; 31L10, la Grande-Côte II, supplementary papers, no. 73 (3 Sept.); 42L99, summary of interrogation of Bédor, n.d. [an II]).

Le Griffon II

Binard *l'aîné* (AD 31L26 (see preceding note); 42L45, no. 32, Dossier de l'Armée lyonnaise, d. Binard, requisition signed by him, 21 Sept.).

Plat-d'Argent

Étienne Serve (gimp-maker) (AD 31L49, minutes of Plat-d'Argent, 1 June; 42L12, fo. 286, CJP, interrogation of Serve, 8 frimaire, an II; 42L49, no. 263, CPR papers, 19 Sept.).

In some cases additional information was drawn from AC 1²7, Sections révolutionnaires: dénonciations et enquêtes (an II).

APPENDIX XII

Sources Used in Identifying Rebel Activists

The two lists of *officiers municipaux provisoires* (that is to say, the presidents and secretaries of *sections* in office on 30 May who became *officiers municipaux* by order of the Département and the *représentants*): AN AF II43, plaq. 339, no. 6, *Municipalité provisoire ... Liste des présidents et secrétaires de toutes les sections réunies* (Lyon, n.d. [4 June 1793]); AD 42L34, d. A(1), Municipalité provisoire formée par procès-verbal du 31 May et autres subséquens. (The latter was drawn up by the repressive authorities in the year II and also included the names of those who entered the Provisional Municipalité after 30 May.)

A list of the sectional presidents and secretaries published with the address, *Les Sections de la ville de Lyon aux habitants du département et de toutes les municipalités voisines* (Lyon, 2 June 1793).

The individual dossiers (approximately 5,000) assembled in the year II and arranged alphabetically in AD 42L56–154.

The interrogations recorded by the Commission Militaire (vendémiaire–frimaire, an II, AD 42L3, d. 5); the Commission de Justice Populaire (brumaire–frimaire, an II, AD 42L12, d. 17); the Commission Révolutionnaire's correspondence (AD 42L19–22) and decisions (AD 42L24).

Procès-verbaux des séances des corps municipaux de la ville de Lyon, publiés par la municipalité (Lyon, 1904), iv. 275–444.

Registre du Secrétariat-Général des sections de la ville de Lyon 2 août–11 octobre 1793, ed. G. Guigue (Lyon, 1907).

Procès-verbaux and correspondence of the *sections*, May–Oct. 1793: AD 31L1–49; AC I²4.

A. Portallier, *Tableau général des victimes et martyrs de la Révolution en Lyonnais, Forez et Beaujolais* (Saint-Étienne, 1911). (This work contains a nearly complete alphabetical list of those condemned by the Revolutionary Tribunals of Lyon and Feurs.)

Liste des citoyens éligibles aux places municipales de la ville de Lyon (Lyon, 1790).

Amongst the individual dossiers in the AD, there are extremely valuable lists of prisoners, suspects, and fugitives drawn up after the siege, by the *Comités Révolutionnaires* of each *section*. They have the advantage of covering people who escaped the Terror and are therefore not on the lists published by the Revolutionary Tribunals. Written by men who knew the *quartier* and the rebel sectional personnel better than the outsiders who sat on the tribunals, they are more reliable sources for the occupations of the rebels and their roles in the revolt than the printed lists. The possibility that personal vendettas might have resulted in the inclusion of some innocents cannot be ruled out. But the fact that there were twelve men involved in compiling the lists meant that there was less chance of blatant misrepresentation, particularly in cases where it was simply a matter of stating who had served in the rebel committees and *sections*, which would be a matter of common knowledge in the *quartier* and usually verifiable by reference to sectional registers. Denials and appeals for mercy were generally based on claims of having taken up a post during the rebellion to help oppressed *patriotes* or to succour the poor. In some cases, such as that of the committee of Port-Affranchi (formerly Port du Temple), great pains were taken to examine the rebels' reasons for serving (loyalty to his leaders, ignorance, gullibility, counter-revolutionary tendencies, fanaticism, or plain stupidity), and to counsel clemency even for those who, in patriotic sincerity, had served as president of a *section* (which was in practice a capital offence for the repressive authorities—see AD 42L101, Prisonniers du Bataillon-affranchi'). The *côtes* for these sectional lists are: AD 42L96, 97, 99–102, 107, 109, 112, 113, 116.

Almanachs de Lyon, 1789–92.

Actes d'accusation drawn up by the rebel authorities in June and July.

AC 1²6, Commission temporaire: certificats de non-rébellion (an II).

AD 1L87, Certificats d'arrestation (an II).

AC 1²3, Petit registre de dénonciation (June–July, 1793).

It would be tedious to document in detail the hundreds of individual references used to acquire the information tabulated in these appendices. Appendix XI provides an example of full documentation.

Bibliography

A. PRIMARY SOURCES

Manuscript

Archives communales de Lyon
F⁴, F¹², F¹⁴;
G (unclassified), *Contribution mobilière*, 1791, 1792, 1793;
I¹154, I¹242, I²2, I²3, I²4, I²5, I²6, I²7, I²16–I²29, I²46, I²46 *bis*, I⁴1.

Archives départementales du Rhône
Bp 3530, 3536;
1L205, 1L372–3, 1L375–7, 1L392, 1L466, 1L482, 1L493, 1L504, 1L557, 1L646,
  1L818, 1L820, 1L985–8, 1L991, 1L1193, 1L1202, 2L9–10, 2L43, 2L87, 2L90,
  2L98, 2L103, 31L49, 31L56–7, 31L61, 34L1–7, 36L9, 36L50, 36L57, 42L3,
  42L12, 42L32–9, 42L44–6, 42L56–60, 42L62–154, 42L160–2.

Bibliothèque de Lyon
Fonds général (a few manuscripts of the revolutionary period);
Fonds Coste, Desvernay et Molinier (contains an invaluable collection of manuscripts relating to the principal figures in Lyonnais politics in 1792 and 1793).

Archives de la guerre
B³103*, Armée du siège de Lyon.

Archives nationales
AA53, AFII43, AF*II12, BIII75, BB3, DIII216, DXXIX *bis*, F¹ᵃIII, Rhône 8,
  F¹ᵃ431, F¹ᵃ548, F¹ᵃ550, F¹ᵃ557, F¹ᶜIII, Rhône 6–7, F⁷3296, F⁷3352, F⁷3686⁶,
  F⁷4412, F⁷4590, F⁹6, F¹¹217, F¹¹1173–4, F¹²1440–1, M669.

Hampshire Record Office
Wickham Papers.

Printed

ADAM et al., *Les Citoyens de la ville de Lyon à leurs frères des districts ... de Rhône-
et-Loire, et à tous leurs frères de la République française* (Lyon, [June] 1793).

*Adresse à la Convention nationale par la Société de Brutus ci-devant la Pêcherie, à
Lyon, département de Rhône-et-Loire* (Lyon, 1792).

*Adresse à MM. les volontaires ci-devant libres maintenant esclaves des officiers
féodaux du quartier du Griffon* (Lyon, [1789]).

*Adresse aux armées, aux citoyens et à tous les départements de la République françoise
par les autorités constituées réunies à Lyon, chef lieu du département de Rhône-
et-Loire* (Lyon, [June] 1793).

Adresse de la Société populaire de Commune-Affranchie. A tous les Jacobins Montagnards de la République (Commune-Affranchie, year II).

Adresse de remercimens ou Roi à l'occasion de la décision portée par sa Majesté, en son Conseil, le 27 décembre 1788 (Lyon, 1789).

Adresse des 32 sections de la ville de Lyon . . . aux habitants de la campagne (Lyon, 1793).

Adresse du club de rue Neuve le 2 octobre 1791 (Lyon, 1791).

Adresse du Conseil-général de la commune de Lyon, lue à l'Assemblée nationale dans la séance du 13 février 1792 (Lyon, 1792).

Adresse du peuple de Lyon à la République françoise (Lyon, 1793).

Almanach astronomique et historique de la ville de Lyon et des provinces de Lyonnais, Forez et Beaujolais (Lyon, 1781, 1789–92).

Almanach astronomique et historique de la ville de Lyon et du département de Rhône-et-Loire (Lyon, 1790, 1791, 1792).

Archives parlementaires de 1787 à 1860, Série 1 (Paris, 1868–92).

AULARD, F.-A. (ed.), *La Société des Jacobins: Recueil de documents pour l'histoire du club des Jacobins de Paris* (Paris, 1889).

—— *Recueil des actes du Comité de salut public avec la correspondance officielle des représentants en mission et le registre du Conseil exécutif provisoire* (Paris, 1891–1933).

Avis aux citoyens (Lyon, 1789).

Avis de la plus grande importance pour tous les ouvriers de la ville de Lyon. Par plusieurs compagnons de différentes professions, de la même ville. Du 23 juillet 1790 (Lyon, 1790).

Barbaroux à ses commettants (Lyon, 1793).

[BÉRAUD, P.-E.], *Relation du siège de Lyon contenant le détail de ce qui sn'y est passé* (Neuchâtel, 1794).

—— *Sur le siège de Lyon et sur les malheurs qui l'ont suivi. En Allemagne, 1794* (n.p., n.d.).

BERNASCON and LAURAS, *La Vie, la mort et le triomphe de Chalier* (Paris, [1794]).

BILLEMAZ, F., *Discours prononcé au Comité central . . . le jeudi 16 août l'an IV* (Lyon, 1792).

—— *Le Grand Bailliage* (Lyon, 1788).

—— *Jugement du tribunal du district de la ville de Lyon en faveur du citoyen Denis Monnet prononcé ensuite du plaidoyer du citoyen François Billiemaz, homme de loi, défenseur officieux* (Lyon, 1791).

BOITEL, L. (ed.), *Lyon vu de Fourvières: Esquisses physiques, morales et historiques* (Lyon, 1833).

—— *Lyon ancien et moderne, par les collaborateurs de la Revue du Lyonnais* (Lyon, 1838).

Cahiers des États généraux classés par lettres alphabétiques de Bailliage ou Sénéchaussée, ed. J. Mavidal and B. Laurent (Paris, 1868).

CARON, P. (ed.), *Rapports des agents du Ministre de l'Intérieur dans les départements, 1793–an II* (Paris, 1951).

CHALIER, J., *Adresse de Joseph Chalier officier municipal de la ville de Lyon à l'Assemblée nationale* (Paris, 1792).

[CHASSAGNON, J.], *Offrande à Chalier* (Lyon, 1793).

Les Citoyennes de Lyon (n.p., [1793]).

Les Citoyens de la ville de Lyon à leurs frères de la République françoise (Lyon, n.d.).

COLLOT d'HERBOIS, J. M., *Rapport fait au nom du Comité de salut public sur la situation de Commune-Affranchie par J. M. Collot d'Herbois. Le 1 nivôse* (Paris, year II).

Les Commissaires des sections de la ville de Lyon réunies en comité les 29 et 30 mai 1793 (Lyon, 1793).

Copie de l'adresse du bataillon de la Juiverie au Conseil général de la Commune provisoire de Lyon, du 30 mai 1793 (Lyon, 1793).

Copie de la lettre écrite par les administrateurs du Conseil-général du département de Rhône-et-Loire ... à la Convention nationale sur les événements antérieurs à ceux du 29 mai dernier (Lyon, 4 June 1793).

Courrier de Lyon.

COURTOIS, E. B., *Rapport fait au nom de la commission chargée de l'examen des papiers trouvés chez Robespierre et ses complices ...* (Paris, year III).

DELANDINE, A. F., *Tableau des prisons de Lyon, pour servir à l'histoire de la tyrannie de 1792 et 1793* (Lyon, 1797).

DELANT, *Adresse à tous les bons patriotes* (Lyon, [1790]).

DERVIEU DU VILLARS, *Lettre de M. Dervieux, commandant de la Garde nationale de Lyon* (Lyon, 1790).

Détail de ce qui s'est passé à Lyon les 28 et 30 mai 1793 (extrait du Journal de Carrier), (Lyon, [1793]).

Discours prononcè par le président du département de Rhône-et-Loire, le premier juillet 1793 ... à l'ouverture de la première séance des députés nommés par les Assemblées primaires de ce département ... (Lyon, 1793).

Discours prononcé par M. Tolozan de Montfort, prévôt des marchands de Lyon, dans la loge des Changes, à l'ouverture du paiement des Rois, le premier mars 1788 (Lyon, 1788).

Discours prononcé par un citoyen de la Société populaire des amis de la Constitution de la section de l'Hôtel-Dieu (Lyon, 1791).

DODIEU, M., *Mémoire à consulter* (Lyon, 1792).

Doléances des maîtres-ouvriers fabricants en étoffes d'or, d'argent et de soie ... adressées au Roi et à l'Assemblée nationale (Lyon, 1789).

DOPPET, A., *Mémoires politiques et militaires du Général Doppet* (Carouge, 1797).

DUBOIS-CRANCÉ, E.-L.-A., *Discours prononcé au Comité central de la ville de Lyon le 4 mars 1792. Par M. Dubois de Crancé* (Lyon, 1792).

—— *Discours sur le siège de Lyon, prononcé au Club des Jacobins à Paris ...* (n.p., [Year II]).

—— *Première et deuxième parties de la réponse de Dubois-Crancé aux inculpations de ses collègues Couthon et Maignet* (n.p., n.d.).

DUBOIS-CRANCÉ, E.-L.-A., ALBITTE, and GAUTHIER, *Proclamation des représentants du peuple envoyés près l'Armée des Alpes* (Grenoble, 3 July 1793).

DU VERO (pseud.), *Lettre à Monsieur Roland de la Platière sur sa brochure intitulée: Municipalité de Lyon. Du Vero, citoyen inactif de Lyon ce 5 avril 1790* (Lyon, 1790).

EDGEWORTH, R. L., *Memoirs of Richard Lovell Edgeworth, Esq., Begun by Himself and Concluded by his Daughter Maria Edgeworth* (London, 1820), i.

État des membres qui composent la Société des amis de la Constitution établie à Lyon le 12 décembre 1789, et affiliée à celle de Paris (Lyon, 1791).

EXPILLY, ABBÉ, *Dictionnaire géographie, historique et politique des Gaules et de la France* (Paris, 1766), iv.

Exposé de tout ce qui s'est passé relativement à l'organisation de la Garde nationale du district de la ville de Lyon, depuis le mois de mars jusqu' au 9 mai 1792. Présenté à l'Assemblée nationale, et aux corps administratifs du département de Rhône-et-Loire, par les chefs de légions, adjutants et sous-adjutants-généraux (Lyon, [1792]).

Extrait des registres de la section de la Convention (Lyon, 1793).

Extrait des registres des délibérations des maîtres-ouvriers fabricants en étoffes ... de soie ... prises dans l'église cathédrale de Saint-Jean le 5 mai 1790 (Lyon, 1790).

Extraits du registre des délibérations du Directoire du département de Rhône-et-Loire (Lyon, [6 Feb.] 1793).

FROSSARD, B. J., and CHALON, *Pétition faite à la barre de la Convention nationale par B. J. Frossard et Chalon, députés extraordinairement par les 3 corps administratifs de Lyon ... novembre 1792* (n.d., n.p.)

GARAT, J., *Mémoires* (Paris, 1862).

GENET-BRONZE, PELZIN, and BADGER, *Rapport et pétition sur les troubles arrivés à Lyon, présentés et lus à la barre de la Convention nationale, le lundi 15 avril 1793* (Lyon, 1793).

GILIBERT, J.-E., *Jean-Emmanuel Gilibert à ses concitoyens* (Lyon, 1793).

GLOVER, M., *Collection complète des jugements rendus par la Commission révolutionnaire établie à Lyon par les représentants du peuple en 1793–1794* (Lyon, 1869).

GONCHON, C., *Gonchon aux citoyens de la section des Quinze-Vingts, fauxbourg Saint-Antoine* (Lyon, [14 June] 1793).

GRANDCHAMP, J., *Qu'est ce que le Comité central des 31 clubs des sections de Lyon?* (Lyon, 1791).

GRIMOD de la REYNIÈRE, *Peu de chose: Hommage à l'Académie de Lyon* (Neuchâtel, 1788).

[GUILLIN, D.], *A Messieurs les officiers municipaux de la ville de Lyon* (Lyon, n.d. [1790]).

GUILLON de MONTLÉON, A., *Lyon tel qu'il étoit et tel qu'il est, ou Tableau historique de sa splendeur passée, suivie de l'histoire pittoresque de ses malheurs et ses ruines* (Paris, 1797).

HIDINS, R., *Hidins au genre humain* (Lyon, 1792).

IMBERT-COLOMÈS, J., *Aux citoyens de Lyon* (n.p., [1790]).

—— *Lettre écrite à Bourg, le 29 février 1790, par M. Imbert-Colomès ci-devant chargé du commandement de la ville de Lyon, à MM. les officiers municipaux de Bourg* (Lyon, 1790).

Institution des citoyennes dévouées à la Patrie (Lyon, 1791).

Journal de Lyon, ou Moniteur du département de Rhône-et-Loire.

Journal des Sociétés populaires des amis de la Constitution de Lyon.

Journal de Ville-Affranchie et des départements de Rhône et Loire. Rédigé par D'Aumale.

Lettre à MM. les capitaines-pennons de la milice bourgeoise de Lyon non encore réformée (Lyon, 1789).

Lettre des commissaires de la ville de Lyon près la ville de Bordeaux à leurs concitoyens, Bordeaux, le 26 juin 1793 (Lyon, 1793).

Lettre d'un citoyen de Lyon à son ami sur les événements de la journée du 29 mai 1793 (Lyon, 1793).

Lettre écrite à l'auteur d'un journal très-connu (Lyon, [1790]).

Lettres à ma fille sur mes promenades à Lyon (Lyon, 1810).

'Lettres inédites de Louis Vitet', *Revue d'histoire de Lyon*, 4 (1905).

Liste des citoyens éligibles aux places municipales de la ville de Lyon (Lyon, 1790).

Liste des neuf juges de paix, que la Cabale fait circuler dans toutes les sections de la ville, avec les notes impartiales d'un PATRIOTE *sur les postulants* (Lyon, 1790).

Livre rouge de la municipalité de Lyon: Premier Cahier (Lyon, 1790).

Les Lyonnois à l'armée dirigée contre eux par Dubois-Crancé (Lyon, n.d.).

Manifeste. Marseille aux républicains français. 12 juin 1793. Délibéré au Comité général des 32 sections de Marseille (Marseille, 1793).

MAYET, E., *Mémoire sur les manufactures de Lyon* (Paris, 1786).

Mémoire de la ville de Lyon au Roi . . . signé Servant, Terret, députés de la ville de Lyon (Paris, 1788).

Mémoire des électeurs fabricants d'étoffes en soie de la ville de Lyon (Lyon, 1789).

Mémoire du Club de rue Neuve le 2 octobre 1791 (Lyon, 1791).

Mémoire justificatif des citoyens de la Société populaire des amis de la Constitution de la section de rue Neuve (Lyon, 1791).

Mémoire pour les volontaires nationaux de la ville de Lyon (Lyon, 1790).

METZGER, A. (ed.), *Centenaire de 1789: Lyon en 1789* (Lyon, 1882).

—— and VAESEN, J. (eds.), *Lyon en 1792: Notes et documents* (Lyon, n.d.).

MONTLUEL, M. DE, *Quelques moyens proposés pour contribuer au rétablissement des manufactures et au bonheur des ouvriers de Lyon* (Lyon, 1789).

[NOLHAC], *Lettre aux citoyens de Lyon* (Lyon, [1790]).

Observations sur le rapport fait par deux commissaires du département du Jura, à l'Assemblée générale de la Commission populaire, républicaine et de salut public de Rhône-et-Loire (Lyon, 1793).

Opinion de la Chambre de commerce de Lyon sur la motion faite le 27 août 1790 . . . pour la liquidation de la dette exigible de l'État (Lyon, 1790).

Opinions impartiales des officiers municipaux sortis par la voie du sort (Lyon, 1790).

Ordonnance de M. l'Archevêque de Lyon, primat des Gaules (Lyon, 1791).

PAILLET, J., *Manifeste des sans-culottes de la République, aux messieurs de la ville de Lyon* (n.p., n.d.).

P[ASSERON], 'Mémoires d'un pauvre diable', *Revue du Lyonnais*, 3 (1838).

PELZIN, M.-A., *Observations, réclamations, motions, pétitions, justifications de la Société populaire des amis de la Constitution de Lyon, de la section des Terreaux* … (Lyon, 1791).

Pétition adressée aux citoyens législateurs … avec la réponse des commissaires en députation auprès d'eux (n.p., n.d.).

Pétition à l'Assemblée nationale par plusieurs négocians, fabricans et autres citoyens de la ville de Lyon, le 18 décembre 1791 (Lyon, 1791).

Plaidoyer du compère Mathieu pour les habitants du canton de Pierre-Scize (Paris, 1790).

PRESSAVIN, J.B., *Avis aux citoyens de la ville de Lyon sur les octrois* (Lyon, 1790).

Procès-verbal du Conseil du district de Lyon, en permanence à l'Hôtel Commun [29–30 mai] (Lyon, 1793).

Procès-verbaux de l'Assemblée des trois ordres de la ville de Lyon … le 17 juillet 1789 (Lyon, 1789).

Procès-verbaux des Conseils généraux du département de Rhône-et-Loire, des districts de Lyon et de la campagne de Lyon relatifs à l'événement du 29 mai 1793 (Lyon, 1793).

Procès-verbaux des événements passés à Lyon, les 29 et 30 mai 1793. Apportés par les députés extraordinaires de Lyon … à la Convention nationale (Lyon, 1793).

Procès-verbaux des séances de la Commission populaire, républicaine et de salut public de Rhône-et-Loire, 30 juin–8 octobre 1793, ed. G. Guigue (Lyon, 1899).

Procès-verbaux des séances des corps municipaux de la ville de Lyon 1787–an VIII (Lyon, 1900–4).

Procès-verbaux du Conseil-général du département de Rhône-et-Loire, ed. G. Guigue, 2 vols. (Trévoux, 1895).

Rapport fait au Conseil-général de la commune provisoire de Lyon, par l'un des commissaires de section … à Paris (Lyon, [June 1793]).

Rapport du Bureau d'administration de l'emprunt de trois millions pour l'approvisionnement de la ville de Lyon. Fait à l'Assemblée générale des actionnaires le 22 mars 1793. Présidée par le citoyen maire (Lyon, 1793).

Rapport fait au Conseil-général de la Commune de Lyon (Lyon, 1793).

Récit sanglant de ce qui s'est passé à Lyon, le 3 juillet, au sujet des réjouissances occasionnées par la réunion des trois ordres. Le 8 juillet 1789 (Lyon, 1789).

Réflexions d'un citoyen patriote, pour les ouvriers en soie de la ville de Lyon (Lyon, 1789).

Registre du Secrétariat-général des sections de la ville de Lyon 2 août–11 octobre 1793 suivi des délibérations de la section de Porte-Froc 26 mai–10 octobre 1793, ed. G. Guigue (Lyon, 1907).

Règlement pour la Société populaire des amis de la Constitution des XXXI sections de la ville de Lyon (Lyon, 1790).

Règlements de la Société populaire de Commune-Affranchie (Commune-Affranchie, [24 floréal], year II).

Réimpression de l'Ancien Moniteur (Paris, 1858), vols. i–xvii.

Réponse des citoyens des 13 [sic] *sections à la lettre de M. Dervieux, commandant de la Garde nationale de Lyon* (Lyon, n.d.).

Requête au Roi par les habitants de la ville de Lyon (Lyon, 1789).

REVERCHON, J. M., and LAPORTE, S., *Au nom du peuple français. Les Représentants du peuple envoyés à Commune-Affranchie pour y faire cesser l'oppression ...* (Commune-Affranchie, year II).

La Révolution du Lyonnois (Lyon, 1789).

Les Révolutions de Paris, xxx (30 Jan.–6 Feb. 1790).

RICHARD, J., *Détail de la vie de M. Monnet, qui a découvert l'infâme complot de contre-révolution qui devoit s'opérer dans toute la France—ruses admirables qu'il a mis en usage—couronne civique et pensions qu'on doit lui décerner, &c. &c. &c* (Lyon, 1791).

ROCHES, J.-B.-M., *Discours dans la cause de neuf hommes, accusés d'être les auteurs ou participes des attentats horribles exercés, le 19 juillet 1790, pendant 6 heures, sur un soldat du régiment suisse, de Sonnemberg, en garnison à Lyon* (Lyon, 1791).

ROLAND, J.-M., *Municipalité de Lyon: Apperçu des travaux à entreprendre et des moyens de les suivre* (Lyon, 1790).

—— *Discours prononcé à la Société centrale par J.-M. Roland le 6 janvier 1791* (Lyon, 1791).

ROLAND, M., *Lettres de Madame Roland*, ed. C. Perroud (Paris, 1900), vols. i–ii.

La Section Rousseau à ses concitoyens (Lyon, n.d.).

Les Sections de la ville de Lyon aux habitants du département et de toutes les municipalités voisines (Lyon, 1793).

La Société populaire de la section de Port du Temple à toutes les autres Sociétés populaires des amis de la Constitution de Lyon, Salut (Lyon, 1791).

Le Surveillant, par une Société de patriotes.

TALLIEN, J. L., *Rapport et projet de décret sur les troubles arrivés à Lyon* (Paris, 1793).

TISSOT, *Observations sur les causes de la mort des blessés par des armes à feu dans la journée du 29 mai 1793 à Lyon* (Lyon, 1793).

VERNINAC, R., *Description physique et politique du département du Rhône* (Lyon, an IX).

VITET, L., *Adresse à l'Assemblée nationale* (Lyon, [1792]).

—— *Vitet député du département du Rhône à ses concitoyens sur le massacre des prisonniers de Pierre-Scize* (n.d.)

Voyages en France de François de la Rochefoucauld (1781–1783) (*Société de l'histoire de la France: Série antérieure à 1789*, ed. J. Marchand; Paris, 1933), vol. i.

B. SECONDARY WORKS

ANDREWS, R. M., 'Réflexions sur la conjuration des égaux', *Annales: Économies Sociétés Civilisations*, 29 (1974).

—— 'Social Structures, Political Elites and Ideology in Revolutionary Paris, 1792–94: A Critical Evaluation of Albert Soboul's *Les Sans-Culottes parisiens en l'An II*', *Journal of Social History*, 19 (1985).

BALLAGUY, P., 'La Guillotière contre Lyon', *Revue du Lyonnais*, 9 (1923).

BOULOISEAU, M., *La République jacobine 10 août 1792–9 thermidor an II* (Paris, 1972).

BUSSIÈRE, G., *Une famille anglaise d'ouvriers en soie à Lyon (1753–1793)* (Lyon, 1908).

CHARLÉTY, S., *Département du Rhône: Documents relatifs à la vente des biens nationaux* (Lyon, 1906).

CHÂTELAIN, A., 'La Formation de la population lyonnaise: L'Apport d'origine montagnarde (XVIIIᵉ–XIXᵉ siècles)', *Revue de géographie de Lyon*, 29 (1954).

CHAUMIÉ, J., *Le Réseau d'Antraigues et la contre-révolution* (Paris, 1965).

COBB, R., *Les Armées révolutionnaires: Instrument de la Terreur dans les départements, avril 1793–floréal an II* (Paris 1961–3).

—— 'La Commission temporaire de Commune-Affranchie (brumaire–germinal an II): Étude sur le personnel d'une institution révolutionnaire', in *Terreur et Subsistances 1793–1795* (Paris, 1965).

—— *The Police and the People* (Oxford, 1970).

—— *Reactions to the French Revolution* (Oxford, 1972).

COBBAN, A., *The Social Interpretation of the French Revolution* (Cambridge, 1964).

—— *Aspects of the French Revolution* (London, 1971).

CROOK, M. H., 'Federalism and the French Revolution: The Revolt of Toulon in 1793', *History*, 65 (1980).

DARNTON, R., *The Great Cat Massacre and Other Episodes in French Cultural History* (London, 1984).

DAWSON, P., *Provincial Magistrates and Revolutionary Politics in France 1789–1795* (Cambridge, Mass., 1972).

DE FRANCESCO, A., 'Montagnardi e sanculotti in provincia', *Studi storici*, 19 (1978).

—— 'Conflittualità sul lavoro in epoca pre-industriale: Le agitazioni degli operai cappellai lionesi (1770–1824)', *Annali della Fondazione Luigi Einaudi*, 13 (1979).

—— 'Le Quartier lyonnais de la Croisette pendant les premières années de la Révolution (1790–1793)', *Bulletin du Centre d'histoire économique et sociale de la région lyonnaise*, 4 (1979).

—— *Il sogno della repubblica: Il mondo del lavoro dall'Ancien Régime al 1848* (Milan, 1983).

DOYLE, W., *Origins of the French Revolution* (Oxford, 1980).

EDMONDS, B., '"Federalism" and Urban Revolt in France in 1793', *Journal of Modern History*, 55 (1983).

—— 'A Study in Popular Anti-Jacobinism: The Career of Denis Monnet', *French Historical Studies*, 13 (1983).

—— 'A Jacobin Débâcle: The Losing of Lyon in Spring, 1793', *History*, 69 (1984).

—— 'The Rise and Fall of Popular Democracy in Lyon, 1789–1795', *Bulletin of the John Rylands University Library of Manchester*, 67 (1984).

EGRET, J., *La Pré-Révolution française* (Paris, 1962).

FAURÉ, C., and LACOUR, R., *Archives départementales du Rhône: Répertoire numérique de la série L* (Lyon, 1950).

FORREST, A., 'The Federalist Movement in Bordeaux', D.Phil. thesis (Oxford, 1970).

—— *Society and Politics in Revolutionary Bordeaux* (Oxford, 1975).

FUOC, R., *La Réaction thermidorienne à Lyon (1795)* (Lyon, 1957).

FURET, F., *Penser la Révolution française* (Paris, 1978).

—— *Interpreting the French Revolution*, trans. E. Forster (Cambridge, 1981).

GARDEN, M., *Lyon et les Lyonnais au XVIIIᵉ siècle* (Paris, 1970).

—— 'La Révolution et l'Empire', in A. Latreille (ed.), *Histoire de Lyon et du Lyonnais* (Toulouse, 1975).

GODART, J., *L'Ouvrier en soie: Monographie du tisseur lyonnais. Étude historique, économique et sociale. Première partie: La Règlementation du travail, 1466–1791* (Lyon, 1899).

GODECHOT, J., *Les Institutions de la France sous la Révolution et l'Empire* (Paris, 1968).

GOODWIN, A., 'The Federalist Movement in Caen in the Summer of 1793', *Bulletin of the John Rylands University Library of Manchester*, 42 (1959–60).

GRAND, A., *La Croix-Rousse sous la Révolution* (Lyon, 1926).

GREER, D., *The Incidence of the Terror during the French Revolution: A Statistical Interpretation* (Gloucester, Mass., 1935).

GUILLEMAIN, C., 'Histoire de la commune de Vaise, faubourg de Lyon', *Albums du Crocodile*, 29 (1961).

GUILLON de MONTLÉON, A., *Mémoires pour servir à l'histoire de la ville de Lyon pendant la Révolution* (Paris, 1824).

GUTTON, J.-P., *La Société et les pauvres: L'Exemple de la généralité de Lyon 1534–1789* (Paris, 1970).

HAMPSON, N., *A Social History of the French Revolution* (London, 1963).

—— *The Life and Opinions of Maximilien Robespierre* (London, 1974).

HERRIOT, E., *Lyon n'est plus* (Paris, 1938–40).

HIGONNET, P., *Class, Ideology, and the Rights of Nobles during the French Revolution* (Oxford, 1981).

HUNT, L., *Revolution and Urban Politics in Provincial France: Troyes and Reims 1786–90* (Stanford, 1978).

HUNT, L., *Politics, Culture, and Class in the French Revolution* (London, 1984).

HYSLOP, B. F., *A Guide to the General Cahiers of 1789* (New York, 1936).

JAURÈS, J., *Histoire socialiste: La Constituante* (Paris, 1901).

JOLY, A., 'Pierre-Jacques Willermoz', *Albums du Crocodile*, 6 (1938).

KAPLOW, J., *The Names of Kings: The Parisian Laboring Poor in the Eighteenth Century* (New York, 1972).

KENNEDY, M. L., *The Jacobin Clubs in the French Revolution: The First Years* (Princeton, 1982).

KLEINCLAUSZ, A., DUBOIS, L., and DUTACQ, F., *Histoire de Lyon*, ii. (Lyon, n.d.).

KUSCINSKI, A., *Dictionnaire des conventionnels* (Paris, 1917).

LA CHAPELLE, S. de, *Notice sur l'Abbé Laussel* (Lyon, 1882).

LAFERRÈRE, M., *Lyon, ville industrielle* (Paris, 1960).

LA GORCE, P. de, *Histoire réligieuse de la Révolution française* (Paris, 1922).

LATREILLE, A. (ed.), *Histoire de Lyon et du Lyonnais* (Toulouse, 1975).

LEFEBVRE, G., 'Compte rendu: E. Herriot, *Lyon n'est plus*, t. I', *Annales historiques de la Révolution française*, 15 (1938).

—— 'Compte rendu: E. Herriot, *Lyon n'est plus*, t. III', *Annales historiques de la Révolution française*, 18 (1946).

—— *La Révolution française* (Paris, 1957).

LÉON, P., 'La Région lyonnaise dans l'histoire économique et sociale de la France: Une esquisse (XVIe–XXe siècles)', *Revue historique*, 237 (1967), 42.

LEROUDIER, E., *La Décadence de la Fabrique lyonnaise à la fin du XVIIIe siècle* (Lyon, 1911).

LÉVY, J. M., 'Les Recensements dans le département du Rhône en 1793 et en l'an II', *Cahiers d'histoire*, 8 (1963).

LITTRÉ, E., *Dictionnaire de la langue française* (Paris, 1863–74).

LONGFELLOW, D. L., 'Silk Weavers and the Social Struggle in Lyon during the French Revolution, 1789–1794', *French Historical Studies*, 12 (1981).

LUCAS, C., 'Nobles, Bourgeois and the Origins of the French Revolution', *Past and Present*, 60 (1973).

—— *The Structure of the Terror: The Example of Javogues and the Loire* (Oxford, 1973).

Lyon ancien et moderne par les collaborateurs de la Revue du Lyonnais, ed. L. Boitel (Lyon, 1838).

LYONS, M., *Revolution in Toulouse: An Essay on Provincial Terrorism* (Berne, 1978).

MANSFIELD, P., 'The Missions of Collot d'Herbois: A Study in his Political Career', Ph.D. thesis (Macquarie University, 1985).

—— 'Collot d'Herbois and the Dechristianizers', *Journal of Religious History*, 14 (1986–7).

—— 'The Repression of Lyon, 1793–4: Origins, Responsibility and Significance', *French History*, 2 (1988).

MARION, M., *Dictionnaire des institutions de la France aux XVIIe et XVIIIe siècles* (Paris, 1923).

MATHIEZ, A., *The French Revolution*, trans. C. A. Phillips (New York, 1962).

METZGER, P., *Le Conseil supérieur et le Grand Bailliage de Lyon (1771–1774, 1788)* (Lyon, 1913).

MORINEAU, M., 'Mort d'un terroriste ... Prolégomènes à l'étude d'un juste: "Aristide" (ci-devant Georges) Couthon, précédé d'un coup d'œil sur ses bibliothéques', *Annales historiques de la Révolution française*, 55 (1983).

PALMER, R. R., 'Popular Democracy in the French Revolution: Review Article', *French Historical Studies*, 1 (1960).

PARISET, E., *Histoire de la Fabrique lyonnaise* (Lyon, n.d.).

PATRICK, A., *The Men of the First French Republic: Political Alignments in the National Convention of 1792* (Baltimore, 1792).

PELAT, H., and CAYROL, M., 'Tableau de la contre-révolution à Lyon d'après 1901 condamnations à mort prononcés à la suite du siège de la ville', DES thesis (Université de Lyon, n.d.).

PORTALLIER, A., *Tableau général des victimes et martyrs de la Révolution en Lyonnais, Forez et Beaujolais* (Saint-Étienne, 1911).

REICHARDT, J. F., *Un Prussien en France en 1792: Strasbourg—Lyon—Paris. Lettres intimes de J. F. Reichardt*, trans. A. Laquiante (Paris, 1892).

REINHARD, M., *La Chute de la royauté: 10 août 1792* (Paris, 1969).

[RICARD-CHARBONNET], *Mémoires d'un Lyonnais de la fin du XVIIIᵉ siècle: Précis de la vie de l'auteur* (Lyon, 1838).

RIFFATERRE, C., *Le Mouvement anti-jacobin et anti-parisien à Lyon et dans le Rhône-et-Loire en 1793* (Lyon, 1912–28).

ROSE, R. B., *The Enragés: Socialists of the French Revolution?* (Melbourne, 1965).

—— 'How to Make a Revolution: The Paris Districts in 1789', *Bulletin of the John Rylands University Library of Manchester*, 59 (1977).

ROUSSET, J., 'Un chirurgien jacobin: L'Infernal Achard', *Albums du Crocodile*, 32 (1964).

RUDE, F., 'Du nouveau sur le socialisme de L'Ange: La Découverte du "Remède à tout" ', *Cahiers d'histoire*, 15 (1970).

RUDÉ, G., *The Crowd in the French Revolution* (Oxford, 1959).

—— *Paris and London in the Eighteenth Century* (London, 1970).

SCHATZMANN, J., 'La Révolution de 1793 à Lyon vue par un témoin oculaire, Jean-Solomon Fazy', *Annales historiques de la Révolution française*, 7 (1940).

SCOTT, S. F., 'Problems of Law and Order during 1790, the "Peaceful" Year of the French Revolution', *American Historical Review*, 80 (1975).

SCOTT, W., *Terror and Repression in Revolutionary Marseilles* (London, 1973).

SOBOUL, A., *The French Revolution 1787–1799*, trans. A. Forrest and C. Jones, 2 vols. (London, 1974).

STEYERT, A., *Nouvelle Histoire de Lyon et des provinces de Lyonnais, Forez, Beaujolais, Franc-Lyonnais et Dombes*, iii. (Lyon, 1899).

SUTHERLAND, D. M. G., *France 1789–1815: Revolution and Counterrevolution* (London, 1985).

SYDENHAM, M. J., *The Girondins* (London, 1961).

SYDENHAM, M. J., 'The Republican Revolt of 1793: A Plea for Less Localized Local Studies', *French Historical Studies,* 12 (1981).

Thompson, J. M., *Robespierre* (New York, 1968).

TRÉNARD, L., *Lyon, de l'Encyclopédie au préromantisme* (Paris, 1958).

—— 'La Crise sociale lyonnaise à la veille de la Révolution', *Revue d'histoire moderne et contemporaine,* 2 (1955), 5–45.

VALLÈS, J., *Réflexions historiques sur quelques chapitres d'un ouvrage de M. l'Abbé Guillon, de Lyon, ayant pour titre: Mémoires pour servir à l'histoire de Lyon pendant la Révolution* (Paris, 1825).

VINGTRINIER, E., *Le Théâtre à Lyon au XVIIIᵉ siècle* (Lyon, 1879).

WAHL, M., 'Joseph Chalier: Étude sur la Révolution française à Lyon', *Revue historique,* 34 (1887).

—— *Les Premières Années de la Révolution à Lyon, 1788–1792* (Paris, n.d.).

WALLON, H., *La Révolution du 31 mai et le Fédéralisme en 1793 ou la France vaincue par la Commune de Paris* (Paris, 1886).

Index